African Foreign Policies

This book explores, at a time when several powers have become serious players on the continent, aspects of African agency, past and present, by African writers on foreign policy, representative of geography, language and state size.

In the past, African foreign policy has largely been considered within the context of reactions to the international or global "external factor". This groundbreaking book, however, looks at how foreign policy has been crafted and used in response not just to external, but also, mainly, domestic imperatives or (theoretical) signifiers. As such, it narrates individual and changing foreign policy orientations over time—and as far back as independence—with mainly African-based scholars who present their own constructs of what is a useful theoretical narrative regarding foreign policy on the continent—how theory is adapted to local circumstance or substituted for continentally based ontologies. The book therefore contends that the African experience carries valuable import for expanding general understandings of foreign policy in general.

This book will be of key interest to scholars and students of Foreign Policy Analysis, Foreign Policy Studies, African International Relations/Politics/Studies, Diplomacy and more broadly to International Relations.

Paul-Henri Bischoff is Professor of International Relations and erstwhile long-standing Head of Department of Political and International Studies at Rhodes University, Grahamstown-Makhanda, South Africa.

Routledge Studies in African Politics and International Relations

Series Editor: Daniel C. Bach
Emile Durkheim Centre for Comparative Politics and Sociology, Sciences Po Bordeaux

African Migrants and Europe
Managing the Ultimate Frontier
Lorenzo Rinelli

Africa in Global International Relations
Emerging Approaches to Theory and Practice
Edited by Paul-Henri Bischoff, Kwesi Aning and Amitav Acharya

Regionalism in Africa
Genealogies, Institutions and Trans-State Networks
Daniel C. Bach

China's Aid to Africa
Does Friendship Really Matter?
Zhangxi Cheng and Ian Taylor

African Border Disorders
Addressing Transnational Extremist Organizations
Edited by Olivier J. Walther and William F.S. Miles

Political Trust and the Politics of Security Engagement
China and the European Union in Africa
Benjamin Barton

Human Rights and the Judicialisation of African Politics
Peter Brett

The Finances of Regional Organisations in the Global South
Follow the Money
Edited by Ulf Engel and Frank Mattheis

African Foreign Policies
Selecting Signifiers to Explain Agency
Edited by Paul-Henri Bischoff

For more information about this series please visit: https://www.routledge.com/Routledge-Studies-in-African-Politics-and-International-Relations/book-series/RSAPIR

African Foreign Policies

Selecting Signifiers to Explain Agency

Edited by Paul-Henri Bischoff

Routledge
Taylor & Francis Group
LONDON AND NEW YORK

First published 2020
by Routledge
2 Park Square, Milton Park, Abingdon, Oxon OX14 4RN

and by Routledge
605 Third Avenue, New York, NY 10017

First issued in paperback 2022

Routledge is an imprint of the Taylor & Francis Group, an informa business

Publisher's Note
The publisher has gone to great lengths to ensure the quality of this reprint but points out that some imperfections in the original copies may be apparent.

British Library Cataloguing-in-Publication Data
A catalogue record for this book is available from the British Library

Library of Congress Cataloging-in-Publication Data
Names: Bischoff, Paul, 1954- editor, author.
Title: African foreign policies: selecting signifiers to explain agency/
edited by Paul-Henri Bischoff.
Description: New York: Routledge, 2020. | Includes bibliographical
references and index.
Identifiers: LCCN 2019054106 (print) | LCCN 2019054107 (ebook) |
ISBN 9780367348281 (hardback) | ISBN 9780429328237 (ebook)
Subjects: LCSH: Africa–Foreign relations–1960- | Africa–Politics and
government–1960-
Classification: LCC JZ1773 .A9168 2020 (print) |
LCC JZ1773 (ebook) | DDC 327.6–dc23
LC record available at https://lccn.loc.gov/2019054106
LC ebook record available at https://lccn.loc.gov/2019054107

ISBN 13: 978-1-03-240026-6 (pbk)
ISBN 13: 978-0-367-34828-1 (hbk)
ISBN 13: 978-0-429-32823-7 (ebk)

DOI: 10.4324/9780429328237

Typeset in Times New Roman
by Deanta Global Publishing Services, Chennai, India

Dedicated to Woineshet, Helina and Olivia

Contents

Contributors

Korwa Gombe Adar is Professor of International Studies, Department of Political and Administrative Studies, University of Botswana, Gaborone, Botswana. He received his BSc and MSc in Political Science at Indiana State University, Terre Haute, Indiana, United States, followed by an MA and PhD in International Studies at the University of South Carolina, Columbia, United States. He is the author of many articles published in internationally recognized refereed journals as well as numerous peer reviewed book chapters. His areas of research interest include: International Relations Theory; African International Relations; Foreign Policy Analysis; Human Rights; and International Law & Organization. His recent co-edited volumes include: *Building Regionalism from Below: The Role of Parliaments and Civil Society in Regional Integration in* Africa (2018); *African Foreign Policy, Diplomacy and Leadership: Reflections of Diplomats and Scholars* (2016); *Cooperative Diplomacy, Regional Stability and National Interests: The Nile River and Riparian States* (2011); and *State of Africa: Parameters and Legacies of Governance and Issue Areas* (2010).

Olumuyiwa Amao obtained his MA (cum laude) and PhD of Philosophy degrees in Politics from the University of KwaZulu-Natal, South Africa, and the University of Otago, New Zealand, respectively. His PhD thesis titled "From Freetown to Kinshasa: Reassessing Nigeria and South Africa's Foreign Policy Behaviour and Conflict Intervention Roles in Africa", argued for the decolonization of the foreign policy literature on Africa to reflect the role of "agency" rather than "structure". His current research focuses on the application of the meta-theoretical approach of analytic eclecticism to the understanding and interpretation of the foreign policy and intervention behaviour of regional powers in Africa. His publications have appeared in a number of leading scholarly journals focused on Africa. These include: "Nigeria, Afro-centrism and Conflict Resolution: Five Decades after—How Far, How Well?", *African Studies Quarterly*, 2015; "South Africa's Emerging 'Soft Power' Influence in Africa and Its Impending Limitations: Will the Giant Be Able to Weather the Storm?", *African Security*, 2016, and "Nigeria and South Africa's Foreign Policy and Intervention Behaviour in Africa: A Structural Realist Analysis", *South African Journal of International Affairs*, 2019.

Kwesi Aning is Director of the Faculty of Academic Affairs and Research at Kofi Annan International Peacekeeping Training Centre. He specialises in peacekeeping economies, hybrid security/political orders and organised crime. Recent publications include: 2016—"Africa in global International Relations: emerging approaches to theory and practice" (P. Bischoff and A. Acharya eds.); 2018—"Exploring peace formation security and justice in post-colonial states" (A. Brown, C. Hunt, V. Boegge); and in 2018—"Deep commitment, high expectations: the values of the next generation of African security sector leaders", *Africa Defence Forum*, 12 July, Vol XI/2.

Paul-Henri Bischoff is Professor and erstwhile long-standing Head of Department of Political and International Studies at Rhodes University, Grahamstown-Makhanda, South Africa, having held previous appointments at the Universities of Papua New Guinea and Swaziland and as Visiting Professor at Jinan University in Guangzhou, China. A graduate of the Universities of the Witwatersrand, Lancaster and Manchester, his research interests revolve around South African foreign policy, African regional organisation and transnational relations between Africa and Asia. Recent publications include "Model, driver and norm entrepreneur or just another participant? The international relations of South Africa's National Assembly and SADC" in: K. Adar, A. Meyer and G. Finizio (eds.), *African Regional Integration Process: Regional, National Parliamentary and Civil Society Dimensions* (Bern, Peter Lang, 2018); *Africa in Global International Relations: Emerging Approaches to Theory and Practice*, with K. Aning and A. Acharya (eds.), (London, Routledge), 2016; "How much its own and to what end? SADC and the culture of security and regional organisation in Southern Africa" in S. Aris and A. Wenger (eds.), *Regional Organisations and Security: Conceptions and Practices* (Routledge, 2014); and with R. Chipaike, "Chinese Engagement of Zimbabwe and the Limits of Elite Agency", *Journal of Asian and African Studies*, Vol 54/7 (2019), pp. 947–964. "A challenge to conventional wisdom: Locating agency in Angola and Ghana's economic engagements with China" (with Ronald Chipaike), *Journal of Asian and African Studies* ,Vol 53/7 (November 2018); "African Transnationalism in China: At the interface of local, transnational, bilateral and multilateral responses", *Journal of Asian and African Studies*, Vol 52/7 (November 2017).

Kwaku Danso is a Research Fellow at the Kofi Annan International Peacekeeping Training Centre. He is also the deputy editor of the *Journal of African Peace and Security*. Kwaku holds a PhD in International Conflict Management from Kennesaw State University, Georgia, USA, and an MSc in African Studies from the University of Edinburgh, UK. His research interests cover global-regional peacekeeping, transitional and relational justice, DDR, political violence, human security and elections. He has a number of publications on peace and security in Africa.

Tshepo Gwatiwa a lecturer in the Department of International Relations at the University of the Witwatersrand. I was previously a lecturer at the University of Botswana and an adjunct lecturer at the BDF DCSC.

Mercy Kathambi Kaburu is Lecturer in International Relations at United States International University (USIU)-Africa. She holds a PhD in International Relations from United States International University-Africa, and an MA of Arts degree in International Conflict Management from the Institute of Diplomacy and International Studies, University of Nairobi, Kenya. Her research areas of interest include foreign policy analysis, and regional peace and security among others.

Kabelo M. Mahupela holds an MA of Arts degree in International Studies, a BA of Arts with Honours in Political and International Studies, as well as a BA of Arts degree from Rhodes University, Grahamstown, South Africa. He has worked as a researcher at the Centre for Human Rights in Botswana (DITSHWANELO) and is currently under the employ of DPC & Associates, a consultancy of development experts who operate in the governance and private sectors, with a focus on Monitoring and Evaluation services. DPC & Associates has been involved in numerous projects to capacitate Regional Economic Communities such as SADC, COMESA, and the African Union Commission, who benefit from support obtained from international development partners such as GIZ, USAID, the EU and UKAid.

Mike Mavura graduated with a PhD in International Studies from Rhodes University, Grahamstown, South Africa, in 2017. Currently he is Change Agent and Lecturer in the Visual Studies Department at the Academy of Design and Photography at the University of Stellenbosch, South Africa. From 2011 to 2017, he worked as Visiting Lecturer at Rhodes University in the Department of Political and International Studies where he taught International Relations at both undergraduate and post-graduate levels. With a research interest in transnational migration and its political ramifications, he was part of a joint project between the Department of Political and International Studies at Rhodes and the School of International Relations at Jinan University in Guangzhou to conduct research on African migrants living in China. He has worked as a researcher on South African immigration policy for the Scalabrini Institute for Human Mobility in Africa (SIHMA) in Cape Town where he co-published "The Evolution of Migration Policy in Post-Apartheid South Africa" report. He is a "Thought Leader" article contributor to South Africa's weekly *Mail and Guardian.*

Cecilia Lwiindi Nedziwe is Lecturer in the Department of Anthropology and Development Studies at the University of Johannesburg (UJ), South Africa. She has also held several senior positions as a research coordinator/policy analyst, regional coordinator, director of operations and fundraiser, among other positions at the Centre for Peace Initiatives in Africa in Zimbabwe, the International Peace Research Institute (PRIO) in Norway and the UJ's

Institute for Pan-African Thought and Conversation (IPATC). Nedziwe holds a doctorate in Political and International Studies from Rhodes University where she studied as the CODESRIA African Pathways and South Africa's National Institute for the Humanities and Social Sciences (NIHSS) fellow, as well as the Carnegie Next Generation Social Science Research Council (SSRC) scholar. She also holds a master's degree in International Studies, Peace and Conflict Resolution from the University of Queensland in Brisbane, Australia, where she studied as a Rotary Peace Scholar; and a BA (honours) degree in International Economics from Don-State Technical University in Russia. Nedziwe has published articles and policy briefs on migration, education policy, curriculum transformation and on South Africa's foreign policy. Her interests include: regional politics (integration) and development; international organisations, civil society; and gender.

Eugenio Njoloma is Lecturer in the Department of Governance, Peace, and Security Studies of Mzuzu University, Malawi. Prior to obtaining this position, he taught Political Studies at the Catholic University of Malawi between 2013 and 2015. This position succeeded his earlier role as a Project Coordinator of Tigawane Project for Street Kids in Balaka, Malawi. In 2011, he received his MA of Social Science degree in International Studies from Rhodes University, South Africa. Eugenio's research interests embrace the areas of Conflict Management, Terrorism, and Security and Development. He has extensively published topical articles in Malawi's leading magazine, *The Lamp*. Other publications include "The Effects of Politicised Ethnicity on National Cohesion in Malawi", *Journal of the Southern African Peace and Security Studies*, Vol 6/2 (May 2019) and a co-authored book chapter focusing on "The Socio-economic Impact of Tourism on the Local Community in Nkhata Bay District, Malawi," *The Routledge Handbook of Tourism Impacts: Theoretical and Applied Perspectives*, by Dogan Gursory and Robin Nunkoo (eds.) (London, Routledge, 2019).

Mzukisi Qobo is Associate Professor in International Business and Strategy at the Wits Business School at the University of the Witwatersrand, Johannesburg, South Africa, after appointments at the University of Johannesburg (where he was Deputy Director at the SARCHI Chair on Foreign Policy and African Diplomacy) and the University of Pretoria. He has held the position of Chief Director: Trade Policy, at the Department of Trade and Industry, where he helped develop South Africa's trade policy. His expertise is in the domains of International Political Economy, global governance and rising powers. He obtained his PhD from the University of Warwick, UK; MA from the University of Stellenbosch, South Africa; and BA from the University of Cape Town, South Africa. Publications include co-authored with Garth Le Pere, "Between Resource Extraction and Industrialising Africa", in Alden, Chris and Farge (eds.), Dan, *New Directions in China-Africa Studies*, London: Routledge, 2018; Mashele, Prince and Qobo (2014). *The Fall of the ANC: What Next?* Johannesburg: Pan Macmillan (Picador Books); co-authored with Garth Le Pere, "The Role of China in Africa's Industrialization: The Challenge of Building Global Value Chains", *Journal of Contemporary China*, Vol 27/10, 2018, pp.208–228; "South Africa's Foreign Policy and Nation-Branding: Regional Leadership and its Discontent", *Journal of Strategic Review for Southern Africa*, Vol 39/1, May 2017; co-authored with Mills Soko, "Economic, Trade, and Development Relations between South Africa and the European Union: The End of Strategic Partnership? A South African Perspective", *South African Journal of International Affairs,* Vol 24/2, 2017, pp.137–157; co-authored with Nceku Nyati, "Ubuntu, Public Policy Ethics and Tensions in South Africa's Foreign Policy", *South African Journal of International Affairs*, 2016, Vol 23/4, 421–43.

Ahmed Ali Salem is Associate Professor and Associate Dean in the College of Humanities and Social Sciences at Zayed University, United Arab Emirates. He is also a senior research associate and currently a visiting professor in the Department of Political and International Studies at Rhodes University, South Africa. He earned his PhD in Political Science, an MA in African Studies from the University of Illinois at Urbana-Champaign, USA. and a BSc in Political Science from Cairo University, Egypt. His research interests include mainstream, critical and non-Western theories of international relations; foreign policies of Muslim and Western states towards each other; and Muslim reformist and political thoughts. He authored, edited and translated numerous books, book chapters and journal articles in Arabic and English, and made countless presentations in international fora. Recent publications include: "Promoting or Resisting Change? The United States and the Egyptian Uprising, 2011–2012", in Geoffrey F. Gresh and Tugrul Keskin (eds.), *U.S. Foreign Policy in the Middle East: From American Missionaries to the Islamic State*; "A Critique of Failing International Relations Theories in African Tests, with emphasis on North African Responses", in Paul-Henri Bischoff, Kwesi Aning and Amitav Acharya (eds.), *Africa in Global International Relations: Emerging Approaches to Theory and Practice*; "Localizing Islam in the West: Mazrui's Journey from the Study of African Politics to Global Cultures," in the *American Journal of Islamic Social Sciences*; and the 2016 book *Collective Security in the League of Arab States between the Realist and Constructivist Theories.*

Issaka K. Souaré has been a member of the UN Standby Team of Senior Mediation Advisors since March 2016; a Senior Research Associate in the Department of Political and International Studies at Rhodes University in South Africa since May 2018; and a Visiting Lecturer in the Department of Political Science at the General Lansana Conté University of Sonfonia in Conakry, Guinea, since mid-2017. He previously served as Special Advisor to the AU High Representative for Mali and the Sahel from March 2013 to February 2016 after a stint at the AU Commission in Addis Ababa as Expert on Early Warning and Preventive Diplomacy. He previously worked at the Pretoria office of the Institute for Security Studies (2007–2012), both as a Senior Researcher and Programme Head. With a PhD in Political Science from the University of Quebec in Montreal, Canada, Dr Souaré's several publications include *Opposition Political Parties in Africa: The quest for power* (in French, Montreal, 2017); *Somalia at the crossroads* (co-edited, London, 2007); *Africa in the United Nations System, 1945–2005* (London, 2006); and *Civil Wars and Coups d'Etat in West Africa* (Lanham, 2006).

Makonnen Tesfaye is Senior Consultant at MTec Economic Research & Consultancy in the UK. Previously, Makonnen worked for the United Nations Conference on Trade and Development as Inter-Regional Advisor and International Consultant, and for the London Council, Camden Borough, as a Senior Economic Advisor. He holds undergraduate and graduate degrees in Economics, Economic Institutions and Planning from the London School of Economics and Political Science, University of London, and the University of Essex in the UK. Makonnen is a regular contributor to the AigaForum, EthioFora and East African Affairs online platforms, writing on Ethiopia and Horn of Africa economic development, politics, foreign policy and diaspora affairs.

Acknowledgements

A remark made by external examiner and colleague, Maxi Schoeman, that the Department of Political and International Studies at Rhodes University was producing good MA theses on foreign policy studies at a time when little foreign policy work on the continent was being produced, gave birth to the idea of this book. I am grateful that some contributors to this book come out of having done their postgraduate studies in International Relations at Rhodes, but also, that many other contributors in this book teach, research and live on the continent. For assisting with individual contributors, my thanks go to Eduard Jordaan, my colleague at the department, Tim Murithi in Cape Town, Kwesi Aning in Accra and Tesfachew Taffere in Addis Ababa. A very warm thank you to Jean Schäfer for her dedicated proofreading and helpfulness in preparing the manuscript for Routledge. A note of special thanks to Jaine Roberts, the Director of the Research Office at Rhodes University, for her support in bringing this book to be print-ready. I am grateful to Andrew Taylor of Routledge and Professor Daniel Bach of the University of Bordeaux, the series editor for the Routledge Studies in African Politics and International Relations, and two anonymous reviewers for Routledge for their valuable criticisms and suggestions. Sophie Iddamalgoda, who expertly handled the contract and editorial process, deserves a note of appreciation.

Acronyms

ACHPR	African Commission on Human and People's Rights
AEC	African Economic Community
AFISMA	African-Led International Support Mission for Mali
AFPLAN	Regional Food Plan for Africa
AHSG	Assembly of Heads of State and Government
AMDC	African Minerals Development Centre
AMISOM	African Union Mission in Somalia
AMV	Africa Mining Vision
ANC	African National Congress
APRM	African Peer Review Mechanism
ASF	Africa Standby Force
AU	African Union
AUC	African Union Commission
BLS	Botswana, Lesotho and Swaziland
BRICS	Brazil, Russia, India, China, South Africa
CAP	Common African Positions
CADSP	Common African Defence and Security Policy
CEDAW	Convention on the Elimination of all Forms of Discrimination Against Women
CET	Common External Tariff
COMESA	Common Market for Eastern and Southern Africa
CONSAS	Constellation of Southern African States
CPP	Convention People's Party
CSSDCA	Conflict Security Stability and Development Conference in Africa
DBSA	Development Bank of Southern Africa
DJAF	Djibouti Armed Forces
DRC	Democratic Republic of Congo
EAC	East African Community
ECCOSOC	Economic and Social Council
ECOMOG	Economic Community of West African States Monitoring Group
ECOWAS	Economic Community of West African States

ESF	ECOWAS Standby Force
EEAS	European External Action Service
EEC	European Economic Community
EEZ	Exclusive Economic Zone
ELF	Eritrean Liberation Front
ENDF	Ethiopian National Defence Force
EPA	Economic Partnership Agreements
EPLF	Eritrean People's Liberation Front
EPRDF	Ethiopian People's Revolutionary Democratic Front
EU	European Union
FLS	Frontline States
FOCAC	Forum on China–Africa Cooperation
FPA	Foreign Policy Analysis
FRELIMO	Mozambique Liberation Front
GAF	Ghana Armed Forces
GCC	Gulf Cooperative Council
GDP	Gross Domestic Product
GL	Gender Links
GNU	Government of National Unity
GSU	General Service Unit
IBSA	India, Brazil, South Africa
IC	International Community
ICC	International Criminal Court
ICJ	International Court of Justice
ICU	Islamic Courts Union
IDC	Industrial Development Cooperation
IFI	International Financial Institution
IGAD	Intergovernmental Authority on Development
IGASOM	IGAD Mission for Somalia
IGO	Intergovernmental organisations
IMET	International military education and training
IMF	International Monetary Fund
INGO	International non-governmental organisations
IR	International relations
ISDSC	Inter-State Defence and Security Committee
ISIS	Islamic State of Iraq and al-Sham
KDF	Kenyan Defence Force
LAPSSET	Lamu Port, South Sudan, Ethiopia Transport
LGBTI	Lesbian, gay, bisexual, transgender and intersex
LGBTQ	lesbian, gay, bisexual, transgender, questioning
LPA	Lagos Plan of Action
MAP	Millennium Africa Recovery Plan
MDG	Millennium Development Goals
MFA	Ministry of Foreign Affairs

MINUSMA	UN Multidimensional Integrated Stabilization Mission in Mali
MK	Umkhonto we Sizwe
MNC	Multinational Corporations
MOD	Ministry of Defence
MP	Members of Parliament
NAM	Non-Aligned Movement
NATO	North Atlantic Treaty Organisation
NCA	National Constituent Assembly
NDC	National Democratic Congress
NEPAD	New Partnership for African Development
NGO	Non-governmental organisation
NPC	National Planning Commission
NPP	New Patriotic Party
OAU	Organization of African Unity
OECD	Organisation for Economic Cooperation and Development
OLF	Oromo Liberation Front
ONUC	Operation of the United Nations in Congo
OPDSC	SADC Organ on Politics, Defence and Security Cooperation
PAC	Pan-Africanist Congress
PAP	Pan-African Parliament
PFMA	Public Finance Management Act
PME	France's General Confederation of Small and Medium Companies
PRC	Permanent Representatives Committee
PSC	Peace and Security Council
REC	Regional Economic Communities
RISDP	Regional Indicative Strategic Development Plan
SACU	Southern African Customs Union
SADC	Southern African Development Community
SADCC	Southern African Development Coordination Conference
SAP	Structural Adjustment programmes
SDG	Sustainable Development Goals
SIPO	Strategic Indicative Plan for the Organ
TDCA	Trade Development and Cooperation Agreement
TFG	Transitional Federal Government
TPLF	Tigray People's Liberation Front
UAE	United Arab Emirates
UCLOS	United Nations Convention on Law of the Sea
UIC	Union of Islamic Courts
UN	United Nations
UNIP	United National Independence Party
UNO	United Nations Organisation
UNSC	United Nations Security Council
UPDF	Uganda People's Defence Force

US	United States
USA	United States of America
WTO	World Trade Organisation
ZANLA	Zimbabwe African National Liberation Army
ZANU-PF	Zimbabwe African National Union-Patriotic Front
ZAPU	Zimbabwe African People's Union

1 Introduction

African foreign policy studies—selecting signifiers to explain agency

Paul-Henri Bischoff

Introduction

The study of foreign policy is about individual and collective agency, where agency is "directed, meaningful, intentional and self-reflective social action" or the faculty or state of acting or exerting power (Chabal, 2009: 7; Buzan, Jones & Little, 1993: 103) in a particular context. Of necessity, it looks at official or officially enabled leaders, decision-makers and role players with their profiles and identities uniquely responding to changing domestic, regional and international contexts. Foreign policy is a "set of ideas or actions designed to solve a problem or promote some change in the policies, attitudes or actions of other states, in non-state actors … in the international economy or the physical environment of the world" (Holsti, 1995: 83).

At first blush, the study of agency in African foreign policy is the search for a broad aggregation of interests and a foreign policy strategy both at an individual and collective level with the aim of achieving sustainable security, welfare and development to mitigate the structural impediments of a hierarchical world order and world economy. Often though, scholarship has plotted the local response to impulses crowding in from the outside. The "external factor" envelops foreign policy description. The post-colonial state's architecture, descriptions of its elite as authoritarian and comprador or neo-colonial in character has helped drive this type of analysis. A limited political and constitutional base for the conduct of any meaningful state-society relations, compounded by a rigid North-South divide and growing encroachments by the forces of globalisation, ever further driving the capitalist integration of the continent with that of the world market, enfeebled African sovereignty, economic self-determination and African agency.

When considered, agency most often described presidential acts and personalities driving an elite foreign policy disposition. In addition, explanations were sought for the type of agency, which had states engage in paradoxical behaviour—where, for purposes of legitimacy and recognition, international norms and institutions were signed onto, only, in practice, to decry them. Found to be seemingly irrational or schizophrenic is explained in terms of the dilemma faced by marginalised states caught in a position of structural inequality (Sabrow, 2019: 1–2).

To arrive at a comprehensive understanding, foreign policy agency needs to be studied on its own and within context. This is because we are aware that "Africans were never the passive and apathetic actors they are typically made to be in discourses of marginalisation".[1] There is also the observation that African agency can be said to have helped to materially change our contemporary world. Amy Niang suggests that Africa's anti-colonialism and de-colonialism, for instance, helped shape today's global commons. African struggles contributed to present day global notions of freedom, human rights and solidarity amidst the ethical collapse of a dying imperial world (2016: 458).

Foreign policy agency, traceable in the period from independence, however broad or limited, we suggest, should be studied as consequential, self-reflective action encompassing the domestic.

After the initial euphoria around nation building faded, African regimes sought to buy social peace and stability. A foreign policy objective of obtaining international support from big powers became key. In the context of a rentier state, established social strata continue to have an interest in the upkeep of an inherited economic structure dependent on the near to exclusive extraction of raw materials and commodities owned by Multinational Corporations (MNC) from Western economies and that of a neo-colonial relationship with Western powers. Foreign policy change to these elites could and can only mean, "with different degrees of urgency" to make these relations "more beneficial to themselves" (Nolutshungu, 1982: 401). It encouraged a foreign policy of staff (free) riding and extraversion or the soliciting of external support to stabilise domestic security.

While a characterisation of foreign policy dependent on the external factor in part still holds true—albeit with the caveat that China in places may have replaced the West as the most hoped for source of benefice—African scholars cognisant of history, culture and the opening up of democratic spaces with new voices, have begun to take a broader view. Domestic rather than external sources are the key explanandum on continuities, and change for the conduct and effectiveness of foreign policy elites over time. The domestic now includes the degree of democratic organisation and plurality of expressed interests influencing foreign policy issues, when relating with outside powers such as China (Chipaike & Bischoff, 2018). Moreover, at a time when liberal global governance and world order is disrupted by the illiberalism in the leadership of big and regional powers or the politics of the environment, the accompanying fluidity allows all other states, regions and civil society actors to appear on scene. A rapidly changing domestic, regional and international environment means expressions of (economic) power, such as the North-South divide, are being debated, renegotiated and re-configured (Acharya, 2018: 17). Here, Africa seeks participation alongside others; to be part of constructing narratives and formulating policy agendas. Such participation assists in structuring relations and creating new realities to reshape existing structures, or create new ones.

Against this background, the African state and society face choices for which agency and its study is called for. The African foreign policy agency of the past can throw light on explanations for the present. It is also opportune to ask what needs to inform the choice of strategic, independent and diverse foreign policy goals on the African continent.

It is to enquire what foreign policy has gone before and to what extent it ever took a deep, holistic look at domestic factors informing (the rediscovery of) agency. Overall, scholarship is to identify the signifiers that in consistent and fresh ways represent the character and ideas that emerge from the domestic. This, in order to prompt full descriptions, ideally of a credible foreign policy that has integrity and carries legitimacy. It is to bring to the surface ordinary African voices and the plurality of meanings, agents of African foreign policy, portray or signify over time into our present.

Signifiers

The signifiers to represent African foreign policy agency emerge from the following issue areas:

One, where the analytical focus has shifted from one of the study of external dependence and asymmetries with the West to either a more dedicated adaptation of existing knowledge or the radical epistemological decolonisation of knowledge. Firstly, this can mean the eclectic selection and application of existing theoretical knowledge to relate African choices or, secondly, with a new theoretical focus in mind, to make endogenous African voices central to analysis in what is an evolving context of glocal and transnational realities. Both approaches serve the need for new ways of explaining African events for International Relations (IR). In the context of a Westphalian framework, the referent in the first approach invariably is the nation-state or the Intergovernmental Organisation (IGO) as foreign policy actor. While the referent remains unchanged, the description of setting and emphasis do change. This is to allow for new or added ways of explaining domestic and regional sources of policy. The second approach talks to referent points other than the imported Euro-centric nation-state model and its representatives, to find the previously marginalised moving to the centre of international life.[2] As such, the contribution of African women, communities or indigenous society actors as voices and actors demanding dignity and recognition as agents, contribute to national, regional and international understandings of history, development and governance. They, as referents, are seen to make up the fabric of international events and need to stand at the source and centre of descriptions of the international (Magadla, 2013).

The overall concern generally, however, is to broadly begin to also look at the lived experiences of the (African) majority, how it conceives of political community (Bischoff et al., 2016: 15) and the way this, by extension, for our purposes here normatively shapes (elite) foreign policy decision-making. Invariably, African scholarship wants to highlight foreign policy as seen through the prism of alternate accounts of history and culture. In other words, how the majority lives, believes and sensitises its leaders, or how leaders anticipate reactions by the opinion of a significant majority, needs to inform our understanding of foreign policy agency. As such, "thinking foreign policy" is social and cultural, as much as it is political, economic or strategic.

Two, where a collective regional societal awareness, in this case, a Pan-Africanist mindfulness, informs the study of foreign policy. Even though states highly prize the norm of sovereignty, they also heavily rely on the multilateral support given by Pan-African institutions at sub-regional and regional levels on a continent that regionally and inter-governmentally is well networked and integrated. As such, the study of individual foreign policy wants to pay heed to shared (Pan-African) norms espoused by evolving regional organisation and its modus operandi. This, at a time when a body such as the African Union (AU) has real powers (Tieku, 2004: 250) to help pattern regional organisational norms and processes, yet finds itself in a setting where Africa lacks continental sovereignty (Kornegay & Landsberg, 2009). Where individual states exploit this cleavage to depart from collective norms, this additionally forms the basis for signifying new avenues of foreign policy explanation.

Three, the need for anticipating and responding to the growing density of relations with the outside world is an additional signifier for agency. In this new century, there is the new or increasing post-Western engagement with a diverse host of resourceful non-Western foreign policy actors in search of mineral, energy, agricultural and other resources on the African continent (China, India, Turkey, Brazil, Iran, Israel, Russia, United Arab Emirates, South Korea for instance). The states involved generally pay heed to a conventional script mindful of state sovereignty and the principle of non-interference. These openly pursue their respective national interest in competition with others, and African states and the AU are often at a strategic comparative disadvantage with the bigger of these actors. The engagement with states in a geo-political and geo-economic taut environment of different bidders—including those Western players willing to engage with the newcomers—demands, more than ever before, for Africans to take advantage of ascendant alliances to formulate their own distinctly informed, strategic national and collective foreign policy responses.

Four, in a world of emerging geo-political regions, the African foreign policy response is of global relevance and signifies a demand for agency. Existing individual polities and regional societies of states in both countries of the North and those of the Global South face sideways and bottom-up pressures from push-and-pull factors to do with transnationalism, cosmopolitanism, identity politics, culture, populism, migration and nationalism. In the post-2008 period of economic crisis radiating out from the West, nationalism, ethnicity and religion have mobilised communities within and across borders. "When the politics of exclusive collective identity … seek a facetious regeneration of *Gemeinschaft* in an increasingly remote *Gesellschaft*" (Hobsbawm, 2008: 93), domestic and transnational challenges from this, call for foreign policy understanding on the responses taken. There is the long-standing African experience of dealing with the ability of a weak Westphalian state to cope with transnational and bottom-up pressures. Here, Africa's deep primordial experiences, the construction of primordial attachments and the relationship between politics and culture is of interest to global scholarship. The late Ali Mazrui (2000: 37, 49) pointed to ethnicity and religion as the two primordial forces operating in Africa and how as transnational forces, these come to be internationalised. Ethnicity and religion are powerful mobilisers of political sentiment. These phenomena affect international relations worldwide and calls for the study of a compendium of foreign policy initiatives and foreign policy responses.

Where transnational and domestic forces, as never before since 1945, challenge the core of the Westphalian state system and regional organisation, long-standing African experience and Africa's often tolerant response bears lessons. For instance, mass migration and displacement on the continent itself advances normative lessons on how the International Community (IC) and individual states and their societies ought to promote responses based on principles of empathy, tolerance and solidarity practised in Africa itself. At the same time, African reactions to long-standing transnational security threats are a source of understanding of now similar, more recent threats elsewhere in the world.

In sum, as political, economic and social forces encroach in new ways, the long historical African experience of being open to the world (Davidson, 1974; Buettner, 1979) is instructive for states and societies in general. The entire post-colonial African foreign relations experience opens itself up to general enquiry.

The contributors to this volume talk to ontological, epistemological, social, sociological, ideological and cultural signifiers of foreign policy, to accompany, complement or substitute political, economic or strategic analyses. This, while acknowledging that overall, agency remains conditioned by asymmetry and the constraints of a (post-) Westphalian structure. Generally, however, the concern expressed is that foreign policy description needs to aim at more holistic accounts of (African) foreign policy. Domestic sources of foreign policy need preeminent consideration.

To unearth African-centred foreign policy actorness, Chapter 2 by Paul-Henri Bischoff sketches the continuities and discontinuities in descriptions up to the present. Where African foreign policy was once largely perceived in terms of the dependence on a predominant West that inhibited African foreign policy agency, the analytical focus has shifted. Where actors have multiplied and regional organisation has grown, there is greater political and ideological space for different expressions of (African) actorness. South Africa and the African Union (AU) serve as illustrations for this. The study of African foreign policy also ought, more than ever, to inform the general study of foreign policy. African specificities test and expand on the validity of general mainstream claims and bear lessons for the world in a Western-led academy largely still extrapolating from Western experience.

Foreign policy agency: Individual and collective

Individual foreign policy agency is about self-reflective action involving identity, norms, coordination and developing organisation. Kabelo Mahupela contends that constructivism allows for an analysis of the social space for agency, one expansive and unrestricted by hierarchy or structure, inclusive of small states and their ability to manipulate their external environment. Throughout its history since independence, Botswana has been able to succeed as a small African state in an international arena dominated by Western ideals. As such, it has lived and visibly espoused liberal democratic values for most of the period since independence. This, in opposition to the general trends in the region and where other states were less successful than Botswana in projecting foreign policy and earning credit and status.

While the early literature on Botswana's foreign policy is dominated by neorealist perceptions positing Botswana as a "client", "captive" or "hostage" state to apartheid South Africa, Mahupela starts from another premise, that Botswana's foreign policy is seen to flow from a set of principles labelled as "principled pragmatism" ascribed to the country's founding father, Sir Seretse Khama. It is held that principled pragmatism implies that Botswana expresses its agency by a set of principles informed by the socio-cultural identity of the country. Driven by a liberal democratic ethos, the stance has had the country prepared to isolate itself from others in defence of its principles, even where African counterparts have chosen to turn a blind eye towards violations of international law and the norms that govern their collective institutions. To this end, Botswana's intervention in Lesotho, the chastisement of Mugabe for bringing about the Zimbabwean electoral crisis of 2009 and its dissenting stance when the African Union (AU) sought to sideline the ICC (International Criminal Court), serve as examples of the principled projection of identity in international affairs.

Collective foreign policy agency implies that rather than any automatic adherence to global norms, the South either adapts global norms to suit itself or provides its own regional sub-sets of norms to inform foreign policy behaviour. Ever since the 1955 Bandung Conference, states of the Global South have come together on common issues to exercise agency. This was buttressed, by the existence, first, of the Organisation of African Unity (OAU) followed by that of the AU, complementing a host of sub-regional organisations, trade treaties and regimes. A collective regional societal Pan-African awareness is informed by the social, political and diplomatic interactions around regional organisation and the goals pursued by states and civil society organisations. The consequence, regional societies of states or non-state actors evolving norms and processes at the levels of regional or sub-regional organisation, speaks to the effect this has on foreign policy agency.

Tsepho Gwatiwa talks to the AU as the primary multilateral institution in Africa, responsible for collective diplomacy on the continent. Responsible as it is for negotiating and implementing agreements on global issues such as international trade, international law, international security and other important crosscutting issues such as migration, humanitarian aid and protection of vulnerable groups, he looks at the degree to which the organisation optimises the available political space to express collective foreign policy agency. He finds that acting under the shadow of coloniality and stymied by member states who engage in mimicry rather than authenticity, the organisation is both limited and self-limiting in its agency. Precepts and codes are incepted and developed elsewhere. Nigeria and South Africa hinder the development of collective and effective agency by their lack of wherewithal to express any persistent type of hegemony. All this occurs against the fault lines of enduring African schisms. Above all, the personalisation and individualisation of AU policy is a major drawback. It prevents progressive institutionalisation and the build-up in the autonomy of the AU as a collective foreign policy agent.

Cecilia Nedziwe expresses the need to deepen and broaden the analysis about collective African agency, one that lies beyond the traditional linearity inherent in a state-centred, Westphalian study of international relations. In looking at the Southern African Development Community (SADC), she argues that SADC as an inter-governmental organisation has an external policy of getting members to implement policies taken at the regional centre. As such, it engages in a "foreign policy" whose prior policymaking processes at the level of SADC involve the participation of non-state actors. This, despite the fact that SADC as an institution does not have any outstanding autonomy as a body and largely remains an instrument of its state members. Her points of reference are gender-based civil society actors; what allows them to interface with SADC on policy. She details how, for non-state actors to participate in supporting the evolution of policy on a wider interpretation of security, the history of the evolution of regionalism in Southern Africa is necessary. Nedziwe explores how the history and specifics of regional organisation in the South opens the way for new and alternative understandings of collective foreign policy internal to a region that embraces non-state participants. As such, the author looks at how, since the mid-1970s, SADC foreign policymaking processes have evolved, and how the interface of state-non-state regionalism promotes a sense of growing regionness that has contributed to improved (human) security and development as regards gender security.

Eugenio Njoloma references constructivism in positing that norms of behaviour advocated for by international or regional organisations shape state identities and interests and signify foreign policy preferences. Malawi, in adhering to collective norms and principles advanced by African regional organisation, is a case in point. Yet, despite this assumption, Malawi offers evidence for inconsistencies by individual states in demonstrating any agreement or solidarity with regional positions over time. As such, he demonstrates that since attaining independence the state has pursued a foreign policy path characterised by both convergence and divergence from developing norms around African unity, in the face of the forces of colonialism, apartheid and neo-imperialism, also helping to shape Malawi's foreign policy positions.

In the absence of democratic or bureaucratic controls or political predictability, the personal factors in leadership often assert itself. Olumuyiwa Amao asserts Nigeria's foreign policy and intervention behaviour is substantially leader dependent. Nigeria, with its self-declared pedigree as a champion for Africa, is the prime example for the study of Afro-centric and intervention-minded foreign policy leadership on the continent and beyond. From championing decolonisation and national liberation struggles in (Southern) Africa, to intervening to stabilise West African security, Nigeria has been unequivocal in its desire to provide leadership roles and challenge Western-led power. Given

Nigeria's imperial presidency, foreign policy is the exclusive preserve of the big man in Abuja. Nigeria has a history of military rule with its unidirectional impulses, state command of material resources and the poorly institutionalised nature of its foreign policymaking. This opened up the space for individual leadership idiosyncrasies to dictate the shape and direction of foreign policy. In the last ten years, domestic constraints have had Nigeria suffer an authority deficit, notably in light of its failure to resolve effectively its decade-long Boko Haram insurgency. This has affected the leader in his capacity to project Nigeria as a hegemonic agent in Africa's international relations. Under civilian administrations, sensitive to domestic constraints, especially with advancing economic and security pressures, foreign policymaking and the articulation of foreign policy tends to follow a multi-directional process. Similarly, Ethiopian foreign policy under Prime Minister Meles, on the other hand, sought to aid the strategic (neo-liberal and Pan-Africanist) vision of Mbeki's "African Renaissance". It successfully managed to balance relations with the West, China and the rest of the world, all of whom were interested in contributing to Ethiopia's security and economic renewal. Since the departure of Meles, Ethiopia, bereft of strategic allies on the continent and beset by governance and security issues, has confined itself to its own backyard, the Horn of Africa.

Culture and ideology expressed in foreign policy

Mike Mavura looks at de-colonial signifiers that take us beyond formal state-citizen relations when considering domestic sources of African foreign policymaking. Culture, as embodied by organised society over time, with which leaders interact, is one unnoticed driver of foreign policy. A cultural perspective to do with spirituality, at odds with the rational logic often associated with mainstream foreign policy study based on the Western experience, informs his reading. In looking at Zimbabwe, he considers modes-of-being-in-the-world that lie outside conventional mainstream analysis. With this in mind, his chapter indicates the need for a new epistemology to signify another, generally hidden, source of foreign policy. In conceptualising de-colonial signifiers to understand African modes of being, *seeing and acting* are seen to be important in providing an alternative avenue for foreign policy explanation. Mavura's "cultural turn" in foreign policy study looks at Zimbabwe's external relations within the framework of its main actors, former President Robert Mugabe and current President Emmerson Mnangagwa. The proposition put forward is that a culturally grounded analysis of foreign policy falls outside the hegemonic norms of conventional foreign policy analysis. Thus, while normatively Mugabeism translates into one conceptual tool by which to analyse Zimbabwe's foreign policy from an actor-centric perspective, what may still be lacking from such an approach are the culturally grounded viewpoints that inform "Mugabeism" and, ultimately, the kind of study of foreign policy that emerges from such analysis.

Similarly, Makonnen Tesfaye, concerned with providing a holistic explanation of African foreign policy, uses history and culture as signifiers of foreign policy.

He can point to Ethiopia, which has defined and redefined its national interest in terms of long-standing historical and cultural experience. This has predisposed the country towards certain strategic alignments. Using a strategic culture approach, he demonstrates that periods of strategic misalignment only confirm the general rule of what the strategic alignment of the country really means. When considering Ethiopia's foreign policy towards Israel and Middle Eastern Arab countries, historical, cultural, strategic and *realpolitik* foreign policy determinants are considered. This is with a view to developing a holistic understanding of foreign policy. The author finds that the domestic sources of foreign policy are preeminent in deciding foreign policy strategy towards the Middle East: domestic security and political pressures largely decide on the cordiality or otherwise with Israel or Arab and Muslim countries in the Middle East. Overall, the historically and culturally embedded Ethiopian state in a geo-politically important region can allow itself a credible but differentiated foreign policy, where close and intensive relations on an economic and political front with China are balanced with collaborative ties with the USA on the military and security front and economic and aid relations with European Union (EU) countries.

Changes in ideological orientation, occasioned by changing domestic environments, make a difference to foreign policy orientation. Democratic South Africa at the onset embraced neo-liberalism with aspirations at some economic redistribution. It also held itself up to Africa and the South as a paragon of reconciliation, consensus building and constitutionalism. In the 1990s and early 2000s, this was of hope to liberal democrats and social democrats looking towards the growth of wealth, democracy, greater equity and the advance of a culture of human rights—a transforming Global South—worldwide. Under President Thabo Mbeki, the emphasis changed: Africanist concerns to shore up the African state and consolidate inter-governmental organisations with a strategic outlook and the attempt to "Africanise neo-liberalism" meant looking for all types of allies, displacing any deeper concern for the advancement of constitutional democracy or human rights on the continent. Building on the legacy and prestige left by the iconic President Nelson Mandela, Mbeki sought to position the country as a global and regional norm entrepreneur able to contribute to global and regional governance.

The policy framework of these two periods remained and still has resonance. The political recognition of the General Assembly electing South Africa for a third time since 1994 to the United Nations Security Council for the period 2019–2021 attests to this. Yet, at the same time, notwithstanding China's invitation to join Brazil, Russia, India, China, South Africa (BRICS) in 2010, South Africa lost credibility, standing and influence globally and on the continent. In Janus-faced fashion and drawing on ideological strands in the ruling African National Congress' (ANC) Cold War past, the country dropped its neo-liberal stance in Africa that appealed mainly to Western sensibilities (having championed economic and political initiatives such as the New Partnership for African Development (NEPAD) and African Peer Review Mechanism (APRM)). Instead, it rather abruptly switched its sympathies towards emerging authoritarian big powers such as China or Russia. By joining the chorus led by largely non-democratic states for diversifying core decision-making at the global level, it sought to take advantage of the shift away from Western predominance. A mechanical ideological posture and ham-handed diplomacy accompanied the venal introspection, political, social and economic decline and growing inequities of the Zuma presidency (2009–2018). This substantially tainted South Africa's independent actorness both on the African continent and in global affairs. Since then, President Cyril Ramaphosa has engaged in efforts to salvage South Africa's reputation, reverse decline and return the country to projecting the values of the Mandela era abroad.

Mzukisi Qobo asserts that while the pillars of the country's foreign policy have stayed much the same, the points of emphasis and the priorities of various leaders have shown that foreign policy is not a static art, but one subject to contingencies. It reflects on the importance of a leader's preferences in changing domestic political, institutional and economic contexts. The foreign policy under President Jacob Zuma amounts to one of a change in orientation from principled strategy seeking to engage the West and others, to one of unprincipled pragmatism occasioned by an anti-Western posture. It is the contention that during this presidential term of office, South Africa's foreign policy lost its moral authority. The ratcheting up of anti-Western views and the adherence to a displaced anti-imperialist reflex harking back to the Cold War period was a departure from the more nuanced Pan-Africanist perspective of the Thabo Mbeki years. This is when the country sought to position itself more as a bridge-builder and middle-power by seeking recognition as a "good international citizen", occupying a reformist middle-ground and advancing multilateralism worldwide. During Zuma's time, there was a marked shift away from the normative signifiers under Mbeki. What featured glaringly was an unhinged approach; despite its economic and normative interconnectedness with the West, the stance was one of decided anti-Westernism. At the same time, there was the lack of agency, independence and confidence. Zuma's anti-Westernism was a political diversion from the growing internal problems of governance, legitimacy and economic management in the country. South Africa gravitated towards the orbit of China and Russia. The danger, however, was of having its foreign policy fall under the sway of the geo-political and commercial interests of these powers. This, even though beyond an unfathomable scepticism towards the West, a democratic, at times politically raucous South Africa normatively shared little in common with both these authoritarian states.

The agency of small states: Balancing, rhetoric, role conceptions

The agency of a small state like Guinea since independence comes from the ideological sweeps, combined with varying expressions of dynamism, by the different leaderships of its three sets of regimes.

Issaka Souaré in writing on Guinea's foreign policy dispositions invokes strategic foreign policy considerations. Informed by *realpolitik* thinking, one disposition involves changing sets of allies combined with a commitment to multilateral and Pan-African regional integration. The country serves as an example of where an initial realist postulate on the national interest and alliance building precedes considerations of applying a mix of both realist and liberal inspired foreign policy positioning. Under the First Republic and facing French and Francophone hostility from its sub-region, Guinea showed agency as a small state aware of its weaknesses in striving to overcome its encirclement. In a balancing act, often tilting towards the Soviet bloc—not necessarily because its members were communist, but because the grouping happened to stand for the same principles on a number of issues such as anti-colonialism and the fight against apartheid—in West Africa the country forged its own distinct foreign policy stance. All the while, Sekou Toure nevertheless endeavoured to court the Western bloc as an extra source of aid, able potentially to offer far greater development assistance than the socialist bloc. This was realism at its core—no permanent enemy or friend, with everything circling around an entirely self-interested notion of the national interest. In addition, the first leaders of independent Guinea had a natural disposition for regional if not continental integration. As such, Guinea's foreign policy orientations made sure that it played a pivotal role in processes aimed at achieving Pan-African unity.

In a later, more liberal foreign policy phase, Guinea's involvement in continental affairs during the Second Republic saw a long decline. This accounted for the country's absence in the major debates on the continent in the 1990s and, in the lead up to the constitution of the AU at the turn of the century.

Rhetoric devoid of practical substance marks the post-revolutionary government in Tunisia. The revolutionary governments led by An-Nahdha adopted a soft policy towards France, the erstwhile coloniser and prop for the Ben Ali regime the Tunisian revolution overthrew in 2011. This does not correspond to normative political theory that expects post-revolutionary governments to adopt radical foreign policies, especially towards the states they perceive as adamant supporters of the deposed dictator. Only over time, the foreign policies of revolutionary governments become more moderate and accommodative. Tunisia is thus an anomaly that Ahmed Salem sets out to explain. In applying a neoclassical realist and non-structural constructivist approach to An-Nahdha's soft policy towards France, Ahmed Salem finds that ideology and domestic political calculations need consideration. He asserts that An-Nahdha's ideology has never been that of a revolutionary party. As such, post-revolutionary Tunisia missed the opportunity of its revolutionary momentum by not re-establishing its relations with France on a more balanced and equitable footing.

After the political foreign policy prominence of the Nkrumah era, the search for a new nationally determined role for the small state of Ghana in international affairs is of concern to Kwaku Danso and Kwesi Aning. Role theory rests on the claim that individuals or actors define their specific roles and behaviour based on social experience and social learning. In response to acting out an identity given by one's role produces expectations in others. The external posturings by Ghanaian governments are all informed by the fundamental national role conceptions adopted in the first decade following independence. Typically, these have included Pan-Africanism, positive neutrality, non-alignment, good neighbourliness and economic diplomacy (Chazan, 1984). The essence of Nkrumah's foreign and defence policies was assuming the role of an African unifier, informed by Pan-Africanism set on eradicating all forms of colonialism. In assuming this role, the intention was to transform the weak and subordinate image of Ghana and those of all other states on the continent. It gave Ghana a number of closely linked identities that had the country's foreign policy obtain global recognition. Identities included those of being a high-profile continental bloc leader, radical liberation supporter and a standout Pan-Africanist unifier. After Nkrumah, Ghana's security and broader international relations have been far from static, and various policymakers from diverse regimes have differed widely in their responses to domestic and global issues. Over time, individual administrations experimented with multiple and sometimes contrasting (foreign) policy choices. However, in recent years, Ghanaian foreign and defence policies came to advocate an international commitment to peacekeeping. Yet, unlike the commitment to anti-colonialism and anti-imperialism, this has not lent itself to giving Ghana a prominent international identity. With the goal of Pan-African unity a chimaera, Kwaku Danso and Kwesi Aning find that it is not at all clear what specific national role conceptions Ghana can currently identify with and what additional roles its diplomatic and military conduct can internationally fill. As an international peacekeeper, the country is yet to develop a new and positive international identity. Yet, transforming Ghana's identity from a troop contributor to a peacekeeper requires the elevation of Ghanaian peacekeeping from that of a functional imperative to that of cognitive orientation. Only a broad intellectual undertaking to consolidate elite perceptions and policies around conflict, peace and security will allow for a more rounded identity for Ghana as an international pacifier to emerge.

Agency and anti-agency: Strategic choices informed by realism

Korwa Adar and Mercy Kathambi Kaburu's study interrogate the thrust of Kenya's foreign policy towards its immediate region, in a context where the state confronts a neighbouring country that is without a functioning or accountable state with all the attendant informal security issues. The chapter proceeds from the premise that Kenya's regional and continental foreign policy follows its national interest, defined in realist terms. This is the Kenyan state's long-term response to long-standing Somali irredentism, whose most recent manifestation comes in the guise of *al-Shabaab* and its quest for a transnational emirate. The authors argue that irrespective of Kenya's seemingly multilateral diplomatic approach, seen by its participation in the African Union Mission in Somalia (AMISOM) peacekeeping mission to Somalia, a clear realist reading of Kenya's strategic setting and of its national interest scripts its foreign policy behaviour. The analysis contextualises the factors that have determined Kenya's strategic thinking in relation to its strategic environment. The threat of the vicissitude of *al-Shabaab*'s frequent incursions into Kenya's territory that were seen to threaten the country's territorial integrity and *raison d'etre* culminated in the deployment of the Kenyan Defence Force (KDF) to Somalia. This, against a background where Kenya's geo-strategic and geo-political interests in the Horn of Africa have remained consistent throughout its history from independence. The protracted internal military efforts directed against the *shiftas* that go back to the 1960s–1970s and the emergence of *al-Shabaab* and its terrorist incursions account for the evolution of Kenya's foreign policy response over a considerable period of time.

Conclusion

Writing on foreign policy involving post-colonial Africa initially revolved around four principal ideas or approaches:

One, the African element in international relations or the African voice was often discounted; two, foreign policy accounts have traditionally described the engagements with the former colonial overlord or other, big outside powers; three, foreign policy actions were seen as reactive, intended to push back the "external factor" and assert non-alignment in attempts at (often collective) foreign policy actions; and four, individual African states in their overall dispositions, to do with their history, culture and society, were often "not seen".

Political and economic structuralism simply treated African states as plugged into systems from which they could make few, if any, domestic and foreign (economic policy) choices. In the light of a shift towards a less hierarchical world, one of parallel pluralities or "multiplexity" (Acharya, 2018: 29) and the growth, scope and intensity of global and international forces engaging Africa, there is a perceived need to enhance (African) foreign policy understanding.

It is to isolate the signifiers at a domestic level to expand our understanding of a variety of different foreign policy responses. Foreign policy elites do reflect on both short- and long-term reasons of state when making foreign policy choices. While political survival has been an important key to foreign policy understanding, agency in the context of domestic norms, beliefs and cultural practices are the stuff to reveal foreign policy patterns over time. African foreign policy writing wants to proceed from the premise of the type of agency that moves along an active and reactive spectrum, where a large number of variants provide a composite understanding of foreign policy agency.

This edited collection proceeds with four sequences in mind. These include foreign policy writing, the foreign policies of the collective continental IGO, big states, sub-regional states, small states and sub-regional IGO intra-regional policy formulation and implementation. The first chapter looks at past and present African foreign policy concepts and practices, followed by a chapter on the African Union as the prime collective foreign policy actor. This is followed with descriptions of South Africa, Ethiopia and Nigeria as key powers of influence. Zimbabwe's and Kenya's expressions of symbolic power and a diplomatic and military presence in their respective regions makes them significant. The next four chapters deal with the external affairs of small states, including those of a state situated both in Francophone Africa and that of the Maghreb. Lastly, the external relations of a regional organisation, SADC, in its external relations of implementing its regional security policy, is considered.

Notes

1 Niang (2016).
2 Magadla (2013).

References

Acharya, A. (2018). *Constructing Global Order*. Cambridge: Cambridge University Press.

Bischoff, P., Aning, K., & Acharya, A. (eds.). (2016). *Africa in Global International Relations*. London: Routledge.

Buettner, T. (1979). *Afrika, Geschichte von den Anfaengen bis zur Gegenwart*. Cologne: Pah-Rugenstein.

Buzan, B., Jones, C., & Little, R. (1993). *The Logic of Anarchy*. New York: Columbia University Press.

Chabal, P. (2009). *Africa: The Politics of Suffering and Smiling*. London: ZED.

Chazan, N. (1984). Ghana. In: T. Shaw & O. Aluko (eds.), *The Political Economy of African Foreign Policy: Comparative Analysis*. London: Gower.

Chipaike, R., & Bischoff, P. H. (2018). A Challenge to Conventional Wisdom: Locating Agency in Angola's and Ghana's Economic Engagements with China. *Journal of Asian and African Studies*, *53*(7): 1002–1017. doi:10.1177%2F0021909618763922.

Davidson, B. (1974). *Africa in History*. St. Alban's: Paladin.

Hobsbawm, E. (2008). *Globalisation, Democracy and Terrorism*. London: Abacus.

Holsti, K. J. (1995). *International Politics*. Englewood Cliffs: Prentice Hall.

Kornegay, F. A., & Landsberg, C. (2009). Engaging Emerging Powers: Africa's Search for a Common Position. *Politikon*, *36*(1): 171–191. doi:10.1080/02589340903174717.

Magadla, S. (2013). The Personal Is the International: For Black Girls Who've Considered Politics When Being Strong Isn't Enough. *Politikon*, *40*(3): 585–596. doi:10.1080/02589346.2013.856568.

Malaquias, A. (2013). Reformulating IR Theory: African Insights and Challenges. In: K. C. Dunn & T. M. Shaw (eds.), *Africa's Challenge to IR Theory*. Basingstoke: Palgrave.

Mazrui, A. A. (2000). Transnational Ethnicity and Subnational Religion in Africa's Political Experience. In: K. Goldmann, U. Hannerz & C. Westin (eds.), *Nationalism and Internationalism in the Post-Cold War Era*. London: Routledge.

Niang, A. (2016) The Imperative of African Perspectives on International Relations (IR). *Politics*, *36*(4): 453–466. doi:10.1177%2F0263395716637092.

Nolutshungu, S. (1982). African Interests and Soviet Power: The Local Context of Soviet Policy. *Soviet Studies*, *XXXIV*(3): 397–417.

Sabrow, S. (2019). Peripheral States and Conformity to International Norms: The Dilemma of the Marginalized. *Third World Quarterly*, *41*(2): 187–206. doi:10.1080/01436597.2019.1637728.

Tieku, T. K. (2004). Explaining the Clash and Accommodation of Interest of Major Actors in the Creation of the African Union. *African Affairs*, *103*: 249–267.

2 African agency

Past into present African foreign policy concepts and practices

Paul-Henri Bischoff

Introduction

Agency has not always resonated with African foreign policy writing.[1] While authors have acknowledged how "African elites have treated foreign policy as a way for nation-states to become effective participants ... in the international arena" (Khadiagala & Lyons, 2001: 1), overall, foreign policy writing on Africa in terms of agency remained limited until comparatively recently. "The bulk of the literature on African foreign policy for long remained a-theoretical, ideological and policy-oriented" (Adogamhe, 2003: 82). Moreover, the study of the hierarchical, Western-led liberal global governance initiative accompanying globalisation initially left little room for contemplating African agency. Economic structuralism in a North-South divide left few, if any, African foreign policy choices to consider (Kraus, 1994). All this happened against a wider panoply of the predominance of political structuralism.[2] The latter's focus on ascertaining aggregate material power relative to others and consequent "rational" readings of power relations in the study of foreign policy excluded studying small or weak states including those in Africa (Elman, 1995: 171).

Foreign policy writing involving post-colonial Africa initially revolved around four principal ideas or approaches:

First, general foreign policy writing focused on Africa and the global system without describing the African element in the relationship (Wright, 1999: 1). A colonial approach had the African voice discounted.

Second, foreign policy studies considered engagements with the former colonial overlords or other, big outside powers. The prime foreign policy aim was to secure the state and offer one's services as a broker in order to extract benefit (Clapham, 1985: 113). Issues of aid relations with the West and its institutions in the context of external penetration and dependency (Harbeson & Rothchild, 2000: 213–224) largely fall into narratives of engagement.

Third, was the description of foreign policy actions as one of pushing back the "external factor" and asserting non-alignment in often (collective) foreign policy actions.

Fourth, the prevalence of world systems theory and the dependency school saw African states plugged into the world market economy which was seen to leave them with few, if any, domestic and foreign (economic) policy choices to make (Cardoso 1979: 2; Bischoff, 1990: 9).[3]

Overall, then, individual African state agency was often "not seen": The structural constraints in which African political economies operated did not ostensibly give them the room for agency and substantive decision-making. Even though diplomacy was seen to emanate from presidential agency, the foreign policies of individual African states were regarded largely as symbolic and reactive: in speaking about Zambia, Steven Chan, for instance, could state, "Zambia's foreign policy has always been reactive … a foreign policy that has appeared vague, contradictory, tailored to benefit the Zambian elite, or simply naïve; … there have been few initiatives in which Zambia has laid down the ground rules for another's reaction" (Chan, 1987: 223). However, importantly, African states, collaborating in Afro-Asian groupings and then in the African group at the United Nations, demonstrated "actorness,"[4] where they "tended to encourage a continental evaluation of African states in international affairs, rather than an evaluation on the basis of single nation-states" (Nolutshungu, 1975: 20). But even when it came to collective foreign policy, mainstream writing mainly associated regional organisation actorness with that of Europe and the European Economic Community (EEC) or the European Union (EU) rather than with Africa and its Organisation of African Unity (OAU) or African Union (AU) (Drieskens, 2017: 1538).

This chapter first looks at descriptions of individual and collective foreign policies or African actorness over time[5] in order to unearth African-centred foreign policy descriptions and to sketch continuities and discontinuities in descriptions up to the present. Second, it sketches how actors have multiplied and regional organisation has grown to allow for greater political space and new individual and collective expressions of (African) agency and actorness, including that by a middle power South Africa. In concluding, it is held, that with the waxing and waning in collective African foreign policy, individual African state agency and the practice of African economic diplomacy at a time of "multiplexity" gains ground.

African foreign policy practice—Then into now

Foreign policy has a state-actor devise a strategy to affirm or enhance its sovereignty. It implies the careful aggregation of interests across an individual polity. The vision accompanying the strategy and its execution carries import for other states. Whereas some states use foreign policy as a tool to accumulate and display power on the world stage, others simply use the credibility sought with it to achieve more modest domestic goals. Most African countries fall into the second category: "many African countries craft and execute their foreign policies as a critical instrument to secure external assistance to solve their domestic problems" (Malaquias, 2011: 5). "Omnibalancing" explained African or Third World alignments where leaders sought to counter internal and external threats to their rule (David, 1991: 233).

When, after independence, constitutionalism and parliamentary democracy largely gave way to one-party states, politics very much centred on the governing state party and its political elite. The elite and authoritarian character of the colonial state and its narrow base for state-society relations reproduced itself in the post-colonial state with its one-party state. When the initial euphoria around nation building after independence began to fade, African regimes sought to buy social peace and stability. A foreign policy objective to obtain international support from big powers became key. Foreign policies were oriented towards obtaining support from the West, many unable or fearful to break the connection with the West that had structurally deeply penetrated (Noluthshungu, 1982: 401) in neo-colonially or informally "captured" individual African states. It encouraged foreign policies of staff (free) riding, bandwagoning, extraversion or soliciting external support aimed at the stabilisation of the domestic situation.

Accompanying a pro-Western disposition was the rentier state. Established social strata had an entrenched interest in the upkeep of relations with the West and flow of a rentier income. To these elites, foreign policy change could only mean "with different degrees of urgency" to make these relations "more beneficial to themselves" (Nolutshungu, 1982: 401). Largely authoritarian states engaged in patron-client relations with the industrialised world. The head of the executive, president or individual leader as dealmaker often became the official agent in relating with the outside and the personification of patron-client relationships at home (Clapham, 1985: 125).

As a consequence, foreign policy, instead of being "a dynamic process of interaction between the changing domestic demands and supports and the changing external circumstances" (Frankel, 1975: 9), became personalised, exclusive and elitist or static. "The charismatic leader became the source, site and embodiment of foreign policy" (Khadiagala, 2001: 5). This, at a time when in the West, mainstream studies assumed rational, bureaucratic or democratic foreign policy descriptions of leadership in foreign policy.

The Cold War between East and West drew African states into dependent relationships with one or the other side, with only some, say Egypt or Tanzania, able to extract benefit from dealing with both sides by omnibalancing. There were exceptions where individual African foreign policies made a real difference to the pattern of development and broke with the prevalent structure of relations. Sam Nolutshungu pointed out that since independence the African environment was one of *ambiguity* expressed in "the tension between the associative (and, generally, conservative) tendencies encouraged by underdevelopment, and the "dissociative" tendencies implicit in decolonisation" (1975: 24). Algeria, with its record of struggle against colonialism, for instance, had a foreign policy that succeeded in partially disengaging from the Western system (Mortimer, 1984: 1–22).

Despite general weakness at home during phases of the Cold War, there seemed to be no barrier to the conduct of African foreign policy since the times "favoured the ascription to African states of a prestige in excess of their physical capabilities". Trade or economic factors aside and unable to enforce their will at a global level, they were, however, able to rely on pressure-group tactics to achieve their ends (Nolutshungu, 1975: 20–21). Ghana on the global stage aspired to play the role of an intermediary in ending the conflict in Vietnam and, to the disquiet of the West, on ending minority rule in settler Rhodesia and apartheid South Africa, while Tanzania played a central role in promoting national liberation on many fronts (Pinkney, 2001: 24). Nigeria created a revulsion against apartheid in Nigerian society. Flush with oil money, the government gave material and financial support to national liberation movements in Southern Africa. Diplomatically, the country pushed for the establishment of an Eminent Person Group at the Commonwealth to facilitate talks for the dismantlement of the apartheid regime (Egedo, 1987: 31). Mengistu Haile Mariam's Ethiopia, Siad Barre's Somalia or, arguably, John Vorster's apartheid South Africa, could, more or less, exploit the strategic rivalry between East and West to obtain from one or the other side political, ideological, economic and military benefits.

African foreign policy found global resonance with its mobilising and garnering of international and transnational support against colonial Portuguese, settler Rhodesian and apartheid South African rule. The Africa Group in 1969 promoted the UN General Assembly Resolution 2202a (XXI) declaring apartheid to be a crime against humanity (Chipaike & Knowledge, 2018: 5). This was a profound marker for the conduct of international affairs; as evidenced by the eventual adoption of the Responsibility to Protect (R2P) principle by the UN much later in 2005, it helped breach the sanctity of the principle of sovereignty and opened the way for internationalising what had been ostensibly domestic human (in)-security issues. Similarly, the collective mass break-off in diplomatic relations by twenty-five African states with Israel in 1973 was a singular demonstration of collective global African resolve to which even a pro-Israeli Ethiopia had to submit to (see Chapter 5). Yet, with the West in the ascendant and colonialism and apartheid as political constructs in recession, African states became ever more caught in the economic, financial and political vice of North-South relations. This is when African states reverted to largely being respondents in international affairs. The international debt crisis of the 1970s–1980s exemplified this. It put paid to original African, Asian and Latin American demands for structural global reform as seen with the proposals for a New International Economic Order (NIEO), for a body of international development law or recognition for a "human right to development" in 1986, something that industrialised (Western) states simply did not want to see happen (Salomon, 2013: 46, 31).

In the wake of the oil crisis of 1973, African state agency was on the decline. On the economic front, growing indebtedness meant regional African remedies at state-centred attempts to economically integrate the continent (whose origins are traceable to the Bandung Conference of 1955 where the Global South for the first time asserted its actorness by collectively meeting and addressing issues of neo-colonialism and underdevelopment), including the Lagos Plan of Action (LPA) or the Regional Food Plan for Africa (AFPLAN), faded away. Western opposition to redress issues of development outside the international capitalist system (Heidhues & Obareby, 2011: 56) was accompanied by African submission to the policy strait-jacket of neo-liberal International Financial Institution (IFI) rule under the Structural Adjustment Programmes (SAPs) after 1982.[6] African (economic) foreign policy decision-making was constrained by this. Throughout the 1980s and beyond, the Washington Consensus complemented by a Western Group G7 states setting the agenda for the Global South spelt far reaching donor conditionality regimes. This global regime controlled and limited access to markets, finance, aid and any seemingly benevolent largesse.

Other than this, the African condition simply periodically intruded onto the international scene. Africa's agency expressed itself in terms of victimhood, the taking of a socio-psychological stance as a victim of colonialism entitled to assistance (Ayoob, 1989) or, as that of an erstwhile sufferer and hapless bystander deserving redress and justice. France was accused of "forgetting" African combatants on the side of the Free French in the Second World War; Britain of ignoring atrocities committed against Kenyan civilians during the "Mau-Mau" resistance to colonial rule and Namibia demanded reparations for the German perpetration of genocide against Herero and Namaqua communities in the early twentieth century. Moreover, the West was held responsible for instituting a one-sided, extractive world economic system accompanied by uneven development whose consequence was structural African poverty. The genesis for the African condition was said to lie with colonial repression and the one-sided development of the extractive sector amidst the balkanisation of the continent. To the rest of the world, the continent was also seen as the source of unfathomable real or unreal threats around epidemic diseases such as HIV/AIDS or Ebola.

Structural Adjustment, with its political and economic conditionality, faltered. Apart from the programme's own ineffectuality in delivering growth or prosperity, the actions of recalcitrance, together with global civil society criticism (Fidler, 2000: 387), cumulatively eroded the mantle of the SAPs. It came to be seen as inappropriately "apolitical" and economistic, developmentally regressive, characterised by excessive conditionality, as well as by the absence of any genuine ownership by the countries concerned (Heidhues & Obareby, 2011: 59). Ultimately, it failed amidst calls for a more human face to capitalism on the continent and African incapacity/resistance. There "was incomplete, half-hearted, and 'stop-and-go' implementation" by African governments (Heidhues & Obareby, 2011: 60). On the realisation that "if the groups most affected by a reform process do not feel that they 'own' it, generally it will not succeed … reform cannot be 'bought' through donor support alone" (World Bank, 2001).

Resistance from Africa and the South and a new plurality of forces engaging with the continent meant African collective action and individual choices helped erode the neo-liberal global policy framework and structure. The eventual reformulations of SAPs by the IFIs[7] happened against a developing scenario where African states chose to embrace China's major diplomatic and economic overtures after 2000. Ostensibly premised on principles of mutual sovereign respect, non-interference and state-led strategies for development, the idea of a "Beijing Consensus" eschewed the modalities of economic and political conditionality imposed by the "Washington Consensus."

Moreover, issues of regional security helped trigger a revival of collective African state agency and new assertiveness. After the fall of the Berlin Wall, the preoccupation of a unilateral world order intent on penetrating the former communist Second World, marginalised Africa emerging from its Third World status. The global neglect of African issues in the 1990s was marked by the growth in African conflict, poverty and discord, a crisis scenario symbolised by the momentous Rwandan genocide with its million victims and Africa's own "First World War" over the Democratic Republic of Congo (DRC). Without the ability to rely on a UN peacekeeping force as was the convention, this led to Africa's own unilateral collective military foreign policy intervention in West Africa.

After the Western-led UN Security Council failed to attend to the Liberian crisis, an Economic Community of West African States Monitoring Group (ECOMOG) force under the Economic Community of West African States (ECOWAS) led by Nigeria intervened in the civil war conflicts of Liberia in 1990 (and later in Sierra Leone in 1997 and Guinea-Bissau in 1999). African actorness was in evidence in subsequent negotiations to find a modus operandi and partnership with the United Nations on joint peacekeeping and conflict resolution measures. Concerted African foreign policy moves at region-building accompanied initiatives to consolidate democracy and promote an African agenda in global politics. The high point of this was the constitution of the AU in 2002, "meant to be better equipped than the OAU to promote African unity" (Saxena, 2004: 164).

African foreign policy activism after the constitution of the AU in 2002, in the area of peace and security involving military and humanitarian interventions, continued apace with peacekeeping and peace-making interventions in the Comores, Somalia and Darfur (Anning & Edu-Afful, 2016: 121). States formally and politically recognised new actors at regional and continental levels, broadened the scope of regional organisations and were committed to adopting, adapting or creating norms to do with African integration, Pan-African unity and collective African responses to global forces.

The constitution of the AU with its broad institutional plan and architecture invigorated the erstwhile idea of Pan-African unity and actorness. Through constructing and planning for bodies such as the Peace and Security Council (PSC), Pan-African Parliament (PAP), the Economic, Social and Cultural Council (ECCOSOC) or the Regional Economic Communities (RECs), the scope for concerted efforts at security cooperation and social and economic integration increased substantially. With this institutional base, the AU Commission engaged in external relations, grew Africa's international presence and demonstrated actorness.[8] This took place in a context where, with the institution of democracy and of neo-liberal (economic) reforms, a plurality of actors became visible and increasingly heard. New actors in the shape of institutions (parliaments, political parties and interest groups), civil society (social movements and non-governmental organisations (NGOs)) and individuals (in society and business) appeared.

African re-imagining and actorness: The African Renaissance and South Africa

The constitution of the AU offered the prospect of shaping an inclusive African multilateralism from the bottom up (Bischoff, 2008: 181). It was a context where, as Acharya (2009: 30) notes, "Local actors operating out of historically formed normative contexts often redefine and reconstruct international norms in accordance with their beliefs and norms". These beliefs and norms constitute a state's imagining (Patience, 2014: 214); here it amounted to a continent's re-imagining of itself.

African discursive re-imagining of itself revolved around the narrative of an "African Renaissance" put forward by President Thabo Mbeki during his presidency (2000–2007). Together with input from Nigeria, Senegal, Algeria and others, the idea gave currency to a renewal of African actorness in a pluralised Pan-Africanism that embraced the participation of state and non-state actors. In the words of Landsberg (2013: 3):

> The decade 1998–2008 will go down as the golden decade of African agency and diplomacy in world affairs, a period that was certainly on par with the height of decolonisation in the 1950s and 1960s. A combination of moral imperatives—decolonisation, apartheid, genocide and strategic aims—political and economic—and Afrocentric diplomatic stratagems, propelled the case for a new continental regime in Africans, crafted in the main by Africans ... During this decade we saw a revival of African attempts to strengthen their voice, greater influence and attention, and a world order that would be more favourable to them

South Africa, under Mbeki (1999–2008) "introduced a vigorous reformist programme aimed at improving the fortunes of developing countries in general and Africa in particular", the aim being that "the extreme and blatant forms of discrimination against Africa are diminished" (Nel, 2006: 116). Under the leadership of South Africa, Nigeria, Senegal and Algeria, the Pan-African initiative to create the AU in 2002 was the most important collective foreign policy decision undertaken since the founding of the OAU in 1963. Accompanying this was promoting good governance and better state-society relations (Achieng, 2014: 54).

The New Partnership for Africa's Development (NEPAD) and the African Peer Review Mechanism (APRM) as part of the AU are examples of African agency, a response to the social and economic ravages of the Western-imposed SAPs. They marked an attempt at regionalising decisions on major investments coming to the continent and redefining African relationships with the outside world, albeit on neo-liberal terms.

South Africa's role was strategic and agenda driven, propagating norms and values of renewal, an attempt in the words of a South African cabinet minister at the time of launching "a Pan-African transnational democratic revolution"

(Bischoff, 2008: 183). The APRM allowed for a plurality of participants; national civil society actors commenting on national government performance and the Economic and Social Council (ECOSOCC) composed of civil society organisations, including gender-based organisations and members of the African diaspora advising the AU.

The advent of South Africa's entrepreneurial presence as a rising middle power at international fora and in BRICS[9] (intended as a counter-hegemonic project led by China and Russia) had South Africa in concert with others, diplomatically pursue the democratic reform of international institutions such as the United Nations Organisation (UNO) or World Trade Organisation. The expanse in Sino-African relationships made individual African states such as Angola, Zimbabwe, South Africa, Ethiopia and Sudan less prone to Western influence and opened up the space to a tentatively qualitatively differently structured set of inter-continental South-South relations that allowed for demonstrations of African agency (Chipaike & Bischoff, 2018).

The strategic African initiative shown in and around the UN's Millennium Development Goals (MDGs); the constitution of the AU, the African response to neo-liberalism and globalisation; with President Thabo Mbeki's "African Renaissance" initiative and African participation at meetings at the G7/G8 were all signifiers of African actorness. To add to this, the exponential growth in diplomatic, trade, commercial and financial relations with China after 2000 heralded a different type of partnership with the outside world. Unlike the US-led, Western Washington Consensus, the Chinese-led Beijing consensus eschewed political conditionality regimes.

Accompanying this was the appearance of South Africa as an aspirant emerging middle power—albeit of a different type—with asymmetrical capacities from the traditional middle power within a Western-led international order (Jordaan, 2003). South Africa emerging from apartheid was keen to uphold the kinds of norms of universally acceptable standards of behaviour that had played their part in the political struggle to win democratic freedom. Keen to play the role of a good international citizen on the global stage, the country advocated human rights norms supplemented by the advocacy of norms in areas of security and the economy (Geldenhuys, 2006: 93). As Janis van der Westhuizen (2009) noted during the period of the Mandela presidency:

> South Africa used its reconciliation process as the basis for its role as a global bridge builder, mediating in conflicts far from home, such as East Timor, the Middle East, Northern Ireland, and the Lockerbie incident. It played a crucial role in getting African support for the international campaign to ban land mines and was instrumental in extending the Nuclear Nonproliferation Treaty. In fact, shortly before U.S. involvement in Iraq, Colin Powell in his address to the UN Security Council heralded South Africa's decision to unilaterally disassemble its nuclear capacity as a model for Iraq to follow. South Africa occupied a degree of symbolic power disproportionate to its size.

Ultimately, even though during the Mbeki presidency this global diplomatic presence came to be felt, with it being an active member of the World Trade Organisation (WTO) or chair of the Non-Aligned Movement (NAM), Pretoria could claim very little influence over substantive or procedural matters or suggest appropriate action, in part because of its inexperience (Lee, 2006: 69–70; Morphet, 2006: 96). Overall, South Africa was cautious when it came to its willingness to confront the core structure of the global political and economic order of the time (Nel, Taylor, & van der Westhuizen, 2001: 124).

At the United Nations, the country drove a "self-conscious Africa-centred UN policy, at least rhetorically" but there were contradictions and tensions with other major African players (Cornelissen, 2006: 47). In positing itself as a force for peace on the African continent to the world, the demands of African peace operations challenged its capabilities—the inability to persuade other African states to buy into the sorts of peace operations required could mean that South Africa was "left playing a leadership role often without African followers"(Williamson, 2006: 201). When Nkosazana Dlamini-Zuma became Chair of the AU Commission in 2013, her role was a contested one since some saw her enabling South Africa in using the AU as a foreign policy tool to punch above its own weight (Landsberg, 2018: 258).

By the end of the presidency of Thabo Mbeki, the country had dented its credibility on the world stage. This had to do with Mbeki's denialism of mainstream scientific understandings on HIV/AIDS, a stance that resulted in government inaction and the loss of many lives in South Africa (Taylor, 2005: 138–145). With his government's shoring up of the Mugabe regime and an express inability to positively intervene to arrest an escalating political, economic and human rights crisis in Zimbabwe after 2000 (Landsberg, 2016), this contributed to the Mbeki government lacking the soft power "to sell the West his ambitious agenda of a kind of Marshall Plan for Africa" (Van der Westhuizen, 2009). Under President Jacob Zuma (2009–2018), there was a marked decline in the socio-economic fabric and the integrity of governance in the country. It accompanied South Africa's receding independent international presence. This also palpably diminished her influence on the continent (Lobo, 2014).

During this time, the preoccupation of strategic actors such as Nigeria, Ethiopia, Kenya, Egypt and Libya with their own major domestic concerns added to the retreat of African diplomacy. Symbolic for this was the marginalisation of the AU's normative agency and its diplomatic failure in Libya in 2011. The United Nations Security Council (UNSC) preferred the Arab League's position over that of the AU with the latter unable to pre-empt the military intervention by the North Atlantic Treaty Organisation (NATO) joined by Qatar. The AU's response was considered feeble at best and called into question its ability to assert its normative agency on issues of critical importance regarding regional peace and security (Swart, 2015: 121, 138–9; Corten & Koutroulisy, 2013: 59).

Conclusion

Descriptions of African foreign policy traditionally revolved around acts of resistance, transactional or symbolic responses to mostly Western state initiative or Western-led institutions. In addition, for those strategically placed, advantage could also be obtained from playing both sides in the Cold War. But few, if any, were able to use foreign policy to change their development trajectory. If at all, African state agency featured most prominently in collective foreign policy actions. But indebtedness and the consequence of SAPs diminished Africa's collective presence.

Africa's global exposure to a neo-liberalising world after 1990 eventually increased global interest. On the continent, this opened up greater foreign policy choices for both state and non-state actors. Indicative of this was the far-reaching state-to-state engagement with China and the constitution of the AU as a normative agent in Africa's international relations. While after the economic crisis of 2008, a pluralising international system, now in flux, did not create scope for major acts of agency in the hope of substantial gains and a more equal, redistributive international order, the period has shown it did not preclude that absolute gains for weak or emergent states were possible (Andreasson, 2019: 25).

Interestingly, successful foreign policy responses even by small states can be based on state-non-state alliances to complement foreign policy weakness: the instance of the "Cotton Four" is where state-non-state actor collaboration successfully boosted the foreign economic bargaining capacity of a coalition of small West African states at the WTO (Lee, 2009: 197–202). It meant that "small state diplomacy … provided traditionally perceived weak small state with the capacity to say "no" and, therefore, to block multilateral trade agreements" (Lee, 2009: 195).

Contemporary global neo-liberal economic policy thinking encouraged economic strategising. "The idea of African agency, where the state is pro-active in helping to create markets, capacities and incentives interacting with private actors has gained ground" (Besada, Xu, Mathers, & Carey, 2017: 19). Where states act as "market-states" they conduct individually assertive, economically driven foreign policies intended to woo international finance and investors. If combined with a strategic agenda to structurally transform the economy, such agency has real potential for effecting structural change and releasing new sources of surplus (Ethiopia serves as an example here). With reference to countries such as Botswana, Rwanda, Mauritius or the Seychelles, small states were able to develop economic and political strategies to overcome their vulnerabilities (Prasad, 2009: 43).

This strategic neo-liberal turn bolstered African actorness regarding participation in development matters. Thus, Bretton-Woods institutions devolved strategic discussions on aid and development to African Ministers of Finance and Planning and the World Bank's Special programme for Africa came to be administered by NEPAD (in turn, NEPAD was supported on this by the UN Economic Commission for Africa). African actorness on the economic front can be described in terms such as the "African Platform for Development Effectiveness"—composed of the AU Commission, the African Development Bank, UN Economic Commission for Africa and the United Nations Development Programme (UNDP) Regional Bureau for Africa—consulted at a national, regional and continental level in order to articulate common African positions (CAPs) for the UN Financing for Development Conference in Addis Ababa in 2015. The conference agreed to seventeen sustainable development goals (SDGs) up to 2030. African agency is also in evidence at a global level when Africans were invited to sit on the High-Level Panel of Eminent Persons for determining the Post-2015 Development Agenda. The spin-off from this has been that the SDGs underpin Africa's Agenda 2063 and FOCAC's Action Plan (Besada et al., 2017: 21–22, 24), the latter involving China.

In re-imagining itself at the turn of the century, the continent subscribed to an open form of Pan-Africanism whose product is the AU. The AU is key to describing African agency (Lyons, 2010: 123). Its own deliberations and complex links with its sub-regions, the RECs, and quest to push integration has promoted a plurality of actors, all of which serve as examples of African actorness. This actorness is not without challenge. The AU's diplomatic failure over Libya or its inability to collectively resist or abrogate the design and implementation of the Economic Partnership Agreements (EPAs) with the EU (Ukpe, 2010: 212) here are evident. Both instances amounted to failures in collective agency in asserting African positions on peace, security and (continental) economic integration.

Overall, the plurality of African international relations, not least encouraged by neo-liberal reform, multiplied the number of non-state foreign policy actors and widened the scope and depth of interactions across borders. This is set against the backdrop of the pluralisation of international politics and power shifts at the international level. The multiplication of actors and the depth and scope of what they do on the continent is set against an international context that has begun to shift towards multiplexity. This pluralising international system Amitav Acharya characterises as a "multiplex world" with multiple layers of authority and leadership that constitute a plurality of actors, including open regions, regional powers and regional institutions (Acharya, 2019), all express agency or normative power, sometimes in parallel, sometimes in competition with each other. In such a scenario, global challenges need to be understood through regional narratives and individual or regional (foreign policy) agency emanating from regions such as Africa.

Notes

1 The study of foreign policy is about individual and collective agency, where agency is "directed, meaningful, intentional and self-reflective social action" or the faculty or state of acting or of exerting power (Chabal, 2009: 7; Buzan, 1993: 103) and its context. It necessarily looks at official or officially enabled leaders, decision-makers and role players with their profiles and identities uniquely responding to changing domestic, regional and international contexts. Foreign policy is regarded as a "set of ideas or actions designed to solve a problem or promote some change in the policies, attitudes or actions of other states, in non-state actors …, in the international economy or the physical environment of the world" (Holsti, 1995: 83).

2 Political structuralism or neo-realism assumes that "international constraints influence state behaviour. In general, international pressures will override domestic interests, internal political struggles and the characteristics of particular states in foreign-policy decision-making. Given that the international system is anarchic and that states must consequently ensure their own security, the exigencies of the international environment will be paramount in decision-makers' calculations. Accordingly, a state's behaviour is viewed as a response to the constraints and incentives of its aggregate power relative to others (i.e. the distribution of capabilities) or the degree of aggressive intent on the part of external actors (i.e. the balance of threat). Neo-realists assume that statesmen will respond rationally to these preconditions and will choose that foreign-policy course which is most likely to maximize security benefits and minimize security risks"(Elman, 2009).
3 Cardoso (2009). Cited after Tausch & Heshmati. (2009). Bischoff (1990).
4 Gunnar Sjöstedt defined as: "the capacity to behave actively and deliberately in relation to other actors in the international system" (Sjöstedt, 1977, p. 16). He thus connects actorness with the ability to respond effectively to others' needs and to act accordingly in a given context. Bretherton & Vogler (1999). See Richard & van Hamme (n.d.).
5 "Actorness is assessed by examining the extent of identification among member states, the formal institutions and informal practises that govern collective decision-making, the homogeneity of member states' preferences on a given issue and the resources available to a region for putting decisions into action" Hulse (2018).
6 "Although African countries, in a document called the Declaration of Tripoli on the World Bank Report entitled 'Accelerated Development in Sub-Saharan Africa: Agenda for Action' rejected the study as inconsistent with the Lagos Plan of Action and contrary to Africa's interest in diversifying its economy, their objections fell upon the deaf ears of the Bretton Woods organizations and their allies. In their frustration of powerlessness against the Bretton Woods Organizations and their allies, the humiliated African countries were tactically compelled in July 1986 to compromise their position in Africa's Priority Program for Economic Recovery (APPER), which embodied the essential elements of the Accelerated Development while casting the elements of the Lagos Plan of Action into the garbage can" (Tetteh, 2000).
7 International Financial Institutions.
8 "Any polity – state, non-state, or quasi-state – has a self-image in international affairs, which may or may not be recognised by other actors in the global system ... This implies that actorness varies along several lines: First, it is dependent on the respective counterpart" (p. 12) "... It has to have a clear self-conception as an actor with regard to the respective subject matter and it must be recognised as an actor. Neither of the two dimensions is a sufficient indicator for actorness on its own. A reason for this is that perceptions of a polity's role (and indeed any perceptions) are inherently subjective and therefore 'Actor A's self-image may or may not correspond to actor B's image of A' (Bengtsson, 2010). "I claim that both dimensions are equally constitutive for the concept of actorness; it can only be achieved when the interplay of internal and external factors support it" (p.15) (Scheler, 2014).
9 Brazil, Russia, India, China, South Africa.

References

Acharya, A. (2009). *Whose Ideas Matter? Agency and Power in Asian Regionalism*. Ithaca, NY: Cornell University Press.

Acharya, A. (2019). From the Unipolar Moment to a Multiplex World. https://yaleglobal.yale.edu/content/unipolar-moment-multiplex-world (Accessed 23 June 2019).

Achieng, R. M. (2014). Can We Speak of African Agency? APRM and Africa's Agenda 2063. *African Sociological Review / Revue Africaine de Sociologie 18*(1): 49–64.

Adogamhe, P. G. (2003). African Foreign Policy: Integrating Political Economy and Decision-Making Perspectives. In: J. A. Braveboy-Wagner (ed.), *The Foreign Policies of the Global South*. Boulder, CO: Lynne Rienner.

Andreasson, S. (2019). Elusive Agency: Africa's Persistently Peripheral Role in International Relations. *Mimeo*: 1–25. http://works.bepress.com/stefan_andreasson/16. (Accessed 23 June 2019).

Aning, K. & Edu-Afful, I. (2016). African Agency and R2P. *International Study Review 18*: 120–133.

Ayoob, M. (1989). The Third World in the System of States: Acute Schizophrenia or Growing Pains. *International Studies Quarterly 33*: 67–79. doi:10.2307/2600494.

Bengtsson, R. (2010). *The EU and the European Security Order: Interfacing Security Actors*. London and New York: Routledge.

Besada, H., Xu, J., Mathers, A. & Carey, R. (2017). Advancing African Agency in the 2030 Transformative Development Agenda. *African Geographical Review 36*(1): 19–44. doi:10.1080/19376812.2016.1138232.

Bischoff, P. H. (1990). *Swaziland's International Relations and Foreign Policy: A Study of a Small African State in International Relations*. Bern: Peter Lang.

Bischoff, P. H. (2008). Pan-African Multilateralism: Transformative or Disconnected? *Politikon 35*(2): 177–195. doi:10.1080/02589340802366968.

Bretherton, C. & Vogler, J. (1999). *The European Union as a Global Actor*. London: Routledge.

Buzan, B., Jones, C. & Little, R. (1993). *The Logic of Anarchy*. New York: Columbia University Press.

Cardoso, F. H. (1979). *Development under Fire*. Mexico, D.F.: Instituto Latinoamericano de Estudios Transnacionales, DEE/D/24 i, Mayo (Mexico 20 D.F., Apartado 85–025).

Chabal, P. (2009). *Africa – The Politics of Suffering and Smiling*. London: ZED.

Chan, S. (1987). Zambia's Foreign Policy. *The Round Table 302*: 223–233.

Chipaike, R. & Bischoff, P. H. (2018). A Challenge to Conventional Wisdom: Locating Agency in Angola and Ghana's Economic Engagements with China. *Journal of Modern Asian and African Studies 53*(7): 1002–1017. doi:10.1177%2F0021909618763922.

Chipaike, R. & Knowledge, M. (2018). The Question of African Agency in International Relations. *Cogent Social Sciences 4*: 1–16. doi:10.1080/23311886.2018.1487257.

Clapham, C. (1985). *Third World Politics*. London: Croom & Helm.

Cornelissen, S. (2006). South Africa at the United Nations. In: D. Lee, I. Taylor & P. D. Williams (eds.), *The Multilateralism of South African Diplomacy*. Basingstoke: Palgrave.

Corten, O. & Koutroulis, V. (2013). The Illegality of Military Support to Rebels in the Libyan War: Aspects of Jus Contra Bellum and Jus in Bello. *Journal of Conflict & Security Law 18*(1): 159–193. doi:10.1093/jcsl/krs029.

David, S. R. (1991). Explaining Third World Alignment. *World Politics 43*(2): 233–256. doi:10.2307/2010472.

Drieskens, E. (2017). Golden or Gilded Jubilee? A Research Agenda for Actorness. *Journal of European Public Policy 24*(10): 1534–1546. doi:10.1080/13501763.2016.1225784.

Egedo, I. (1987). Nigeria and Apartheid. *The Round Table 301*: 33–39.

Elman, M. F. (2009). The Foreign Policies of Small States: Challenging Neorealism in Its Own Backyard. *British Journal of Politics 25*(2): 171–217. doi:10.1017/S0007123400007146.

Fidler, D. (2000). A Kinder, Gentler System of Capitulations? International Law, Structural Adjustment Policies, and the Standard of Liberal, Globalized Civilization. *Texas International Law Journal 35*: 387.

Frankel, J. (1975). *British Foreign Policy 1945–1973*. London: Oxford University Press.

Geldenhuys, D. (2006). South Africa's Role as International Norm Entrepreneur. In: W. Carlsnaes & P. Nel (eds.), *Full Flight – South African Foreign Policy After Apartheid*. Johannesburg: IGD.

Harbeson, J. W. & Rothchild, D. (2000). *Africa in World Politics*. Boulder, CO: Westview.

Heidhues, F. & Obareby, G. (2011). Lessons from Structural Adjustment Programmes and their Effects in Africa. *Quarterly Journal of International Agriculture 50*(1): 55–64.

Holsti, K. J. (1995). *International Politics*. Englewood Cliffs: Prentice Hall.

Hulse, M. (2018). Actorness and Trade Negotiating Outcomes: West Africa and the SADC Group in Negotiations for Economic Partnership Agreements. *International Relations 32*(1): 39–59. doi:10.1177%2F0047117817723065.

Jordaan, E. (2003). The Concept of a Middle Power in International Relations: Distinguishing Between Emerging and Traditional Middle Powers. *Politikon 30*(2): 167–169. doi:10.1080/0258934032000147282.

Khadiagala, G. M. & Lyons, T. (eds.). (2001). *African Foreign Policies*. Boulder, CO: Lynne Rienner.

Kraus, J. (1994). The Political Economy of African Foreign Policies: Marginality and Dependency, Realism and Choice. In: T. Shaw & J. Okolo (eds.), *The Political Economy of Foreign Policy in ECOWAS*. New York: Springer.

Landsberg, C. (2013). *Afro-centric Diplomacy: The Golden Decade 1998–2008 and Pan African Agency in World Affairs, Professorial Inaugural Address*. Johannesburg: University of Johannesburg.

Landsberg, C. (2016). African Solutions for African Problems: Quiet Diplomacy and South Africa's Diplomatic Strategy Towards Zimbabwe. *Journal for Contemporary History 41*(1): 126–148.

Landsberg, C. (2018). South Africa's Pivotal Role in the African Union. In: T. Karebo & T. Murithi (eds.), *The African Union*. London: IB Tauris.

Lee, D. (2006). *South Africa in the World Trade Organisation*. Basingstoke: Palgrave Macmillan.

Lee, D. (2009). Bringing an Elephant into the Room: Small African State Diplomacy in the WTO. In: A. F. Cooper & T. Shaw (eds.), *The Diplomacies of Small States*. Basingstoke: Palgrave Macmillan.

Levey, Z. (2008). Israel's Exit from Africa, 1973: The Road to Diplomatic Isolation. *British Journal of Middle-Eastern Studies 35*(2): 205–226. doi: 10.1080/13530190802180621.

Lobo, D. F. O. (2014). Perceptions of South African Foreign Policy in the African Union. MA Thesis, Nelson Mandela Metropolitan University. http://hdl/handle.net/10948/d1020029.

Lyons, T. (2010). African Agency in International Politics. *Journal of Indian Ocean Region 10*(2): 122–123.

Malaquias, A. (2011). Angola's Foreign Policy – Pragmatic Recalibrations. *Occasional Papers 84*: 1–19. Braamfontein: SAIIA.

Morphet, S. (2006). South Africa as Chair of the Non-Aligned, September 1998–February 2003. In: D. Lee, I. Taylor & P. D. Williams (eds.), *The Multilateralism of South African Diplomacy*. Basingstoke: Palgrave.

Mortimer, R. A. (1984). Global Economy and African Foreign Policy: The Algerian Model. *African Studies Review 27*(1): 1–22.

Nel, P. (2006). The Power of Ideas: "Ambiguous Globalism" and South Africa's Foreign Policy. In: W. Carlsnaes & P. Nel (eds.), *Full Flight—South African Foreign Policy After Apartheid*. Braamfontein: IGD.

Nel, P., Taylor, I. & van der Westhuizen, J. (2001). *South Africa's Multilateral Diplomacy and Global Change*. Aldershot: Ashgate.

Nolutshungu, S. (1975). *South Africa in Africa*. Manchester: Manchester University Press.

Nolutshungu, S. (1982). African Interests and Soviet Power: The Local Context of Soviet Policy. *Soviet Studies XXXIV*(3): 397–417.

Patience, A. (2014). Imagining Middle Powers. *Australian Journal of International Affairs 68*(2): 210–224. doi:10.1080/10357718.2013.840557.

Pinkney, R. (2001). *The International Politics of East Africa*. Manchester: Manchester University Press.

Prasad, N. (2009). Small but Smart: Small States in the Global System. In: A. F. Cooper & T. Shaw (eds.), *The Diplomacies of Small States*. Basingstoke: Palgrave.

Richard, Y. & van Hamme, G. (n.d.). *The European Union as an Actor in International Relations*. Cairn.info, International Edition. https://www.cairn-int.info/article_p.php?ID_ARTICLE=E_EG_421._0015 (Accessed 23 September 2019).

Salomon, M. (2013). From NIEO to Now and the Unfinishable Story of Economic Justice. *International and Comparative Law Quarterly 62*(1): 31–54. doi:10.1017/S0020589312000590.

Saxena, S. C. (2004). The African Union: Africa's Giant Step Towards Continental Union. In: J. M. Mbaku & S. C. Saxena (eds.), *Africa at the Crossroads*. Westport, CT: Praeger.

Scheler, R. (2014). *The EU as a Global Actor: A Framework for Analysis*. Paper presented at the ECPR Graduate Student Conference Innsbruck, 3 to 5 July 2014. https://ecpr.eu/Filestore/PaperProposal/87c93b1f-cc56-4796-89d1-ddf8ad37bf0f.pdf (Accessed 20 September 2019).

Sjöstedt, G. (1977). *The External Role of the European Community*. Westmead: Saxon House Westmead.

Swart, G. (2015). An Emerging, Established or Receding Normative Agent? In: P. Bischoff, K. Aning & A. Acharya (eds.), *Africa in Global International Relations*. London: Routledge.

Tausch, A. & Heshmati, A. (2009). *Re-Orient? MNC Penetration and Contemporary Shifts in the Global Political Economy*, September 2009, IZA Discussion Paper No. 4393.

Taylor, I. (2005). *NEPAD*. Boulder, CO: Lynne Rienner.

Tetteh, D. (2000). The Politics of One-Sided Adjustment in Africa. *Journal of Black Studies 30*(4): 515–533. doi:10.1177%2F002193470003000403.

Ukpe, A. (2010). Will EPAs Foster the Integration of Africa Into World Trade? *Journal of African Law 54*(2): 212–231. doi:10.1017/S0021855310000057.

Van der Westhuizen, J. (2009). Has South Africa Lost Its Soft Power? *Foreign Policy* 10 April. https://foreignpolicy.com/2009/04/10/has-south-africa-lost-its-soft-power/.

Williamson, P. D. (2006). South Africa and Peace Operations. In: D. Lee, I. Taylor & P. D. Williams (eds.), *The Multilateralism of South African Diplomacy*. Basingstoke: Palgrave.

World Bank (2001). Adjustment from Within. Lessons from the Structural Adjustment Participatory Review Initiative, A contribution from the World Bank to the Second Global SAPRI Forum, July 30–31. http://documents.worldbank.org/curated/en/386221468332448978/pdf/359150rev0WB1SAPRI1Report.pdf (Accessed 4 September 2019).

Wright, S. (1999). *African Foreign Policies*. Boulder, CO: Westview.

3 The African Union as a foreign policy player

African agency in international cooperation

Tshepo Gwatiwa

Introduction

The African Union (hereafter AU) is a complex organisation at the interstices of bilateral and multilateral foreign policy execution in Africa. In the first instance, the African continent's future largely rests in the hands of the AU Commission. The AU is the face of Africa and represents continental interest when it negotiates and implements [international] agreements on issues such as international trade, international law, international security and other important issues. However, most of the precepts and codes in these issue areas are developed elsewhere, both in the West, and often also in the East. The challenge for the AU is to reconcile what are pre-determined, different forms of foreign funding and support, with African preferences and interests. As such, the organisation demonstrates externally oriented agency in its attempts to reconcile international agendas, while it incepts its own new regimes for the continent. This epitomises an organisation that finds itself in the perennial quest to protect African foreign policy agency in international politics, while it forges a unique and actionable course for African multilateralism and regionalism.

According to Wight, as cited in Brown (2012), agency is defined as the ability to do something. Article 3(e) of the AU Constitute Act vests a foreign policy obligation on the AU by requiring that it "encourage[s] international cooperation, taking due account of the Charter of the United Nations" (AU, 2000: 5). Giving the AU this emphasis makes it easier for both Africa and the international community to relate since it reduces the transaction cost of having to deal on a bilateral basis (see Abbott & Snidal, 1998).

This chapter considers the role of the AU as a foreign policy actor in global politics. It makes use of the concept of "agency" as an empirical element and dimension of the continent's foreign policymaking and implementation. It mainly focuses on how the AU projects foreign policy. It argues that the AU projects its foreign policy through agency.

This chapter unfolds in three broad parts. The first part contextualises the notion of agency as a function of foreign policy. It operationalises the concept at both the abstract and empirical level in the AU foreign policy process. Thereafter, African agency is juxtaposed against coloniality and imperialism, thereby elucidating the historical and structural context in which AU foreign policy agency obtains. In a second part, the role of agents or elites shaping African agency is discussed. It pays special attention to the role of summitry through which agents seek to give African agency meaning and intentionality. The processes through which various actors seek to exert agency are described. A third part looks at African agency in the AU's international partnerships. Finally, two major instances of collective diplomacy that put African agency to the test are analysed in order to illustrate the current limits of the AU as a foreign policy actor.

Foreign policy as African agency and African agency as foreign policy

Foreign policy is typically ascribed to states as opposed to multilateral institutions. However, in the recent decades regional organisations such as the European Union (EU), the North Atlantic Treaty Organisations (NATO) and others have all pursued a foreign policy of sorts. The most salient example is the EU, which has its "Common Foreign and Security Policy" enforced by the European External Action Service (EEAS). As a supranational organisation it has assumed many characteristics of a hybrid of state and multilateral organisation (Carta, 2013). Although the EU has been keen to export its model of regionalism to other organisations, especially its protégé the AU, there is yet to be such an approach as regards foreign policy (Rüland, Hanggi, & Roloff, 2006). However, in order to understand foreign policy agency in itself, it is important to first consider it at a state level.

Foreign policy is difficult to define, but mostly identifiable in the manner in which decision-makers—such as heads of state and government, ministers and [international] diplomats—conduct diplomacy in an international milieu. Elman posits that "a state's behaviour is viewed as a response to the constraints and incentives of its aggregate power relative to others (i.e. the distribution of capabilities) or the degree of aggressive intent on the part of external actors [i.e. the balance of threat]" (Elman, 1995: 172). This means that foreign policy is, among other things, primarily concerned with survival pursued in relation to existing resources and capabilities. These capabilities get harnessed to carefully influence other elements of diplomacy such as norm suasion and entrepreneurship (Payne, 2001). In order for states (or more recently regions) to play a meaningful role in international affairs, their "national interest"—defined as "the perceived needs and desires of one sovereign state in relation to other sovereign states comprising the external environment"—play a crucial part in defining the nature and extent of foreign policy pursued by that actor (Nuechterlein, 1976: 247). In order for the national interest to be relevant and achievable, it ideally should be matched with domestic policy (Simon, 1985) because the dichotomous policy must embody the values espoused by the referent polity (Mead, Erwin, & Goldstein, 2006). The design and implementation of a foreign policy is the preserve of a set of decision-makers—or foreign policy elites (Hafner-Burton, Hughes, & Victor, 2013: 369).

When elites collate their preferences to form a robust policy, they do this based on their perception of the international milieu. In order to have a meaningful role in international affairs, states often adopt a unique rhetoric laced with subjective meanings, as well as interpretations of world politics or "the linguistic construction of reality" (Doty, 1993: 302–305). For instance, this has been a particularly useful technique in African multilateralism at the United Nations, especially when it dealt with sensitive or controversial subjects such as colonialism, apartheid and other issues related to African sovereignty.

Preferences and interests form a key component of foreign policy. These interests can be categorised into those that relate to survival, are vital or important and peripheral to determine how to allocate resources (Mead et al., 2006). In most cases, when elites design foreign policies they consider military and economic capabilities as well as the competing interests of the elites and other constituents in that polity (Brecher, Steinberg, & Stein, 1969).

The notion of (elite) agency designing foreign policy implies that there are social agents acting within a structure. Brown (2012) argues that human agents such as individuals, groups and organisations inject meaning and intentionality into structure. This invites us to highlight the actions of the various decision-making elites. These are heads of state, ministers (especially of foreign affairs), the Chairperson of the AU Commission, the Commissioner of Peace and Security, diplomats and others. During a highlight period, [i.e. circa. 1998–2008] in which the role of political elites in advancing African agency had great effect and prominence, there were key human agents. They included President Thabo Mbeki (South Africa), President Olusegun Obasanjo (Nigeria), Abdelaziz Bouteflika (Algeria), Muammar Gaddafi (Libya), Abdoulaye Wade (Senegal) and the then Chairperson of the AU Commission Alpha Konare, among others. Mbeki was arguably the most vocal promoter of African agency in global politics to promote African agency. Theirs was a constant battle against post-coloniality in order to forge a unique African identity with intentionality and meaning.

Solidarity is a very important aspect of Africa's ability to carry out its regional projects with or against the international community. A careful examination of Mazrui (2006) and Zondi (2012) suggests that common positions promoting solidarity among AU member states aim at fostering collective diplomacy initiatives at the AU level. Examples include the Solemn Declaration on Common African Defence and Security Policy and the African Union Non-Aggression and Common Defence Pact, both of which address solidarity within the continent so as to secure the territorial and juridical integrity of the continent (AU, 2004, 2005). African states' compliance with these positions is debatable but their existence is an indication of an attempt to lay a threshold for agency in international politics.

AU: Foreign policy actor and foreign policy maker

The AU occupies an important role and position in (African) foreign policy agency. As the primary multilateral institution in Africa, it focuses on collective diplomacy in the continent. This foreign policy mandate derives from the Constitutive

Act [of the AU], which states that the AU shall "promote and defend African common positions on issues of interest to the continent and its peoples" as well as "encourage international cooperation" and "establish the necessary conditions which enable the continent to play its rightful role in the global economy and in international negotiations" (AU, 2002: 5–6).

There is no rigid template as to who can conceive common African positions. However, most of what results as common positions often emanates from the preferences designed prior at the national level, or from those proposed by an incumbent AU Commission Chairperson.[1] Thereafter, various heads of state and government and ministers (the Executive Council) convene to forge common positions for the entire continent (Bah et al., 2014). Finally, implementation is the preserve of the AU Commission (AUC) Chairperson's cabinet [comprising of his/her deputy and commissioners], working closely with the Permanent Representatives Committee (PRC) to focus on the implementation of those common positions. However, once the AU has codified its position, the AUC Chairperson often works closely with the AU Chairperson (a nominated head of state or government) who acts as the diplomatic face of the AU in international affairs.

As such, the AU's Constitutive Act gives the AU foreign policy agency with the Chairperson of the AU Commission as the de facto chief diplomatic figure. Nevertheless, a number of other foreign policy actors are found across the AU's structure and attendant procedures. The primary actors include the Assembly of Heads of State and Government (AHSG), the Executive Council (of Ministers), the PRC, and commissioners in various tiers of the AU Commission (AU Commission, 2015). All these actors are responsible for coordinating and reconciling interests and preferences between sub-regional organisations (or Regional Economic Communities/Regional Mechanisms), member states, civil society organisations, business entities and other interest groups.

This task of harmonisation and reconciliation of the various interests and preferences amounts to an act of framing and implementing the foreign policy positions for the continent. At the same time, being an organisation driven by its member states, its collective foreign policy is determined by which member states enjoy influence at any given time and to what extent they can be successful in forging a common and durable consensus across particular issues. However, an incumbent AU Chairperson and/or Chairperson of the AU Commission does not necessarily influence these positions, but they are often a result of consensus building between all member states (Hardt, 2014: 47). This consensus creates buy-in for various common positions.

African agency: Concept and practice

Agency can be defined as the "faculty or state of acting or exerting power", in "a more nuanced notion" that can accommodate "a variety of entities … differentiate between them, and can locate agency in relation to the social contexts from which it arises and which shape, enable and constrain it" (Brown, 2012: 1894).

This implies purposive action, which, among other things, is representative. This representation takes place within an international structure, involving a social dimension that has "both meaning and intentionality" (ibid.). Yet, structurally Africa is on the periphery of the international order. This comes with the cost of having to emulate or depend on other regions and powers in international affairs (Bach, 2013: 7–11). Perhaps missing from Wight and Brown's accounts, but often inferential in most International Relations (IR) texts, is the structural imbalance in which African agency takes place.

African agency has several characteristics. First, agency is a political action. It is relayed through both rhetoric and action. Brown (2012) mainly focuses on the action and leaves out rhetoric. In an international political space and with limited resources, given the relatively weaker material and financial position in international affairs, rhetoric (however soft) plays an important, greater role than material considerations in African agency in international affairs. A key example is the popular rhetoric of "African solutions for African problems"—the basis for negotiations with the United Nations Organisation (UNO) on the modalities of peacekeeping for instance—and concomitant African attempts to build institutions which Esmenjaud (2014) considers anti-imperial phantoms.

Second, the anti-imperialist posture and anti-colonial intellectual activism around, say, Pan-Africanism and an African Renaissance—from whence the rhetoric emanates—is not mere discourse but one with a purpose to spur African agency in the immediate and long term. Such discourse is useful in "othering" other actors in an anarchic international milieu of self-help. It is evinced by the promulgation of Pan-African positions (often backed by intellectual activism) in efforts to co-design and disseminate norms and regimes in global politics. Correspondingly, Niang (2016: 458, 459) posits that the

> global commons [such as freedom, solidarity, human rights] was [not] an outflow of imperial undertakings as assumed by international intellectuals ... African political actors viewed their responsibility as global and their vocation as universal ... taking into account both the specificity and the universality of African concerns, values and aspirations.

More recently, African internationalists have significantly influenced prevalent international norms, even though often, the credit accrues to others, elsewhere. For instance, the African, Francis Deng, was instrumental in shaping the notion of "sovereignty to protect" and the first to coin the "sovereignty as responsibility" norm (Evans, 2008: 35–37).

Third, the ability of the AU as a foreign policy actor to "exert power" in global terms is currently an aspiration rather than a reality. Africa was a relative latecomer to international politics that is largely driven by world regions with which it has an acrimonious past. Hence, the organisation has inadvertently been drawn into institutionalised international partnerships mainly designed by the outside. These aim to build up the institution and achieve reconciliation with thriving international organisations. As a result, the AU reproduces itself in the image of its counterparts such as the EU and the UN.[2] As a corollary, it has limited latitude to exert agency based on its very own interests.

The AU's quest for African agency is not only a question of contestation but also one of overcoming coloniality and of making positive contributions to international cooperation.

The context of Africa's agency in international relations: Post-coloniality, identity and ideology

Africa's agency in international relations obtains, under the shadow of empire, post-coloniality and networks of patronage.[3] "Post-coloniality" or the "post-colonial condition" refers to "a global phenomenon of interactions based on unequal power relations in an era that goes beyond the world of colonialism but that has been (and continues to be) decisively shaped by the logic of coloniality" (Hönke & Müller, 2012: 385). The power differential lent by the logic of coloniality incites a form of political resistance—through rhetoric, shirking and slippage—amounting to agency. This resistance is mostly a result of the incompatibilities between the former colonisers and relatively underdeveloped post-colonial states where both sides differ on the meaning of politics and security (Ayoob, 1997; Acharya, 1997; Barkawi & Laffey, 2006; Franke & Ganzle, 2012).

In light of the above disparities, African agents and organisations frequently invoke the agency of resistance, say at the UN, which is largely controlled by former colonisers and neo-imperial nations such as France, Italy, UK, Germany and the US—even though most UN missions are in Africa. But at the same time African states rely on UN normative leadership and funding on development and security programmes, something that influences Africa's institutional and programme design and implementation (Aggarwal, 1998; Brosig, 2013, 2015). This then takes away from agency.[4]

Needed to overcome post-coloniality and assert influential agency are new structures. Identity and ideology build regional agency and with institutionalisation contribute to a process of regional organisation. Institutionalisation in a bureaucratic sense is an important component of predictability and the basis for adjusting enduring international cooperation.[5] Building structure through institutionalisation in turn, again, is further enabling of agency in international relations.

Typically, a process of bureaucratisation creates homogeneity through a process of structuration that involves mimicry, coercion and normative suasion (DiMaggio & Powell, 1983). Agency based on homogeneity creates a unique identity. This attracts meaning and intentionality and allows for the projection of values and norms in international affairs. For instance, the enlargement of NATO took into account the values and norms of East European states (Schimmelfennig, 1998). At the same time, the new states were admitted into NATO if they did not deviate from the identity of NATO as an organisation. Correspondingly, for (collective) African agency to work, there needs to be the projection of a unique, corporate African identity accompanied by its own set of norms of values. This can drive and inform African regionalism and international cooperation.

However, it is difficult to locate the role of (African) identity in the AU's international engagements because African multilateralism lacks ideational and structural authenticity. In most cases, African bureaucrats find themselves transliterating ideas and initiatives from elsewhere. This can be partly attributed to external funding but it is also an African problem because Africans have virtually surrendered a significant portion of institutional design to external actors, even when they do have the resources to carry out certain tasks. For instance, the OAU Charter was drafted by a retired Irish general (OAU archives, no date), despite the availability of a significant number of Africans educated in the West at that point in time. The OAU had an unflinching streak for dependency and mimicry to the extent that it was the organisation to develop Africa using a "tripartite approach … involving Arab money, African resources and Western technology" (Gassama, 2013: 25). This meant that both the OAU and its successor organisation, the AU, at (different) times never took into account Africa's unique political and sociological experiences as a source to build its own differentiated thinking and institutional responses. Even where common African positions are held to be signifiers of agency (Zondi, 2012), these are often mimicked. Thus, the Common African Defence and Security Policy (CADSP), for instance, bears a striking resemblance to the European Security Defence Policy (ESDP). This creates a binary challenge for the AU (or other sub-regional organisations), because on the one hand, African policies lack authenticity and, on the other, these inauthentic policies create structures through which it becomes difficult to obtain traction and implement programmes in countries with different histories, systems and aspirations.

Ideologically, African multilateralism is so bereft of identity that even the ideologies that seek to give its international institutions meaning are not distinctly African-grown. Pan-Africanism, the hallmark of African discourse and rhetoric, is an imported ideology, the brainchild of Henry Sylvester-William (a Trinidadian) and others who suffered racism and oppression outside Africa (see Shepperson, 1962).[6] Yet, the power and reach of the movement of Pan-Africanism and its ideology should not be underestimated. Doubtlessly, the ideology served as an effective rallying point for greater African agency in the struggle for independence immediately after the Second World War and also drove early African multilateralism (see Abdul-Raheem, 1996; Mazrui, 1996). On another level, it provided a somewhat African-centred view of the world. However, Pan-Africanism has not sufficiently been refined to match the aspirations of the AU.

Pan-Africanism was articulated by prominent heads of states such as Robert Mugabe and Muammar Gaddafi, who represented a conservative state-centred old guard in the OAU. This stood in contrast to the ideology of an African Renaissance, popularised by Thabo Mbeki, with its reformist and transformative aspirations on non-state participation under the AU (Mboya, 2006; Mangu, 2006; Bischoff, 2008). In this, Pan-Africanism served as a "background ideology", overshadowed by the template of an African Renaissance in the AU era. The failure to entrench

Pan-Africanism meant the ideology existed more in rhetoric than in action. This can be traced to the foundation of the OAU at two levels—identity and early attempts to build continental institutions.

First, as regards identity, a close examination of early speeches at the OAU reveals a lack of clarity on what constitutes an African. From the inaugural speeches of the OAU, it is evident that states such as Madagascar or Ethiopia and those from the Maghreb strongly emphasised the uniqueness of their own experiences by differentiating them from those of black Africa (see OAU, 1963). This implied that from the onset there were cognitive fissures.

Second, concerning the building of continental institutions, African states failed to reify the idea of a continental army in the 1970s. In the early 1970s, Nigeria and Sierra Leone submitted a proposal for an African Defence Organisation (ADO), which would be a "continental clearinghouse for national armies" earmarked within countries and available on request by the OAU (Fasehun, 1980: 55). The idea did not materialise as member states jealously guarded their sovereignty. Similarly, in July 1978, the Frontline States (FLS)—forerunner to SADCC—submitted a proposal for a more powerful African army to the 31st Ordinary Session of the Council of Ministers (Agbi, 1986). Notwithstanding this imperative, Pan-Africanism was unable to pay heed to the proposed continental institution.

African agency hovered, oscillating between aspirations and practical quandaries despite the fact that the OAU was still sorely concerned with "[promoting] unity and (the) solidarity of the African States … [defending] their sovereignty, their territorial integrity and independence" (OAU, 1963). Nevertheless, in spite of these divisions and apathy, African regionalism thrived.

Schisms tend to affect African regionalism and periodically appear to trump "shared" norms and values. In African identity, regional identity loyalties play a crucial role in African collective action. African regional elites are aware of the impact of identity on African agency in Africa and beyond. Gassama (2013: 79) argues that:

> regionalism still remains a factor … particularly when it comes to matters such as the hosting of new institutions, offices and projects and the election of the Chairperson, his/her Deputy and Commissioners as well as selection of candidates for positions in the UN System.

Ironically, the regional schisms are not just a question of identity but seemingly a premise for African agency. African regionalism is strongest at the sub-continental level. Some perceive the relatively newer AU project as secondary to Africa's regional integration. This is shown by the way various regions approached the [supposed] augmentation of the AU regional project.

Negotiations to collate sub-regional preferences for African regional integration in the early 2000s revealed two major undercurrents regarding general attitudes towards the AU. According to one of the diplomats involved in Africa-EU partnership negotiations, there was a general feeling that compared to its sub-regional counterparts, the AU project was an experiment. Moreover, there was the sanguine conviction that the AU was relatively more susceptible to intrusion and control by international partners in pursuit of neo-imperialism (read: former colonial powers) and sub-imperialism (read: emerging powers) (Tomaz Salomao, *Personal Communication*, 2016: Johannesburg). This reveals a seemingly contradictory approach to continental African regionalism.

The concern about foreign power intrusion into Africa's international relations is real. The reason why sub-regional organisations jealously guard their "sovereignty" is because neo-imperial intrusion is more salient in some regions than others. For instance, due to the post-colonial agreements that Charles De Gaulle forced on former French colonies (Mays, 2002; Schmidt, 2013), French intrusion is much stronger in West and Central Africa. Despite this, this has not diminished the importance of solidarity as an important aspect of both individual and collective African foreign policy.

Agents, elites and African summitry as drivers of African agency

African agency, when captured in an [inter]regional context, derives from intergovernmental cooperation on the continent. Ideally, regional agency depends on the role of regional powers; thus, for instance, European regional security depends on the leadership of the United Kingdom and France (Howorth, 2007). Some scholars use the problematic concept of hegemons or powers when dealing with their role in African regionalism (see Adebajo & Landsberg, 2003; Alden & Soko, 2005). Ideally, Nigeria and South Africa, through their heads of state, remain two main legitimate, de facto agentic pivots linking the continent with the rest of the world. Arguably, it is comparatively easier for a charismatic leader of one of these two "pivotal powers" to be an effective agent in African agency than of a smaller state. However, in reality, the empirical fuzziness of the notion [of leadership] in Africa strongly indicates that African agency is not anchored on the leadership specific countries but, instead, shifts periodically. African foreign policy agency has centred on different states such as Algeria (Bouteflika), Uganda (Museveni), Rwanda (Kagame), Ethiopia (Zenawi), Libya (Gaddafi) and others, depending on the issue area at hand. Here, summitry has often determined which country's head of state would lead a particular regional project.

The quest for African agency at a continental level began in earnest in the 1980s through summitry and promulgations. The push for agency normally is attributed to the "Kampala Movement". In 1991, the likes of Olusegun Obasanjo (Nigeria), Arap Moi (Kenya) and Omar Al-Bashir (Sudan) promulgated a range of security and governance reforms for the African continent. They realised African agency could only start from within the continent. According to Akuffo (2011), these reforms culminated in the Conference on Security, Stability, Development and Cooperation in Africa (CSSDCA), grudgingly endorsed by the Organisation of African Unity (OAU). It included the idea of a new outlook on peace and security that was to culminate in the present African Peace and Security Architecture (APSA) as part of the AU as a successor body of the OAU.

It took a concerted effort between retired and incumbent heads of state and government to translate the CSSDCA into a continental policy. In fact, the CSSDCA only gained buy-in subsequent to the political fallout following the Rwandan genocide of 1994. Obasanjo, a former Nigerian military leader and key figure in the Kampala Movement, teamed up with Presidents Thabo Mbeki of South Africa and Abdel Aziz Bouteflika of Algeria to engage diplomatically with their counterparts in Europe and elsewhere. By the time all three had become heads of state in 1999, they were instrumental in ensuring that the CSSDCA gained political buy-in in different parts of the continent where they wielded political influence.

Libyan leader Muammar Gaddafi helped reify the CSSDCA later in the late 1990s. This lent credence to creating a successor organisation to the OAU and strengthened a new collective continental position on peace and security. A number of African states were opposed to the idea of transition from the OAU to the AU. Gaddafi made concessions and side-payments to thirty-two states that were either opposed or ambivalent to the transition. It took two years of backroom negotiation and bargaining and involved making economic and financial concessions to opponents of the AU project as promoted by Gaddafi and the pivotal states of Nigeria, South Africa and Algeria.

At the same time, Gaddafi was a controversial figure, with sub-imperial ambitions. In order to curb his enormous financial influence, AU member states came up with a number of rules. One of the rules was that fiscal contributions by the so-called Big Five (Algeria, Nigeria, South Africa, Egypt and Libya) could not equate into political control (Maphoi Komanyane, *personal communication*, Geneva: 2013). This did not deter Gaddafi from assuming a key role in African summitry and becoming an African voice in international affairs.

Key African summits can be hailed as milestones in crafting African agency. Their legacy transcends the political ambitions of various political agents during the initial process. The Sirte Declaration of 1998, hosted by Gaddafi, was a landmark summit that gave birth to the AU. Gaddafi strongly sought to increase his political influence at this point. The backroom diplomacy and closed-door negotiations in and around these summits pitted Gaddafi, who had "hegemonic ambitions", against Mbeki and Obasanjo, who preferred a gradualist approach to African regionalism (Makinda & Okumu, 2008: 23). Once African states had signed the landmark Sirte Declaration, Obasanjo ensured that most of the components of the CSSDCA were incorporated into the new multilateral organisation by hosting another conference in Abuja in 2000. Such competition by different elite leaders vying for ideological and policy prominence in these summits shaped a number of perceptions and rivalries that continue to affect Africa's collective diplomacy.

Constituting actors and processes at AU: African foreign policy making

Collective positions and diplomacy are the pivot for Africa's engagement with the rest of the world. The echelon of African collective diplomacy is the AHSG. It incepted international partnerships with the EU, the UN, the US and South America (most of which were signed as a result of two key heads of state—President Thabo Mbeki (South Africa) and President Olusegun Obasanjo (Nigeria)) working alongside a handful of others (AU, 2014). However, the bargaining also requires the active involvement of the Chairperson of the AU Commission. During the early period of the AU, the leading heads of state worked closely with then Chairperson Alpha Konare to successfully oversee regional common positions (AU, 2002). Konare, a former head of state, was a particularly astute diplomat who oversaw robust partnerships with NATO and the EU, where African agency trenchantly expressed itself on matters of norms and principles—evinced by the Cairo and Lisbon summits of 2000 and 2007, respectively.

The success of African collective diplomacy in international cooperation also depends on the role of an incumbent Chairperson of the AU Commission. The chairman of the Commission is essentially the chief diplomat. According to Gassama (2013), the capability of the OAU/AU largely depends on the diplomatic fortitude of the chief of the AUC. Correspondingly, in the domain of peace and security, the Protocol on the Peace and Security Council (of 2002) mandates the Chairperson of the AU Commission to incept and pursue partnerships for peace and security. It was for this reason that Alpha Konare worked with then NATO Secretary General, Jaap de Hoop Scheffer, to sign the first AU-NATO partnership in 2005. Years later, Nkosazana Dlamini-Zuma as AUC Chairperson exercised the same privilege to incept and sign a new strategic partnership with Norway even though the AU had imposed a moratorium on new partnerships, because they were deemed too numerous. It is important to realise that African agency also depends on the individual officeholder in question and, as such, on the AUC Chairperson's ability to mobilise a majority of AU member states to adhere to African common positions.

In recent years, AUC chairpersons have had a harrowing time getting African countries to adhere to African common positions in international affairs. In 2006, AU member states signed the Banjul Formula whereby they agreed to collate their bilateral preferences through the AUC. This, in order for the Commission to speak and act on behalf of the continent—especially in forums such as the Forum for China–Africa Cooperation (FOCAC), the Tokyo International Conference on African Development (TICAD) and Korea-Africa Economic Cooperation (KOAFEC). However, AU member states have gradually shown increasing reluctance to abide by the Banjul Formula. This, because the majority of small states felt that their bilateral interests were being neglected in favour of those of the major member states (Sanqu Bassu, *personal communication*, Addis Ababa: 2016).

Overall, however, inter-state bargaining and the negotiations of the 1990s shaped the notion of "leadership" within Africa's collective diplomacy. During this period, Nigeria and South Africa emerged as de facto lead states. In order to isolate Gaddafi, as well as create an ad hoc burden-sharing formula, the two states signed a memorandum of understanding (MOU) which exhorted the two states' ministries of foreign affairs to compare notes before representing the continent in international affairs. Both states had something to offer to Africa's collective diplomacy: "while South Africa under Mbeki brought a sense of urgency to African diplomacy, Nigeria … brought history and diplomatic experience, as well as a sense of legitimacy to South Africa's post-apartheid role in Africa" (Landsberg, 2008: 205). The other members of "the Big Five"—such as Algeria and Egypt—with the exception of Libya—appeared less interested in this continent-wide influence. But this arrangement did not last.

For instance, Africa's aspiring "hegemons" have faced enormous challenges in the area of peace and security, especially in regard to role playing and burden sharing. Compared to the first decade of the AU, African states have generally reduced their commitment to a common agency on African security. The hegemonic aspirants—Nigeria and South Africa—no longer contribute as many resources to African security as they used to in the early 2000s.[7] African leadership during the early 2000s evinced regional agency in international politics. However, the present trend portends a reduction in regional agency.

This further signifies the inability to rely on the idea of African hegemony as a sustainable pillar propping up continental organisation and informing continental foreign policy agency in any way.[8] In the period since, Nigeria, Libya, Senegal, Algeria, Ethiopia and South Africa, mostly for domestic reasons, have taken less interest in strengthening the AU and its agency with the outside.[9] Given the nominalism of the Zuma presidency in all other respects, South Africa exceptionally played a key role with Nkosazana Dlamini-Zuma at the helm of the AUC (2012–2017) to actualise the AU's "Agenda 2063" (Landsberg, 2014). Lately, a figure like President Paul Kagame could inject new energy and urgency into promoting collective African agency when Rwanda played a meaningful role in actualising the African Continental Free Trade Agreement (AU, 2018).

Leadership at state level in African regionalism is a complex issue. This manifests in the difficulty with which big and/or capable states are unable to provide regional leadership. It is imperative to note that in order for Africa to pursue an effective foreign policy at the global level, it must first primarily tackle the issue of strategic leadership and "strategic citizenship".[10] By example, the latter has been attended to and become standard practice in the way the EU executes the Common Foreign and Security Policy (CFSP) (Howorth, 2007), or the cases of NATO and other organisations (Leurdjik, 2003; Rieker, 2006). However, in the case of Africa, the issue remains a challenge.

As such, collective African foreign policy agency is significantly hampered by the lack of ever-present, ever-committed and recognised regional hegemons whose far reaching capabilities are able to consistently sustain continental postures. "Hegemony" connotes leadership. Ideally, regional hegemons should meet the following five-point criteria: there should be a delimited region with political, economic and cultural links; a willingness and preparedness of the hegemon to assume regional leadership; the hegemon possessing material and ideational capacities should influence the region; provision of collective public goods for the region; and acceptance by other states in the region (Flemes & Nolte, 2010: 1–14). Based on these criteria at least continent-wide, there is no

African state to qualify as a regional hegemon. This is despite Nigeria and South Africa harbouring hegemonic ambitions.

As such, the early prominence given to the AU as a foreign policy actor when supported by bigger member states early on did not last. Perhaps most important of all, the strategic interventions did not leave African agency depersonalised. The AU and its processes remain personality-driven. Certainly, human agents play a pivotal role in foreign policy, yet the lack of depersonalisation of African agency—especially at the level of the AHSG—has a far-reaching effect.

With personalisation and individualisation comes the risk of failure to institutionalise solutions to the problems confronting the organisation. It is the challenge of achieving sustainability and predictability in one's interactions with others. One explanation is that the founding group for a collective continental organisation in 1963, heads of states such as Kwame Nkrumah, Julius Nyerere, and others came to espouse the idea of life presidencies or one-party states which revolved around personality cults. In other words, even beyond the OAU, few, if any, had an interest in a depersonalised or institutionally more autonomous AU. The successors to the founders who oversaw the CSSDCA, the Constitutive Act, and survived Gaddafi's bid for leadership of the organisation failed to appreciate the imperative to depersonalise the different dimensions of African agency.

The result was that AU foreign policy agency rose and declined with certain strong personalities such as Thabo Mbeki, Olusegun Obasanjo, Meles Zenawi and Abdelaziz Bouteflika, let alone strong AUC chiefs such as Alpha Konare. The strategic partnerships the AU has embarked on attest to this.

AU foreign policy on international cooperation: The record on partnerships

AU declarations form an important aspect of African agency. Zondi (2012) posits that African agency in international affairs largely depends on African common positions and declarations. This suggests that common African positions are an important element of the AU's foreign policy engagement in that they set the tone and terms of engagement with the rest of the world. However, the evidence suggests that the divided positions of African states on certain central issues affect the AU's ability to formulate durable collective foreign policy position.

African agency has been something of an anthem at the AU, encapsulated in the phrase "African ownership and leadership". Historical evidence shows that by the time Africa renegotiated the Lomé Agreement with Europe in the late 1990s, the OAU was concerned with the salience of African agency in this significant inter-regional partnership. Concerning the renewed partnership agreement, the negotiating team was advised "[it] is important that there is no Eurocentric perspective of these essential elements. The ACP must give their perspective of these elements which takes on board the social, cultural, historical, political and economic specificities of our states" (OAU, 1999: 9).

In the resulting *Joint Africa-EU Strategy of 2007*, the two parties highlighted the enhanced status of African agency by stating the need to "move away from a traditional relationship and forge a real partnership characterised by equality and the pursuit of common objectives" (European Union, 2007). Accounting for the largest share of African inter-regional relations, the Africa-EU partnership set a precedent for subsequent partnerships in particular, by purveying the notion of African "leadership" and "ownership". Significantly, African experts had a large input in most of the documents that shaped the design and implementation of the APSA (Ademola Abbas, *personal communication*, Addis Ababa: 2015). Moreover, for the most part the European Commission paid close attention to the objections of its African counterparts. This ushered in an altogether new measure of African agency, which was not easily found in other Western partnerships.

Partnerships with the East (and South Asian) economic powerhouses such as China, Japan, India and South Korea seem to provide leeway for African agency. A yet-to-be-published evaluation of the AU's international partnerships ranked the above-mentioned above the Africa-EU partnership (AU, 2014). The partnerships were ranked in terms of their efficiency and outputs. Going by the measure of partnership effectiveness provided by Setainidi, these partnerships are efficient in terms of factors including high-level diplomatic engagement, managerial complexity, preference and interests linkage, as well as resource disbursement and directionality. The reason why these variables are highly efficient owes to a lack of colonial history as well as a shared history in the multilateralism of a Global South—this is especially true where China, India and South Korea are concerned.

In the case of the EU, this does not apply. Africa's partnership with the EU became an uneasy one. This was due to the Economic Partnership Agreements (EPA) that directly impacted on and disrupted the AU's own Regional Economic Community (REC) integration schemes. The EPA became a source of political divisions among AU member states, especially Southern African Customs Union (SACU) and Southern African Development Community (SADC) states (Flint, 2009: 87–89). But the general perception created is that there was a resurgence in neo-colonial impulses by a number of lead states within the EU.

In fact, France's intrusion into African multilateralism has become ever more palpable in the area of security and in economic terms. This is traceable to the history and politics of French decolonisation in Africa. Prior to decolonisation, France demarcated its African "sphere of influence" into three zones, which marked the strategic prioritisation of these regions. First was the "Active Zone"—a top priority zone stretching from Senegal to the Democratic Republic of Congo (DRC); second, the "Passive Zone"—comprising of small former Belgian colonies; and third and finally the "Mixed Zone", comprising of former colonies along the Mediterranean Sea and the Red Sea (Zartman 1984, as cited in Mays, 2002). Since the inception of this system, to-date, African states have been run through "ad hoc structures in Paris … [rather] than … normal diplomatic channels" and "many aspects [are] kept out of public or parliamentary view" Moncrieff (2012: 360). Interestingly, these zones currently constitute the most unstable and conflicted regions of the continent, accounting for a majority of AU political and security missions.

Beyond partnerships: African collective diplomacy in action

There are instances wherein crucial issues in global politics require African states and organisations to form strong positions in order to enact a new order and for the continent to defend its territorial or juridical integrity. Two instances stand out that have shown weakness and loopholes in Africa's collective diplomacy.

Libya

African states were unable to arrive at a common position on Libya during the popular uprisings of North Africa in 2011. The debate between the leaders Meles Zenawi, Goodluck Jonathan and Jacob Zuma on Libya took too long, only to culminate in a non-committal compromise position (Mehari Maru, *personal communication*, Addis Ababa: 2015). The common but politically tenuous position opened up the space for the AU to be sidelined when it absented itself from meetings of the 35-member strong Libyan Contact Group in London. This, in turn, enabled the controversial (NATO and US AFRICOM) military actions in Libya sanctioned by the Arab League and the UN.

However, even if there had been a more solid common African position on Libya, it would not have been a match for Western diplomatic manoeuvres. In a typical case of Western jingoism-in-action—something which Adler-Nissen and Pouliot (2014: 902–904) describe as "skilful diplomacy", France worked with the US and UK to undermine African preferences within the UN Security Council by isolating Nigeria, South Africa and their sympathisers (Russia, China and Brazil), in order to legitimise a military intervention in Libya. This major global event substantially weakened the AU as a foreign policy actor in global politics.

UN reform

Sometimes, even where there are common positions, these are insufficient to exert foreign policy agency. A lack of compliance and adherence by the more powerful African states undermines them. For instance, when the then UN Secretary General, Kofi Annan, proposed United Nations Security Council (UNSC) reforms, AU member states adopted a common African position called the *Ezuwlini Consensus* of 2005. The consensus demanded "full representation of Africa in the Security Council … [with] no less than two permanent seats with all prerogatives and privileges of the permanent membership including the right to veto … [and] five non-permanent seats" (AU, 2005). Deservedly, the AU was acting in line with the opportunity for the much wanted reform of the UN, but this reform would not be necessarily useful. If the UN had met AU demands, the two permanent non-veto seats would not have made much difference because Africa, under the current system, does always have non-veto representation in the UNSC. Moreover, while they do not have permanent seats in the AU Peace and Security Council (PSC), it is not clear how two African states having permanent seats in the UNSC would benefit overall African agency. It is surprising that despite forming the largest voting bloc at the UN General Assembly, the AU has not pressed for far more important and far reaching reforms, such as including widely-spoken African languages (as with Swahili) to the list of UN official languages. Adding African languages at the UN would give greater weight to African agency by promoting African identity and, by extension, endogenous African ideologies. The approach to UN reform showed that African states are more concerned with symbolism rather than substantive projections of agency.

Conclusion

This chapter discussed African agency under the auspices of the AU as a function of foreign policy in international affairs. African agency is the ability of the AU as a foreign policy actor "to do something" or achieve in international affairs. With particular reference to neo-colonialism and neo-imperialism, the historical and structural environment in which this agency unfolds clearly matters. Yet, even though these conditions allow for an understanding of the context, they do not necessarily allow for an appreciation of the AU's "ability". To understand this ability, it is important to identify the key agents that make up its agency and to understand their role.

The foreign policymaking roles of the heads of government, the chief of the AU Commission and other role players in exercising African international relations are varied, as they are complex. As an inter-governmental organisation, the part played by leaders and major states such as Nigeria and South Africa and their ability to collate various preferences and interests and forge common positions for Africa in international positions is disputed by smaller members, periodic and not sustained. In addition, there are difficulties that emanate from the inevitable appetite for self-help and the unspoken challenges of freeriding by a number of states. The intercessory role of identity, ideology and solidarity in African agency plays into this mix. Most importantly of all, the consolidation of African foreign policy agency at the level of the AU is hamstrung by a lack of political will to depersonalise, depoliticise, institutionalise and build greater institutional autonomy to accompany evolving common foreign policy agency.

Overall, it is demonstrated that African agency has outgrown its honeymoon phase. In its early years, the role of heads of states was identifiable through the various processes as in the international partnerships where the international community (IC) pledged to respect African ownership and leadership. Yet, since the 2010s, the efficiency of this level of high-level diplomacy has waned. While the role of the Chairperson of the AUC has remained relatively unchanged, no one since Alpha Konare (2003–2008) has matched his fortitude.

Most pointedly, member states have been reluctant to adhere to the Banjul Formula that envisages the AUC Chairperson spearheading the collation and projection of African interests with major powers such as the US, China, Japan and Korea. This is primarily because most member countries feel the AUC is unable to adequately represent their interests. Against a background where identity and ideology periodically cause schisms within the AU, this in corollary implies member states prefer to focus their collective efforts and energy at the sub-regional level. Where the AU or Africa has to deal with other world regions, this has grossly undermined the idea of African solidarity. African agency and the AU's foreign policy presence may have waxed and waned, yet the potential to strengthen and consolidate itself into the future seemingly remains.

Notes

1 It is important to differentiate the African experience from a phenomenon described by Tana Johnson (2013) and other scholars (Barnett & Finnemore, 2004) whereby some inter-governmental organisations, although created by states, tend to assume a life of its own wherein international bureaucrats can insulate those organisations from state control. In Africa, states still exercise tight control of inter-governmental organisations. As a matter of fact, if an AUC Chairperson is perceived as too strong, they are voted out in the next election (Gasamma, 2013).

2 For a background reading on international institution building and reconciliation, see Vinod Aggarwal (ed.) (1998), *Institutional Designs for a Complex World: Bargaining, Linkages and Nesting*, Ithaca & London: Cornell University Press.

3 The literature is awash with explanations of the formation of the African state as a post-colonial entity (Clapham, 1992). It also explains how coloniality influenced the way the African state approaches international relations (Mbembe, 1992, 2006). Galtung (1971) insists that there are networks between elites in the developed and developing states which support a political economy of patronage.

4 Even today, due to its uniqueness, African regionalism is treated as an oddity and a source of intrigue to enterprising theorists. Mbembe (2006: 2) argues that:

> It is in relation to Africa that the notion of 'absolute otherness' has been taken farthest. It is now widely acknowledged that Africa as an idea, a concept, has historically served, and continues to serve, as a polemical argument for the West's desperate desire to assert its difference from the rest of the world. In several respects, Africa still constitutes one of the metaphors through which the West represents the origin of its own norms, develops a self-image, and integrates this image into the set of signifiers asserting what is supposed to be its identity.

5 Sociologically, the process of institutionalisation is an isomorphic process that involves a myriad of inputs because "in practice, the distinction between a political institution and a social force is not a clear-cut one" and "the power and influence of social forces varies considerably" (Huntington, 1968: 9).

6 Other progenitors or advocates of pan-Africanism include Kwame Nkrumah, Marcus Garvey, Sékou Toure, W.E. Du Bois, Julius Nyerere and others.

7 This is attributable to two dynamics. First, although nine African states have the capacity for strategic airlift, African states are less motivated to role play because unlike the UN, the AU is unable to reimburse member states for contingent owned equipment (COE). Second, regional hegemons are less inclined to engage in regional projects which are distant from their immediate spheres of influence. This is a radical departure from the early years of the AU where capable states led AU missions (such as the AU Mission in Burundi and the AU Mission for the Support to the Elections in the Comoros) in order to limit foreign states' involvement even when they provided a portion of the funding.

8 Nigeria espoused the notion of a "Pax-Nigeriana" in the 1970s. According to Adebajo (2008), *Pax-Nigeriana* informed three military interventions in Chad between 1979 and 1982. On the other hand, post-apartheid South Africa also espoused continental leadership even though it was never able to make progress without Nigeria which had more

experience in African regionalism and security. However, none of these have influence outside their sub-continent. There has been some fierce competition between the two countries. Even when these two engage in joint efforts, their capabilities and actions rarely transcend the hortatory rhetoric that has hitherto dwarfed African agency in various issues. This is more illustratable in the area of peace and security.

9 Finally, the capacity for effective hegemony is encumbered by the aspirants' competition in global politics. In spite of the "twin-hegemony" of the 2000s, the aspirants succumbed to temptations of grandeur and influence through candidature for a permanent (non-veto) seat in the United Nations Security Council. According to Landsberg (2008: 205), initially South Africa was not a strong contender for the UNSC permanent seat but enjoyed support from US statesmen and diplomats such as Henry Kissinger, Gwendolyn Mikell and Princeton Lyman. This implies that South Africa was "encouraged" to augment its global ambition at the expense of regional imperatives. As a result, competition between South Africa, Nigeria and Egypt intensified. Adebajo (2008: 26) states that the three contenders "entered a Byzantine contest ... Cynics dismissed Nigeria as too 'anarchic', Egypt as too 'Arab' and South Africa as too 'albinocratic'". This competition revealed a key weakness in African states' individual and collective foreign policy—a poor ordering of priorities.

10 The term "strategic citizenship" is an extrapolation of Eckstein's (1992) conception of citizenship whereby civic reciprocity is expected between a constituent and their geopolitical cleavage, through mechanisms such as compliance to rules and roles or dissent through self-exclusion. Thus, a discussion of strategic citizenship in Africa entails discussions of how states of a particular size and capabilities play their role and share burdens of regional security.

References

Abbott, K. W. & Snidal, D. (1998). Why States Act through Formal International Organizations. *The Journal of Conflict Resolution*, 42(1): 3–32.

Abdul-Raheem, T. (ed.). (2006). *Pan Africanism: Politics, Economy and Social Change in the Twenty-First Century*. New York: New York University Press.

Acharya, A. (1997). The Periphery as the Core: The Third World and Security Studies. In K. Keith Krause & M. C. Williams (eds.), *Critical Security Studies: Concepts and Cases*, pp. 299–327. Minneapolis, MN: University of Minnesota Press.

Adebajo, A. & Landsberg, C. (2003). Nigeria and South Africa as Regional Hegemon. In M. Baregu & C. Landsberg (eds.), *From Cape to Congo: Southern Africa's Evolving Security*, pp. 171–203. Boulder, CO: Lynne Rienner.

Adebajo, A. (2008). Hegemony on a Shoestring: Nigeria's Post-Cold War Foreign Policy. In A. Adebajo & A. R. Mustapha (eds.), *Gulliver's Troubles: Nigeria's Foreign Policy After the Cold War*, pp. 1–37. Pietermaritzburg: University of Kwazulu-Natal Press.

Adler-Nissen, R. & Pouliot, V. (2014). Power in Practice: Negotiating the International Intervention in Libya. *European Journal of International Relations*, 20(4): 889–911.

African Union. (2002). *Protocol Relating to the Establishment of the Peace and Security Council of the African Union*. Addis Ababa: AU Commission.

African Union. (2004). *Solemn Declaration on a Common African Defence and Security Policy*. Addis Ababa: AU Commission. Retrieved from http://www.peaceau.org/uploads/declaration-cadsp-en.pdf.

African Union. (2005). *African Union Non-Aggression and Common Defence Pact*. Addis Ababa: AU Commission. Retrieved from https://au.int/sites/default/files/treaties/37292-treaty-0031_-_african_union_non-aggression_and_common_defence_pact_e.pdf.

African Union. (2014). *Evaluation of the Africa's Strategic Partnerships Draft Final Revised Report*. Addis Ababa: UNDP/AU.

African Union. (2015). The Permanent Representatives Committee. Retrieved from http://www.au.int/en/organs/prc.

African Union. (2018). Statement by President Paul Kagame, Chairperson of the African Union at the Closing Ceremony of the 10th Extraordinary Summit of AfCFTA. Retrieved from https://au.int/fr/node/34035.

African Union. (2015). The Executive Council. Retrieved from http://www.au.int/en/organs/council.

Agbi, S. O. (1986). *The Organization of African Unity and African Diplomacy, 1963–1979*. Ibadan: Impact Publishers.

Aggarwal, V. (1998). Reconciling Multiple Institutions: Bargaining, Linkages and Nesting. In V. Aggarwal (ed.), *Institutional Designs for a Complex World: Bargaining, Linkages and Nesting*, pp. 1–3. Ithaca, NY/London: Cornell University Press.

Akuffo, A. (2011). Human Security and Interregional Cooperation between NATO and the African Union. *Global Change, Peace & Security*, 23(2): 223–237. doi:10.1080/14781158.2011.580962.

Alden, C. & Soko, M. (2005). South Africa's Economic Relations with Africa: Hegemony and Its Discontents. *Journal of Modern African Studies*, 43(3): 367–392.

Ayoob, M. (1997). Defining Security: A Subaltern Realist Perspective. In K. Krause & M. C. Williams (eds.), *Critical Security Studies: Concepts and Cases*, pp. 121–146. Minneapolis, MN: University of Minnesota Press.

Bach, D. C. (2013). Africa in International Relations: The Frontier as Concept and Metaphor. *South African Journal of International Affairs*, 20(1): 1–22. doi:10.1080/10220461.2013.783283.

Bah, A. S., Chogo-Nyangoro, E., Dersso, S., Mofya, B. & Murithi, T. (2014). *The Africa Peace and Security Architecture: A Handbook*. Addis Ababa: Friedrich-Ebert-Stiftung.

Barkawi, T. & Laffey, M. (2006). The Postcolonial Moment in Security Studies. *Review of International Studies*, 32: 329–352. doi:10/1017S0260210506007054.

Barnett, B. & Finnemore, M. (2004). *Rules for the World: International Organisations in Global Politics*. Ithaca, NY/London: Michael Barnett.

Bischoff, P. H. (2008). Pan-African Multilateralism: Transformative or Disconnected? *Politikon*, 32(2): 177–195. doi:10.1080/02589340802366968.

Brecher, M. B., Steinberg, B. & Stein, J. (1969). A Framework for Research on Foreign Policy Behaviour. *Journal of Conflict Resolution*, 13(1): 75–94. doi:10.1177%2F002200276901300105.

Brosig, M. (2013). The African Union: A Partner for Security. In S. Biscop & R. G. Whitman (eds.), *The Routledge Handbook on European Security*, pp. 292–301. Oxon: Routledge.

Brosig, M. (2015). *Cooperative Peacekeeping in Africa*. London/New York: Routledge.

Brown, W. (2012). A Question of Agency: Africa in International Politics. *Third World Quarterly*, 33(10): 1889–1908. doi:10.1080/01436597.2012.728322.

Carta, C. (2013). *The European Union Diplomatic Service: Ideas, Preferences and Identities*. London/New York: Routledge.

Clapham, C. (1996). *Africa and the International System: The Politics of State of Survival*. Cambridge: Cambridge University Press.

Council of European Union. (2007). *The Africa-EU Strategic Partnership: A Joint Africa-EU Strategy*. Brussels: Presse 291.

DiMaggio, P. J. & Powell, W. W. (1983). The Iron Cage Revisited: Institutional Isomorphism and Collective Rationality in Organizational Fields. *American Sociological Review*, 48(2): 147–160. doi:10.2307/2095101.

Doty, R. L. (1993). Foreign Policy as Social Construction: A Post-Positivist Analysis of U.S. Counterinsurgency Policy in the Philippines. *International Studies Quarterly*, 37(3): 297–320. doi:10.2307/2600810.

Eckstein, H. (1992). *Regarding Politics: Essays on Political Theory, Stability, and Change*. Berkeley, CA/Oxford: University of California Press.

Elman, M. F. (1995). The Foreign Policies of Small States: Challenging Neorealism in Its Own Backyard. *British Journal of Political Science*, 25(2): 171–217.

Esmenjaud, R. (2014). The African Capacity for Immediate Response to Crisis: Conceptual Breakthrough or Anti-Imperialist Phantom? *African Security Review*, 23(2): 172–177. doi:10.1080/10246029.2014.898589.

Evans, E. (2008). *The Responsibility to Protect: Ending Mass Atrocity Crimes Once and For All*. Washington, DC: Brookings Institution Press.

Fasehun, O. (1980). Nigeria and the Issue of an African High Command: Towards a Regional and/or Continental Defence System. *Afrika Spektrum*, 80: 3.

Flemes, D. & Nolte, D. (2010). Introduction. In D. Flemes (ed.), *Regional Leadership in the Global System: Ideas, Interests and Strategies of Regional Powers*, pp. 1–14. Farnham: Ashgate.

Flint, A. (2009). The End of a "Special Relationship?" The New EU-ACP Economic Partnership Agreements. *Review of African Political Economy*, 36(119): 79–92. doi:10.1080/03056240902863595.

Franke, B. & Ganzle, S. (2012). How "African" Is the African Peace and Security Architecture? Conceptual and Practical Constraints of Regional Security Cooperation in Africa. *African Security*, 5(2): 88–104.

Galtung, J. (1971). A Structural Theory of Imperialism. *Journal of Peace Research*, 8(2): 81–117. doi:10.1177%2F002234337100800201.

Gassama, M. (2013). *From the OAU to the AU: The Odyssey of a Continental Organization*. Serrekunda, Gambia: Fulladu Publishers.

Hafner-Burton, E. M., Hughes, D. A. & Victor, D. G. (2013). The Cognitive Revolution and the Political Psychology of Elite Decision Making. *Perspectives on Politics*, 11(2): 368–386. doi:10.1017/S1537592713001084.

Hardt, H. (2014). *Time to React: The Efficiency of International Organizations in Crisis Response*. Oxford/New York: Oxford University Press.

Hönke, J. & Müller, M. M. (2012). Governing (In)Security in a Postcolonial World: Transnational Entanglements and the Worldliness of "Local" Practice. *Security Dialogue*, 43(5): 383–401. doi:10.1177%2F0967010612458337.

Howorth, J. (2007). *Security and Defence Policy in the European Union*. New York: Palgrave Macmillan.

Huntington, S. P. (1968). *Political Order in Changing Societies*. New Haven, CT: Yale University Press.

Johnson, T. (2013). Institutional Design and Bureaucrats' Impact on Political Control. *The Journal of Politics*, 75(1): 183–197. doi:10.1017/s0022381612000953.

Landsberg, C. (2004). *The Quiet Diplomacy of Liberation: International Politics and South Africa's Transition*. Johannesburg: Jacana Media.

Landsberg, C. (2008). An African "Concert of Powers?" Nigeria and South Africa's Construction of the AU and NEPAD. In A. Adebajo & A. R. Mustapha (eds.), *Gulliver's*

Troubles: Nigeria's Foreign Policy After the Cold War. Pietermaritzburg: University of Kwazulu-Natal Press.

Landsberg, C. (2014). Dr Dlamini-Zuma and the AU's Agenda 2063. Africa-EU. Retrieved from http://www.africa-eu.com/2014/11/zuma-au-agenda-2063.html.

Leurdjik, D. A. (2003). The UN and NATO: The Logic of Primacy. In M. C. Pugh & W. P. S. Sidhu (eds.), *The United Nations and Regional Security: Europe and Beyond*, p. 57. Boulder, CO/London: Lynne Rienner.

Makinda, S. M. & Okumu, F. W. (2008). *The African Union: Challenges of Globalization, Security and Governance*. London/New York: Routledge.

Mangu, A. B. (2006). Democracy, African Intellectuals and African Renaissance. *International Journal of African Renaissance Studies, Multi, Inter- and Transdisciplinarity*, 1(1): 147–163. doi:10.1080/18186870608529711.

Mays, T. M. (2002). *Africa's First Peacekeeping Operation: The OAU in Chad, 1981–1982*. Westport, CT/London: Praeger.

Mazrui, A. (2006). Global Africa: From Abolitionists to Reparations. In T. Abdul-Raheem (ed.), *Pan Africanism: Politics, Economy and Social Change in the Twenty-First Century*, pp. 123–143. New York: New York University Press.

Mbembe, A. (1992). Provisional Notes on the Post-Colony. *Africa*, 62(1): 3–37. doi:10.2307/1160062.

Mbembe, A. (2006). *On the Postcolony*. Berkeley, CA/London: University of California Press.

Mboya, M. M. (2006). Mbeki and the Peace Process in Africa: A Contribution to Africa's Renaissance. *International Journal of African Renaissance Studies*, 1(1): 80–90. doi:10.1080/18186870608529707.

Mead, W. R., Erwin, S. & Goldstein, E. (2006). The United States: Inextricably Linked with Nations across the Globe. *e-JournalUS*, 5–8.

Moncrieff, R. (2012). French Africa Policy: Sarkozy's Legacy, and Prospects for a Hollande Presidency. *South African Journal of International Affairs*, 19(3): 359–380. doi:10.1080/10220461.2012.741104.

Niang, A. (2016). The Imperative of African Perspectives on International Relations. *Politics*, 36(4): 453–466. doi:10.1177%2F0263395716637092.

Nuechterlein, D. E. (1976). National Interests and Foreign Policy: A Conceptual Framework for Analysis and Decision-making. *British Journal of International Studies*, 2(3): 246–266.

OAU. (1963). Proceedings of the Summit Conference of Independent African States. Addis Ababa: OAU Secretariat.

OAU. (1999). 'Key Issues in the Current ACP-EU Negotiations', Technical Report No.1 Prepared for African Negotiators by OAU Advisory Panel of Experts on ACP-EU Negotiations. Addis Ababa: OAU.

Payne, R. A. (2001). Persuasion, Frames and Norm Construction. *European Journal of International Relations*, 7(1): 37–61.

Rieker, P. (2006). *Europeanization of National Security Identity: The EU and the Changing Security Identities of the Nordic States*. London/New York: Routledge.

Rüland, J., Hanggi, H. & Roloff, R. (2006). Interregionalism: A New Phenomenon in International Relations. In J. Rüland, H. Hanggi & R. Roloff (eds.), *Interregionalism and International Relations*, pp. 3–14. Oxon/New York: Routledge.

Schimmelfennig, F. (1998). NATO Enlargement: A Constructivist Explanation. *Security Studies*, 8(3): 198–234. doi:10.1080/09636419808429378.

Schmidt, E. (2013). *Foreign Intervention in Africa: From the Cold War to the Present*. Cambridge: Cambridge University Press.

Simon, H. (1985). Human Nature in Politics: Dialogue of Psychology and Political Science. *American Political Science Review*, 79(2): 293–304.

Zondi, S. (2013). Africa in Multilateral Negotiations: A Critique of African Common Positions. In W. Brown & S. Harman (eds.), *African Agency in International Politics*. London: Routledge.

4 Unprincipled pragmatism and anti-imperialist impulses in an interconnected world

The Zuma presidency, 2009–2017

Mzukisi Qobo

Introduction

Despite the same party, the African National Congress (ANC), leading the country from 1994 onwards, South Africa's foreign policy has markedly changed over the years. While the major (ideological) pillars of the country's foreign policy have ostensibly stayed much the same, the points of emphasis and the priorities of various leaders have considerably differed. It has shown that foreign policy is not a static art, but one subject to contingencies, which reflect on a leader's preferences and the character of institutions. I extend this conceptual view to what I characterize as unprincipled pragmatism under President Jacob Zuma, which is essentially a foreign policy stance that cloaks personal and particularistic interests as a country's own interests, and that has no anchorage in any defined set of ideas. Much of this has been amplified in South Africa's anticolonial rhetoric. Essentially, a foreign policy stance that cloaks personal and particularistic interests to mimic the country's own interests. It has no anchorage in any defined set of ideas even though foreign policy pronouncements were amplified by the superficial use of anti-colonial rhetoric.

It is the contention of this chapter that during the period from 2009 to 2018, South Africa's foreign policy lost its moral authority. The sources for this drift are varied. In the main, they lie in domestic institutional erosion, governance failure and economic mismanagement, all of which drained the country's confidence as a global actor during the period. It is no coincidence that the loss of South Africa's moral weight abroad and the confident articulation of its foreign policy became glaring at a0 time when governance failures and economic underperformance were deepening, with growing concerns domestically about the rise of corruption. On the African continent South Africa also lost moral influence. It has failed to be a positive force for change in spite, if not because, of the country's insistence on nominating its own candidate to head the African Union Commission, as well as the country's lethargic role in the continent.

The foreign policy rhetoric during the Zuma period emphasised anti-colonialism and anti-imperialism. This was in tandem with the ratcheting up of the language on "radical economic transformation" domestically. Arguably, this "radical" turn in foreign policy was an attempt to divert attention from the government's domestic failings and to mask the decline in South Africa's moral authority in international relations.

The loss of moral authority was evident not only in the neglect of the human rights pillar in the country's foreign policy and voting record at the United Nations, but also in various policy pronouncements, especially when it came both at a state level and party-to-party level, to overstressing relations with China and Russia. As such, Zuma's foreign policy orientation diverged normatively from the administrations of President Nelson Mandela (1994–1999) and President Thabo Mbeki (1999–2008). In order to better understand the meaning of unprincipled pragmatism under Zuma, this chapter will draw some parallels with foreign policy dispensation under Mandela and Mbeki era, as well as to examine its features on their merits.

Consider, for example, the gravitation of foreign policy towards China and Russia. Zuma's strong embrace in extensively close relations with these two major authoritarian and state-capitalist countries was not based on any justifiable strategic calculations or the concerted pursuit of economic diplomatic goals. On economic grounds, especially in light of the global redistribution of leadership and the need for generating economic benefits for the country, closer relations with China would have been justifiable. However, there was no systematic policy framework on the part of South Africa to cast the relationship in such terms and harness it towards serving the country's deep-seated developmental challenges.

While the ideological signifiers in the preceding Mandela and Mbeki eras were markedly different, say on the articulation of human rights idealism (viz. Mandela) vis-à-vis the emphasis on Africanism (viz. Mbeki), there were varying doses of pragmatism with both administrations. Both Mandela and Mbeki understood the imperatives of the interconnectedness of the world, the importance of global cooperation and the need to diversify platforms of diplomatic engagement. There was a great deal of overlap in the terms of office of these two leaders: even when Mandela was president, Mbeki played a role akin to that of a prime minister, playing an active role in shaping economic policy thinking domestically and foreign policy through his signature plan of African Renaissance abroad. During this time, South Africa's trade and investment relations were diffused across the world. Much of its diversified exports were destined for the US and Europe. In addition to its active role in the African Union – with Mbeki having pioneered the relaunch of the Organisation of African Unity to the African Union with a renewed focus – South Africa was also keen to deepen relations with Europe and the US. Early after democratic elections, South Africa negotiated a very detailed trade and development cooperation agreement.

It should be underlined that at this time, South Africa's pragmatism was grounded on principle: it maintained and jealously guarded South Africa's independence in international relations, it cultivated an Africanist focus, and kept relations with other African countries on cordial terms. South Africa was keenly aware South Africa was keenly aware of its changing identity in close alignment with the developmental interests of the broader African continent and the need to play an active role as a system stabiliser. To this end, it pursued a diplomacy aimed at bridging the divides between the North and the South, as well as strengthening multilateral institutions.

The Zuma administration departed from this vision of an interconnected world. It worked off a foreign policy paradigm that in practice was markedly different to that of both previous governments. Zuma's foreign policy conduct can be characterised as one of unprincipled pragmatism. What underlined this unprincipled turn were several factors: absence of animating ideas about South Africa's place in the world and the African continent, and Zuma's more transactional brand of leadership and urge towards populism. South Africa's progressive internationalism suffered during this era as Zuma privileged relations that would reinforce transactional bargains of crony capitalism in South Africa. In looking at this foreign policy phase, the chapter casts a spotlight on three crucial divergences that signify a departure from the country's prior foreign policy conduct: South Africa's deferential relationship with China, its personalised, informal approach to commercial diplomacy with Russia and growing cavalier attitude towards international law.

The ANC's conceptual approach to foreign policy

The ratcheting up of anti-Western views in South African foreign policy under Zuma is a departure from the more nuanced Pan-Africanist perspective of the Thabo Mbeki years. Under Mbeki, the more populist voices within the governing party had been drowned. South Africa was set on a path that broadly converged with neo-liberal perspectives and international openness. Mbeki walked a tight rope. He did not pursue a neo-liberal order for its own sake, but worked within its constraints to project South Africa positively in international relations and carve a space of for North-South engagements in ways that would benefit the African continent. The New Economic Programme for Africa's Development (NEPAD) set out Mbeki's objectives in engaging with the world. Not so with Zuma who, in the course of his term, did not develop a sound ideational framework that would define South Africa's external relations. Further, his foreign policy practices diverged from Mandela's normative focus on human rights. Both leaders who preceded Zuma valued independence more than any narrow ideological alliances in international relations. At the same time, they were aware of South Africa's burden of responsibility towards the African continent. Nonetheless, even though South Africa emphasised its "South" credentials and Pan-Africanist outlook especially under Mbeki, it still sought to position itself more as a bridge builder. This led to some characterising this posture as that of a middle-power (Nel, Taylor and van der Westhuizen, 2001).

Middle powers tend to be known for their neutrality in international affairs, blending the normative with pragmatic positions. Scholars such as Cooper (1997) regard middle powers as countries that are imbued with traits that condition them to act as "good international citizens" or multilateralists. This, of course, is not without its challenges in an international system characterised by the pursuit of national interest to maximise relative power—or in the case of economic goals—to aggregate wealth.

During Zuma's administration, there was a marked shift in South Africa's foreign policy conduct away from these normative signifiers. What featured glaringly in Zuma's foreign policy was its unhinged approach—at times decidedly anti-Western, at other times showing a lack of independence and confidence. It was apparent how South Africa's interests increasingly came to be tied to those of China and Russia, especially during Zuma's second term of office (2014–2018).

In the early years of South Africa's democracy and when the country rejoined the international community after decades under isolation, the new South Africa forged deep relations with both the Western and the non-Western world. As part of its foreign pillars, South Africa acknowledged the importance of strengthening relations with the countries of the North. Promoting exports on a diversified basis, attracting foreign direct investment and benefitting from technology spillovers were some of the calculations for maintaining relations with Western countries. As such, the first ever-comprehensive bilateral trade agreement South Africa entered into post-1994 was with the European Union, supplemented by the Trade Development and Cooperation Agreement (TDCA) with the European Union. The trade deal was signed in October 1999 after five years of intense negotiations.

On the multilateral front, South Africa was actively involved in both regional bodies such as the Southern African Development Community (SADC) and the Organisation of African Unity (OAU), now the African Union (AU), as well as in international processes beyond the continent, such as the Non-Aligned Movement, the World Trade Organisation and the United Nations. South Africa's commitment to multilateralism also had its source within the pillars of the struggle propagated by the ANC in exile, especially normative commitments to international solidarity and the rights-based discourse (Alden & Le Pere, 2006). Under Zuma, South Africa had strained relations with its African partners.

Despite the unwritten rule that major countries in the continent, South Africa and Nigeria would not seek office in the African Union Commission, South Africa pushed for its own candidate—Nkosazana-Dlamini Zuma—in 2012. Dlamini-Zuma is a powerful South African politician who was once the country's minister of foreign affairs and who is someone with presidential ambitions. Her campaign for the AU Commission was seen by some as divisive as it pitted the two powerhouses on the continent—South Africa and Nigeria—against each other. Ultimately, Dlamini-Zuma's record at the helm of this body was a mixed one. Despite the fact that she spearheaded the launch of African Union's Agenda 2063, she was mostly absent from the AU and very slow to react to crises such as those in Mali and the Sahel or the Ebola outbreak in West Africa.

Dlamini-Zuma was certainly not the cause of these crises, while the complexity of politics at the AU, which give very little room for any head to bring in reforms, should be acknowledged. However, every leader that takes up the cudgels should appear able to bring forth their creativity, diplomatic skills and political acumen to effect noticeable institutional reform. There is no evidence to show that after her term she left a legacy of leaving a stronger and independent institution behind.

This was in part because South Africa in the first place did not have any strategic perspectives in bringing about reforms at the AU. As part of promoting Dlamini-Zuma's candidacy, there were no objectives or priorities articulated. If at all, these were to emerge as rationalisation after the fact.

South Africa and external relations

On the international front, South Africa had been active during the Mandela and Mbeki eras to forge relations everywhere with other developing, emerging and advanced industrial economies. The India, Brazil, South Africa (IBSA) cooperation arrangement was one of such arrangements established during the Mbeki era, as a reformist platform to counter-balance the dominance of the G8 (with Russia then a member) in global governance. The IBSA group was made up of significant democracies in the developing world, pivotal states in their regions and countries that are very active in global governance processes. Rather than being constrained within narrow alliance structures, South Africa kept its remit of engagement in international relations open. Later this was to happen with its accession to the BRICS, comprised of Brazil, Russia, India and China. Alongside organisations such as IBSA, South Africa participated in deliberations with the G8 under the G8+5 discussions in the early to mid-2000s or contributed to enhancing OECD engagement between advanced industrial economies and emerging economies. Even in the context of multilateral trade negotiations, South Africa maintained membership of the Africa Group, the Cairns group that included both developed and developing countries and the G20 formation, predominantly made up of developing countries. Simultaneously, the country continued to maintain membership of various international groupings such as the Socialist International, the Non-Aligned Movement (NAM) and the G77 Group of developing countries at the United Nations, which had their roots in the anti-colonial struggle during the Cold War era.

In sum, South Africa sought to pursue an open, independent and values driven, yet pragmatic foreign policy. This is not to suggest that South Africa's foreign policy did not suffer incoherencies. Aberrations such as the embrace of the Libyan dictator Muammar Gadaffi or siding with China in opposing sanctions on Myanmar were some of the examples of the moral weakness in the foreign policy during Mandela's time. However, this was not a salient or common feature of South Africa's diplomacy. Overall, South Africa wanted to be seen doing the right thing—promote human rights and international peace. The country's leaders were vocal on human rights issues, actively championing its constitution and the ideals of constitutionalism. They also believed that the best way to resolve tensions internationally was through dialogue and mediation rather than military conflict. In tandem, South Africa sought to take advantage of international goodwill to forge relationships that would generate economic value for the country.

The Zuma era reflected the drawing of the curtain on principled pragmatism. To be fair, the signs that South Africa's lustre was waning began just before Zuma took over. When in January 2007, South Africa voted at the United Nations

Security Council against a resolution reprimanding the Myanmar government's use of military force against civilians in ethnic minority regions, it presaged the end of an era in South Africa's foreign policy. Mbeki had just over a year before he was about to be unceremoniously recalled from office. The spectre of Zuma was already hovering, with the governing party, the African National Congress (ANC), signalling a more radical posture in foreign policy, a stance that was to be adopted at the end of 2007 during the party's elective conference where Zuma was elected its president. The South African government used procedural points in justifying its dubious vote on the Myanmar issue, protesting that the UN Security Council was the wrong platform to raise this issue (Fabricius & Donnenfeld, 2018).

It would be another decade before South Africa could slowly recover its bearings on human rights issues and attempt to rectify its previous positions. In December 2018, under the Ramaphosa presidency, the country voted in support of the passing of the resolution on the issue of human rights in Myanmar at the UN General Assembly. This about-turn was face-saving and confirmed that Zuma's approach to human rights issues had been out of kilter with South Africa's long-term foreign policy commitment to promoting human rights. This tallied with the Zuma era where there was a consistent sense of the institutional erosion, governance failure and weakening commitment to constitutionalism in South Africa.

While the two presidents that preceded Zuma were both modernists and embraced the virtues of constitutionalism, having both played a key role in South Africa's negotiations for a new constitutional dispensation, Zuma on the other hand was more of a traditionalist with little respect for institutional strictures. His conception of the state was one of the state as an extension of personalised (executive) power. This accounts for why, under his leadership, there was little sign of a guiding philosophy or a coherent set of ideas. Much foreign policy activity was driven by whimsical considerations accompanied by inexplicable voting patterns on human rights at the United Nations Security Council.

Even on regional matters, South Africa's foreign policy displayed a new precedent of dissonance with the country's constitutional and liberal leanings on human rights issues. In 2018, the South African Constitutional Court ruled against Zuma in a judgement that was a reprimand for his role in undermining the powers of the SADC Tribunal. This judgement followed a similar judgement indicting Zuma's presidency, where the courts found that government breached its constitutional obligation in failing to arrest the Sudanese President Al-Bashir on a visit to South Africa, despite the fact there was a warrant for his arrest issued by the International Criminal Court of Justice (ICC).

The SADC Tribunal existed in terms of the SADC Treaty to which South Africa is a signatory, as a regional adjudicating body to promote human rights, democracy and the rule of law. This body adjudicates between states but also between natural or legal persons and states. The judgement of the SADC Tribunal ruled that the action of the South African government in signing a protocol in 2014 which effectively neutralised the Tribunal was unconstitutional, unlawful and irrational. Here the court played the role of upholding South Africa's commitment to international human rights. Again, this confirmed the South African government's cynicism towards human rights, especially in articulating foreign policy.

In instances where states have committed excesses against individuals or companies, aggrieved parties should have recourse and procure resolutions. Constraining or undermining the SADC Tribunal would therefore erode the nascent rights-based legal framework in the region and deny citizens an avenue for protection and redress outside of the domestic legal framework, which in other countries is weak. The challenges of the Tribunal began around 2010 when Zimbabwe was not complying with its decisions. Instead of forcing Zimbabwe to comply, the SADC Summit decided in May 2011 not to renew the term of office of the Tribunal members and further prohibited the body from taking any more cases, thus neutering it.

A new protocol was concluded in 2014. This effectively changed the terms of the SADC Tribunal and limited its remit over adjudication of human rights cases brought about by individuals on human rights issues (Weiner, 2018). South Africa was part of this regressive decision, which was inconsistent with its long-standing human rights commitments as enshrined in its constitution. Civil society bodies in South Africa brought an application before the Constitutional Court, contending that Zuma's action in ratifying the new protocol that throttled the Tribunal was contrary to the spirit of the treaty that established the SADC in 1994, in particular its commitment to human rights, democracy and the rule of law; and that this was an irrational action.

The Constitutional Court ruled that the decision by the South African government to endorse the suspension of the Tribunal undermined South Africa's legal obligation and that the executive had no power to unilaterally terminate an international treaty. In keeping with the doctrine of the separation of power, it was the remit of parliament to terminate an international treaty. This showed, once again, that Zuma was not an institutionalist, and his administration lacked a grasp of constitutionalism. Thus its foreign policy conduct was, in significant ways, unprincipled. The Zuma administration and the governing party conceived of themselves as pursuing a grand, meta-struggle to achieve radical economic goals at home, and an anti-imperial drive abroad, with everything else—here human rights and constitutionalism—being subsumed under this epic effort.

South Africa's democratic transition in the early 1990s leaned heavily on soft instruments of the constitution, and placed emphasis on a rights discourse. Zuma's administration represented a break with this tradition, and inaugurated a regressive new way of behaviour. Its foreign policy behaviour stood in stark contrast to that pursued by both the Mandela and Mbeki administrations. Ever since 1994, South Africa under the first two sets of governments was, according to Deon Geldenhuys (2008: 1), pursuing international norm entrepreneurship, with the country establishing "an exemplary record in respecting universal norms both domestically and in its foreign relations". Trenchant in this is the example, where, immediately after the end of Mandela's presidency, South Africa became a signatory to the Rome Statute (1998), adopted to establish the International

Criminal Court (ICC) in order to discipline the excesses of state elites in acting against their own citizens.

South Africa would accede as a member in 2002, after instruments of ratification were deposited in its own parliament. This was a major step in expressing South Africa's commitment to international law and a rule-based multilateral order. South Africa's refusal to abide by the ruling of the court later, on a matter concerning Sudanese President Omar Al-Bashir's visit to South Africa, would be one of the signs of South Africa's unprincipled pragmatism (see discussion below). During its phase of idealism, the South African government participated actively in the United Nations Human Rights Committee, and acted consistently with its normative commitments to human rights—a stance that would later be turned on its head under Zuma.

As Mills (2000) points out, during the democratic transition in the early 1990s, there were three assumptions about South Africa's foreign policy present: that government would develop a coherent set of foreign policy goals with a strategy to achieve these. First, morality, in contrast to the apartheid past, with a particular accent on human rights, would occupy centre stage in South Africa's foreign policy. Second, South Africa in the age of globalisation would offer an exportable model of development to the rest of the continent and third, South Africa would provide a leadership role in Southern Africa and the broader African continent. However, under Zuma, morality and a policy on human rights could not be sustained and would later pivot regressively towards unprincipled pragmatism.

Under President Zuma, foreign policy was bereft of the ideas and strategic intent that reflect a distinct national interest. It departed from idealism and normative commitments that were a hallmark of Mandela's era, and lacked the ideas-driven edge that was epitomised by the Mbeki administration, especially in its clear packaging and articulation of Africa's developmental interest in engagements with both the North and the South.

Weakening moral authority

Apart from the above examples, one of the signs that South Africa was lacking confidence on the global stage, and that it was no longer relying on moral authority to participate in international relations, was when the country lobbied in 2009 to allow it entry to the BRIC (Brazil, Russia, India and China) club. This body established as the BRIC at Yekaterinburg, Russia, initially did not contemplate South Africa's participation. In an aspirant South Africa, presumably a crisis of confidence set in.

Opportunistically, China took up South Africa's cause and ensured the country's acceptance into this elite club of economically influential emerging economies. This is something that made South Africa feel indebted to China. As such, South Africa's participation in the BRICS group was in large part motivated by cultivating closer relations with China. This indebtedness was revealed when it came to the example of the Dalai Lama. Whereas the Dalai Lama had visited

South Africa on several occasions after 1994, after South Africa joined BRIC, on three occasions he no longer was permitted to enter the country. In 2009, the South African government refused to grant the Dalai Lama a visa, claiming that this would detract attention from the mega sporting event, the 2010 World Cup, planned for the following year. Again, in 2011 South Africa failed to grant the Dalai Lama a visa to attend the birthday celebrations of a civil society luminary, Archbishop Desmond Tutu, in Cape Town. The following year the court ruled that officials acted unlawfully in failing to grant the visa. The third time he was refused entry was at the 14th World Summit of Nobel laureates that was to take place in Cape Town in October 2014. South Africa put up hurdles that made the visa approval impossible. Given the absence of rational explanation for this jettison, it is probable that South Africa did not want to offend China, a country that the South African government increasingly viewed as a repository of largesse and lessons on development.

Although over time, participation in the BRICS would prove valuable since it enabled South Africa to participate in institution building at the BRICS. South Africa was technically active in developing institutional pillars such as the BRICS Bank, the Contingency Reserve Account and the Public-Private Partnership infrastructure financing model. However, at the time of its lobbying, South Africa had no clearly defined goals and there were signs of a weakening normative base.

Joining BRICS had other consequences. After South Africa acceded to the BRICS membership, IBSA, established at the Heads of State level in 2006 as a platform for a democratic South, began to weaken. By this time, South Africa was no longer an active champion of human rights, democracy and rule of law. Domestically, rule of law was weakening with corruption and impunity on the rise. As a result of cultivating proximity to China and Russia, South Africa's foreign policy largely lost its independence.

This, whilst other developing countries showed a more confident and independent foreign policy. They had the ability to stand up to China when they held a different view on a foreign policy or trade issue. For example, despite being part of the BRICS, Brazil confronted China for manipulating its currency between 2012 and 2013. China was accused by Brazil of artificially devaluing its currency in order to bolster its exports of manufactured goods to the detriment of jobs in manufacturing sectors in other middle-income countries. In the tariff spat, Brazil took a hard line and slapped import tariffs on Chinese steel to protect its own domestic steel sector. Unlike the South African government, Brazil understood its strategic interests and chose to protect its industries and workers instead of maintaining a relationship with China at all costs. That is not to say that South Africa should have applied a muscular posture in its relationship with China, but that it should not have allowed its interests to have been subordinated to those of China (or, for that matter, any other country), something which happened for much of the Zuma years.

An obsequious foreign policy towards China did not necessarily help South Africa to power its economy and create jobs. Instead, it witnessed the decline of its manufacturing, especially in the clothing and textile sectors, and China continued to run hefty current account surpluses vis-à-vis South Africa.

Turning away from the West

The main emphasis of Zuma's administration—and indeed that of the ANC in Luthuli House—has been to de-emphasise relations with the West, and to forge closer ties with China and Russia, a calculation driven by geo-strategic considerations, as well as more narrow commercial interests that became most associated with President Zuma.

Zuma would view structures such as the BRICS as important fora on which to cast his own foreign policy legacy, even though he did not set out distinct and unique ideas about South Africa's purpose in the world. He also tended to see countries such as China as one of several possible allies outside of the West. This, without so much even considering South Africa's long-term economic interests.

Mbeki too had been wary of the West, but he had strong open channels to working with Western countries in order to find solutions to the complex developmental challenges facing Africa. Mbeki was able to balance anti-imperialism and cooperation with the West in ways that Zuma could not. In Mbeki's calculation, programmes such as the NEPAD offered a redemptive platform for the West to pay for its historical debt to developing countries. Zuma, on the other hand, pursued a vulgar form of anti-colonialism, not grounded in any principled position or framework of ideas. For Mbeki, it was important to maintain relations with the West to keep it wedded to its historical responsibility towards Africa's development. For example, when he was deputy president, Mbeki enjoyed a strong relationship with US Vice-President Al Gore, under President Bill Clinton's Democratic Administration. They both chaired the Bi-national Commission established in 1995. He enjoyed a cordial relationship with Republican President George W. Bush. Mbeki was a member of the Progressive Governance Forum. This is where he joined Britain's Prime Minister Tony Blair, the US's Bill Clinton and Sweden's Goran Persson, a group of enlightened leaders that sought to renew social democracy or the "Third Wave". This ideological project was one where the states and markets would co-reinforce each other in delivering economic efficiencies, infrastructure and social equity.

Before Zuma, South Africa's foreign policy straddled many fronts. It would narrow significantly in the years between 2009 and 2018, with Zuma preferring to work closely with non-democratic and state-capitalist states such as China and Russia. Hostility to the West rather than defining a positive agenda became the hallmark of South Africa's policy.

Noting South Africa's shift towards a close embrace with China, *The Economist* newspaper pointed out the relationship with China: "The ANC seems to think that commerce with China will flourish only if South Africa is hostile to the West" ("South Africa's Foreign Policy: Clueless and Immoral". *The Economist*, 2015). A milder view of shifts in South African foreign policy was offered by Garth Le Pere: "The Zuma era has thus been adaptive and continuous in terms of the normative charters which guided his predecessors, with the centre of gravity less concentrated in the Presidency than was the case during the Mbeki years" (Le Pere, 2014: 33).

There are clear signs that under President Zuma's administration, foreign policy acutely tilted towards countries such as China and Russia. At the same time, foreign policy was in thrall to party rhetoric at Luthuli House—the headquarters of the ANC. Accordingly, as a signal of where greater priority in diplomatic relations was gravitating, the ANC cemented its party-to-party relations despite its right-leaning credentials with Vladimir Putin's United Russia as well as the Communist Party of China.

If it were not for the absence of the strategic signifiers of the pillars of its foreign policy, especially from a commercial point of view, South Africa's diversification of its foreign relations to privilege China would be understandable. No country today can afford to ignore China's economic weight and the imperative of deepening trade and investment links with this behemoth. As one edition of *The Economist* newspaper points out: "All countries struggle to balance principles and national interests. Yet, South Africa's revolutionary foreign policy [under Zuma] serves neither" (ibid.).

The danger for South Africa in cultivating closeness with China and Russia is that its foreign policy could well be subsumed under the geo-political and commercial interests of the two big powers. Yet, beyond scepticism towards the West, there is no shared normative agenda between South Africa and these countries. South Africa needs to fashion a relationship based on a clear view of its (strategic) economic interests and leverage these to advance its own position in various global processes. This continues to be vague in as much as South Africa has not had a domestic security and economic framework to pertinently inform its foreign policy goals.

The emphasis on party-to-party relations between the ANC and the ruling parties of China and Russia under Zuma did not bode well for the pursuit of pragmatic relations that could avoid mediation by narrow party or personal interests. Russia and the symbolism of a right-leaning party, United Russia, presided over by strongman Vladimir Putin, stands in great contrast to the historical virtues of a governing ANC which professes to be a social democratic party or a party situated on the broad left. Except for memories of a history that no longer holds, when the communist Soviet Union (USSR) offered the ANC moral and material support during three decades of exile, there are no threads of ideological principle to bind the two countries. Today's Russia is a fundamentally different reality than that which existed during the Cold War.

There is a sense that the motivation of Zuma's administration in choosing new diplomatic friends had less to do with South Africa's collective interests or even ideology than with enhancing the welfare of the ruling party. The establishment of party-to-party relations between the ANC and United Russia in October 2013, as well as between the ANC and the Chinese Communist Party, were not based on any obvious sense of normative convergence.

South Africa cultivated a relationship of subservience and pandered to Russia's commercial interests from 2012 and 2015. This pertained to Zuma's manoeuvres to procure Russia's nuclear technology with no accountability to the public. The attempt meant that procurement bypassed the sacrosanct procurement rules of the Public Finance Management Act (PFMA). The highly secretive nature of the agreement between South Africa and the Russians raised disquiet within South Africa, with concerns that procurement procedures were being circumvented to give the Russians a front-run advantage vis-à-vis other potential contenders. The push for this commercial agreement had no rational basis: the country's National Planning Commission was cautious about going nuclear. Since the revised Integrated Resource Plan 2010–2030 that would guide the country's energy needs and the balance between various energy inputs had not been finalised, there was at the time no guiding policy framework in place.

Another stark example of unprincipled pragmatism to show up South Africa's declining moral authority under Zuma was in respect of the Sudanese leader Omar al-Bashir and his attendance of the AU Summit in South Africa in June 2015.

A signatory to the Rome Statute of the ICC, South Africa was obligated to arrest Omar al-Bashir for crimes against humanity and genocide committed in Sudan between 2003 and 2005. The ICC had issued a warrant of arrest for al-Bashir in 2009 and 2010. Article 86 of the Statute obligates states to "cooperate fully with the court in its investigation and prosecution". South Africa's non-arrest of al-Bashir was a violation of this Article as well as its own constitution.

In 2002, the South African parliament passed the Implementation of the Rome Statute of the International Criminal Court Act 27, which effectively domesticated the ICC legal instrument in line with the country's own, making this international agreement binding on South Africa. South African NGO, the South African Litigation Centre, brought an urgent application before the North Gauteng High Court to petition it to compel the South African government to arrest al-Bashir.

Upon hearing the matter, the court prohibited al-Bashir from leaving South Africa until this case was to be fully heard and settled. A day later, in defiance of the court, the South African government facilitated al-Bashir's passage out of the country. Subsequently, the ruling ANC made threats that it could call on the government to withdraw from the ICC. Three months after government defied the courts, Zuma met with al-Bashir on the sidelines of victory celebrations in China and committed to strengthening ties. Yet at the time, the matter of al-Bashir's escape out of South Africa and the government's defiance of the courts was still to be settled in court.

Zuma was not an institutionalist leader in the way that his predecessors were. With the judiciary having come under attack several times from the ruling party, his leadership did not exhibit any deep commitment to constitutional principles. In international relations he far preferred informal relationships to those mediated by the strictures of institutions and formal codes. His language of diplomacy converged with non-Western, kleptocratic and state-capitalist countries. It explained why he was keen to shift South African foreign policy priorities in the direction of cultivating stronger ties with countries such as China and Russia. Zuma and the ANC used the anti-imperialist cloak in order to mask what was its declining moral authority in South Africa's foreign policy. Taking an anti-Western stance and preferring one-sided alignment with China and Russia, however, constrained

South Africa's options in international relations. This made South Africa vulnerable to being used to further the interests of these countries.

Conclusion: The future shape of South Africa's foreign policy

The two successive administrations of Mandela and Mbeki enunciated clear ideas on what South Africa's foreign policy represented or sought to achieve, especially during the Mandela era, even if this was not always coherent and well-coordinated. It is difficult to assert the same about Zuma. There was quite a lot of activity, but little clarity on ideas. There are, however, some elements of continuity, such as, for example, the emphasis and focus on the African continent.

There were areas that began to fade further during his terms in office, such as the discourse on human rights—a reality already evident in Mbeki's era. The ANC as a party seemed to play a greater role in foreign relations, and this blurred the lines between party and state regarding where the nerve centre of policy lies. Accompanying this was something peculiar to all three administrations—a discernible lacuna in having a set of clearly articulated domestic economic priorities and its consequence, an economic diplomacy strategy.

While the rhetoric about foreign policy deployed in the service of achieving domestic goals such as poverty reduction and job creation—as well as advancing Africa's development interests—features strongly in various policy statements, this does not find its concrete and dedicated expression in foreign policy activity and its outcomes.

In 2012, the National Planning Commission (NPC) released its National Development Programme (National Planning Commission, 2012). This contained a dedicated chapter on South Africa's foreign policy. The NPC made several critical statements:

First, it called for foreign relations to be driven by the country's domestic economic, political and social demands in meeting the challenges of eradicating poverty, lowering inequality and creating jobs. Accordingly, it recommended that the country define its national priorities.

Second, it asserted that South Africa should aggressively expand trade and investment in its region, across the continent and the globe. If there were better coordination across different government agencies dealing with economic issues, enhanced interaction with industry and sufficient technical capacity within the foreign ministry to drive economic diplomacy, this would be achievable. However, this coordination has been lacking.

The National Planning Commission (NPC: 237) decries what it sees as South Africa's "relative decline in power and influence in world affairs", further noting that "South Africa lost a great deal of the moral authority—as a power source—that the country enjoyed in the period immediately after the 1994 elections" (ibid.). The NPC went on to state that South Africa's foreign relations are becoming ineffective, with the country experiencing a drop in global competitiveness and moral standing. It attributes this decline to what it calls "the overall demise of the golden age of [South Africa's] African diplomacy, spanning 1998 to 2008" (ibid.: 238).

According to the NPC's assessment, even on the African continent, South Africa's standing has declined, with the country having a weak grasp of Africa's geo-political situation, and with "policy makers vacillating between leading and muddling through on issues of integration and cooperation". This trenchant critique did not go down well with the foreign ministry. What is clear is that South Africa's foreign policy under Zuma has weakened. By the time Cyril Ramaphosa took over as President in 2018, the importance of domestic economic priorities underpinning foreign policy had become more urgent than ever as the country faced multiple and serious economic challenges.

From the Zuma presidency one observation can be made about the foreign policy choices of leaders and parties. It is that foreign policy choices always flow from the character of leadership and the institutional make-up of a country. This determines its strategic priorities and whether or not it can demonstrate confidence on the international stage. Zuma's anti-Western or anti-imperialist stance was not grounded on any coherent framework of ideas. There was no set of positive ideals that South Africa sought to attain during this period. Whenever countries' institutions are in decline and their confidence is waning, it appears that leaders amplify their anti-Western and anti-imperialist rhetoric, both to divert attention from institutional decadence and to allow leaders to use foreign policy in the pursuit of parochial ends.

References

Alden, C. & Le Pere, G. (2006). South Africa's post-apartheid foreign policy. In: N. Phillip & W. Carlsnae (eds.). *Full Flight: South African Foreign Policy After Apartheid.* Midrand: Institute of Global Dialogue.

Fabricius, P. & Donnenfeld, Z. (2018). SA prepares for a historic about-turn on human rights foreign policy. *ISS Today*, 23 November 2018. www.issafrica.org.

Geldenhuys, D. (2008). South Africa's international norm entrepreneurship. *Acta Academia*, *40*(2): 1–27.

Le Pere, G. (2014). Critical themes in South Africa's foreign policy: An overview. *Strategic Review for Southern Africa*, *36*(2): 31–56.

Mills, G. (2000). *The Wired Model: South Africa, Foreign Policy and Globalisation.* Cape Town: Tafelberg.

National Planning Commission. (2012). *National Development Plan 2030: Our Future, Make it Work.* Pretoria: National Planning Commission.

South Africa's Foreign Policy: Clueless and Immoral. (2015). *The Economist*, 5 September 2015. https://www.economist.com/leaders/2015/09/03/clueless-and-immoral [Accessed: 15 October 2018].

Weiner, J. (2018). On the SADC Tribunal case. *Politicsweb*, 16 March 2018.

5 Towards a strategic culture approach to understanding and conceptualising Ethiopia's foreign policy towards Israel and the Middle Eastern Arab countries

Makonnen Tesfaye

Introduction and context

Ethiopia, in the "Horn of Africa", occupies a geo-politically and strategically important position *vis-à-vis* the Arab states and Israel. This is due to its proximity to the Middle East, Europe, the Gulf of Suez, the Gulf of Aden trade route, the Red Sea and the Indian Ocean; and its size, being the second most populous country and eighth biggest economy in Africa (IMF, 2018). Long-standing strategic alignments persistently informed by history and culture characterise Ethiopia's foreign policy. This is helped by the long-standing existence of its monarchy that traces its legitimacy by lineage and symbolism through association with Africa, the Middle East, Palestine and modern-day Israel, providing a milieu for three world religions—Christianity, Judaism and Islam. Ethiopia has been a bridge between African and Middle Eastern civilisations, cultures, trade and commerce for over two millennia (Trimingham, 1952; Giday, 1991; Levin, 1974; Marcus, 2002; Crummey, 2000; Houston, 1985). Ethiopia also stands at the interface of a number of ideological streams that include Pan-Africanism, Marxist and nationalist anti-imperialism, Zionism and Pan-Arabism (Markakis, 1990; Markakis & Ayele, 1978; Tareke, 1996; Kendie, 1990). This context and background, have over time, conditioned and driven the country's foreign policy agency towards the Middle East and Africa as well as the global powers.

The way in which Ethiopia positioned itself in the Middle East has been as varied as it has been complex. Comprehending Ethiopia's foreign policy towards the region has, however, been insufficiently understood.[1] The way it has defined and redefined its national interest has been informed by historical and cultural experiences. This has predisposed it towards certain strategic alignments interspersed with periods of strategic misalignment which only confirm the general rule. Thus, under the regimes of Haile Selassie and Mengistu Haile-Mariam during the Cold War, the country's stance was often ambivalent, strategically misaligned and conflicted. Under Meles Zenawi's *Developmental State* and in a changing global order, foreign policy became more consistent, non-aligned and pragmatic (Haggai, 1994, 2016; Bishku, 1994; Hussain, 1997; Lefebvre, 1996; Mohammed, 2007; Schmidt, 2013; Schwab, 1978; Tesfaye, 2017).

A strategic culture approach to understanding Ethiopia's foreign policy towards Israel and Middle Eastern Arab countries allows for the integration of historical, cultural, and strategic and *realpolitik* foreign policy determinants.[2] This is with a view to developing a holistic understanding and obtaining an overarching conceptualisation of Ethiopia's foreign policy.

It was only in those periods when domestic pressures challenged the regime's security that the strategic behaviour of the state became closely aligned with a pro-Israeli foreign policy. Conversely, when the state domestically felt relatively secure, this spelt the conduct of cordial relations with neighbouring Arab and Muslim countries (Mengistu, 2004; Clapham 1988; Spencer, 2006; Henze, 1996; Haggai, 2016; Meles, 2017).

It is Ethiopia's strategic culture combined with geo-politics and the material forces of its national interest that provides a consistent and overarching understanding of Ethiopia's changing and complex foreign policy towards Israel and Middle Eastern Arab countries. It is in terms of Ethiopia's long enduring strategic culture that the strategic alignment or misalignment of its foreign policy objectives under the regimes of Haile Selassie, Mengistu and Meles are described and assessed.

A strategic culture framework for conceptualising Ethiopia's Middle Eastern foreign policy

Strategic culture theory in International Relations and Foreign Policy Analysis

The concept of strategic culture broadly refers to a nation's domestic political culture and institutions, history and traditions, values and norms, patterns of behaviour, habits and symbols, and particular ways of strategic thinking with regard to war, peace and strategic behaviour (Snyder, 1977; Gray, 1981; Booth, 1990; Bloomfield, 2012; Klein, 2007; Stone, 2006; Lantis, 2005; Howlett, 2005). Strategic culture is articulated and institutionalised by ruling elites, is semi-permanent and evolves only in response to major internal and external shocks. Jack Snyder (1977) and Colin Gray (1981, 1986) put forward the strategic culture approach to the strategic study of states especially with regard to the nuclear strategies of the superpowers at the height of the Cold War in the 1970s and 1980s.

According to Colin Gray (1999), rather than explaining causes for behaviour, strategic culture provides a contextual understanding of strategic behaviour and geo-political thinking. John Glenn (2009) argues for the feasibility and utility of theoretical and empirical synthesis, a cross fertilisation between strategic culture and realist positions. Although it does not necessarily exclude material determinants, the concept of strategic culture with its emphasis on context provides an alternative foreign policy explanation to mainstream realism and pluralism.

Since cultural variables are difficult to define and operationalise, strategic culture is a contested concept. Moreover, there are epistemological issues on how we can analyse state behaviour using subjective factors under an objective category. Positivists postulate that strategic behaviour can be distinctively defined and explained by independent strategic culture variables (Johnston, 1996), whereas constructivist/interpretivist writers (Gray, 1981) argue the importance of a contextual understanding of strategic behaviour, in particular its interpretive as distinct from its explanatory or predictive value.

This chapter takes a broad approach to strategic behaviour. It argues that strategic culture variables such as history, geography, culture and identity, ideology and religion, and domestic politics and institutions, together with material factors such as preponderant military power, technology, demography or economic resources, influence national security decisions and strategic behaviour (Morgenthau, 1978; Waltz, 2010; Keohane, 1984; Keohane & Nye, 1977) and both need to be considered to understand Ethiopia's foreign policy. As an alternative, though complementary approach to conventional explanations, the strategic culture approach provides an overarching understanding in conceptualising Ethiopia's national security decisions and its strategic behaviour towards Israel and the Middle Eastern Arab countries.

Ethiopia's strategic culture and foreign policy objectives

Ethiopia's strategic culture has the following broad characteristic contextual features (MFA, 2002; Haile Selassie, 1999; Mengistu, 2004; Haile-Melekot, 2000; Giday, 1991; Meles, 2017; Lipsky, 1967; Haggai, 1997, 2007; Rubenson, 1991; Levin, 1974; Ullendorff, 1965, 1968; Brooks, 1998; Zewde, 2001, 2008; Sbacchi, 1985):

i. A belief of being an ancient civilisation and independent country with an unrealised potential for development and "greatness" if it were not for mainly external threats, but also internal challenges. Throughout the ages the destiny of Ethiopian independence and the mystical and transcendental belief of being "favoured" children of God have been propagated by the state, the *Ethiopian Orthodox Tewahedo Christian Church*[3] and the *Kebra Nagast* (Brooks, 1998) based on biblical references, such as that Ethiopia kneels/stretches her hands only to God and not earthly powers, or Ethiopians as Israelites favoured by God. Biblical Verses about Ethiopia include (King James Bible online, 2018):

> "Princes shall come out of Egypt; Ethiopia shall soon stretch out her hands unto God"
>
> (Pss.68)

and

> "Are ye not as children of the Ethiopians unto me, O children of Israel? saith the LORD. Have not I brought up Israel out of the land of Egypt? and the Philistines from Caphtor, and the Syrians from Kir?"
>
> (Amos.9)

ii. A heightened awareness of colonial and neo-colonial machinations, hence a tradition of active diplomacy and strategic alliances to counter threats to national security and territorial integrity.
iii. An inspiration and desire to play a leadership role in Africa, promoting Pan-Africanism and anti-colonial struggle, as expressed, for example, in Nelson Mandela's biography, *Long Walk to Freedom* (1994):

> "Ethiopia has always held a special place in my own imagination, and the prospect of visiting Ethiopia attracted me more strongly than a trip to France, England, and America combined. I felt I would be visiting my own genesis, unearthing the roots of what made me an African".
>
> (Mandela, 1994, p. 348)

iv. It stands at the cross-roads and provides a link between African and Middle Eastern Asian cultures and civilisations offering opportunities for trade and commerce.
v. The country possesses a cultural familiarity with major world religions since it is a long-established home for Christianity, Islam and Judaism. As such, it has the requisite experience in navigating inter-religious tensions and issues of religious-ethnic identity.
vi. Has a deep sense of being "a Non-Arab and predominantly Christian country island surrounded by a sea of Arab and Muslim countries"; hence a perception of being surrounded and "besieged" by real and perceived hostile neighbours.
vii. Holds an existential fear, particularly among the ruling elites, of the dismemberment of the country whose heterogeneity makes it susceptible to external threats.

Ethiopia's own strategic culture permeates its whole society, and is articulated and institutionalised by its political, economic and faith-based elites. At its core, the repository of its strategic culture is formulated by the political leadership as well as its religious authority, primarily the Ethiopian Orthodox Tewahedo Church (Perham, 1969; Mathew, 1974; Markakis, 1972; Kebede, 1999; Pankhurst, 1968, 1990; Lata, 1999; Zewde, 2001, 2008).

Since the second half of the 20th century, and within the context of its prevailing strategic culture and geo-political thought, Ethiopia's foreign policy has sought to achieve the following objectives (Haile Selassie, 1999; MFA, 2002; Mengistu, 2004; Berhanu, 2010; Meles, 2017): This is in order to

i. maintain its national sovereignty and territorial integrity, in particular securing and maintaining an outlet to the sea (pre-Eritrean independence in 1993);
ii. forge alliances with one super power to secure economic and military support in order to promote national sovereignty, preserve domestic power alignments and consolidate class rule;
iii. counter real and perceived threats to national security, mainly emanating from Arab and Muslim countries;

iv. project African leadership roles, promoting Pan-Africanism and the OAU/AU, as well as promoting international institutions and multilateralism; and
v. pursue an *inside-out* (domestically-focused) foreign policy that (since the advent of the *EPRDF*[4]) facilitates economic development, poverty alleviation, democracy and regional peace and stability. A key feature of the *Inside-out* foreign policy is economic diplomacy whose focus is to maximise foreign investment and technology for internal economic development and the promotion of regional economic integration conducive for regional peace and stability.

The impact of Ethiopia's strategic culture on its strategic behaviour and geo-political thought, in particular on the strategic alignment or misalignment of its foreign policy objectives vis-à-vis Israel and Middle Eastern Arab and Muslim countries under the regimes of Haile Selassie, Mengistu and Meles are discussed in the following sections.

Ethio-Israeli relations

Background and context

Ethiopia and Israel have regarded each other as important partners historically, politically and geo-strategically. Ethiopia was the first African country—other than apartheid South Africa—to establish diplomatic relations with Israel. The early Zionist leaders of Israel supported Africa's anti-colonial struggle and were keen to express solidarity and establish diplomatic relations with newly independent African countries, in particular with Ethiopia. This against the background of long-standing historical and cultural links. Historically and culturally, the state and society in Ethiopia have a strong sense of shared heritage, emotional attachment and a "special relationship" with Israel dating back to the era of the *Queen of Sheba*[5] and the emergence of the *Solomonic Dynasty*[6] in the First Millennium AD.

> The Lion of Judah has always been the symbol of the Ethiopian Monarchy and the links between the Jews and Ethiopia have always been unique.
> (Golda Meir, 1975, p. 341)

There is also a strong religious kinship between the Ethiopian Orthodox *Tewahedo* Church and Judaism. The Judo-Christian link manifests itself both symbolically and religiously by the spiritual significance attached to the Ethiopian Orthodox *Tewahedo* Church's custodianship of the *Ark of the Covenant*[7] in Axum, Ethiopia. Furthermore, *Ethiopian Jewry*[8] (Bete-Israel) provides an important historical, cultural and kinship link between the two countries. Before the *Aliyah* (return) of Ethiopian Jews to Israel in 1984–85 and 1991 under *Operations Moses* and *Solomon* respectively, Ethiopia had the largest Jewish community in Sub-Saharan

Africa after that of South Africa (Haggai, 2016; Bishku, 1994; Kessler, 1996; Summerfield, 2003).

In addition, geo-politics and strategic factors play an important role in an enduring link between Ethiopia and Israel. Prior to the independence of Eritrea in 1993, Ethiopia, apart from Somalia and Djibouti, was the only non-Arab country to have access to the Red Sea, Israel's principal maritime link (via the Israeli port of Elat in the Gulf of Aqaba) to the eastern hemisphere. Under Haile Selassie and Mengistu, Ethiopia and Israel therefore had the common objective of countering the political and military influence of the Arab League countries, in particular the latter's support for the Eritrean liberation movement and Somalia's claim to the Ogaden region of Ethiopia.

The bipolar global order and Cold War rivalry between the USA and the USSR in the Middle East and the Horn of Africa provided the context and subtext that drove the geo-politics of the region. Ethiopia found itself in the Western camp during the regime of Haile Selassie and the Soviet camp during the Mengistu era (Yordanov, 2016; Patman, 1990; Ottaway, 1982; Lefebvre, 1991, 1998). In the post-Cold War period, the relations between the regime of the EPRDF under Meles Zenawi and Israel became cordial, spanning security, technical and economic matters, in particular regarding strategic cooperation and the fight against terrorism in the Horn of Africa region.

Importantly, Ethiopia's geo-political behaviour and thinking towards Israel under the regimes of Haile Selassie and Mengistu Haile-Mariam often did not strategically align with the country's national security objectives. Here strategic cultural variables, in particular, domestic political pressure, played a decisive role in driving and shaping the stops and starts of continuing or discontinuing the relationship with Israel.

Ethio-Israeli relations under Haile Selassie

Despite Emperor Haile Selassie's claim to be "the Lion of Judah", something that signified his kinship with the Israelites, it is a paradox that Ethiopia's first foreign policy decision on Israel was to abstain on the UN resolution in 1947 establishing the state of Israel. The rationale behind this was not to antagonise Arab and Muslim countries at a time when Ethiopia sought the unification of Eritrea with Ethiopia from the UN. This amounted to tactical positioning and did not represent a departure from Ethiopia's basic strategic alignments.

The grand strategy of the state under Haile Selassie was to position the country in the Western camp under the wing of the USA and by extension, that of Israel. To this effect, Ethiopia provided troops for the Korean War in 1951 under the command of the USA military. This was followed in 1953 by an agreement with the USA to set up the Kagnew Military Station for Communication in Asmara and the use of the port of Massawa by the US military. In return, Ethiopia received \$279 million in military and \$350 million in economic assistance from the US (Bishku, 1994). Moreover, the strategic alliances with the USA and Israel were largely also motivated by the conservative and anti-communist domestic objectives of the monarchy.

Following the establishment of the state of Israel in 1948, Ethiopia was nevertheless keen to establish a diplomatic relationship with the government of Israel, in particular after the Nasserite Egyptian Revolution in 1952, the ensuing 1956 Suez Crisis and the war between Egypt and the Israeli, British and French alliance. Haile Selassie was particularly concerned about the spread of *Nasserite Pan-Arabism*, which he considered hostile to the territorial integrity of the country. As such, Ethiopia and Israel established formal diplomatic relations in 1956.

In the late 1950s and early 1960s, these relations developed into a strategic partnership between Israel and Ethiopia; the latter becoming party to Israel's "Peripheral Strategy",[9] a "secret" strategic alliance between Israel, Ethiopia, Iran and Turkey set up to counter the politico-military encirclement of Israel by hostile Arab countries (Bishku, 1994; Haggai, 2016). This dovetailed with the Ethiopian state's own strategic culture based on a "siege mentality" with the country having a sense of encirclement from hostile Arab and Muslim countries. From the late 1950s to the 1973 *Yom Kippur War* between Israel and Middle Eastern Arab countries, the relationship between Ethiopia and Israel was both strategic and comprehensive. This included widespread cooperation in military, intelligence, political and economic affairs (Bishku, 1994; Haggai, 1994, 2016; Hussein, 1997).

The strategic alliance with the USA and Israel allowed the emperor to thwart the 1960 *coup d'état* against his government by a section of the Ethiopian military (Greenfield, 1965; Bishku, 1994; Haggai, 2016). It also emboldened him in 1962 to annex Eritrea by cancelling the Ethio-Eritrean Federation (Iyob, 1995). Yet, increasingly this strategic alliance with Israel conflicted with Ethiopia's leadership on Pan-African initiatives; the country became a founding member of the Organisation of African Unity (OAU) whose seat in 1963 came to be in Addis Ababa. This meant expressing solidarity with North African Arab countries, in particular with Egypt, against Israel's occupation of the Sinai following the Arab-Israeli war in 1967. Following the Yom Kippur War in October 1973, the pressure on Ethiopia by the OAU countries, especially from Egypt, Libya and Algeria, became intense.

The art of diplomatic duplicity or appeasement, susceptibility to petro-dollar bribery and the subordination of strategic national interest to tactical alliance aimed at subduing domestic political pressure, are inherent characteristics of the statecraft and strategic culture of the Ethiopian feudal aristocracy (Kapuscinski, 1983; Levin, 1974; Lockot, 1992; Bishku, 1994; Haggai, 2016). This in large part signals the change in strategic behaviour. An additional, secondary reason for Ethiopia's change or abandonment of its strategic alignment with Israel was shaped by both its fears of Pan-Arabism and the leadership opportunities offered by the OAU to create a Pan-African organisation:

> But although Ethiopia is a Christian (predominately) country, it is part of Africa and as such, was subjected for years to strong anti-Israel pressure by

> the Arabs. For a long time, however, Haile Selassie warily trod a tight-rope, many of his dealings with Israel were kept secret, and we sent an ambassador only in 1961.
>
> (Meir, 1975, p. 341)

The emperor, along with a majority of OAU member states, severed diplomatic relations with Israel in 1973. This constituted a major strategic misalignment, given that Israel was the single most effective supporter of Ethiopia's territorial integrity and reliable ally against hostile Arab countries.

> Even Ethiopia, with which we had a very special relationship for so many years, broke with us ... I was immensely disappointed when even Haile Selassie—for all of his own experience with appeasement (by League of Nations)—did not stand by us. It proved to me once again—though I didn't need very much proof by then—that one can never count on anyone but self.
>
> (Meir, 1975, p. 341)

A strategic alliance with the conservative regimes of Egypt, Sudan and Saudi Arabia in the early 1970s happened at the expense of Israel, but Haile Selassie became increasingly concerned with domestic political pressures. These included a looming domestic social, economic and political crisis that culminated in the Ethiopian Revolution and the end of the monarchy in 1974. This, despite the emperor's desperate but belated secret request for Israeli and US interventions to suppress the revolutionary upsurge (Bishku, 1994; Henze, 1996; Mengistu, 2004; Spencer, 2006; Haggai, 2016).

The emperor's strategic behaviour towards Israel was inconsistent with a realist geo-political interpretation in the wake of hostile acts by Arab states that supported the Eritrean national liberation fronts and the irredentist Somali state that expected Ethiopia to side with Israel in order for the latter to help safeguard the country's territorial integrity.

To what extent the severance of diplomatic relations with a strategic ally was consistent with the strategic interests of the country is a matter of academic debate—in order to address domestic political pressure or express Pan-African solidarity (Haggai, 2016; Bishku, 1994; Lefebvre, 1996). Ironically, Haile Selassie's strategically misaligned Middle Eastern foreign policy was presented as realist and pragmatic, yet it failed to achieve the twin objectives of safeguarding the principle of territorial integrity and the survival of the monarchical state.

The OAU and the Arab-Israeli conflict and the role of Emperor Haile Selassie

Following the Arab-Israeli War in June 1967, the OAU supported the UN Security Council Resolution 242 that called for the withdrawal of Israeli forces from all occupied Arab territories. Yet many African countries, including Ethiopia, continued to maintain bilateral relations with Israel. Following the Heads of State and Government Summit in Addis Ababa in 1971, the OAU at the suggestion of the Zambian President Kenneth Kaunda set up a committee of ten "Wise Men", including Emperor Haile Selassie, to help mediate between the Arabs and Israel (Gitelson, 1973). Four heads of state—Presidents Leopold Senghor of Senegal, Ahmadu Ahidjo of Cameroon, Mobutu Sese Seko of the former Zaire (now the Democratic Republic of the Congo) and Yakubu Gowan of Nigeria—were selected to visit the belligerent countries with a view to supporting a diplomatic effort by then UN General Secretary U Thant. Due to the irreconcilable positions of the two parties in the dispute, a lack of diplomatic advantage and the complexities of the regional and global power politics of the Cold War era, the mission failed to achieve its goal of facilitating a peaceful settlement in the Middle East. Following the June 1972 OAU Summit in Rabat, the OAU position became noticeably pro-Arab, and by 1973, following the Yom Kippur War in October, further hardened against Israel, resulting in many African countries breaking off diplomatic relations (Levy, 2008; Miller, 1975; Cervenka, 1974). During this period the role of the emperor mainly followed the general trend rather than being of influence or one to lead from the front. This can in part be attributed to Arab mistrust of the emperor and his strategic ambivalence, derived from his presumed mixed African and Judaic heritage.

Ethio-Israeli relations under the Derg[10] *and Mengistu Haile-Mariam*

Globally and regionally, the Ethiopian Revolution in February 1974 and the overthrow of the imperial government brought about a major shift in Ethiopia's strategic alignment. Between 1975 and 1978, the Derg regime maintained clandestine relations with Israel, partially reversing Haile Selassie's more recent policy stance towards Israel. The relationship between Israel and the Derg was described by Golda Meir (1975) as:

> at the time of which I write (1975) the ties were still very strong, although never publicized by the Ethiopians and therefore also no(t) by us.
>
> (Meir, 1975, p. 340)

The Derg abstained on the UN General Assembly Resolution 3379 in November 1975 that "characterised" Zionism as a "form of racism and racial discrimination". At the same time, the Derg sought and obtained support from Israel in its counter-insurgency war fought against the Eritrean liberation movement and other nationalist forces, including the TPLF (Tigray People's Liberation Front)[11] and OLF (Oromo Liberation Front).[12]

However, with the complete seizure of power by the Mengistu faction within the Derg in February 1977 and the onset of the *Ethio-Somali War* over the Ogaden in July 1977, the Derg switched its global alliance from the US camp to the one led by the USSR. The aim was to undercut political pressure from popular opposition forces led by civilian left-wing organisations and nationalist elements. By the late 1970s and early 1980s, the Derg regime's "Red Terror" suppression campaigns had silenced many of these critics (Markakis & Ayele, 1978; Legum & Lee, 1979; Lefort, 1983; Schwab, 1985; Iyob, 1995; Tiruneh, 1993; Mengistu, 2004).

In 1978–79, with the weakening of domestic opposition forces and the growing predominance of the Derg under Mengistu Haile Mariam, Ethiopia expelled Israeli personnel and became increasingly antagonistic towards Israel (*The New York Times*, 1978). As such, Mengistu's foreign policy towards Israel was strategically misaligned with national security objectives, given Israel's track record of supporting Ethiopia's territorial integrity. Moreover, regionally, Ethiopia was seen as pro-USSR and at loggerheads with the conservative regimes of Sudan, Egypt and Saudi Arabia, all of which intensified their support for the Eritrean liberation struggle; only Southern (socialist) Yemen and Ghadhafi's Libya were aligned with Mengistu's regional foreign policy (Clapham, 1988; Keller, 1991; Henze, 1996; Shehim, 1988).

Yet, by the mid-1980s, when domestic pressure from nationalist forces gathered momentum, threatening the survival of his regime, Mengistu again chose to establish clandestine links with Israel. These secret military and intelligence relations with Israel led to some cooperation. As a result, by 1984–85, Mengistu had agreed to "Operation Moses Project" that saw the clandestine permanent shipment of 7,000 to 8,000 Ethiopian Jews to Israel (Bishku, 1994). The relationship between Mengistu and Israel, however, amounted to too little too late for the Ethiopian regime and could not be elevated to a strategic level. Israel's main objective in maintaining links with the Derg were only tactical. This was to safeguard "the return" of Ethiopian Jews to Israel. Strategically, Israel had concluded that the opponents to the Mengistu regime, the EPRDF and EPLF,[13] would be the eventual victors in the civil conflict. Moreover, the reckoning was that both movements would not necessarily be hostile to Israel's geo-political objectives in the Red Sea and the Horn of Africa. In May 1991, the Mengistu regime collapsed after having agreed with Israel to the airlifting of 14,500 Ethiopian Jews to Israel in return for securing Mengistu's own personal safety in Zimbabwe and a payment of US$35 million (Bishku, 1994; *The Baltimore Sun*, 1991).

Mengistu's ambivalent, discontinuous and strategically misaligned foreign policy towards Israel was inconsistent with a realist imperative for the primacy of safeguarding Ethiopia's national sovereignty or territorial integrity. Both with Haile Selassie and Mengistu, the foreign policy choice of strategic misalignment contributed significantly to the downfall of these regimes.

The OAU and the Arab-Israeli conflict and the role of Mengistu Haile-Mariam

Throughout the Mengistu period, Ethiopian foreign policy towards the Arab-Israeli conflict was to follow the prevailing trend within the OAU. This was preferred to any of its own steering or leading from the front. A characteristic outcome of Ethiopia's strategic culture, the position taken was similar to the Haile Selassie's period, one of strategic ambivalence in Ethiopia's foreign relations with

Israel and Middle Eastern Arab countries. Overall, the OAU position on the conflict was pro-Arab and against Israel. Here, Mengistu's "Anti-Zionist and Anti-Imperialist" rhetoric was reflective of this general trend (Mazuri, 1979; Quinn, 2010; Bishku, 1994, 2015). The 1985 OAU Council of Ministers resolution on the situation in the Middle East was particularly strong against Israel:

> Noting with concern that the alliance between the Zionist regime of Israel and the racist regime of South Africa is aimed at promoting the policy of terrorism and the liquidation of the Palestinians and Arabs in the occupied territories on the one hand and of the majority black population of South Africa and Namibia on the other.
>
> (OAU, 1985)

Yet, all the same, most members of the OAU, including Ethiopia, maintained bilateral relations with Israel or had re-established formal diplomatic ties by the end of the 1980s (Shehim, 1988).

Ethio-Israel relations under the EPRDF and Meles Zenawi

By the late 1980s, it was apparent to Israel and the USA that the EPRDF was on course to defeat the Derg's army. There was a tacit recognition that the EPRDF was not ideologically antagonistic to the USA since the EPRDF, while maintaining a progressive "revolutionary democracy" outlook, had largely abandoned its Marxist-Leninist ideology (Henze, 1990). Further, the EPRDF was not strategically hostile to Israel, nor in alliance with the USSR (Henze, 1996; Lefebvre, 1996; Meles, 2017). Indeed, cognizant of the prevailing global power and ideological realignments after the Cold War, the de-facto independence of Eritrea and the changing geo-politics of the region, the EPRDF led by Meles Zenawi pursued a non-aligned and pragmatic foreign policy course towards the countries of the Middle East and towards the USA (Abraham, 1994). The EPRDF's relations with Israel soon became cordial and included cooperation agreements on technical and economic matters.

Following the 9/11 war on global terrorism, Ethiopia forged a strong strategic/security partnership with Israel alongside that of the USA. The aim was to combat terrorism, in particular to fight *al-Shabaab*'s terrorism that threatened Ethiopia, as well as regional peace and stability.

The OAU and the Arab-Israel conflict and the role of Meles Zenawi

Meles Zenawi pursued a strong bilateral relationship with Israel, in particular on security and strategic matters. During his visit to Israel in 2004 and 2005, Meles expressed his wish to work as a bridge between Israel and Africa (Sharon, 2004, 2005). Since the advent of the AU in 2002, Meles successfully fought against Libya's Gaddafi, who sought to move the headquarters of the AU from Addis Ababa because of Meles' close relationship with Israel, in particular with former

Prime Minister Yitzhak Rabin. However, Meles was unable to garner a majority in favour of Israel retaining its "Observer Status" at the AU as offered to the Palestinian government. This was in part due to South Africa's and Libya's strong objections. Following Prime Minister Benjamin Netanyahu's visit to Ethiopia in 2016, Zenawi's successor, Prime Minister Haile-Mariam Desalegn, expressed Ethiopia's endeavour, along with Kenya, Rwanda and Uganda, though to no avail, to continue to support Israel in its quest for obtaining observer status at the AU (Yihunbelay, 2016).

Ethiopian and Middle Eastern Arab relations

Background and context

Ethiopia's geography underscores the vitality of the physical link with the near Middle Eastern Arab and Muslim countries, in particular Sudan, Saudi Arabia, Yemen and Egypt. Following the *First Hegira*,[14] the immigration of the persecuted followers of the Prophet from the Arabian Peninsula to Ethiopia in the 7th century AD, Islam established itself in the country. Welcomed by the kings of Ethiopia in AD 725, and consistent with the teachings of the Prophet Muhammed Ibn Ishaq, Muslims have peacefully co-existed with fellow Ethiopian Christians for the better part of 1,300 years. Ethiopia is the site for one of the most revered mosques in the world (the fourth after Mecca, Medina and Jerusalem), located in the town of *Negash*, in the Tigray region. Demographically, 33.9% of Ethiopians are Muslims[15] (Central Statistical Agency, 2010) who provide a bond for those abroad with whom they share similar cultural, religious and heritage links. This is a source of enduring people-to-people relations. Yet, the experiences of conscious long-standing interactions between Ethiopia and Middle Eastern Arab/Muslim countries finds expression in two major historical and contradictory narratives (Haggai, 1994, 2007, 2016; MFA, 2002).

The dominant narrative for the entire historical period is a positive discourse based on the Prophet's edict of peaceful co-existence with Ethiopia, including prohibiting "Jihad" against Ethiopia (The Hadith, n. d.). A secondary narrative, dominant in history up to contemporary times, is often expressed by sections of "fundamentalist Muslims". It portrays Ethiopia negatively as a bulwark against the spread of Islam or as antagonistic to Muslims in Ethiopia and its neighbouring countries. There were two major instances for this view. They include a period during the early 16th century when there was a jihadist campaign to convert Ethiopia to Islam. A similar episode happened in the second half of the 19th century when there were Ottoman Turks and Egyptian incursions into Northern Ethiopia and present-day Eritrea (Trimingham, 1952). Overall, however, historical interactions between Ethiopia and Middle Eastern Arabs can be characterised as mainly peaceful, promoting mutually beneficial trade and cultural links. Yet, despite only these brief interludes of mutual antagonism, both narratives have, nevertheless, come to shape Ethiopia's strategic culture to the present-day.

Ethio-Egyptian relations

Ethio-Egyptian relations base themselves on historical and regional geo-politics, as well as *hydro-politics*. Bilateral relations revolve around competing for the strategic resource of water and the history of relations regarding ecclesiastical, political and military affairs. Given that the Nile is Egypt's only source of water, Egypt has its own special, existential fears on the issue of Ethiopia's ability, for the purposes of economic development and poverty alleviation, to control and regulate the flow of the Abay (Blue Nile).

It was for more than a millennia-and-a-half until 1959 that the Ethiopian Orthodox *Tewahedo* Church was administered by the *Egyptian Coptic Orthodox Church of Alexandria* when it secured its own independent *Patriarch*. Historical resentment abounds about the Egyptian Church's meddling in Ethiopian domestic affairs during different points in time. This often pertained to the anointment of Ethiopian dynastic successions and power struggles between regional principalities. Egyptian intervention under Ottoman ruler Ismail Pasha in the latter part of the 19th century meant the occupation of a large swathe of territory in Northern Ethiopia, something which only ended with Ethiopian victories against Egypt in 1875 and 1876.[16]

Throughout the 20th century up to the present, Ethio-Egyptian relations have been conditioned by five conflicting factors:

i. Pan-African solidarity and the common objective of promoting decolonisation in Africa, as well as interactions based on shared religions, cultures and traditions.
ii. Pan-Arabism, in particular radical Nasserite Arab nationalism that appeared to threaten Ethiopia's national sovereignty and territorial integrity. This became evident in the early 1960s by Egypt's support for the Eritrean Liberation Front (ELF)[17] and Somalia's claim to the Ethiopian Somali region, the Ogaden. Included here is politico-religious hostility towards Ethiopia from the *Egyptian Muslim Brotherhood* in particular.
iii. Ethiopia's strategic alliance with the USA and Israel, and Egypt's pro-USSR positioning during Haile Selassie's rule in Ethiopia and Nasser's in Egypt, and the subsequent reversal of this positioning when Mengistu and Sadat/Mubarak assumed power in Ethiopia and Egypt respectively.
iv. Mutual fear and suspicion regarding the use and regulation of the Blue Nile. Egypt's default position has been, if need be, to seek to destabilise, or even dismember Ethiopia. As such, Egypt supports opposition and secessionist nationalist forces in Ethiopia; issues veiled and unveiled military threats and has an active policy of preventing Ethiopia from acquiring technology and external development finance for the Nile basin (Tilahun, 1979; MFA, 2002; Mohammed, 2007; Kassu, 2012; Meles, 2017; Tesfaye, 2017).
v. Mutual interest to counter the threat of terrorism, in particular the ones originating from the Horn of Africa (*al-Shabaab*) and the Arabian Peninsula (*al-Qaida*).

Ethiopian and the Arabian Peninsula countries' relations

Ethiopia's relations with Arabian Peninsula countries, in particular Yemen and Saudi Arabia, have been characterised by geographical, historical, cultural and religious factors. Historical and cultural links date back to the advent of Islam. This has resulted in strongly shared cultures and traditions with Yemen in particular. Prior to the Ethiopian Revolution, tens of thousands of Yemenis resided in Ethiopia.

The three countries bordered the Red Sea prior to Eritrean independence in 1993 and had an interest in the strategically important *Strait of Bab el-Mandab* as well as the *Gulf of Aden- Suez Canal* trade route. The emperor cultivated cordial relations with Saudi kings, in particular King Faisal. As conservative states, both were firmly within the USA camp. This changed after 1977 when Ethiopia and Yemen both became allies of the USSR.

With the end of the Cold War, after 2000 in particular, the relations between Ethiopia and Arabian Peninsula countries experienced new geo-political developments and emerging economic cooperation ventures that included (Tesfaye, 2017):

i. Increasing investment and trade links between Gulf Cooperative Council (GCC) countries and Ethiopia.
ii. The rise of militant Jihadist terrorism, in particular from *al-Qaida*, *ISIS and al-Shabaab*, and the need to form security alliances regionally and globally.
iii. The politicisation and spread of *Wahhabism* to the Horn of Africa sponsored by Saudi Arabia, including the political spillovers of schisms in *Sunni Islam*, in particular amongst *Wahhabists*, *Salafists*, *Sufists and al-Ahbashists*.
iv. The *Ethio-Eritrean War* of 1998–2000 and the ensuing state of "no war no peace" between the regimes and its negative impact on domestic politics in Ethiopia and the stability of the Horn of Africa.
v. The *Ethio-Somali War* of 1977–1978, the ensuing civil war and regime failure in Somalia and its destabilising impact on Ethiopia and the Horn of Africa.
vi. The *Saudi-Iranian* regional rivalry, including over the control of the Red Sea and its geo-political impact on Eritrea, Ethiopia, Sudan, Djibouti, Somalia and Yemen.

Shift in Ethiopia's strategic culture and foreign policy under the EPRDF and Meles

After the end of the Cold War during the rule of the EPRDF under the leadership of Meles Zenawi, Ethiopia's non-aligned, more consistent and strategically aligned foreign policy towards Israel and Middle Eastern Arab countries reflected a shift in strategic culture. The radical reading of threats from neighbouring Arab and Muslim countries had changed, as had the state itself, and with it, domestic political and religious power alignments (MFA, 2002; Meles, 2017).

The establishment of a *Federal Democratic Republic* in 1991 enhanced the country's internal socio-political cohesion and economic development. This induced a shift in strategic culture. It was predicated on a number of factors, including a reduced sense of siege, a more rational analysis of regional threats, a more inclusive domestic discourse and a preoccupation with domestic developmental priorities. All this happened against the background of a less constrained global environment that provided opportunities to pursue a non-aligned foreign policy.

The *Foreign Affairs, National Security Policy, and Strategy of Ethiopia* principally authored by Meles Zenawi, further elucidated Ethiopia's strategic culture and its foreign policymaking implication:

> It should also be noted that the foreign policies of past governments were, in part, founded on a "siege mentality" which considered the country to be surrounded by enemies. Its effects on the psychology of the people and its adverse impact on our relations with the outside world cannot be underestimated. This is, however, not to say that the country does not have external enemies, or that all past policies directed against those who were arrayed against the country were wrong. What is essential is the necessity to carry out appropriate studies and assessments to distinguish between those whose interests would be negatively affected by our development and democratization efforts, and those who mistakenly believe that their interests would be negatively affected in this way. It would subsequently be proper to pursue a policy and strategy that would reduce the dangers and threats while ensuring that speedy economic development and democratization.
>
> (MFA, 2002, p. 7; Meles, 2017)

The "Inside-out" foreign policy of the EPRDF under Meles Zenawi as opposed to Haile Selassie's, or Mengistu's "Outside-in" foreign policies, is one element in the shift in strategic culture during the 1990s and 2000s. Ethiopian security and strategic policy underscored the primacy of national sovereignty, security and defence goals, and also emphasised the critical role of domestic policy, in particular the alleviation of poverty, the imperatives of economic development and democratisation, as a basis of the country's security, defence and foreign policy.

> There is no point in trying to pursue a foreign relations and national security policy to be implemented externally without a major and effective in-country effort to realize our vision of development and democratization.
>
> (MFA, 2002, p. 7; Meles, 2017)

The EPRDF and Meles successfully navigated regional geo-political and multipolar global power alignment divides by establishing concomitant, non-aligned relations with both Israel and Arab and Muslim countries regionally, and with powers such as the USA, China, Russia and the EU globally. Strategically, Ethiopia under the EPRDF and Meles pursued active security alliances and economic diplomacy benefitting from opportunities presented by the current Middle Eastern geo-political equilibriums between Saudi Arabia, Israel and Iran on the one hand and between the USA and Russia on the other.

Conclusion

In summary, this chapter has argued that to best understand Ethiopia's international relations and foreign policy one should look at the country's strategic culture and its impact on strategic behaviour and geo-political thinking. The country's strategic culture, derived from history, religions, culture, identity, geography, as well as domestic political and institutional factors, presents itself differently over time. This offers a fuller explanation than those offered by realism and pluralism.

Haile Selassie's and Mengistu's fear of Pan-Arabism and Muslim encirclement on the one hand and need to demonstrate African solidarity with Egypt and North African Arab countries against Israel's occupation of the Sinai on the other, explains Ethiopia's ambivalent and often strategically misaligned foreign policy vis-à-vis these countries. Similarly, Haile Selassie's ambivalent and strategically misaligned foreign policy towards Israel, as demonstrated by Ethiopia's severance of diplomatic relation in 1973, or Mengistu's disjointed and misaligned diplomatic relations with Israel in the period 1975–1991, are best explained by strategic culture variables. These include Ethiopia's balancing of African solidarity with a pro-Israel policy based on historical/cultural legacies, its geography and its often conflicting Christian-Judaic-Islamic identity and traditions (Bishku, 1994; Spencer, 2006; Haggai, 2016; MFA, 2002; Mengistu, 2004; Meles, 2017).

Perhaps more importantly, it was the exigencies of domestic policy, in particular pressures from nationalist, multi-nationalist, or religious forces rather than the safeguarding of national sovereignty, that impacted most on Haile Selassie's and Mengistu's preferences for foreign alliances. It is only in those periods when domestic pressures challenged the regime's security under Haile Selassie during the 1960s and 1974 or Mengistu in 1975–1978 and 1989–91, that the strategic behaviour of the state became closely aligned with a pro-Israel foreign policy (Mengistu, 2004; Spencer, 2006; Haggai, 2016). Conversely, when Haile Selassie and Mengistu felt domestically relatively secure they were able to conduct cordial relations with neighbouring Arab and Muslim countries. Ethiopia's strategic culture combined with geo-politics and material forces of national interest provide a consistent and overarching understanding of Ethiopia's complex foreign policy towards Israel and Middle Eastern Arab countries.

The country's strategic culture, in particular domestic political and religious pressures, therefore provides the contexts and subtexts for a more or less successful foreign policy. As such, under Meles Zenawi, the state for a time was under less domestic pressure and Ethiopia could follow a fully aligned strategic behaviour that consistently optimised its national interest. It meant successfully engaging all of the Arab Middle East, as well as Israel, Russia, China and the USA. This compares with the foreign policies under Haile Selassie or Mengistu, which, driven by outside-in considerations, but also because of domestic pressures, were often inconsistent; ambivalent and strategic behaviour was misaligned with national security objectives.

The Inside-out strategy provides the foundation for a strong and effective foreign and defence policy, aimed at reducing domestic vulnerabilities and outside threats. An active and non-alignment policy that followed from this enabled the regime to pursue pragmatic, non-exclusive and cordial relations with Israel and Middle Eastern Arab countries as well as with global power blocks, such as the USA, China, Russia and the EU. Alternatively, and when complemented with conventional analysis of state interests based on power and material calculations, this approach better explains and conceptualises the country's often ambivalent and strategically misaligned foreign policy towards Israel and Middle Eastern Arab countries.

The dynamics of strategic culture, regionalism and a changing post-Cold War global order provide developing countries such as Ethiopia with opportunities to pursue relatively autonomous, non-aligned and "win-win" foreign policies that are better aligned with their domestic policies (MFA, 2002; Meles, 2017; Sanubi, 2012). Ethiopia's experience and achievements under the EPRDF and Meles suggest that this is possible. The adoption of a more self-conscious strategic approach to foreign policy by African states, by interrogating their own strategic cultures and unique historical legacies, in an emerging multipolar environment can therefore arguably usefully serve as a template for the study of foreign policy in Africa, as elsewhere.

Notes

1 The dominant IR theories of realism and pluralism have hitherto served as the basis for a partial explanation of Ethiopia's foreign policy towards Israel and the Middle East (Haggai, 1994, 1997, 2007, 2016; Lefebvre, 1996; Bishku, 1994). As such, following a realist script, Ethiopia's strategic alliance with the USA and Israel during the reign of Emperor Haile Selassie and with the USSR, Yemen and Libya during the era of Mengistu are explained by the regimes' desire to safeguard the country's territorial integrity. Similarly, consistent with liberal institutionalist theories of IR, Ethiopia's active diplomacy and participation in international institutions are seen aimed at safeguarding its national sovereignty and territorial integrity.

2 As such, Ethiopia's foreign policy is not necessarily based on a realist script where the national interest is informed solely by rational and material considerations of strategy, nor is it based on objective economic considerations alone as a liberal approach would suggest.

3 The majority religion of Ethiopia, which is a branch of the Eastern (Coptic/Orthodox) Christian Church. According to the Ethiopian Population and Housing Census of 2007, 43.5% of Ethiopians are adherent of the Orthodox Tewahedo Christian Church; Protestants make up 18.5%; and Catholics 1%, making up 63% of Christian population. In contrast, Muslims make up 33.9% and traditional religions 3% of the population (CSA, 2010).

4 The Ethiopian People's Revolutionary Democratic Front is a coalition of four regional parties led by Meles Zenawi that overthrew the Mengistu regime, and has ruled Ethiopia since 1991.

5 According to Ethiopian and Biblical legend, Queen Sheba was a powerful Ethiopian queen who ruled over Ethiopia and across the Red Sea c. 965–931 BC. She travelled to Jerusalem to visit King Solomon of the Israelites from whom she bore a son, Menelik I, who became the first Solomonic monarch of Ethiopia.

6 The Solomonic Dynasty is, according to Ethiopian legend/history, the succession of Ethiopian monarchs who claimed their ancestry to King Solomon of Israel, through his son Menelik I, and the Queen of Sheba of Ethiopia. It is claimed that Emperor Haile Selassie was the last Solomonic monarch of Ethiopia.
7 The Ark of Covenant contains the Stone Tablets of the Ten Commandments, which is of great religious significance to Judaism and the Ethiopian Orthodox Tewahedo Church. According to Ethiopian legend and history, the Ark of Covenant was brought to Ethiopia by Queen Sheba. It is preserved in the Church of Mary of Zion in the ancient city of Axum, Ethiopia.
8 Ethiopian Jews who settled in the country from the times of Queen Sheba of Ethiopia about beginning c. 10 centuries BC.
9 A strategic and geo-political doctrine developed by David Gurion in the late 1950s. It was discontinued after the overthrow of Haile Selassie in 1974 and the Shah of Iran in 1979.
10 The Military Council, led by Mengistu Haile-Mariam, that overthrew the Haile Selassie regime and ended the Ethiopian Monarchy in 1974, and ruled the country until 1991.
11 The Tigray People's Liberation Front, led by Meles Zenawi, is one of the coalition parties of the EPRDF and played the leading role in the defeat of the Derg and the establishment of a Federal Democratic state in Ethiopia in 1991.
12 The Oromo Liberation Front is one of the oldest national liberation forces in Ethiopia, representing the single biggest nationality in Ethiopia.
13 Eritrean People Liberation Front, a front that led and won the Eritrean independence in 1991. It was renamed the People's Front for Justice and Democracy (PFDJ) in 1994, and has ruled Eritrea since 1991.
14 The emigration from the Arabian Peninsula of the persecuted followers of the Prophet to Ethiopia in the 7th Century AD, where they were given refuge and allowed to keep their religion and live in peaceful coexistence with Ethiopian Christians.
15 The second major religious community in Ethiopia, making up 33.9% of the population according to the Ethiopian Population and Housing Census 2007 (CSA, 2010).
16 The Egyptian invasions were subsequently defeated at the battles of Gundet in 1875 and Gura in 1876 by an army led by Ras Alula Abanega, a general of the then Emperor of Ethiopia, Yohannes IV (Haggai, 1997; Rubenson, 1991; Tilahun, 1979; Marcus, 2002).
17 The Eritrean Liberation Front is the oldest national liberation force in Eritrea that started the armed struggle for the independence of Eritrea in the early 1960s.

References

Abraham, K. (1994). *Ethiopia: From Bullets to the Ballot Box—The Bumpy Road to Democracy and the Political Economy of Transition*. Lawrenceville, NJ: The Red Sea Press.

Bard, G. M. (2018). *Israel's International Relations: The Evolution of Israel's African Policy*. Online Jewish Virtual Library. A Project of AICE. Accessed 29 November 2018. https://www.jewishvirtuallibrary.org/the-evolution-of-israel-rsquo-s-africa-policy (Accessed 29 November 2018).

Berhanu, T. (2010). *An Introduction to Ethiopia's Foreign Policy: Its Progress and Reflections Pre-1991*. Addis Ababa, Ethiopia: Printing by Far East Trading.

Bishku, B. M. (1994). Israel and Ethiopia: From a Special to a Pragmatic Relationship. *Journal of Conflict Studies*, *14*(2). ISSN 1715-5673. Accessed 19 November 2018. https://journals.lib.unb.ca/index.php/JCS/article/view/15180 (Accessed 19 November 2018).

Bishku, B. M. (2015). Ethiopia and Israel: A Long-term Relationship on the Periphery of the Arab and Muslim Worlds. In Lukian Prijac (ed.), *Foreign Relations with Ethiopia: Human and Diplomatic History*, pp. 41–58. Lorient, France: University of Britanny-South and Western France Research Centre.

Bloomfield, A. (2012). Time to Move On: Reconceptualising the Strategic Culture Debate. *Contemporary Security Policy*, *33*(3): 437–461. doi: 10.1080/13523260.2012.727679.

Booth, K. (1990). The Concept of Strategic Culture Affirmed. In C. G. Jacobsen (eds.), *Strategic Power: USA/USSR*, pp. 121–128. London: Palgrave Macmillan.

Brooks, F. M. (1998). *Kebra Nagast (The Glory of Kings)—The True Ark of the Covenant.* Third Printing, 1998 (Translation by M. Brooks). Kingston: Jamaica LMH Publishing Company.

Central Statistical Agency. (2010). *Population and Housing Census of Ethiopia.* Addis Ababa, Ethiopia: Central Statistical Agency.

Cervenka, Z. (1974). *The Emergence and Significance of the African-Arab Solidarity. Instant Research on Peace and Violence.* Tampere, Finland: Tampere Peace Research Institute: University of Tampere.

Clapham, C. (1988). *Transformation and Continuity in Revolutionary Ethiopia.* Cambridge: Cambridge University Press.

Crummey, D. (2000). *Land and Society in the Christian Kingdom of Ethiopia: From the 13th to 20th Century.* Addis Ababa, Ethiopia: Addis Ababa University Press.

Giday, B. (1991). *Ethiopian Civilization.* Addis Ababa, Ethiopia: Belai Giday.

Gitelson, A. S. (1973). The OAU Mission and the Middle East Conflict. *International Organisation*, *27*(3): 413–419. doi:10.1017/S0020818300003581.

Glenn, J. (2009). Realism versus Strategic Culture: Competition and Collaboration? *International Sties Review*, *11*(3): 523–551. doi:10.1111/j.1468-2486.2009.00872.x.

Gray, C. (1981). National Styles in Strategy: The American Example. *International Security*, *6*(2). doi:10.2307/2538645.

Gray, C. (1986). *Nuclear Strategy and National Style*. Lanham, MD: Hamilton Press.

Gray, C. (1999). Strategic Culture as Context: The First Generation of Theory Strikes Back. *Review of International Studies*, *25*(1): 49–69. doi:10.1017/S0260210599000492.

Greenfield, R. (1965). *Ethiopia: A New Political History*. New York: Praeger.

Haggai, E. (1994). *Ethiopia and the Middle East*. Boulder, CO: Lynne Rienner Publishers.

Haggai, E. (1997). *Ras Alula and the Scramble for Africa: A Political Biography – Ethiopia and Eritrea 1859–1897*. Trenton, NJ: Red Sea Press.

Haggai, E. (2007). *Saudi Arabia and Ethiopia: Islam, Christianity and Politics Entwined.* Boulder, CO: Lynne Rienner.

Haggai, E. (2010). *Islam and Christianity in the Horn of Africa*. Boulder, CO: Lynne Rienner Publishers.

Haggai, E. (2016). *Alliance and Alienation: Ethiopia and Israel in Days of Haile Selassie*. Trenton, NJ: The Red Sea Press.

Haile Selassie, I. (1999). *My Life and Ethiopia's Progress: Autobiography of Haile Selassie I.* Research Associates School Times Publication and Frontline Distribution International, Inc. English Translation and Annotation by Edward Ullendorff, 1976. Lansing, MI: Michigan State University Press.

Haile-Melekot, A. (2000). *The Victory of Adowa: The 1st Victory of Africa over Colonialists*. Addis Ababa, Ethiopia: Commercial Printing Enterprise.

Henze, P. B. (1990). *The Tigre People's Liberation Front: Conversation with Meles Zenawi*. Online Archives of California (OAC). Inventory of P. B. Henze Papers. Box/Folder 76:11, April 1990.

Henze, P. B. (1996). Moscow, Mengistu, and the Horn: Difficult Choices for the Kremlin. *Cold War International History Project Bulletin, 8–9*(1996–97): 45–47.

Houston, D. D. (1985). *Wonderful Ethiopians of the Ancient Cushite Empire*. Baltimore, MD: Black Classic Press.

Howlett, D. (2005). Strategic Culture: Reviewing Recent Literature. *Strategic Insights, 6*(10). Accessed 10 January 2020. https://calhoun.nps.edu/bitstream/handle/10945/11212/howlettOct05.pdf?sequence=1&isAllowed=y.

Hussein, A. S. (1997). Islam, Christianity and Ethiopia's Foreign Policy. *Muslim Minority Affairs, 17*(1): 165–208. doi:10.1163/9789004265486_007.

IMF. (2018). *World Economic Outlook (WEO)*. International Monetary Fund, April 2018. Accessed 29 November 2018. https://www.imf.org/external/pubs/ft/weo/2018/01/weodata.

Iyob, R. (1995). *The Eritrean Struggle for Independence: Domination, Resistance, Nationalism 1941 –1993*. Cambridge: Cambridge University Press.

Johnston, I. A. (1995a). *Cultural Realism: Strategic Culture and Grand Strategy in Chinese History*. Princeton Studies in International History and Politics. Princeton, NJ: Princeton University Press.

Johnston, I. A. (1995b). Thinking about Strategic Culture. *International Security, 19*: 32–64.

Kapuscinski, R. (1983). *The Emperor: The Downfall of an Autocrat*. English Translation, London: Quartet Books.

Kassu, W. T. (2012). Religion and Cold War Politics in Ethiopia. In P. Muehlenbeck (ed.), *Religion and the Cold War: A Global Perspective*, pp. 139–157. Nashville, TN: Vanderbilt University Press.

Kebede, M. (1999). *Survival and Modernization: Ethiopia's Enigmatic Present—A Philosophical Discourse*. Trenton, NJ: The Red Sea Press, Inc.

Keller, J. E. (1991). *Revolutionary Ethiopia: From Empire to People's Republic*. Bloomington, IN: Indiana University Press.

Kendie, D. (1990). An Aspect of the Geo-Politics of the Red Sea. *North-eastern African Studies, 12*(2/3): 117–131.

Keohane, O. R. (1984). *After Hegemony: Cooperation and Discord in the World Political Economy*. Princeton, NJ: Princeton University Press.

Keohane, O. R. & Nye, S. J. (1977). *Power and Interdependence: World Politics in Transition*. Boston, MA: Little Brown.

Kessler, D. (1996). *The Falashas: A Short History of the Ethiopian Jews* (3rd ed.). London: Frank Cass & Co. Ltd.

King James Bible Online. (2018). *Bible Verses About Ethiopia*. Accessed 29 November 2018. https://www.kingjamesbibleonline.org/Bible-Verses-About-Ethiopia.

Klein, Y. (2007). A Theory of Strategic Culture. *Journal of Comparative Strategy, 10*(1): 3–23. doi:10.1080/01495939108402827.

Lantis, J. (2005). Strategic Culture: From Clausewitz to Constructivism. *Strategic Insights, 6*(10). Accessed 29 November 2012. https://core.ac.uk/download/pdf/36704606.pdf.

Lata, L. (1999). *The Ethiopian State at the Crossroads - Decolonization and Democratization or Disintegration?* Trenton, NJ: The Red Sea Press, Inc.

Lefebvre, A. J. (1991). *Arms for the Horn: US Security Policy in Ethiopia and Somalia, 1953–1991*. Pittsburgh, PA: University of Pittsburgh Press.

Lefebvre, A. J. (1996). Middle East Conflicts and Middle Level Power Intervention in the Horn of Africa. *The Middle East Journal, 50*(3): 387–404.

Lefebvre, A. J. (1998). The United States, Ethiopia and the 1963 Somali-Soviet Arms Deal: Containment and the Balance of Power Dilemma in the Horn of Africa. *Journal of Modern African Studies*, *36*(4): 611–643. doi:10.1017/S0022278X98002870.

Lefort, R. (1983). *Ethiopia—An Heretical Revolution?* Translated by A. M. Berrett. London: Zed Press.

Legum, C. & Lee, B. (1979). *The Horn of Africa in Continuing Crisis*. London: Holmes & Meier Publishers.

Levey, Z. (2008). Israel's Exit from Africa, 1973: The Road to Diplomatic Isolation. *British Journal of Middle Eastern Studies*, *35*(2): 205–226. doi:10.1080/13530190802180621.

Levin, N. D. (1974). *Greater Ethiopia: The Evolution of a Multi-ethnic Society*. Chicago, IL: The University of Chicago Press.

Lipsky, A. G. (1967). *Ethiopia: Its People, Its Society, Its Culture*. New Haven, CT: HRAF Press.

Lockot, H. W. (1992). *The Mission: The Life, Reign and Character of Haile Selassie I.* London: Hurst & Company.

Mandela, N. (1994). *Long Walk to Freedom: The Autobiography of Nelson Mandela*. London: Little, Brown and Company.

Marcus, G. D. (2002). *A History of Ethiopia* (updated edition). Berkeley, CA: University of California Press.

Markakis, J. (1972). *Ethiopia: Anatomy of a Traditional Polity*. Addis Ababa, Ethiopia: Oxford University Press.

Markakis, J. (1990). *National and Class Conflict in the Horn of Africa*. London: Zed Books Ltd.

Markakis, J. & Ayele, N. (1978). *Class and Revolution in Ethiopia*. Nottingham, UK: Spokesman.

Mathew, D. (1974). *Ethiopia: The Study of Polity: 1540–1935* (original work published 1974). London: Greenwood Press.

Mazuri, A. A. (1979). *Africa and the Arab-Israeli Conflict*. Conference Paper. Bentley Historical Library, University of Michigan, Michigan.

Meir, G. (1975). *My Life: Autobiography of Golda Meir, Former Prime Minister of Israel.* (first American Edition, 1975). New York: G.P. Putnam's Sons.

Meles, Z. (2017). *Ethiopia: The Renewal Journey*. Addis Ababa, Ethiopia: Democratic Developmental State Essays, Meles Zenawi Foundation.

Mengistu, H. M. (2004). *Our Struggle: The Revolutionary History of the Ethiopian People*. Los Angeles, CA: Tsehai Publishers.

MFA. (2002). *Ethiopia's Foreign Affairs and National Security Policy and Strategy*. Addis Ababa, Ethiopia: Ethiopian Ministry of Foreign Affairs.

Miller, C. J. (1975). African-Israeli Relations: Impact on Continental Unity. *Middle East Journal*, *29*(4): 393–408. http://www.jstor.org/stable/43661168.

Mohammed, A. (2007). Ethiopia's Strategic Dilemma in the Horn of Africa. *Inter-Africa Group. Crisis in the Horn of Africa*. Published online on 20 February 2007. Accessed 29 November 2018. https://hornofAfrica.ssrc.org/Abdul_Mohammed/index3.html.

Morgenthau, J. H. (1978). *Politics among Nations: The Struggle for Power and Peace* (5th ed.). New York: Alfred A. Knopf.

OAU. (1985). *Resolution on the Situation in the Middle East*. Resolutions Adopted by The Forty-Second OAU Council of Ministers. Addis Ababa, Ethiopia: Organisation of African Unity Secretariat.

Ottaway, M. (1982). *Soviet and American Influence in the Horn of Africa*. New York: Praeger.

Pankhurst, R. (1968). *Economic History of Ethiopia: 1800–1935*. Addis Ababa, Ethiopia: Haile Selassie I University Press (renamed Addis Ababa University Press).

Pankhurst, R. (1990). *A Social History of Ethiopia – The Northern and Central Highlands from Early Medieval Times to the Rise of Emperor Tewodros II*. Addis Ababa, Ethiopia: Institute of Ethiopian Studies, Addis Ababa University.

Patman, G. R. (1990). *The Soviet Union in the Horn of Africa: The Diplomacy of Intervention and Disengagement*. Cambridge: Cambridge University Press [e-book].

Perham, M. (1969). *The Government of Ethiopia*. London: Faber and Faber.

Quinn, J. J. (2010). African Foreign Policies. *Oxford Research Encyclopedia of International Studies*. Published online on 04 June 2019. https://oxfordre.com/internationalstudies/abstract/10.1093/acrefore/9780190846626.001.0001/acrefore-9780190846626-e-117. doi:10.1093/acrefore/9780190846626.013.11.

Rubenson, S. (1991). *The Survival of Ethiopian Independence* (second reprint). Addis Ababa, Ethiopia: Kuraz Publishing Agency.

Sanubi, A. F. (2012). Assessing Nigeria's African-centred Foreign Policy against an Inside-Out Paradigm: A Proposal for an Alternative Foreign Policy Approach. *Africana Journal*, *6*(1): unpaged.

Sbacchi, A. (1985). *Ethiopia under Mussolini: Fascism and the Colonial Experience*. London: Zed Books.

Schmidt, E. (2013). *Foreign Intervention in Africa: From the Cold War to the War on Terror*. Cambridge: Cambridge University Press [e-book].

Schwab, P. (1978). Cold War on the Horn of Africa. *African Affairs*, *77*: 6–20. doi:10.1093/oxfordjournals.afraf.a096955.

Schwab, Peter (1985). *Ethiopia: Politics, Economics and Society*. London: Frances Pinter (Publishers) Limited.

Sharon, A. (2004). *Address by Prime Minister Ariel Sharon Welcoming Prime Minister Meles Zenawi of Ethiopia*. Jerusalem: Prime Minister's Office, Communications Department, 1 June 2004.

Sharon, A. (2005). *Prime Minister Ariel Sharon Meets with Ethiopian PM Zenawi*. Jerusalem: Prime Minister's Office, Communications Department, 14 November 2005.

Shehim, K. (1988). Israel-Ethiopian Relations: Change and Continuity. *Northeast African Studies*, *10*(1): 25–37. http://www.jstor.org/stable/43661168.

Snyder, J. (1977). *The Soviet Strategic Culture: Implications for Limited Nuclear Operations*. Santa Monica, CA: Rand Corporation.

Spencer, H. J. (2006). *Ethiopia at Bay: A Personal Account of the Haile Selassie Years*. Los Angeles, CA: Tsehai Publishers.

Stone, E. (2006). Comparative Cultures Literature Review (Part 1). *Defence Threat Reduction Agency, USA*; Fort Belvoir, Advanced Systems and Concepts Office; Comparative Strategic Culture Curriculum.

Summerfield, P. (2003). *From Falashas to Ethiopian Jews—The External Influences for Change c. 1860–1960*. Routledge: London.

Tareke, G. (1991). *Power and Protest—Peasant Revolts in the Twentieth Century* (original work published 1991). Trenton, NJ: The Red Sea Press, Inc.

Tesfaye, M. (2017). Strategic and Tactical Issues of Ethiopia's Foreign Policy: Strengths, Weaknesses, Opportunities and Threats. *AigaForum*, October 2017. http://www.aigaforum.com/article2017/strategic-and-tactical-issues-ethiopia-foreign-policy.htm.

The Baltimore Sun. (1991). Freeing Jews cost Israel $35 million. May 29, 1991. Article by R. Ruby. *Jerusalem Bureau of the Sun.* Accessed 29 November 2018. articles.baltimore.com//1991-05-29/news/1991149054_1_ethiopian-jews-addis-ababa-israel.

The New York Times. (1978). Moves to Oust Dayan Is Blocked in Israel. *The New York Times.* Accessed 29 November 2018. https://www.nytimes.com/1978/02/23/archives/move-to-oust-dayan-is-blocked-in-israel.html.

Tilahun, W. (1979). *Egypt's Imperial Aspirations over the Lake Tana and the Blue Nile.* Addis Ababa, Ethiopia: United Printers.

Tiruneh, A. (1993). *The Ethiopian Revolution 1974–1987: A Transformation from an Aristocratic to Totalitarian Autocracy.* Cambridge: Cambridge University Press

Trimingham, J. S. (1952). *Islam in Ethiopia.* Oxford: Oxford University Press.

Ullendorff, E. (1965). *The Ethiopians: An Introduction to Country and People* (2nd ed.). Oxford: Oxford University Press, 1960.

Ullendorff, E. (1968). *Ethiopia and the Bible.* Oxford: Oxford University Press.

Waltz, N. K. (2010). *Theory of International Politics.* Long Grove, IL: Waveland Press. 1979 (original work published 1979).

Yihunbelay, B. (2016). Bibi's Visit, the Arabs and the Geopolitical Dynamics. *The Reporter (Ethiopian).* Addis Ababa, Ethiopia, 16 July 2016. Accessed 4 June 2019. https://www.thereporterethiopia.com/search/node?keys=bibi%27s+visit.

Yordanov, R. (2016). *The Soviet Union and the Horn of Africa during the Cold War.* Lanham, MD: Lexington [e-book].

Zewde, B. (2001). *A History of Modern Ethiopia: 1855–1991.* Eastern Africa Studies (2nd ed.). Oxford: James Currey.

Zewde, B. (ed.). (2008). *Society, State and Identity in African History.* Addis Ababa, Ethiopia: Forum for Social Studies.

6 Nigeria's foreign policy and intervention behaviour in Africa

What role for agency?

Olumuyiwa Amao

> Just as President Monroe proclaimed the American hemisphere free from the military incursions of European empires, so also do we in Nigeria and in Africa insist that African affairs be left to Africa to settle.
>
> (Shagari, 1981: 75)

Introduction

Many analyses in foreign policy literature have focused on the use of structural/institutional and constructivist perspectives in the examination of foreign policy and the intervention behaviour of state actors. While in their own right these approaches have proven useful, their theoretical limitations are evident in their overwhelming focus on institutions, structure and material capabilities. In the process, "agency" as the substructure of foreign policy has not received due attention. At the same time, the extant attempts at highlighting the analytical relevance of agency in the study of Foreign Policy Analysis (FPA) has focused on Western scholarship.

Margaret Hermann has argued that by examining idiosyncrasies, characteristics and personality, predictions regarding foreign policy decision-making are possible since this type of analysis can account for likely personal behaviour (Hermann, 1980). Lloyd Jensen has evinced how a display of high level of interest in foreign affairs, the possession of high decisional latitude, a non-routine situation and unambiguity of the information regarding the situation can shape a state's foreign policy behaviour (Jensen, 1982: 14–15).

Zee Maoz and Annat Shayer have noted that "the role of personality in foreign policy should not be underestimated, as there are significant events in international relations that can be attributed, at least partially, to the ideas and personal actions of key leaders" (Maoz & Shayer, 1987: 576). Edward Yang, drawing references from the leadership traits analysis framework, has demonstrated how

> a leader's level of conceptual complexity interacts with external stimuli (system- and/or domestic-level factors), to affect: (i) the leader's willingness

> to change course in response to policy failure and (ii) the type of changes that the leader is likely to carry out.
>
> (Yang, 2010: 1)

Writing on leadership and foreign policy analysis, John Preston has identified the early literature on foreign policy analysis along four main lines. The first, the "great man" theory of leadership, believes leaders are "born, and not made". The second, situational based theories and critiques focus on "the person and the situation" to explain leadership. The third is the psychology and psychoanalytic theory which explains a state's foreign policy behaviour from a leadership style perspective. The last approach analyses a state's foreign policy behaviour from both a leadership and followership perspective (Preston, 2010: 1–2).

Valerie Hudson (2014), has highlighted a leader's personal characteristics in decision-making, leadership style, level of interest in foreign policy, degree of foreign policy training, level of expertise on a defined issue, level of exposure to group interaction, the nature and extent of a crisis situation and regime-type, as ways through which a state's foreign policy behaviour can be contextualised. Hudson (2014: 40–41) goes further to propose three variables as useful analytic instruments in determining foreign policy agency. These include cognitive-psychological profile of leaders (that is, how they perceive the world and their state's role in it); leadership styles (independent, cooperative or consultative); and a leader's position and role within the bureaucratic and national politics of their states, as useful analytic instruments through which the foreign policy and intervention behaviour of state actors can be analysed from an agency perspective.

With the exceptions of James Rosenau (1980), who highlighted the role personality plays in foreign policy behaviour in "Black Africa", and Felix Kumah-Abiwu (2016), who drew references from the leadership traits theory to examine Jerry Rawlings' foreign economic policy in Ghana in the 1980s, Africa has not sufficiently paid attention to personality and leadership as a signifier of foreign policy agency, particularly, the role of leadership agency in the foreign policy and intervention behaviour of its state actors. This opens an analytical gap, given the demonstrable importance of leaders in the politics of the continent.

This contribution therefore addresses this lacuna in African foreign policy literature, by examining the role of individual leaders, their personality and beliefs in the foreign policy and intervention behaviour of Nigeria, a foremost regional player in Africa. Using Nigeria's leadership agency as the instrument of analysis, the chapter examines how Nigeria's Afro-centric foreign policy and intervention behaviour in Africa between 1960 and 2019 has been shaped by the personality and leadership idiosyncrasies of its leaders. By Afro-centrism, I refer to a commitment to an activist foreign policy orientation which places Africa and its interests at the heart of Nigeria's foreign policy in the course of its engagement with the rest of the world.

To be sure, this commitment to an Afro-centric foreign policy orientation is well enshrined in Nigeria's constitution. Section 2 of its 1999 constitution states, for example, that Nigeria "shall promote African unity, as well as the total political, economic, social and cultural liberation of Africa, and shall combat racial discrimination in all its manifestations".[1] This provision notwithstanding, Nigeria's decision and ability to maintain this policy appears propelled by a number of considerations. The first is the geo-political consideration which sees Nigeria strategically located within the West African sub-region. The second is the demographic explanation, which recognises Nigeria as the most populous black nation in the world, with an estimated population of over 195 million people.[2] The third and last factor is the economic consideration, which positions Nigeria as the largest economy in Africa with an estimated Gross Domestic Product (GDP) of about $397.27 billion.[3]

Conceived as such, the chapter seeks to answer two important questions: 1) to what extent is Nigeria's foreign policy and intervention behaviour leader-dependent? 2) What impact does regime-type have on the shape and direction of Nigeria's foreign policy and intervention behaviour? To address these questions, the chapter situates the leadership idiosyncrasies of Nigerian leaders within the context of Valerie Hudson's (2014: 40–41) three variables: (a) cognitive-psychological profile of leaders (that is, how they perceive the world and their state's role in it); (b) their leadership styles (independent, cooperative or consultative); and (c) their position and role within the bureaucratic and national politics of their states.

The choice of Hudson's approach as our analytical guide is premised on two principal grounds. First, Nigeria's history of military rule and poorly institutionalised nature of foreign policy opens up the space for individual leadership idiosyncrasies to dictate the shape and direction of its foreign policy. Second, given Nigeria's imperial presidency, issues of foreign policy are seen as the exclusive preserve of the *big man* in Abuja. This suggests the individual's personality, beliefs and motives do matter in decision-making.

The chapter has been divided into four parts. Following this introduction, the second section reappraises Nigeria's foreign policy and intervention behaviour in Africa since independence. The third highlights the role of leadership agency in Nigeria's foreign policy and intervention behaviour in Africa. The fourth section offers concluding remarks.

Reappraising Nigeria's foreign policy and intervention behaviour in Africa since independence

From championing decolonisation struggles in Africa to supporting liberation movements in Southern Africa and beyond, Nigeria has been unequivocal of its desire and resolve to provide a leadership role in West Africa and on the African continent (Adebajo, 2000; Amao & Uzodike, 2015; Amao, 2019). This desire, termed by Bolaji Akinyemi as the concept of *Pax Nigeriana*, implies how Nigeria's demographic preponderance, economic and natural endowments, and staggering human resources helped provide leadership for Africa (Akinyemi, 1974). On Nigeria's admittance into the United Nations on October 7, 1960, Sir Abubakar Tafawa Balewa, Nigeria's first prime minister, left no one in doubt as to what the centrifugal and centripetal determinants of Nigeria's foreign policy would be.[4]

Balewa stated that:

> so far, I have concentrated on the problems of Africa. Please do not think that we are not interested in the problems of the rest of the world; we are intensely interested in them and hope to be allowed to assist in finding solutions to them through this organisation, but being human we are naturally concerned first with what affects our immediate neighborhood.[5]

Affirming this further, Balewa noted that:

> it is the desire of Nigeria to remain on friendly terms with all nations and to participate actively in the work of the United Nations Organisations. Nigeria, by virtue of being the most populous country in West Africa has absolutely no territorial or expansionist ambitions. We are committed to uphold the principles upon which the United Nations is founded. Nigeria hopes to work with other African countries for the progress of Africa and to also assist in bringing all African countries to a state of independence.
>
> (Aluko, 1997: 2)

Under Balewa, Nigeria demonstrated a sense of relative commitment to the liberation struggle in South Africa, by leading the campaign which culminated in its expulsion from the Commonwealth in 1963; sent a contingent of Nigerian troops as part of the UN peacekeeping force deployed to the Congo in 1960 and 1964; dispatched troops to quell the Tanganyika rebellion in 1964; and equally facilitated trade deals between the Africa, Caribbean and Pacific (ACP) Group of States and the European Economic Community (EEC) in 1966; Akinboye, 1999; Fawole, 2003). At a stroke, Nigeria's foreign policy under Balewa achieved three things. It demonstrated a willingness and capability to sustain the authority of the new continental organisation; assisted sister-states in mortal danger of civil war and disintegration and demonstrated that Nigeria was solidly committed against neo-colonialist influences in Africa.

Yakubu Gowon's leadership (1966–1975) saw Nigeria maintaining a tripartite foreign policy posture built on (1) African continental issues, (2) a domestic regional policy and (3) a global level policy (Abegunrin, 2003). In Africa, Nigeria increased its strategic and financial support to liberation movements in Guinea-Bissau, Mozambique, Angola, Rhodesia and South Africa (Abegunrin, 2003). On decolonisation, Nigeria was very clear on its stance and this was brought into the fore in the warning handed out to the backers of the remaining vestiges of colonisation in Africa, including apartheid South Africa (Abegunrin, 2003). Gowon warned:

> Let no one deceive himself that South Africa is spending $540 million for defence purposes and seeking to acquire nuclear capability only to come to

> terms with independent Africa and grant the right of self-determination to her African population. South Africa is growing an octopus. It is reaching beyond its territories. It is exporting its racist policies. It is being used by the imperialists' powers to regain their foothold on Africa.
>
> (Abegunrin, 2003: 37)

Nigeria also reaffirmed its commitment to African unity through the Organisation of African Unity, and by encouraging inter-governmental cooperation and multilateralism in West Africa through the formation of the Economic Community of West African States (ECOWAS) in 1975.

Also, and as Adekeye Adebajo aptly puts it,

> the Nigerian civil war between 1967 and 1970, Israel and France's support for the secessionist Biafra group, Britain's hesitant support for Nigeria, and America's condescending dismissal of Nigeria as a British sphere of influence, equally led Nigeria to a more activist, less naïve post-war foreign policy

under the Gowon regime (Adebajo, 2008: 8). An important take-away from Nigeria's foreign policy behaviour under the regime was that Gowon outside of his Nigerian sphere of influence had an uncommon ability to mobilise forces against Western hegemony. Indeed, this uncommon ability represents the most distinguishing factor between the Balewa and Gowon governments. While the former had a challenger personality[6] and foreign policy approach, as strongly reflected in his regime's foreign policy behaviour, the latter had a very reclusive personality and conservative approach to foreign policy, as evinced in his administration's reluctance to act against the interests of Westminster over apartheid Pretoria (Amao & Uzodike, 2015).

Like the Gowon regime, the Murtala Muhammed regime also had a challenger approach to foreign policy issues. Indeed, a key defining foreign policy moment for the regime was Nigeria's stance on Angola's independence. Nigeria called the bluff of Washington, and also threatened to impose an oil embargo on it, over the latter's support for the *União Nacional para a Independência total de Angola* (UNITA) rebels, against the Organisation of African Unity (OAU)-backed *Movimento Popular de Libertação de Angola* (MPLA) (Aluko, 1977). Furthermore, when Pretoria invaded Southern Angola over the ownership of Cunene dam in 1975, Nigeria was unequivocal of its condemnation, and also offered revolutionary support to the MPLA to counter the imperialistic tendencies of Pretoria and Angola's Portuguese colonisers (Hélia, 2008).

Similarly, in Namibia, Nigeria supported the South West African Peoples' Organisation (SWAPO) led by Sam Nujoma, against the other political parties sponsored by South Africa and the West, to victory (Abegunrin, 2003). The South African Relief Fund, the donation of $20 million (USD) to the SWAPO and Patriotic Front of Zimbabwe and other liberation movements in Southern Africa, the military assistance and aid offered to Mozambique to help suppress the Pretoria-backed RENAMO (*Resistência Nacional Moçambicana*) guerrillas, all bear witness to Nigeria's Afro-centric foreign policy commitment under the regime (Gambari, 2008). Nigeria foreign policy and intervention behaviour between 1976–1979, particularly its Africa-centred approach to foreign policy, remained largely defiant and unchanged. Its policy on decolonisation and apartheid were pursued with renewed vigour, as evidenced in its nationalisation of a number of Western assets, particularly Barclays Bank and British Petroleum by the Obasanjo/Yar Adua regime (Hélia, 2008).

During the Shehu Shagari administration (1980–1983), Nigeria continued with its Africa-centred approach to foreign policy. This was manifested for example in the country's dispatch of twenty-one articulated trucks of relief materials to recession-hit Ghana in 1979, its attendance of a six-nation ad-hoc committee meeting on the decolonisation of Western Sahara in Monrovia in 1980 and its role in the resolution of the Chadian conflict in 1980 (Ogunbadejo, 1980: 406). On its decolonisation and anti-apartheid policy in Southern Africa, existing sanctions and seclusions on Pretoria were strengthened, while Nigeria's contribution to liberation movements in Southern Africa rose to about $5 million in aid yearly (Hélia, 2008).

Perhaps, an apt confirmation of Nigeria commitment to the anti-apartheid cause was the diplomatic spat it had with Washington, when the latter asked African states to boycott the 1980 Olympic games in Moscow to protest the Soviets' 1979 invasion of Afghanistan (Ogunbadejo, 1980). Not only did Nigeria attend the games, it also led other African states to Moscow as reciprocation for Africa's lack of support from Washington, when it called for a boycott of the 1976 Montreal Olympics over the unending apartheid rule in South Africa (Ogunbadejo, 1980).

During the Buhari/Idiagbon (1983–1985) regime, Nigeria kept fate with its Afro-centric foreign policy focus and radical stance towards decolonisation and apartheid in Africa, and it also formally recognised the Polisario government in Western Sahara (Saharawi Arab Democratic Republic) (Akinboye, 1999). However, Nigeria's Africa-focused foreign policy approach was called into question when some undocumented citizens from Chad and Niger Republic were expelled, and Nigeria's borders shut to prevent smuggling and money laundering (Gambari, 2008: 58).

Under the Babangida regime (1985–1993), Nigeria's foreign policy and intervention behaviour towards Africa was largely Afro-centric and cooperative. The reversal of the border-closure policy of the Buhari regime, the increased funding of the Technical Aid Corps (TAC) programme, the Concert of Medium Powers initiative and the activation of the ECOWAS Protocol on Free Movement of Citizens under Babangida's chairmanship are all testament to how Africa-centred Nigeria's foreign policy was (Adeniran, 2008). Nigeria equally enhanced its role as the arrowhead of the sub-regional organisation through its intervention in Liberia (1990–1997). In Liberia, for example:

> Nigeria not only provided the bulk of the material and logistic support for ECOMOG operations but also the bulk of the personnel. Apart from the first

> Commander who was a Ghanaian, all subsequent Commanders were from the Nigerian military. That today Liberia is a united country owes much to the foresight and sacrifice of Nigeria … the Babangida regime gave ECOWAS institutional relevance by not only donating land for the building of the ECOWAS Secretariat but also contributed 4.5 million dollars towards its construction.
>
> (Shaw & Ihonvbere, 1996: 31)

In keeping with its Afro-centric foreign policy focus, Nigeria, along with thirty-two other countries, boycotted the Commonwealth games in Edinburgh in 1986 in protest against Britain's patronage of Pretoria. Financial donations were made to major anti-apartheid movements in Southern Africa (Ofoegbu, 1990). US$1.5 million in aid was given to the SWAPO, while the African National Congress (ANC) and the Pan-Africanist Congress (PAC) received donations of US$1 million and US$600,000 respectively (Osaghae, 1998).

Nigeria's foreign policy behaviour under the Abacha regime (1993–1998) was shaped by the global tilt towards liberal democracy, and the international community's stiff opposition to the palace coup, which ousted Ernest Shonekan's interim national government. As a consequence, Nigeria effectively became a pariah state and was expelled from the Commonwealth, in response to the regime's gross human right abuses, particularly the execution of the "Ogoni 9" in 1995.[7] The international community responded to Abacha in kind, with Nigeria's traditional allies—Britain, United States, France, Germany, Canada and South Africa, withdrawing their diplomatic representations from the country, while the Commonwealth also suspended Nigeria's membership (Akintola, 2007).

Responding to his government's isolation from the West and its allies, Abacha turned to Asia and other fringe states for cooperation—a move that further ostracised Nigeria from the rest of the world. This leadership-created international isolation and sanctions were imposed on Nigeria; yet, notwithstanding, Nigeria's Afro-centric approach to foreign policy during this period remained unchanged. In West Africa, Nigeria continued to act as its sub-regional policeman, as evidenced in the intervention role it played in Sierra Leone through ECOMOG, and its continued funding of the OAU (Adebajo, 2008).

Between 1998 and 1999, the concern of Abacha's successor, Abdulsalami Abubakar, was to rescue Nigeria from the self-inflicted international isolation it had been drawn into and to prepare the way for democratic rule. Thus, during this period, Abubakar focused on the pursuance of a policy of rejuvenation, aimed at redeeming Nigeria's battered international image and reputation (Akintola, 2007). This policy saw Nigeria pursuing a resolution-seeking external relations approach, as evidenced in the withdrawal of Nigeria's troops from Sierra Leone (Badmus & Ogunmola, 2017). Nigeria returned to democratic rule in 1999, with Olusegun Obasanjo emerging as president.

Between 1999 and 2007, Nigeria's foreign policy behaviour was set to achieve four important objectives: (1) reposition Nigeria's lost reputation as a formidable force in Africa; (2) strengthen democratic consolidation and political stability in Africa; (3) pursue economic integration and cooperation of Africa; and (4) facilitate the peaceful resolution of conflicts on the continent (Gambari, 2008: 58). On conflict intervention, Nigeria favoured a peaceful approach to conflict resolution. For example, Liberia's Charles Taylor was handed over to the International Criminal Court (ICC); the Mano River dispute between Liberia, Guinea and Sierra Leone was resolved, the Constitutive Act of the African Union with the New Partnership for African Development (NEPAD) as its economic variant was adopted by the African Union (AU); and President Fradique Mendez, who was ousted from office while on a state visit to Nigeria in 2003, was reinstated (Gambari, 2008). Similarly, the Nigerian-South African Bi-National Commission instituted in 1999; the Nigeria-Congo Joint Commission established in 2001; the transitioning of the OAU into the AU, and the formation of the NEPAD, bears witness to the Africa-centred orientation of Nigeria's foreign policy during this period.

Nigeria's foreign policy behaviour under the Yar'Adua administration (2007–2010) gravitated towards a citizen-diplomacy-styled approach, although Africa continued to remain the corner-piece of its foreign policy (Amao & Uzodike, 2015). These ideas had not been fully implemented when Yar' Adua died in office on May 5, 2010, and was succeeded by his deputy—Goodluck Jonathan. Under Jonathan, Nigeria strengthened its diplomatic, economic and security cooperation with the US, through the signing of its first US-Nigeria Bi-national Commission (Alao, 2011); strongly opposed the undemocratic change of government in Mali and Guinea-Bissau in 2011; and also supported the AU resolution seeking to oust Ivory Coast's Lauren Gbagbo and Libya's Muammar Gaddafi as a counterweight to Western hegemony (Amao, 2012). Lastly, when in 2012, the South African government "deported 125 Nigerians, alleging their yellow fever vaccination certificates were fakes, the Jonathan presidency responded with undisguised tit-for-tat deportation of eighty-four South Africans in two days".[8] Jonathan was succeeded by Muhammadu Buhari in 2015, in what was Nigeria's first inter-party transfer of power by an elected government since 1999.

Under Buhari (2015–2019), Africa has continued to remain the centrepiece of Nigeria foreign policy. The signing of the African Continental Free Trade Area Agreement (AfCFTA)[9] to boost in intra-African trade; its role in the resolution of the election impasse in the Gambia in 2017;[10] Nigeria's donation of $500,000 USD towards Guinea-Bissau's general elections;[11] and Nigeria's diplomatic resolution of the xenophobia-related disturbances in South Africa in September 2019 after initially recalling its ambassador from Pretoria[12] bears credence to the country's Afro-centric foreign policy orientation. These commitments notwithstanding, it is imperative to mention that Nigeria's capacity to assert its foreign policy dominance in Africa has been relatively constrained by two main occurrences under the Buhari administration.

The first is Buhari's ill health, which saw him spend a total of 172 days on medical convalescence, the longest by any Nigerian serving president.[13] During this time, Nigeria's foreign policy articulation suffered momentary decline, as the president is seen as the face of the country's foreign policy.

Nigeria barely had any representation in major international summits, and for the first time since the creation of the AU in 2002, Nigeria did not return a candidate for "the Commissioner for Political Affairs position it had always produced, instead Nigeria ran for, and duly lost the position of Commissioner for Peace and Security".[14] Lastly, Nigeria appears to be suffering an authority deficit in the light of its failure to effectively resolve its decade-long (2009–2019) Boko Haram insurgency, and this increasingly diminishing hegemonic capacity portends grave implications for sub-regional security (Amao & Maiangwa, 2017).

In the succeeding section, I will draw references from the empirical example we have expatiated above, to highlight the role of leadership agency in Nigeria's foreign policy and intervention behaviour in Africa.

What role for agency?

Two distinct narratives have emerged from our examination above. First, empirical evidence suggests that Nigeria's foreign policy and intervention behaviour is substantially leader-dependent. Second, despite the enshrinement of its core foreign policy principles in its constitution, there is a nexus between regime-type and the shape and direction which Nigeria's foreign policy and intervention behaviour follow. One plausible explanation for this could be the over-reliance of Nigeria's foreign policy at independence on the intuition and leadership idiosyncrasies of its leaders.

Thus, it is unsurprising that, while Nigerian leaders have made consistent attempts to operate within the ambits of Nigeria's subscription to an Afro-centric foreign policy in their external engagements, the manner in which this policy was/is being pursued is contingent on the leader's personality, beliefs and character. These differences in personality, when situated within the confines of Valerie Hudson's (2014) variables of (a) cognitive-psychological profile of leaders (that is, how they perceive the world and their state's role in it); (b) their leadership styles (independent, cooperative or consultative); and (c) their position and role within the bureaucratic and national politics of their states, leads us to a number of important observations.

For example, although the Balewa administration maintained a firm focus on Africa's interest in world affairs and was vociferous in condemning apartheid, it was reticent and conservative when it came to matching words with action. Balewa's timid and conservative personality explains why while rhetorically condemning apartheid South Africa, his regime fell short in imposing sanctions on Pretoria or challenging Westminster, over the latter's support for Pretoria. Situating Balewa's approach to foreign policy along Hudson's variables suggests that while Balewa seemed well aware of Nigeria's place in the world, as reflected in his rhetoric expressions of Nigeria's desire to lead the rest of Africa, he failed to create an effective leadership role for himself. Given his inability to detach himself from the influence of Westminster meant that Balewa was unable to exert substantial foreign policy independence.

Unlike Balewa, Gowon took a radical stance. This was due to his well-documented challenger personality in foreign policy-related issues. From Hudson's (2014) point of view, Gowon's foreign policy decisions show that he had a succinct and prescient appreciation of how to conduct an effective style of diplomacy for Nigeria in the world. Nigeria's suspension of bilateral relations with France over the nuclear tests it conducted in the Sahara and with Israel (over its support for the secessionist Biafra government) and its strong support for the anti-apartheid movements in Southern Africa demonstrate Gowon's radical foreign policy activism.

Gowon's leadership style epitomises a combination of Hudson's (2014) independent, cooperative or consultative variables. On the latter, there is Gowon's politics of oil diplomacy, where oil was sold at concessionary rates to ECOWAS member states who aligned with Nigeria during its civil war; the concession of the Bakassi Peninsula to Cameroon in 1975; the road projects executed in Benin Republic; the sugar factory constructed in Senegal, among others, are all useful examples of his independent leadership style (Abegunrin, 2003). Similarly, Gowon's cooperative, or consultative leadership style, was also visible in the multilateral ties he forged while in office. The formation of ECOWAS in 1975, and Nigeria's active role in the OAU, bear witness to this.

The challenger personalities of both the Murtala and Obasanjo's regime were brought to bear on Nigeria's foreign policy and its intervention behaviour in Africa. Inarguably, both leaders had bold and strong personalities, together with a well-defined, articulate, coherent and explicit grasp of the substance of Nigeria's foreign policy on Africa. What most exemplifies this attribute was the enforcement of the indigenisation and nationalisation decree of 1977 which led to the Nigerianisation (government takeover) of British assets, following London's continuous support for the regime in Pretoria, and Prime Minister Thatcher's infamous "toothless bull dog" description of the Obasanjo regime's capacity to effect a change in South Africa (Oluleye, 1985; Gambari 1989). Of the two heads of state, however, Murtala Muhammed demonstrated the more radically inclined challenger personality. This reflected in a profound sense of foreign policy activism and sustained commitment to Nigeria's Afro-centric foreign policy orientation.

Situated within the context of Hudson's variables, this leads to a number of observations. First, Yakubu Gowon, Murtala Mohammed and Olusegun Obasanjo's leadership personalities reflect a deep understanding of Nigeria's place in the world, and their role in it. Second, they all maintained an independent individual leadership style, hence their ability to exert a considerable degree of foreign policy authority in their external engagements. Lastly, while in power, they all held a well-established position and clearly defined role within the bureaucratic and national politics of their country. Put differently, the charismatic authority they possessed, and the respect they commanded at home, significantly influenced their exercise of an activist and influential foreign policy abroad. More than anything else, this reinforces the linkage between foreign policy articulation and domestic politics.

Similarly, and in the light of the contrasting difference in personalities, Hudson's (2014) foreign policy variables are further useful to understand the foreign policy and intervention behaviour of both the Shagari and Buhari administrations. First, both Shagari and Buhari lacked the sort of cognitive-psychological profiles which their predecessors had. Second, though their leadership styles were both largely independent, they both failed to achieve the same positive foreign policy effects as those of their predecessors. Lastly, unlike with previous administrations, the domestic climate in Nigeria at the time (which, following Hudson is identified as the position and role of a leader within the bureaucratic and national politics of his state) significantly impacted on many of their foreign policy decisions. For example, when Nigeria's borders were shut against Ghanaians and Chadians without recourse to the ECOWAS treaty on free movement of persons in 1980 and 1983, Nigeria's Afro-centric foreign policy and soft power was significantly dented within the West African sub-region.

Similarly, Hudson's (2014) foreign policy variables are instructive when contrasted with Nigeria's foreign policy and intervention behaviour under the Babangida and Abacha regimes. The case of Babangida's challenger personality showed in his employment of the Nigerian Army as a foreign policy instrument and as a platform for demonstrating Nigeria's capacity to maintain peace within its West African sub-region (Amao, 2012). Babangida, as Adekeye Adebajo argued, saw Nigeria's foreign policy and intervention approach as an avenue to create for himself "an image of a fearless, brave and great leader whose memory he hoped would remain indelible in Nigeria's contemporary history" (Adebajo, 2008: 87).

Abacha, on the other hand, bore the same challenger-oriented approach to foreign policy articulation as Babangida, the only *caveat* being that his overtly ambitious personality impacted negatively on Nigeria's international standing and reputation. Abacha saw foreign policy decision-making as a vital opportunity to "hit back" at his "foreign enemies" and an avenue to crudely act in defiance of international opinion about his regime (Fawole, 1999). The Abacha junta, as is characteristic of tyrannical rule, became confrontational, arrogant, defiant, and, above all, turned a deaf ear to all entreaties. As Fawole argued, "not only was Abacha paranoid at home, he also suspected that there was an insidious international conspiracy against his regime" (Fawole, 2003: 16).

Thus, Abacha's approach to foreign policy was largely reactive and isolationist. Examined from Hudson's (2014) cognitive-psychological profile point of view, both leaders' foreign policy decisions indicate a firm grasp of foreign policy diplomacy, and Nigeria's role in it. Second, they both had an independent leadership approach to foreign policymaking. Lastly, the strength of their imperial presidency at that time meant that they were in firm control of the bureaucratic and national politics of Nigeria at that time.

Since the country's return to civil rule in 1999, subjecting Hudson's (2014) foreign policy variables to the leadership idiosyncrasies of Nigerian leaders evinces a different narrative. The democratic Obasanjo, Yar'Adua/Jonathan and Buhari presidencies have all had a cooperative and consultative approach on issues of foreign policy. When making foreign policy decisions, they have all had to take greater cognisance of Nigeria's prevailing bureaucratic and national politics than under the previous military dispensations. At the same time, the leadership personalities of the three presidencies and their cognitive-psychological profiles could still have a huge impact on Nigeria's Afro-centric presence and intervention policy. Thus, between 1999 and 2007, Olusegun Obasanjo's prominence and leadership personality gave him deep mastery of the intricacies of foreign policy diplomacy, which set him apart from all his other democratic presidential counterparts.

There are a number of possible explanations for this. First, since 1999, the regional environment had changed. The West African sub-region (with the exception of Mali and Côte d'Ivoire in 2011 and the Gambia in 2017), which previously was a hotbed for civil strife and conflict, began to stabilise. As such, unlike that obtained under military rule, ECOWAS performed a sub-regional integration role rather than a conflict intervention role. This meant that Nigeria had a very limited "sub-regional policing role" to play. Second, since Nigeria's return to democratic rule, its leaders have focused more on an economic and citizen diplomacy-themed foreign policy approach.

In interpretive terms, while Afro-centrism remained Nigeria's guiding principle in its engagement with the rest of the world, its history of radical foreign policy has become contingent on the constraints of leadership agency given by civilian rule. This perhaps explains how Nigeria has opened up to international corporate business under the Olusegun Obasanjo (1999–2007), Yar'Adua/Goodluck (2007–2015), and the Muhammadu Buhari (2015–2019) governments.

Lastly, and of no less significance, the oil boom of the 1960s, 1970s, 1980s and early 1990s has waned while Nigeria's economic and security challenges have continued to grow. As such, in contrast to the interventionist approach it favoured in the past, since 2000, Nigeria has adopted a diplomacy-themed approach to resolving conflicts. While an interventionist approach suited the individual imperial demeanour of more-or-less unrestrained military presidential leaders—a function of the idiosyncrasies of leadership—dwindling economic resources over the last twenty-five years (1994–2019) have significantly constrained the state's capacity to deliver on its self-imposed sub-regional policing role in conflicts.

Put differently, Nigeria's ability to commit huge resources to any military intervention within the sub-region has been severely hampered by its home-grown domestic challenges, in particular, a Boko Haram insurgency it has been struggling to contain since 2009. One of the unintended consequences of this insurgency is that Nigeria's image and reputation as a regional power has been severely tainted. Thus, its inability to resolve the decade old insurgency has not only dented Nigeria's erstwhile successful record of peacekeeping operations in Africa and its regional power status, it also puts a question mark on its capacity to provide leadership for the rest of Africa.

Since foreign policy is seen as a continuation and reflection of a country's domestic politics and socio-economic and political environment, it is unsurprising that compared to its aggressive and challenger foreign policy and intervention behaviour under military rule, Nigeria's foreign policy and intervention behaviour post-military rule has sought to maintain a balance between the personal leadership ambitions of democratically constrained presidents and the pursuit of nominal utilitarian goals in an increasingly domestically constrained environment.

Conclusion

This chapter has revisited Nigeria's foreign policy and intervention behaviour in Africa since independence, by contrasting it with foreign policy analysis literature on agency. It finds that regardless of the form of government in power, Nigeria's commitment to an Afro-centric foreign policy orientation remains a permanent feature of state policy and the country's disposition in external affairs. Applying Hudson's (2014) foreign policy analytical variables, the chapter finds that while Nigeria's military, socio-economic and political resources serve as a backdrop to projecting foreign policy influence, the characteristics of individual leadership consistently remain a key driver. This brings to the fore the analytical relevance of signifying a state's foreign policy behaviour from an agency perspective.

In answering the question, to what extent Nigeria's foreign policy and intervention behaviour are leader-dependent, and what impact regime-type has on the shape and direction of Nigeria's foreign policy and intervention behaviour, the answer is twofold. On the one hand, empirical evidence suggests that what determines Nigeria's foreign policy activism is the personality and idiosyncratic sentiments of a materially, bureaucratically and politically relatively unconstrained individual in power. Where Nigeria has had leaders with a firm interest in foreign policy, its foreign policy and intervention behaviour have been very active and pragmatic, as we saw for example during the Yakubu Gowon, Murtala/Obasanjo and Ibrahim Babangida regimes, and under Olusegun Obasanjo as civilian president. Conversely, we have also seen how Nigeria's foreign policy behaviour went into a state of near redundancy under the Shehu Shagari, Abdulsalami Abubakar, and Goodluck Jonathan governments.

Similarly, our exploration equally highlights the influential role played by regime-type. Whether military or civilian, authoritarian versus democratically elected the type of regime influences the country's foreign policy agency and degree of intervention behaviour. There is a noticeable difference in the direction and approach of Nigeria's foreign policy under its military regimes as opposed to its civilian administrations. Under military rule, we observe how unidirectional and autocratic Nigeria's foreign policy and intervention behaviour was. This was because the country's command and control structure rested with the head of state who enjoyed near too absolute authority.

Given the authoritarian nature of military regimes, military heads of states had more scope to significantly influence Nigeria's foreign policy behaviour. In contrast, under civilian administrations, sensitive to domestic constraints, especially with advancing economic and security constraints, foreign policymaking and the articulation of foreign policy tends to follow a multi-directional process. Seen against the type of regime, leadership, organisation and process are arguably considerably more useful than mere structural approaches set on power relations in bringing to light the different degrees of Nigeria's foreign policy and intervention behaviour within West Africa, and on the African continent.

Notes

1 For more on this, see: Constitution of the Federal Republic of Nigeria, 1999. https://publicofficialsfinancialdisclosure.worldbank.org/sites/fdl/files/assets/law-library-files/Nigeria_Constitution_1999_en.pdf (Accessed 13 October 2019).
2 See for example: Nigeria: https://data.worldbank.org/country/nigeria. Accessed 30 October 2019.
3 For more on the enabling factors for Nigeria Africa-centred foreign policy approach, see: Aluko (1977), Abegunrin (2003), Fawole (2003), Gambari (2008), and Adebajo (2008). See also: Nigeria: https://data.worldbank.org/country/nigeria. Accessed 30 October 2019.
4 See Fawole's book on "Understanding Nigeria's Foreign Policy since 1999, Institutions, Structures, Processes and Performance", OAU Press, 2003 and "the Colonial Legacy, and Major Themes in Nigeria's Foreign Policy" in International Relations. Vol. 10 of Nigeria since Independence: The first 25 years A.B. Akinyemi, et al. (Ibadan, Nigeria: Heinemann, 1989) for more on this argument.
5 The extract was part of the speech made by Nigeria's first Prime Minister, Sir Tafawa Balewa, on the occasion of Nigeria's admittance as a member of the United Nations in 1960. It was quoted from: Aluko,(1977, p. 2).
6 A challenger personality develops if an individual or group in an environment succeeds in indicating a political alternative and in effectively mobilising support among their own environment (and/or other environments) against another environment. For more on this, see: Hoogenraad-Vermaak (2001).
7 The Ogoni 9 were members of the Movement for the Survival of Ogoni People (MOSOP). The group sought to champion the cause of the Ogoni people over issues related to environmental degradation. The movement was led by environmental rights activists—Ken Saro-Wiwa, and 8 others, and they were arrested by the Abacha Junta over the killing of some local chiefs. They were found guilty of the murders by military tribunal and sentenced to death in October 1995. The "Ogoni 9" were hanged while Commonwealth heads of government were meeting in New Zealand, a day after the former South African president Nelson Mandela appealed for a stay of execution.
8 See for example, Nigeria, South Africa feud over yellow fever jabs. Reuters 8 March 2012. https://af.reuters.com/article/idAFJOE82700M20120308 (Accessed 7 October 2019).
9 See for example: Nigeria signs African free trade area agreement. 7 July 2019. https://www.bbc.com/news/world-africa-48899701. Accessed 30 October 2019.
10 See for example: Nigerian air force deploys to Senegal as Gambia deadline nears. Reuters, 19 January 2017. https://www.reuters.com/article/us-gambia-politics-force/nigerian-air-force-deploys-to-senegal-as-gambia-deadline-nears-idUSKBN1522OW (Accessed 13 September 2019).
11 Nigeria Donates $500,000, Vehicles to Guinea Bissau for Elections. ChannelsTelevision, 26 April 2019. .https://www.channelstv.com/2019/04/26/buhari-donates-500000-vehicles-to-guinea-bissau-for-elections (Accessed 13 September 2019).
12 Updated: Nigeria recalls Ambassador to South Africa. Premium Times, 4 September 2019. https://www.premiumtimesng.com/news/headlines/350546-breaking-nigeria-recalls-ambassador-to-south-africa.html. (Assessed 13 September 2019).
13 See also, President Buhari beats Yar'Adua record – makes 172-day medical trips in two years. 8 May 2018. https://www.icirnigeria.org/president-buhari-beats-yaraduas-record-%E2%88%92-makes-172-day-medical-trips-in-two-years/ (Accessed 30 October 2019).
14 Ibid.

References

Abegunrin, O. (2003). *Nigerian Foreign Policy under Military Rule, 1966–1999*. Westport, CT: Praeger, USA.

Adebajo, A. (2000). Nigeria: Africa's New Gendarme? *Security Dialogue*, *31*(2): 185–199.

Adebajo, A. (2008). Hegemony on a Shoestring: Nigeria's Post-Cold War Foreign Policy. In A. Adebajo & R. Mustapha (eds.), *Gulliver's Troubles, Nigeria's Foreign Policy after the Cold War*. Scottsville, South Africa: University of KwaZulu-Natal Press, pp. 1–37.

Adeniran, T. (2008). Foreign Policy, External Image and International Relations. In S. Oyovbaire (ed.), *Governance and Politics in Nigeria: The IBB and OBJ Years*. Ibadan, Nigeria: Spectrum Books Ltd, pp. 343–364.

Akinboye, S. O. (1999). Nigeria's Foreign Policy. In Anifowose, R. & F. Enemuo (eds.), *Elements of Politics*. Lagos, Nigeria: Sam Iroanusi Publication, p. 380.

Akintola, B. (2007). Nigeria and the World: A Review of Nigeria's Foreign Policy (1960–2007). *The Nigerian Army Quarterly Journal*, *3*(4): 462.

Akinyemi, A. (1974). *Federalism and Foreign Policy: The Nigerian Experience*. Ibadan, Nigeria: Ibadan University Press, p. 191.

Alao, A. (2011). Nigeria and the Global Powers: Continuity and Change in Policy and Perceptions, South African Foreign Policy and African Drivers Programme. *Occasional Paper Series (SAIIA), No 96*.

Aluko, O. (1977). The Determinant of the Foreign Policies of African States. In O. Aluko (ed.), *The Foreign Policies of African States*. London: Hodder and Stoughton.

Amao, O. B. (2012). Between Afrocentrism and Citizen Diplomacy: The Dilemma of Nigeria's Conflict Resolution Mechanism in Africa. Unpublished Master's Thesis, University of KwaZulu Natal, South Africa, pp. 1–120.

Amao, O. B. & Uzodike, U. O. (2015). Nigeria, Afrocentrism, and Conflict Resolution: After Five Decades – How Far, How Well? *African Studies Quarterly*, *15*(4): 299–319.

Amao, O. B. & Maiangwa, B. (2017). Has the Giant Gone to Sleep? Re-Assessing Nigeria's Response to the Liberian Civil War (1990–1997) and the Boko Haram Insurgency (2009–2015). *African Studies*, *76*(1): 22–43. doi:10.1080/00020184.2017.1285665.

Amao, O. B. (2019). The Foreign Policy and Intervention Behaviour of Nigeria and South Africa in Africa: A Structural Realist Analysis. *South African Journal of International Affairs*, *26*(1): 93–112. doi:10.1080/10220461.2019.1588158.

Badmus, I. A. & Ogunmola, D. (2017). Re-Engineering Nigeria's Foreign Policy in the Post-Military Era: Olusegun Obasanjo's Presidency and Nigeria's African Foreign Policy. *Journal of International and Global Studies*, *9*(1): 56–76.

Fawole, W. (1999). *Paranoia, Hostility and Defiance: General Sani Abacha and the "New" Nigerian Foreign Policy*. Ile Ife, Nigeria: OAU Press Ltd.

Fawole, W. (2003). *Understanding Nigeria's Foreign Policy since 1999, Institutions, Structures, Processes and Performances*. Ile Ife, Nigeria: OAU Press Ltd.

Gambari, I. (1989). *Theory and Reality in Foreign Policy Making*. London: Humanities Press.

Gambari, I. (2008). From Balewa to Obasanjo: The Theory and Practice of Nigeria's Foreign Policy. In A. Adebajo & A. Mustapha (eds.), *Gulliver's Troubles: Nigeria's Foreign Policy after the Cold War*. Scottsville, South Africa: University of KwaZulu-Natal Press, pp. 58–80.

Hélia, S. (2008). "*MPLA (Angola)*": *A Historical Companion to Postcolonial Literatures-Continental Europe and Its Empires*. Edinburgh: Edinburgh University Press.

Hermann, M. G. (1980). Explaining Foreign Policy Behaviour Using the Personal Characteristics of Political Leader. *International Studies Quarterly*, *24*(1): 7–46.

Hoogenraad-Vermaak, S. (2001). The Environment Determined Political Leadership Model: A Comparative Analysis of the Gowon, Babangida and Abacha Regimes. Unpublished Master of Arts dissertation submitted to the University of Pretoria. https://repository.up.ac.za/bitstream/handle/2263/25992/Complete.pdf?sequence=9 (Accessed 7 October 2019).

Hudson, V. M. (2014). *Foreign Policy Analysis: Classical and Contemporary Theory* (2nd edition). Lanham, MD: Rowman & Littlefield Publishers, pp. 1–266.

Jensen, L. (1982). *Explaining Foreign Policy*. London: Prentice-Hall.

Kumah-Abiwu, F. (2016). Leadership Traits and Ghana's Foreign Policy: The Case of Jerry Rawlings Foreign Economic Policy of the 1980s. *The Round Table*, *105*(3): 297–310.

Maoz, Z. & Shayer, A. (1987). The Cognitive Structure of Peace and War Argumentation: Israeli Prime Ministers versus the Knesset. *Political Psychology*, *8*(4): 575–604. doi:10.2307/3790923.

Ofoegbu, R. (1990). The Structure and Processes of Foreign Policy Formulation and Implementation: A Thesis of the Ministry of External Affairs. In G. O Olusanya & R. A. Akindele (eds.), *The Structure and Processes of Foreign Policy Making and Implementation in Nigeria, 1960–1990*. Lagos, Nigeria: NIIA, p. 213.

Ogunbadejo, O. (1980). Foreign Policy Under Nigeria's Presidential System. *The Round Table*, *70*(280): 401–408.

Oluleye, J. (1985). *Military Leadership in Nigeria 1966–1979*. Idaban, Nigeria: Ibadan University Press, p. 29.

Osaghae, E. E. (1998). *Crippled Giant: Nigeria since Independence*. Indianapolis, IN: Indiana University Press.

Preston, J. (2010). Leadership and Foreign Policy Analysis. *Oxford Research Encyclopaedias*, 1–28. doi: 10.1093/acrefore/9780190846626.013.255.

Rosenau, J. (1980). Leadership Change and Foreign Policy Behaviour in Black Africa. *Journal of African Studies*, *7*(3): 138–143.

Shagari, S. (1981). *My Vision of Nigeria*. London/Toronto: Frank Cass, pp. 75–76.

Shaw, C. & Ihonvbere, J. (1996). Hegemonic Participation in Peace-Keeping Operations: The Case of Nigeria and ECOMO. *International Journal on World Peace*, *XIII*(2): 31–60.

Yang, Y. E. (2010). Leaders' Conceptual Complexity and Foreign Policy Change: Comparing the Bill Clinton and George W. Bush Foreign Policies toward China. *The Chinese Journal of International Politics*, *3*(4): 415–446.

7 Zimbabwe and new signifiers

Towards a cultural political economy of foreign policy making

Mike Mavura

Introduction

How do we understand and conceptualise de-colonial signifiers in understanding African modes of being, seeing and acting in foreign policy analysis? The challenge here is to look at culturally grounded conceptual tools to build alternative understandings of foreign policy. This "cultural turn" in foreign policy analysis looks at Zimbabwe's foreign policy within the framework of its main actors—former president Robert Mugabe, current president Emmerson Mnangagwa and the Southern African context—whilst teasing out instructive examples and cases revealing cultural perspectives that seem to be at odds with the rational logic often associated with foreign policy strategies.

It is important to state that my interest here is not to locate culturally grounded foreign policy within either systemic, actor specific (George, 1993) or actor general theory as understood in normative foreign policy theory. Rather, my proposition is that African culturally grounded foreign policy analysis falls outside these hegemonic norms of foreign policy analysis. To illustrate this point, Kenneth Waltz's (1959) "first-image" theory stresses the need to analyse individuals and their behaviour as actors in foreign policy decisions. However, this kind of knowledge is underpinned by a Western understanding of an individual as a rational subject. Lushaba (2017: 2) expands on this when he states that:

> a modern subject is governed by a number of complexes. A citizen is a rational, modern calculative being. To make its claims, the citizen appeals to public reason. More importantly the modern rational subject – better still the citizen-subject has only one way of habiting the world. It does so only through reason.

Lushaba goes on further to ask a pertinent question—the crux of our enquiry here: "What then happens to those whose lives are ordered otherwise than (by the) modern, those whose everyday lives are governed by the logic of ancestral and spiritual intercession—we ask?" (Lushaba, 2017: 2). The subject of Lushaba's enquiry hints at the cultural turn that is advocated here in understanding foreign policy from perspectives beyond Western modernity and rationality. This is important especially as "in international studies, culture was seen as a non-rational element that, like religion and emotion, did not fit nicely in rational models" (Zaharna, 2012: 12). I argue for this cultural turn in understanding foreign policy on the continent because of its distinct default drive, which informs some aspects of foreign policy conduct and how actors operate. Lushaba (2017: 4) illustrates an impasse whereby "modern political reason located in the citizen-subject citizenship works not just as a statutory but as a normative category that precludes certain modes-of-being-in-the-world which are fashioned outside its bounds". It is instructive to look towards Zimbabwe to understand this impasse as well as to expand on the cultural turn framework in foreign policy.

Culture and foreign policy: Mugabe and the use of totemism

Zimbabwe recently experienced tectonic shifts in its politics as a result of the November 2017 coup which ousted President Robert Mugabe, who had been in power since Zimbabwe attained independence in 1980. To all intents and purposes, Robert Mugabe personified and personalised Zimbabwe's foreign policy during his long reign. He fits within Waltz's "first image" level of analysis of foreign policy decision-making that stresses that in order to appreciate and understand international events, we need to look at individuals. Foreign policy includes a range of policies, activities and strategies under which a state interacts with other states and international players. Robert Jackson and Georg Sørensen (2007: 223) observe that foreign policy involves goals, strategies, measures, methods, guidelines, directives, understandings, agreements and so on, by which national governments conduct international relations with each other and with international organisations and non-governmental actors. To get to grips with Mugabe's domestic and foreign political philosophy, Ndlovu-Gatsheni has conceptualised the term "Mugabeism". Mugabeism is understood as:

> a summation of a constellation of political controversies, political behaviour, political ideas, utterances, rhetoric and actions that have crystallised around Mugabe's political life. It is a contested phenomenon with the nationalist aligned scholars understanding it as a pan-African redemptive ideology opposed to all forms of imperialism and colonialism and dedicated to a radical redistributive project predicated on redress of colonial injustices. A neoliberal-inspired perspective sees Mugabeism as a form of racial chauvinism and authoritarianism marked by antipathy towards norms of liberal governance and disdain for human rights and democracy. Mugabeism [is also referred to as] populist phenomenon propelled through articulatory practices and empty signifiers.
>
> (Ndlovu-Gatsheni 2009: 1140)

Normatively, Mugabeism then translates into a conceptual tool to analyse Zimbabwe's foreign policy from an actor-centric perspective. However, what is lacking in this approach are the culturally grounded viewpoints that inform

"Mugabeism" and ultimately the foreign policy analysis that emerges from such analysis. Whereas Robert Mugabe might have been president within the modern political theory understanding of power, he was also generally referred to in Zimbabwe by his totem name *Tsivo Gushungo* (crocodile totem) *of the Karigamombe clan* (the clan that breaks bulls). Mugabe was therefore also known simply as *Gushungo* or *Karigamombe*, totemic and clan names which point towards a reality ulterior to modern political theory. In terms of identity:

> African cosmology dictates that a person is metaphysically conceived as more than just a material or physical object. Totems expand the range of a person's identity to the metaphysical and spiritual via revered animals. Certain species of natural vegetation and wildlife are revered because they are believed to be hosts of spiritual forces. As such, beyond instrumental value, certain animals have significant value because of their spiritual significance as totems. A totem animal thus forms part of one's identity milieu and is aligned to their behaviour, attitude, and way of thinking.
>
> (Machiri & Mavura, 2018)

The spiritual, metaphysical and symbolic force of totemic and clan names in relation to Robert Mugabe offer an alternative analytic window to understand some of the seemingly "illogical" or "ill-informed" foreign policy choices that Zimbabwe has made. Zaharna (2012: 12) reminds us "there are few culturally-informed analytical frameworks that can help us speak constructively about observable differences in public diplomacy and appreciate the significance of those differences for communicating in a multi-cultural global arena". Totems speak to people's stations in society and manifestations of power. Totems provide the link between society and the environment and thus articulate the relationship between people and resources. Robert Mugabe, as *Gushungo* of the *Karigamombe* clan as well as being president, was thus culturally invested with the power to be the ultimate custodian of Zimbabwe. As Mugabe once commented, "there's no African tradition that I don't know. I'm not uncultured" (*The Chronicle*, 2018). Regarding decision-makers in foreign policy, we are reminded to take into account the psychological and societal milieux that envelope decision-makers. Hudson (2005: 10) stresses that:

> The mind of a foreign policy maker is not a tabula rasa: it contains complex and intricately related information and patterns, such as beliefs, attitudes, values, experiences, emotions, traits, style, memory, national, and self-conceptions. Each decision maker's mind is a microcosm of the variety possible in a given society. Culture, history, geography, economics, political institutions, ideology, demographics, and innumerable other factors shape the societal context in which the decision maker operates.

To further understand this cultural angle, and the projections of culture and totems on politics and foreign policy in this case, we need to look into history.

Zimbabwean pre-colonial history tells us that powerful ancestors were represented by the majestic *Mhondoro*/Lion spirit, which possessed mediums tasked with complex tasks. One such powerful spirit was the spirit of *Nehanda*, which only possessed female mediums and only those of the *Mhofu* totem. Her spirit possessed those who were most respected and had leadership skills and qualities. A woman who became Nehanda's spirit medium remained single and was immediately bestowed the spirit name, *Mbuya* Nehanda. When Europeans arrived in Zimbabwe, Nehanda's spirit medium was a woman by the name of Nyakasikana, whose spiritual leadership spanned the entire region of Zimbabwe. Concurrent with *Mbuya Nehanda Nyakasikana*'s mediumship, another great regional Shona spirit medium (*Mhondoro Huru*) Kaguvi, possessed a man by the name of *Gumboreshumba* (the lion's foot), who became known as *Sekuru Kaguvi*. *Mbuya Nehanda (Nyakasikana)* and *Sekuru Kaguvi (Gumboreshumba)* formed the epicentre of resistance and uprising, the First Chimurenga against colonialism in Zimbabwe. Here, the spiritual, metaphysical, physical and symbolic coalesce towards subaltern emancipatory resistance … Put on death row by the colonialists, *Mbuya Nehanda* is said to have prophesied that her bones would rise and liberate Zimbabwe (Machiri & Mavura, 2018).

The bones that rose to fight a guerrilla war that liberated Zimbabwe are embodied in *Gushungo/Karigamombe*, the breaker of bulls. In this sense, Robert Mugabe emerges as the successor of *Ambuya* Nehanda and *Sekuru* Kaguvi and the cultural milieu which underpins power and policymaking in Zimbabwe. How do we discern the weight of this cultural milieu and cultural political economy within the discourse of land and sovereignty which became focal points in the diplomatic fallout with the West?

Mugabe's now infamous "Blair keep your England, and I will keep my Zimbabwe" (Ndlovu-Gatsheni, 2009: 1148) statement signals to a foreign policy of isolationism and disengagement that Zimbabwe adopted in its relations with the West especially after the adoption of the land reform process. In 2003, for example, Mugabe unilaterally disengaged from the Commonwealth group of states over what he called "unfair treatment" over his human rights abuses and democratic shortcomings. Mangwana (2017), commenting on foreign policy under Mugabe, states that:

> now both the United States and the United Kingdom are world powers, who to some extent, can afford to choose or lose friends. But Zimbabwe is not. We are a very small country with a massive budget deficit and suffocating debt overhang. This reality seemed to escape us for a long time as we pursued the massaging of our burgeoning ego, which grew in tandem with our expanding unemployment rate. Our approach to diplomacy was self-defeating.

The point here is that in a conventional sense, this approach to diplomacy indeed appears self-defeating, but the analysis misses the cultural turn; the cultural political economy that underpins what Mugabe means when he says "my Zimbabwe". The spiritual, metaphysical and cultural backdrop of Zimbabwe and the totemic link between society and the environment all coalesce in the *Gushungo* presidency. A *Shona* traditional praise poem speaks of the *Gushungo* totem in terms of the highest reverence: "Tatenda varidzi venyika/ Vakabva Guruuswa/ Varidzi vamazhanje/Maita vokwaZvimba" /"thank you the custodians of the country, who migrated from present day East/Central Africa, the custodians of the fruits, who have now settled in Zvimba" (Mugabe's rural area). What emerges from a cultural political economy and totem narrative is the cultural instruction that informed Mugabe's overriding sense of destiny in relation to Zimbabwean politics and an absolute fearlessness and disregard of the consequences, in pursuit of that destiny.

Lushaba (2017: 3–4) argues that "in the non-European world colonial modernity does not suture society (and we may add foreign policy as well). It does not fully define the norm and ethic of life—there is an excess that escapes it". This history and cultural backdrop serve to illustrate the cultural perspectives that are often excess to consideration and that exist beyond the current available conceptual tools of foreign policy analysis. This is in line with Zaharna's (2012: 22) analysis that:

> Overlooking the cultural component may mean having a limited and potentially distorted understanding of others' behaviours. Analyses that focus only on political, economic, or other traditionally observable factors may provide plausible explanations for the "logical" behaviours of others, but not for the seemingly "irrational" or "unexplained" motivations. To understand what on the surface may appear "irrational", requires public diplomacy moving beyond listening to what Rentsch and her colleagues called "multi-cultural perspective taking". Without an appreciation of the cultural factor, it is difficult to understand the depth of "cultural identity", the challenge of "cultural insecurity", or the implications of "cultural power".

In other words, there are "life-worlds that are constituted otherwise than modern, life-worlds that are at once material, spiritual, mythical, non-rational and ancestral, modern reason does not enjoy an assumed priority" (Lushaba, 2017: 4). However, this cultural envelope that also informs foreign policy is often not easy to decipher in foreign policy readings. For example, under the Mugabe presidency, Zimbabwe's foreign policy objectives were understood to be based on:

> the need to safeguard and enhance the security and prestige of the country as well as geared towards the improvement of quality of life of the Zimbabwean people. This is done through interaction with other countries at various levels in order to influence the behaviour of other actors so that the international environment is conducive to the attainment of these goals.
>
> (Chigora, 2007: 62)

From these objectives, it is difficult to discern the totemic weight and cultural instruction that informed Mugabe's decisions, but this weight and instruction are often what propelled foreign policy practices, especially those that appeared self-defeating or illogical.

Zimbabwe's fallout with the West largely stems from its controversial fast track land reform policy announced in 2000, with the intention of acquiring land from white commercial farmers for redistribution to poor and middle-income landless black Zimbabweans. Mashingaidze (2006: 59) notes in that period:

> land assumed a hegemonic position in day-to-day discourse, political rhetoric, the media, and the country's international relations. Land became the sole signifier of patriotism and sovereignty. Those who seek to question the modalities of Mugabe`s version of land redistribution, are defined as outside the nation, and mere imposters for imperialist designs.

The nexus between the totemism, land and pre-and post-colonial Zimbabwean history in this case speaks to a cultural turn that informs how normative values such as sovereignty are understood and acted upon, using different modes of rationality and worldviews in foreign policy. As a consequence,

> the use of values in public diplomacy may be also controversial … Whilst a value may be "universal" in its appearance, the nature of its expression may vary considerably from culture to culture. Even values that on the surface may be considered basic or fundamental … can be perceived quite differently. Differences in how values are understood and expressed may undermine a campaign's effectiveness.
>
> (Zaharna, 2012: 14)

It may be this conundrum that Mangwana (2018) alluded to in respect to foreign policy under the Mugabe regime being self-defeating.

Regarding Mugabe and the cultural turn in foreign policy, we also have to examine the issue of age. Robert Mugabe was president of Zimbabwe until he was deposed at 93 years old. Menkiti (1984: 173) mentions that as far as African societies are concerned:

> Full personhood is not perceived as simply given at the very beginning of one's life, but is attained after one is well along in society which indicates straight away that the older an individual gets the more of a person he becomes. As an Igbo proverb has it, "What an old man sees sitting down, a young man cannot see standing up." The proverb applies, it must be added, not just to the incremental growth of wisdom as one ages; it also applies to the ingathering of the other excellencies considered to be definitive of full personhood. What we have here then is both a claim that a qualitative difference exists between old and young, and a claim that some sort of ontological progression exists between infancy and ripening old age. One does not just take on additional features such as convergence and divergence from the expected norm, one also undergoes fundamental changes at the very core of one's being.

Within the cultural context of politics, the proposition is that age culturally endowed Mugabe with reverence, which made it difficult for younger statesman to sanction him within the auspices of the Southern African Development Community (SADC) in Southern Africa in particular and Africa in general. To be sure, it is not being suggested that the factor of age alone was the reason behind SADC's seeming inability to act against Mugabe. In addition, within African colonial and post-colonial history, Mugabe has the founding father status of post-colonial Zimbabwe akin to Julius Nyerere in Tanzania, Kenneth Kaunda in Zambia and Sir Seretse Khama in Botswana, amongst others. His role, commitment and sacrifice for the liberation of Zimbabwe, Southern Africa and Africa in general validates his Pan-African credentials within an African lens which understands "being" as fundamentally linked to community via the *Ubuntu* philosophy which dictates that "I am because we are and since we are, therefore I am". This speaks to the "processual nature of "being" in African thought, the fact that persons become persons only after a process of incorporation" (Menkiti, 1984: 172). This also explains the difference and distinction between a *muntu mutupu* (a man of middling importance) and *muntu mukulupe* (a powerful man, a man with a great deal of force—plenitude force at maturation) (Menkiti, 1984: 172).

Africa: Individual and collective foreign policy as expressions of irrationality

It is this cultural turn that enhances our understanding of foreign policy practices as seemingly inimical to reason. In 2013, Mugabe was quoted saying "SADC has no power. Let it be known that we are in SADC voluntarily. If SADC decides to do stupid things, we can pull out" (Mugabe, 2013). This, after SADC had raised concerns over Zimbabwe's intention to hold elections before reforms related to free, fair and credible elections had been put in place. The threat towards unilateralism or disengagement within the SADC context can be understood as plain speech by an elder, warning for the need for cultural modes of African diplomacy and respect akin to quiet diplomacy. In other words, such stunts might be a strategy to communicate that a *muntu mutupu* (a man of middling importance) cannot discipline a *muntu mukulupe* (a man with a great deal of force) in relation to himself and younger SADC statesman.

Mugabe's age and reverence could also be argued to have afforded him cultural power leverage in diplomatic interactions. That reverence, for example, can be linked to South Africa's quiet diplomacy in dealing with Mugabe and the Zimbabwe crisis. South Africa's "quiet diplomacy" approach centred on trying to resolve the crisis in Zimbabwe and influencing positive behaviour by secret negotiation and by refraining from taking specific action such as sanctions. According to Kagwanja (2006), "quiet diplomacy" as a policy was underpinned by the imperatives of African solidarity and peer pressure rather than "megaphone diplomacy" and open criticism of illiberal policies. Quiet diplomacy is an inherently African form of foreign relations that was used to respect Zimbabwe as a sovereign state (Mkhize, 2008: 32) and resonates with the African proverb:

"A matter dealt with gently is sure to prosper, but a matter dealt with violently causes vexation".

This makes sense under the philosophical umbrella of former South African president Thabo Mbeki's African Renaissance project. The African Renaissance was a

> new form of Pan-Africanism which prompted the reformation and establishment of African institutions driven by the need to unite the people and collectively tackle challenges facing the continent ... the African Renaissance was also based on the need to find African solutions to African problems.
>
> (Iroulo, 2017: 2)

Of interest is also the way other southern African countries have engaged in quiet diplomacy in relation to South Africa, especially on the issue of the xenophobic attacks[1] in South Africa. Zimbabwe and the other southern African countries whose citizens were being attacked in South Africa did not intervene or issue strong public condemnations of these attacks. In view of the declared policies of the national interest to protect one's citizens in another country though, interventions could have been expected.

Mugabe is no longer in power in Zimbabwe. A coup led by the current president of Zimbabwe Emmerson Mnangagwa dethroned Mugabe in 2017. The manner of this power shift brings to the fore other aspects in the conduct and practice of foreign policy within African contexts. Such aspects serve to enhance our understanding of the conduct of diplomacy on the continent. Ascending to power via a coup in this day and age would seem to be a worst-case scenario from a diplomacy perspective. Yet, this does not seem to be the case for the new regime in Harare. The African Union (AU) does not look kindly on coup d'états. The AU Constitutive Act states that "governments which shall come to power through unconstitutional means shall not be allowed to participate in the activities of the Union" (African Union, 2000). Furthermore, the Peace and Security Council of the AU is granted the power to "institute sanctions whenever an unconstitutional change of government takes place in a Member State, as provided for in the Lomé Declaration" (Omorogbe, 2010).

Under the Lomé Declaration of 2000, unconstitutional changes of government can be defined as a military coup d'état against a democratically elected government ... According to the AU norm banning unconstitutional changes of government, perpetrators shall not be allowed to participate in elections held to restore democratic order—nor should they be allowed to hold any position of responsibility in political institutions of their state (Ayele-Dersso, 2014, no page number).

In the case of Zimbabwe, there thus seems to be a gap between policy and practice on the part of the AU in respect of the recent, unconstitutional change of government. The events which led to the ousting of Robert Mugabe from power started with the firing of the then Deputy President of Zimbabwe, Emmerson Mnangagwa on November 6, 2017, on accusations of being disloyal, disrespectful and deceitful. Mnangagwa, fearing for his and his family's safety, then fled the country to Mozambique, then to South Africa for "exile". The coup began on November 14, 2017, and by November 24th, Mnangagwa had been sworn in as president. South Africa was the first country that the new president paid a courtesy visit to, to see South African President Jacob Zuma. During his visit in South Africa, Mnangagwa expressed the following:

> I came here to pay my respect to my older brother President Jacob Zuma. Part of the background is that during the war, he (Zuma) was the head of security, both military and civil under MK and I was head of security, military and civil under ZANLA; so we worked together before as brothers in the security sector.
>
> (Mnangagwa, 2017)

Speaking of his escape to South Africa via Mozambique, Mnangagwa pointed out that

> as you know for many years I operated in Mozambique in the department of security. I know the area and it is infested with land mines. Those things are still there, you walk in-between strings to avoid landmines. I did (that) from about 9 pm until about 7:30am the next day. I arrived in Mozambique and we had a lift back to the border to have my passport stamped again on the Mozambican side. Then I phoned a colleague from South Africa that I was on my way to Beira. By the time we arrived in Beira, a small plane had arrived from South Africa to pick me up and I went to South Africa.
>
> (ZimEye, 2018)

Mnangagwa also pointed out that he informed South African authorities that he was in their country through the Speaker of Parliament, Baleka Mbete.

Since then, Mnangagwa has visited all major Southern African countries, Mozambique, Angola, Zambia, Namibi, Tanzania and the Democratic Republic of Congo to appraise these countries on the political developments in Zimbabwe. On his visit to Tanzania, President Mnangagwa visited the "Kaole Art Academy", where he is said to have received military training during the struggle to liberate Zimbabwe. His visit to Zambia revealed further historical ties: the Mnangagwa family had fled from Zimbabwe to Zambia in 1955 in the wake of the Rhodesian repression with President Mnangagwa, later becoming a member of Zambia's United National Independence Party (UNIP).

> He was tasked to help organise the party at Chililabombwe until the end of 1961. He had joined the UNIP student movement at college and was elected into its executive. On his return to Lusaka, President Mnangagwa became Secretary for the UNIP Youth League.
>
> (*The Herald*, 2018)

Mnangagwa's political history in southern Africa is relevant to my proposition for a cultural turn on foreign policy. This cultural turn informs his ascendancy to the presidency in Zimbabwe and the role played by some southern African countries in the process. Hudson (1999) points out that:

> one useful conceptualisation of culture is that of a pre-established set of behavioural competencies, which in turn form behavioural dispositions. According to this variant of culture theory, decision makers faced with new situations will rely on established behavioural competencies in forming an initial policy response. This assumption can also be applied at the nation-state level, where established behavioural predispositions may lessen uncertainty and stress in ambiguous yet salient foreign policy situations. Likewise, observers in one nation-state may be able to identify such behavioural dispositions in other nation-states, lending greater transparency and predictability to international interactions. Do such culturally based action templates exist?

Mnangagwa's process in ascending to the highest office in Zimbabwe points towards a cultural political economy of foreign policymaking in southern Africa. It is not common practice for neighbouring states to harbour high profile political fugitives whilst they are in the process of instituting a coup, a usurpation of power which is against the statutes of SADC and the AU. What this signals is the existence of a strong transnational network of historical interpersonal alliances and relationships between state actors in southern Africa. Such networks were formed within the theatre of decolonising southern Africa with the common understanding that the freedom of one country was meaningless without the freedom of others, an understanding that links back to the cultural ethos of subject-hood and community, premised on *Ubuntu*. It raises the level of interest in these historical transnational alliances amongst political elites in the region. How has a history of cross-border cooperation in the fight against colonialism in the region resulted in intimate political, personal and social alliances which influence foreign policy strategies and positions? As such, we are keen to enquire into what kinds of access these historical relations offer; what sets of leverage this network provides and what kind of dynamism it infuses foreign policy positions and practices in the region with?

We can speculate on these strong historical ties to have had an influence on giving the Harare coup a pass in both SADC and AU fora. In a sense, the Zimbabwe coup leaned on historical ties and alliances to manifest transnationally. It seems odd that Mozambique and South Africa provided passage, bed and breakfast and allowed coup shenanigans on their soil if this was not somehow in their interest. Our interpretation of this odd fact lies in the nature of the person at the centre of this power shift, Mnangagwa himself. This view attributes the individual political actor with cultural currency. In line with this view, Zaharna (2012: 11) points to:

> a nation's culture as one of the three primary elements of its soft power resources that nations can wield to enhance their appeal or attraction. This perspective views soft power as primarily an individual attribute, a resource

> held by an individual political entity. Other conceptions of soft power may be external to the individual entity. In addition to being an individual attribute, soft power could be conceptualised in terms of "relational quality", or emerge through relational dynamics.

In this case, both the individual and the relational seem to coalesce. As alluded to above, Mnangagwa has deep roots in the Southern African political scene. He is part of a transnational network of elite state players bonded by the anti-colonial struggle that enveloped the whole of Southern Africa. It necessitated close cooperation amongst political movements such as the Zimbabwe African National Union-Patriotic Front (ZANU-PF), Zimbabwe African People's Union (ZAPU), the African National Congress (ANC) of South Africa, The Mozambique Liberation Front (FRELIMO), Chama Chama Cha Mapinduzi of Tanzania and the UNIP of Zambia, amongst others. During the anti-colonial struggle this cooperation included intelligence sharing, training, joint security operations and the use of each other's territories for operations, amongst other aspects. The collaboration was informal and below the radar to avoid detection and the thwarting of plans. Stemming from this history, Mnangagwa's dramatic escape and the legitimacy that was afforded by his power grab by regional actors allude to the existence of highly personalised and informal diplomatic channels and machinery.

Conclusion

To conclude, the thoughts expressed in this chapter are an attempt to examine and bring to the fore a range of cultural perspectives that may deepen our understanding of foreign policy and its practice within African settings, using Zimbabwe as an illustrative case. Causal relational dynamics between cultural sensibilities (usually considered to be beyond rationality) and foreign policy practices were explored, in order to highlight cultural political economies that are often at play in diplomatic practices that appear illogical using a normative lens of analysis. The various facets of enquiry on the "cultural turn" are meant to signify the existence of a nascent field of foreign policy analysis grounded in African modes of being, seeing and acting.

Customs, traditions and history permeate diplomatic practice on the continent in ways that have the potential to unsettle norms such as culture being a subsidiary of soft power. A "cultural turn" in the study of African foreign policy also speaks to emancipation as it has the potential to introduce "new" apparatus of coding such as totems and customs, which speaks to lived experiences. Such a "cultural turn" thus not only potentially opens up the field of foreign policy in particular and international relations in general to new signifiers, but also non-traditional participants and experts from other sections of society who carry forms of knowledge beyond the current default drive.

Note

1 In 2008, xenophobic attacks broke out across South Africa over several weeks, within communities as 'community policing and enforcement' took a turn for the worse.

By the time the violence subsided, 62 people had been killed, 670 injured, unknown amounts of property and possessions had been destroyed or looted, and more than 150,000 people had been displaced from their homes across the country (Segatti & Landau, 2011: 10). The latest wave of xenophobic attacks against foreign nationals in 2015 started in the province of KwaZulu-Natal. Thousands were displaced from their homes and up to five people were reported to have been killed when violence spread through the province. It began a week after Zulu king, Goodwill Zwelithini, was reported to have said that foreigners "should pack their bags and go back home". The king later denied making those comments but within days the violence had spread to the country's most populous city, Johannesburg.

References

African Union. (2000). Constitutive Act. Available at: https://au.int/en/constitutive-act [accessed 1 August 2018].

Ayele-Dersso, S. (2014). Abdel Fattah el-Sisi's landslide presidential victory in Egypt presents the African Union with a serious challenge regarding its position on unconstitutional changes of government. Institute for Security Studies. Available at: https://issafrica.org/iss-today/the-au-on-egypt-between-a-rock-and-a-hard-place [accessed 1 August 2018].

Chigora, P. (2007). On crossroads: Zimbabwe's foreign policy and the west. *Journal of Sustainable Development in Africa*, *9*(1): 173–184.

George, A. L. (1993). *Bridging the Gap between Theory and Practice*. Washington, DC: U.S. Institute for Peace.

Hudson, V. M. (1999). Cultural expectations of one's own and other nations' foreign policy action templates. *Political Psychology*, *20*(4): 767–801. Available at: www.jstor.org/stable/3792194.

Hudson, V. M. (2005). Foreign policy analysis: Actor-specific theory and the ground of international relations. *Foreign Policy Analysis*, *1*: 1–30.

Iroulo, L. (2017). Pan-Africanism and the African renaissance through the APRM. *South African Institute of Foreign Affairs Policy Briefing*, *162*: 1–4.

Jackson, R. H. & Sørensen, G. (2007). *Introduction to International Relations: Theories and Approaches*, 3rd edition. Oxford: Oxford University Press.

Kagwanja, P. (2006). South Africa: Breathing new life into "Quiet Diplomacy", electronic briefing paper by centre for international political studies. University of Pretoria. Available at: http://ecommons.hsrc.ac.za/handle/20.500.11910/6347 [accessed 18 August 2018].

Lushaba, L. (2017). Towards a phenomenological critique of modern citizenship: Notes on Heideggerian Seinsverstandnis. *Seminar paper*. University of Cape Town.

Machiri, R. & Mavura, M. (2018). Of totems, history and politics. *The Chimurenga Chronic*. Available at: https://chimurengachronic.co.za/of-totems-history-and-politics/ [accessed 19 July 2018].

Mangwana, N. 2018. The shifting of Zimbabwe's foreign policy. Available at: https://www.herald.co.zw/the-shifting-of-zims-foreign-policy/ [accessed 20 June 2018].

Mashingaidze, T. (2006). The Zimbabwean entrapment: An analysis of the Nexus between domestic and foreign policies in a "Collapsing" militant state, 1990's-2006. *Alternatives: Turkish Journal of International Relations*, *5*(4): 57–76.

Menkiti, I. (1984). Person and community in African traditional thought. In R. Wright (ed.), *African Philosophy: An Introduction*. Lanham, MD: University Press of America.

Mkhize, C. M. (2008). Assessing South Africa's "Quiet Diplomacy" towards Zimbabwe: Strengths and weaknesses. MA Thesis. Pietermaritzburg: University of Kwa-Zulu Natal.

Mnangagwa, E. (2017). Speech to the Zimbabwean Diaspora in Pretoria, South Africa. *Youtube Video, added by 263Now! [Online]*. Available at: https://www.youtube.com/watch?v=V6ZiBDl_iWc [accessed 22 July 2018].

Mugabe, R. (2013). Zimbabwe can pull out of SADC: Mugabe. Available at: http://www.newzimbabwe.com/news-11606-We%20can%20leave%20SADC,%20Mugabe%20warns/news.aspx [accessed 22 June 2018].

Ndlovu-Gatsheni, S. J. (2009). Making sense of Mugabeism in local and global politics: "so blair, keep your England and let me keep my Zimbabwe". *Third World Quarterly*, *30*(6): 1139–1158.

Omorogbe, E. Y. (2010). A club of incumbents? The African union and Coups d'État. *Vanderbilt Journal of Transnational Law*, *44*(123): 124–153.

Segatti, A. & Landau, L. B. (eds.). (2011). *Migration to South Africa: A Regional Development Issue*. Washington, DC: Agence Française de Développement and the World Bank.

The Chronicle. (2018). President now a grandfather. Available at: https://www.chronicle.co.zw/president-now-a-grandfather/ [accessed 21 May 2018].

The Herald. (2018). President details "great escape", poisoning. Available at: https://www.herald.co.zw/president-details-great-escape-poisoning/ [accessed 20 September 2018].

Waltz, K. (1959). *Man, the State, and War: A Theoretical Analysis*. New York: Columbia University Press.

Zaharna, R. S. (2012). *The Cultural Awakening in Public Diplomacy*. Los Angeles, CA: Figueroa Press.

8 Realist conceptions of Kenya's foreign policy and foreign policy behaviour

A theoretical and contextual disposition

Korwa Gombe Adar and Mercy Kathambi Kaburu

Background and introductory context

The ongoing epistemological debate surrounding Kenya's foreign policy and foreign policy behaviour dates back to its independence in 1963 when the country acquired its sovereignty in terms of international law, with rights and duties as well as the capacity to enter into and assume international obligations in international relations. The debate on the nature of Kenya's agency has mainly been advanced through examining Kenya's general diplomatic practice in the global and regional arena (Makinda, 1983; Orwa, 1994; Mwagiru, 2000; Mwanika, 2015). Adar (1994) uses a legal approach to explore the concept of territorial integrity with regard to Kenya-Somalia relations dating back to independence. Using realism as a framework of analysis, this chapter explores the theoretical and contextual disposition of Kenya's foreign policy and foreign policy behaviour with regard to the pursuit of its interests in its region.

Within the Horn of Africa region, particularly in the 1960s–1970s, Kenya was involved in a protracted internal military conflict with *shiftas* (a rebel movement dominated by Kenyan Somalis) who were demanding autonomy in a quarter of the country's territory in the former Northern Frontier District of Kenya. The objective of achieving ultimate unity with Somalia was taking root at a time when Somalia's regional and continental foreign policy priorities and objectives were largely driven by the ideology of *Somaliweyn* (Greater Somalia) or Pan-Somalism (Adar, 1994; Mburu, 2005; and Meredith, 2011).[1] As Meredith (2011) argues, one of the key reasons that led to the overthrow of then Somali president Siad Barre in 1991, as viewed by some in the Somali elite and the Somali foreign policy establishment, was the idea that Barre had betrayed the official, post-independence policy and ideology of Pan-Somalism. It was Pan-Somalism as an internal-cum-regional systemic variable that also drew together the *shifta* movement in Kenya. Kenya viewed this *Somaliweyn* ideology-driven movement as a direct threat to its sovereignty and territorial integrity. This threat constituted the key determinant in Kenya's foreign policy behaviour towards the Horn of Africa in general and Somalia in particular (Adar, 1994).

During the Organisation of African Unity (OAU) Summit in 1981 in Nairobi, President Siad Barre reiterated that Somalia had no ambitions of claiming any part of Kenya's territory (Zartman, 1985: 100). President Siad Barre was conscious of Kenya's long-term foreign policy interests regarding the preservation of its territorial boundaries acquired at the time of independence. The preservation of boundaries in Africa after decolonisation was entrenched under AHG Res. 16(1) at the 1964 OAU Cairo Summit, with *uti possidetis juris* recognised in international law, henceforth becoming the continental guiding normative principle. Specifically, the resolution provided that the Heads of State and Government "solemnly declare that all member states pledge themselves to respect the borders existing on their achievement of national independence" (OAU, 1965, AHG Res. 16 (1), (2)). Shaw (1997: 494) observes that

> the acceptance of the colonial borders by African political leaders and by the OAU itself neither created a new rule nor extended to Africa a rule previously applied only in another continent. Rather it constituted the recognition and confirmation of an existing principle.

This internal *shifta* conflict contained both systemic centrifugal and centripetal factors. In addition, there was Somalia government's drive for the unity of all the Somali speaking peoples in the Horn of Africa, something that influenced President Jomo Kenyatta (Kenya) and Emperor Haile Selassie (Ethiopia) to sign a military pact in 1964. This military agreement has been renewed over the years, namely between the leaderships of Presidents Daniel arap Moi (Kenya) and Maj. Mengistu Haile Mariam (Ethiopia) in 1979, and President Uhuru Kenyatta (Kenya) and Prime Minister Hailemariam Desalegn (Ethiopia) in 2015.

The balkanisation of Somalia into self-proclaimed autonomous regions, including for example, Somaliland, Puntland, and Jubaland, as well as the continued volatility of the successive governments in Somalia, however, put in abeyance the ideology of Greater Somalia (Pan-Somalism). As such, it has featured only intermittently in the pronouncements by, *inter alia*, movements in Somalia such as the Islamic Courts Union (ICU) or the Union of Islamic Courts (UIC) and *al-Shabaab*.[2] *Al-Shabaab* pledges its loyalty to *al-Qaeda* and the Islamic State of Iraq and al-Sham (ISIS) from which the group gets its financial, logistical and training support. By implication, this has given a global dimension to the role of this terrorist movement.

Within the East African regional context, Kenya is one of the founding members of the East African Community I (EAC I, 1967–1977) and the EAC II (1999–present) and the key economic hegemon in the region. It continues to anchor its foreign policy priorities around an economic and politically grounded national interest set against a context of regional stability. The country's foreign policy establishment pursues its economic and political interests, as well as stability within the parameters of the EAC. This is salient to the pursuit of Kenya's immediate foreign policy interests and behaviour. Stability in the Horn of Africa and the EAC regions is understood with a realist conception of the national interest in mind and this view has been key and the cornerstone of Kenya's regional and continental geo-strategic and geo-political interests since independence (Adar, 2007, 2011).

The decision by President Mwai Kibaki in 2011 to invoke the right of *self-defence* enshrined in Article 51 of the United Nations Charter,[3] to deploy, with the acquiescence of the leadership in Somalia, the Kenya Defence Forces (KDF) code-named *Operation Linda Nchi* (Swahili for Operation Protect the Country) in Somalia against the *al-Shabaab* can be understood in this broad context.[4] Other scholars would argue that Kenya's military involvement in Somalia was not carried out within the meaning of Article 51 of the United Nations (UN) Charter (Tams, 2009). However, then UN Secretary General Ban Ki-moon, during his visit to Kenya in December 2011, in many respects sanctioned and gave some elements of legitimacy on behalf of the organisation in relation to Kenya's military engagement in Somalia by dubbing it a "sacrifice" operation.[5] Equally, Kenya's foreign policy decision was informed by the economic threat emerging from the continued attacks by the *al-Shabaab*. In particular, the tourist sector which contributes significantly to the country's economy remained under bewilderment and constant threat with Western states issuing travel advisories (Kenya Defence Forces, 2014; Anderson & McNight, 2015).

What explains *al-Shabaab*'s frequent attacks on Kenya? There are various competing viewpoints with respect to the underlying factors that influence *al-Shabaab*'s incursions into Kenya. One perspective draws our attention to the long-standing objective of the *al-Shabaab* movement to attract support from the ranks of Muslim youths in Kenya, the Horn of Africa, Africa and globally (Botha, 2014). Other scholars place the attacks by *al-Shabaab* on the movement's reaction to Kenya's military involvement in Somalia (Anderson & McKnight, 2015). The global dimension is the more imperative one, mainly because *al-Shabaab* is determined to demonstrate to its followers, sympathisers and the world at large about the level of its commitment to the cause and its whole *raison d'etre*. This global perspective pursued by *al-Shabaab* is similar to that of other terrorist organisations (Chaliand & Blin, 2007; Piazza, 2009). Other scholars yet again argue that the main factors that determine the *al-Shabaab*'s incursions into Kenya are driven by other factors, namely Kenya's proximity to Somalia; Kenya's international status and visibility; the exposure to ready media coverage; the opportunities Kenya as an international tourism destination offers; the existence of Kenyan foreign fighters; the ability to link up with terror cells in Kenya (home grown networks); authoritarianism versus democracy and the vulnerability of democracies[6] as well as operations eased by corruption (Cannon & Pkalya, 2017).

In the minds of Kenya's foreign policy establishment, however, one of the key objectives of *al-Shabaab* is that the terrorist organisation aims to establish a state, the *Islamic Emirate of Somalia*. This is meant to be comprised of Somalia, Somaliland, Puntland, North-Eastern Kenya, Ogaden (Ethiopia), and Djibouti,[7] rekindling the decades old *Somaliweyn* conflict triangulation scenarios in the region associated with the *shifta* movement and the Somali administrations of the 1960s–1990s. As Ali (nd.: 8) observes, "the *Shabaab* traces its roots back to the erstwhile irredentist Islamic movement which for years aimed at recovering Somali-inhabited regions of Ethiopia and Kenya. It continues to use a hybrid of irredentism and global *Jihad*" (holy war). In other words, *al-Shabaab* operates largely on the ethos of international *jihadism*, which is consistent with those of *al-Qaeda* and ISIS.

Within Africa, Kenya's diplomatic engagement has been and is influenced by a number of factors. These include the drive for enhanced intra-African economic trade, a desire for the maintenance of stability in Africa and respect for the territorial integrity and borders. There is also the principle of non-interference in the internal affairs of other sovereign states. This is understood within the meaning of the principle of *uti possidetis juris*[8] recognised under international law, among other continental norms and principles enshrined in the OAU Charter and now the Constitutive Act of the African Union (AU).

We take cognisance of the fact that International Relations theories such as liberalism, neo-realism and constructivism, among others, can provide useful explanatory values when assessing Kenya's foreign policy and foreign policy behaviour. This study, however, proceeds from the premise that Kenya's regional and continental foreign policy and foreign policy behaviour is shaped mainly by its national interest defined in the context of realism. More specifically, the chapter examines the interplay between realism as theory and Kenya's foreign policy and foreign policy behaviour. In other words, it is worth asking what *place* realism and the concepts inherent to it occupy in the formulation of Kenya's foreign policy and its foreign policy behaviour.

The chapter is divided into four sections. The introduction broadly outlines the key issues associated with Kenya's foreign policy and foreign policy interests. The following section puts into perspective the theoretical and conceptual frameworks for the analysis of the study. More specifically, it focuses on the realist conception of the national interest and its relevance to Kenya's foreign policy and foreign policy behaviour. The third section, which is the core of the chapter, covers Kenya's foreign policy and foreign policy interests in Africa using the AU; more specifically, the AU Mission in Somalia (AMISOM) as the key ontological variable which is used herein to assess the relevance of a realist analysis. Using AMISOM as our focal unit of analysis, we examine the extent to which Kenya as a state has effectively used multilateral diplomacy to define and pursue her national interests in Somalia driven by realist theoretical underpinnings.

Even though the merger of the KDF with AMISOM transformed the role of Kenya in Somalia into a continental AU peacekeeping mission and a multilateral diplomatic and seemingly normative driven initiative, we argue that realist national interest conceptions continued *a fortiori* to underpin the country's short-term and long-term foreign policy core objectives and interests. These are centred on the preservation of her territorial sovereignty, secure economic interests and the desire for stability in the region, particularly in Somalia. This study therefore wishes to make an original contribution *ceteris paribus* by drawing attention to the interface between the theoretical explanatory value of realism and Kenya's foreign policy and foreign policy behaviour. Finally, the fourth section puts into proper perspective the summary and conclusion of the study.

Realism: Theoretical and conceptual frameworks for analysis

The realist conception of the national interest dates back to Niccolò Machiavelli, who, in *The Prince*, predicted the importance of the role of interest in international relations. He argued that the prince as a ruler had to be conscious of when and when not to use power (Clinton, 1994). A state's national interest, which defines the *raison d'etat* (reason of state) has dominated foreign policy studies since the inception of the nation-state at the 1648 Treaty of Westphalia. For Hans Morgenthau (1948, 1985), whose works over several decades continued to dominate the epistemological debate surrounding realism, a state's primary or principal concern driven by the national interest remains its *raison d'etre* in international relations. In other words, sovereign states, the dominant actors in international relations (one of the key assumptions of realism), must protect their physical (territory), political (political and economic system) and cultural (historical values and experiences) identities against any interference and encroachment by any other state or actor. Given the anarchic nature of the international system, sovereign states guarding the state's national interest and values are imperative. For realists such as Thucydides, power (military might) which gives a state the means to compel others to do what is in their national interest is an important instrument for the state's survival (struggle for power) in the international system (Connor, 1984; Crane, 1998).[9] It is a state's domestic or national variables that determine its behaviour in the international system. For realists, this provides a clear distinction between domestic politics and international politics.

For the most part of its post-independence history, Kenya hardly involved itself in external military interventions across its territorial boundaries. Instead, its foreign policy and foreign policy behaviour were driven by what has been called "quiet diplomacy" (Makinda, 1983; Orwa, 1994). The deployment of the KDF in Somalia in 2011, therefore, marked a clear paradigm shift in the country's foreign policy and foreign policy behaviour. Of importance to the country, and this study in particular, was the cardinal responsibility for the preservation of its national interest understood from a realist theoretical epistemology.

In the view of the country's foreign policy establishment, the state was threatened by the vicissitude of *al-Shabaab*'s frequent incursions into Kenya's territory. The incursion by *al-Shabaab* into Kenya threated the country's territorial integrity and *raison d'etre*. The Kibaki administration in response invoked the country's military resources at its disposal to ensure that the preservation of Kenya's national interest understood in the context of *realpolik* (power politics) conceptions of stability, was maintained at the national and regional systemic levels. The deployment of the KDF in Somalia provides useful explanatory value in contextualising Kenya's *realpolitik* national foreign policy interest.

From KDF to AMISOM: Realism and Kenya's foreign policy behaviour towards Somalia

By the time Kenya deployed its military in Somalia in 2011, the AMISOM had been in a peacekeeping military operation in the country since 2007. The

Intergovernmental Authority on Development (IGAD) Mission for Somalia (IGASOM) proposed by the member states in 2005 did not materialise. Therefore, AMISOM was established in January 2007 by the AU Peace and Security Council (PSC) and endorsed by the UN Security Council in its Resolution 1744 (2007). AMISOM assumed the peacekeeping responsibilities and was mandated to support, among other things, the:

> Transitional Federal Institutions (TFIs) in their efforts towards the stabilisation of the situation in Somalia and the furtherance of dialogue and reconciliation; to facilitate the provision of humanitarian assistance; and create conducive conditions for long-term stabilisation, reconciliation and development in Somalia.
>
> (AU, 2007, Art. IV)[10]

The establishment of the AMISOM was necessitated by the persistent instability in Somalia that threatened peace and security in Africa, in particular the existence and operational functions of the Transitional Federal Government (TFG) of Somalia. Established in 2004, in Nairobi, Kenya, the TFG remained volatile and incapacitated in the wake of the state collapse of 1991 and the persistent intra-Somali clan conflicts, the rise of the ICU and later the *al-Shabaab*.[11] The unstable TFG, the rise of ICU and *al-Shabaab* led to the prevailing volatility and instability of the strategic environment not only in the Horn of Africa but also in Africa as a whole and beyond. By strategic environment, we mean the realm of advancing individual and/or collective interests through interaction with state and non-state actors. A strategic environment is a complex and interlocking system which has implications on actors therein. The prevailing instability in Somalia and its inherent sub-regional (Horn of Africa) and regional (Africa) ramifications gradually influenced Kenya's persistent military involvement in Somalia.[12] Of the fifty-four member states of the AU, only six countries, namely Burundi, Djibouti, Ethiopia, Kenya, Sierra Leone, and Uganda contributed peacekeeping troops to the AMISOM.[13]

Table 8.1 shows the military contingents and police contributed by the six AU members, with Kenya joining AMISOM in 2012. The six AU member states, it can be argued, have made stabilising and constructive economic, political and military contributions in Somalia. These efforts are driven by the spirit of the AU's neo-Kantian normative principles enshrined in its Constitutive Act which is centred on the continental discourse of African solutions to African problems.[14]

By the time Kenya joined the AMISOM in 2012, the Mwai Kibaki administration was influenced by two main factors. First, the administration considered its main objective as one of largely preventing *al-Shabaab* from making frequent incursions across Kenya's territorial borders. More specifically, it can be said the KDF was integrated into AMISOM following the accomplishment of one of its original objectives, that is, the liberation of Kismayo from *al-Shabaab* forces in September 2012 (Gayathri, 2012). The decision to integrate the KDF into

Table 8.1 AU member states contributing troops and police to AMISOM (countries listed alphabetically)

Country	*Year joined*	*Troops*	*Police*	*Year joined*
Burundi	2007	5432	–	–
Djibouti	2011	960	–	–
Ethiopia	2014	4395	–	–
Ghana	–	–	56	2013
Kenya	2012	3664	21	2013
Nigeria	–	–	140	2010
Sierra leone	2013	850	47	2010
Uganda	2007	6223	402	2010

Sources: Compiled from amisom-au-org. Accessed 16 November 2018 as well as the *Military Balance* (2007–2016) and the *International Institute for Strategic Studies* various years (2007–2016). These figures vary from source to source and the years.

AMISOM is in line with: the long-standing general policy objectives documented by the Ministry of Foreign Affairs and International Trade in 2014 which include, among other foreign policy issue areas:

> Protecting Kenya's sovereignty and territorial integrity;
> Promoting sub-regional and regional integration and cooperation;
> Enhancing regional and global peace and security;
> Advancing the economic prosperity of Kenya and her people;
> Protecting Kenya's image and prestige;
> Promoting international cooperation and multilateralism; and
> Promoting and protecting the interests of Kenyans abroad.
> (Kenya, Ministry of Defence, 2014: 19)

Second, the option of taking a multilateral approach to conflict resolution in Somalia was viewed by the Kibaki administration as more viable than a unilateral one. When contributing to the debate in Kenya's National Assembly on the motion to approve the deployment of the KDF under AMISOM, the Minister for Defence explained to the Members of Parliament (MPs) that:

> the Intergovernmental Authority on Development (IGAD) and African Union (AU) Extraordinary Session attended by Heads of State, called upon Kenya to consider the integration of its forces in Somalia into the African Union Mission in Somalia;… this House approves the deployment of the National Security Forces in Somalia to serve under the auspices of AMISOM, pursuant to provisions of Article 240 (8) (a) (i) and (ii) of the Constitution.
> (Kenya, National Assembly, 2011: 18)

Article 240 (8) provides that "the Council may, with the approval of Parliament (a) deploy national forces outside Kenya for (i) regional or international peace support operations; or (ii) other support operations" (Kenya, 2010: Article 8 (a) (i)(ii)).[15] This is what set the stage for Kenya's decision to join AMISOM and henceforth directly engage in multilateral diplomacy in Somalia. The AMISOM serves dual but complementary multilateral diplomatic roles for Kenya. The AU peacekeeping mission, we argue, was established to promote stability, peace and security in Somalia, in conformity with the continental normative principles enshrined in the Constitutive Act. In other words, multilateral diplomacy driven by the AMISOM not only serves the interests of the AU but also the individual interests of the member states involved in the initiative, Kenya included. It should also be noted that Kenya has remained instrumental in the efforts towards a stable Somalia since the fall of Siad Barre in 1991 and the subsequent state collapse. For example, between 1996 and 2001 President Moi made numerous unilateral attempts to reach out to the warring factions, with the aim of ending the war and establishing structures of governance in Somalia. These efforts were however undermined by claims of exclusion by some clan factions, and also by Ethiopia's parallel negotiation initiative, which was perceived as more inclusive (Menkhaus, 2014). It is, however, notable that Kenya played a prominent role that led to the conclusion of the 2004 Somali peace process (Adar & Yoh, 2006).

Strategic environment and interdependence: Implications on Kenya's foreign policy interests

The analysis in this section attempts, from a theoretical perspective, to contextualise the factors that determined Kenya's strategic setting in relation to the strategic environment culminating in the deployment of the KDF in Somalia. In doing so, realism is used as the theoretical point of departure. We specifically proceed from the premise that Kenya's strategic setting, influenced by the prevailing unstable strategic environment, can be explained within a realist context. By strategic setting, in this context we mean planning and employment of military and economic resources to achieve foreign policy objectives and national interests.[16] O'Loughlin (1989: 292) has aptly argued that since the end of the Second World War, "all nations, regardless of location, history, size, political orientations, leadership style, government form, and military and economic strength, were motivated by the same goal—maintenance of world order according to the logic of power". We argue, *ceteris paribus*, that realism provides useful explanatory values and theoretical tools to epistemologically investigate Kenya's foreign policy behaviour towards Somalia.

Realism comes into play for two main reasons. First, as we have observed in the chapter, preservation of its territory (sovereignty and territorial integrity) remains the key tangible attribute that has historically influenced Kenya's foreign policy and foreign policy behaviour in Africa, particularly in the Horn of Africa. Second, as one of the dominant economies (a key national attribute) in the region, stability, peace and security in the Horn of Africa and Somalia in particular are important ingredients for Kenya's national interest.

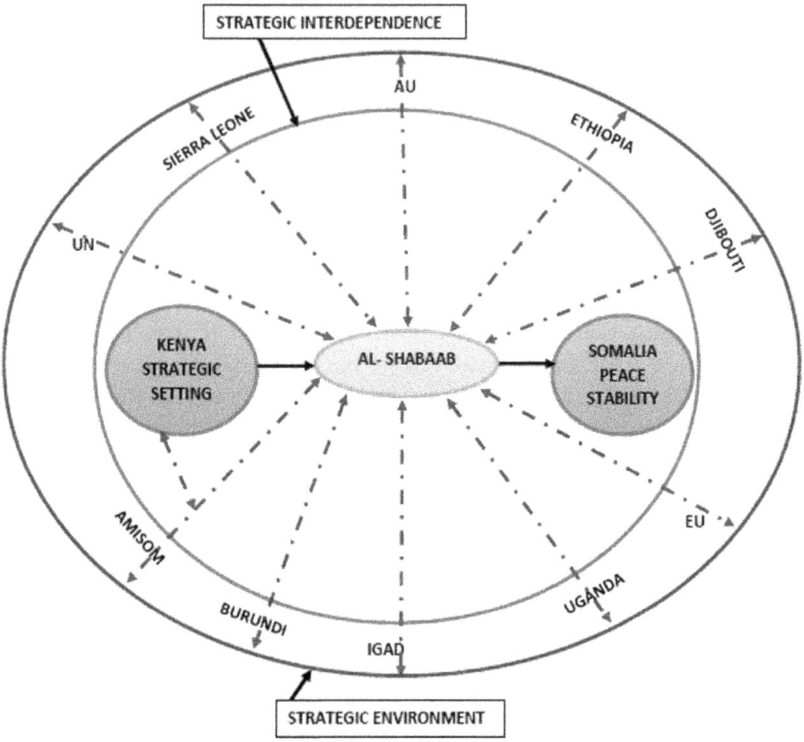

Figure 8.1 Strategic environment and its impact on Kenya's decision to deploy KDF in Somalia. Source: Constructed by the authors (2018).

Figure 8.1 depicts a situation in which the actors such as Kenya and AMISOM are entangled in an interlocking strategic interdependence scenario, by implication influencing their decision to be directly involved in Somalia with the objective of eradicating *al-Shabaab* and promoting peace and stability as well as the viability and durability of the TFG and the TFIs. Strategic interdependence concerns areas of common interest to actors that influence their individual and collective actions, irrespective of their differences, and which by implication lead to mutually beneficial outcomes for the common good. The multiplicity of actors herein, Kenya included, are directed towards one goal. Specifically, the common good in the context of this study is based on the objective of achieving the Lockean conception of stability, peace and security in Somalia as mandated to the AMISOM by the AU.

By strategic interdependence we mean a systemic environment in which actors (in this case, Burundi, Djibouti, Ethiopia, EU, IGAD, Kenya, Sierra Leone, Uganda and the UN, among others) are interconnected as they pursue their individual and/or collective interests. However, in this study the focus is on Kenya as the key actor. We take cognisance of the fact that there are more complex geo-strategic and geo-political, as well as centrifugal and centripetal factors, involving among other elements, a plethora of actors other than those depicted in Figure 8.1. However, the purpose of Figure 8.1 is mainly to provide a picture of the strategic environment, the strategic interdependence and the strategic setting which have entangled Kenya in its unilateral and multilateral military engagement in its quest to eradicate the key intervening variable, that is, *al-Shabaab*, and by implication promoting stability, peace and security in Somalia. As demonstrated in Figure 8.1, Kenya, *al-Shabaab*, and Somalia serve as independent, intervening and dependent variables respectively.

As indicated in Figure 8.1, the individual and/or collective interests include, for example, the elimination of *al-Shabaab* and the stabilisation of the TFG and its TFIs as well as the promotion and consolidation of peace and stability in Somalia in general. As such, it needs to be reiterated that Kenya's military involvement in Somalia in 2011 was not a conventional war *per se* involving state-to-state military exchanges. In other words, Kenya was not at war with Somalia, but was merely engaged in hot pursuit of the *al-Shabaab*.

The debate surrounding Kenya's direct military involvement in Somalia centre around a number of the country's foreign policy interests. Due to uncertainty surrounding the volatility of the TFG that gave space for the growth of *al-Shabaab* and the movement's incursions into Kenya, the KDF action can be characterised as falling within the meaning of *jus ad bello* (just war theory) advanced by St Augustine and St Thomas Aquinas (Kenya, Ministry of Defence, 2014).[17]

The decision to invoke the right to self-defence against *al-Shabaab* was approved by the Cabinet Committee on Security and Foreign Relations on 4 October 2011 (Kenya, Ministry of Defence, 2014: 78). When contributing during the debate in parliament on the question of Kenya's deployment of troops in Somalia, the Minister of State for Defence stated, *inter alia*:

> The KDF in exercise of the right to self-determination under Article 51 of the Charter of the UN engaged the *al-Shabaab*. This was done in defence of the sovereignty and the territorial integrity of the Republic. Consequently, the KDF launched the Operation *Linda Nchi* in hot pursuit of al-Shabaab, crossed into Somalia.
>
> (Kenya, National Assembly 2011: at 19)

The deployment of the KDF into Somalia was therefore meant, among other things, to serve the interests of both Kenya and Somalia. Article 51 of the UN Charter places no limitation on "the inherent right of individual or collective self-defence if an armed attack occurs against a Member of the United Nations" (United Nations Secretariat, 1948: Article 51). We argue that where non-state actors carry out terrorist acts across international borders inflicting damage on the sovereignty of the state, as was the case with *al-Shabaab* against Kenya, the doctrine of self-defence applies. It forms part of general state practice.

The meaning of self-defence and its application as inscribed in Article 51 of the UN Charter, particularly in relation to non-state actors, however, remains contentious among scholars.[18] The concepts of self-determination, sovereignty and territorial integrity inscribed in the Minister of Defence's statement are fundamental for any state's *raison d'etre*, including Kenya's. In practice, states normally invoke the right to self-defence if these same doctrinal principles are threatened by external aggression. Indeed, the protection of citizens is one of the cardinal responsibilities of any sovereign state. In the context of a realist conception of the national interest, military actions conducted in the defence of these same doctrinal principles, implicitly and/or explicitly, promote the prestige of a state in international relations. In its 2014 document, Kenya's Ministry of Foreign Affairs and International Trade outlined the principles that guide the country's foreign policy interests and foreign policy behaviour as follows:

Sanctity of sovereignty and territorial integrity of the Republic of Kenya;
peaceful co-existence with neighbours and other nations;
resolution of conflicts by peaceful means;
promotion of regional integration; respect for equality, sovereignty and territorial integrity of states; and
respect for international norms, customs and laws

(Kenya, Ministry of Foreign Affairs and International Trade, 2014: 19)

These guiding principles are in line with the general spirit of the Constitutive Act of the AU and the UN Charter among other international instruments recognised under international law.

The *Operation Linda Nchi* commenced inside Kenya and continued with hot pursuit operations inside Somalia. Later, hot pursuit actions were jointly carried out with TFG forces (Kenya, National Assembly 2011, at 19).[19] Principally, instability prevailing in the strategic environment and its inherent ramifications in Kenya influenced the decision to deploy the KDF in Somalia after the frequent *al-Shabaab* incursions into the country, particularly in the north-eastern and coastal regions of the country. Examples for the latter include attacks at Dadajabula Police Post (2009); the General Service Unit (GSU) in Liboi (2010); Bula Hawa (2011) and Doble (2011); as well as laying mines in Mandera Town (Kenya, National Assembly 2011, at 19). One MP put the threat of *al-Shabaab* into a broader context, arguing that "the issue of Somalia and *al-Shabaab* is not a Kenyan problem. It is more of an African, problem, and a world problem" (Kenya, National Assembly 2011, at 19). This suggests that national, regional and global security was simultaneously threatened. The issue of Somalia therefore entangled actors, states or other actors in an interlocking strategic interdependence driven by considerations of *realpolitik*.

Kenya's geo-strategic and geo-political interests in the Horn of Africa have remained consistent throughout its independence history (Adar, 2011). The emergence of *al-Shabaab* and its terrorist incursions in the country explains this consistency whose historical origins lie in the protracted internal military efforts directed against the *shiftas* in the 1960s–1970s. In one of its Defence White Papers, the Ministry of Defence outlined Kenya's interests as underpinned by "sovereignty and territorial integrity; national security; economic prosperity and well-being of Kenyans; and national prestige" (Kenya, Ministry of Defence, 2017: 2). The *Operation Linda Nchi* as explained by one MP was to "protect both our strategic economic interests" (Kenya, National Assembly 2011, at 21). In this context, Kenya's *realpolitik*, driven by various attributes of state power which include but is not limited to security, political and economic interests, played key roles in its involvement in Somalia. "The purpose of the operation was to defend the security of the people, the security of the refugees who live among us…; our economy was going to be badly affected" (Kenya, National Assembly 2011, at 22). Specifically, the inflow of refugees into the country from Somalia and the abduction of tourists in Kenya by *al-Shabaab* had the potential of having a negative impact on Kenya's economy and the socio-political well-being of the people (Kenya, National Assembly, 2011, at 52).

The inflow of refugees into Kenya from Somalia not only continued to create an economic burden on the country, but the main refugee centres, particularly Dadaab and Kakuma also became the breeding ground for *al-Shabaab*. Figure 8.2 indicates that by the time the KDF engaged in military operations in Somalia in 2011, the refugee inflow into Kenya had increased markedly, reaching more than 500,000 (after which, between 2013 and 2017, it declined steadily). This is attributable to KDF and AMISOM military operations in Somalia.

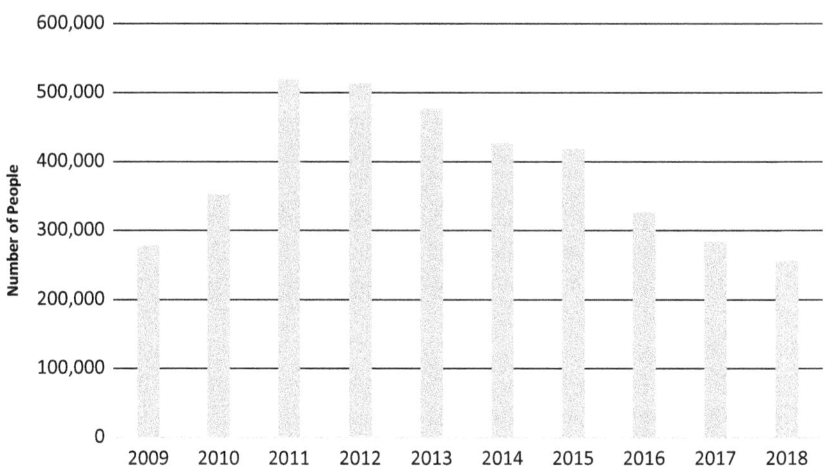

Figure 8.2 Somalia refugee and asylum seekers in Kenya. Source: www.unhcr.org/ke/wp-content/uploads/sites/2/2018/08/Kenya-Statistics-Package-July-2018.pdf. Accessed 18 November, 2018.

Other than the inflow of refugees into the country, the key concern of Kenya's foreign policy establishment centred on the potentially negative impact of the *al-Shabaab* incursions on the tourism industry. Some Western countries such as France, the UK and the USA issued official travel warnings to their citizens against visiting Kenya. However, despite this fear, the inflow of tourists remained steady during these years. For example, in 2008, 2009 and 2010, the number of tourists who visited Kenya reached 1,203,224; 1,490,448; and 1,609,110 respectively.[20] This accounted for an average of about 4.4% of Kenya's Gross Domestic Product (GDP). The travel warning by the Western countries as well as the KDF military involvement in Somalia notwithstanding, in 2010 and 2011 the number of tourists who visited Kenya increased from 1,822,900 to 1,873,752 respectively, which amounted to an average of 4.7% of the country's GDP. These figures declined steadily from 2013 to 2015 (1,434,000 to 1,261,000 to 1,114,000 international visitors respectively) and started rising again in 2016 with 1,268,000 visitors and 2017 with 1,364,000 visitors accounting for an average of 3.9% GDP within this period.

It is important to note that these *al-Shabaab* related issue areas, with their global, continental and sub-regional (Horn of Africa) strategic interdependence scenarios, characterised by social, economic and political dimensions, have had implications on Kenya's foreign policy behaviour towards Somalia.

Al-Shabaab remains the key variable that determines strategic interdependence in Somalia, the Horn of Africa and Africa in general, despite the rivalry of the AMISOM troop-contributing countries. In what can be considered as spheres of influence against *al-Shabaab* in Somalia, the troop-contributing countries are responsible for specific regions within Somalia. In Figure 8.3, while the Burundi National Defence Force (BNDF) contingent is responsible for Bay and Bakool regions (Sector 5), the Djibouti Armed Forces (DJAF) contingent is assigned the Hiiraan and Galgaduud areas (Sector 4). On the other hand, the Ethiopian National Defence Force (ENDF) contingent operates in the Bay, Bakool and Gedo regions (Sector 3), with the KDF contingent responsible for Lower and Middle Juba regions (Sector 2) and the Uganda People's Defence Force (UPDF) has been assigned Banadir (Mogadishu) and Lower Shabelle areas (Sector 1). The specific areas which the KDF captured between January and September 2012 and controlled thereafter, include Hoosingo town-Lower Juba, the main gateway for *al-Shabaab*; Fafadun town-Gedo region, Afmadhow town, Miido town, Harbole and Biibi towns, Sooyac and Jana Cabdala towns and Kismayo (Kenya, Ministry of Defence, 2014).

Most of these sectors (as they are known in AMISOM operational and institutional circles) have been liberated, with *al-Shabaab* engaging in guerilla and terrorist tactics. Kenya's *realpolitik* interests shifted from its original unilateral military engagement through the deployment of the KDF in 2011, to one driven by multilateralism and AU AMISOM peacekeeping Track One diplomacy. Track One diplomacy simply means an official or formal interaction of state-to-state, or by representatives of International Governmental Organisations (IGOs) such as the UN, and regional organisations, as well as the Vatican (Mapendere, 2006).

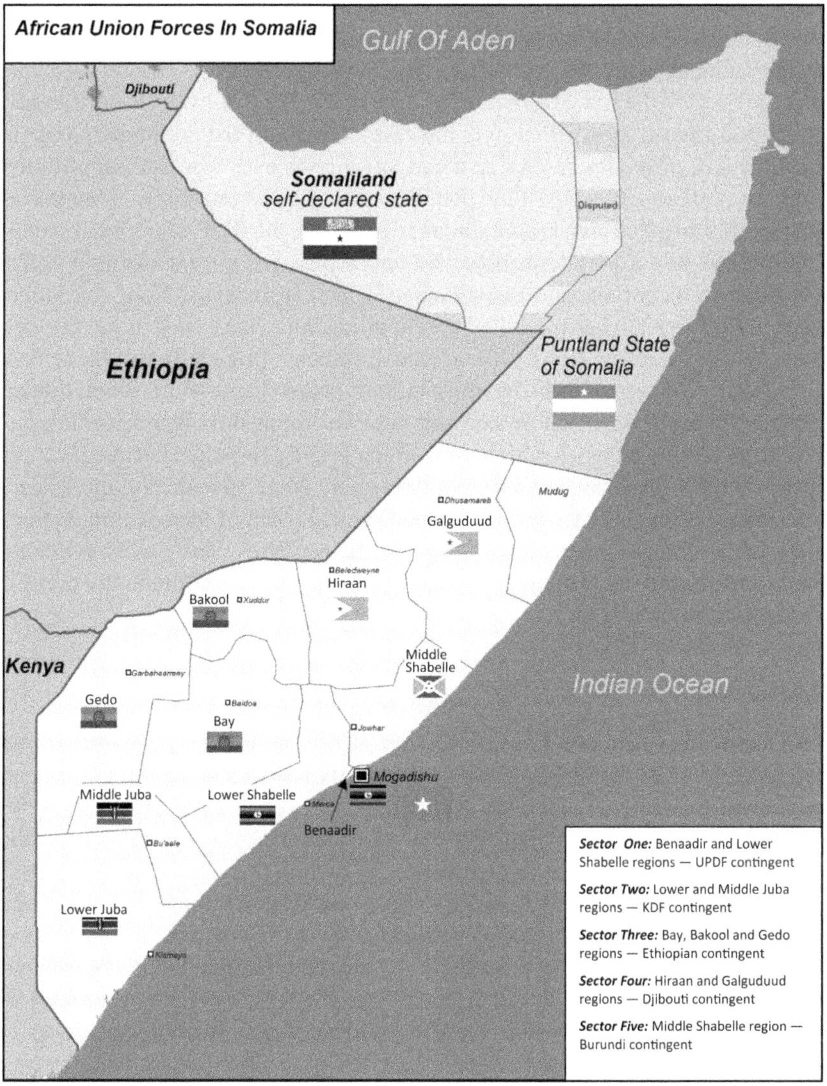

Figure 8.3 AMISOM military contingents' operational sectors. Source: By Ingoman (James Dahl) own work, public domain, https://commons.wikimedia.org/w/index.php?curid=2832784

Kenya joined the AMISOM in 2012 following the adoption of the United Nations Security Council (UNSC) Resolution 2036 (2012) (UNSC Doc. S/RES/2036 (2012)).

Although the short-term objective of Kenya's military involvement in Somalia was based on the need to protect its territory and citizens from threats posed by the *al-Shabaab*, the emerging interest in oil exploration along the Kenya-Somalia coastal region was another one of Kenya's long-term objectives. Conflicts relating to the Exclusive Economic Zone (EEZ) prompted Somalia to sue Kenya in 2014 at the International Court of Justice (ICJ). The TFG argued that its coastal EEZ border is in line with the UN Convention on Law of the Sea (UCLOS). Kenya argued that the ICJ had no jurisdiction over the case. Kenya lost the preliminary case in which the ICJ, *inter alia*, ruled that it had jurisdiction over Somalia's application on the delimitation of the maritime boundary dispute between the two countries.[21] Notably, this disputed area is contiguous to Jubaland, the KDF operational sector.

Kenya has had a long-term objective and aspiration of establishing a buffer zone between its borders and Somalia, particularly in Jubaland along the Indian Ocean area. The KDF has used the Somali militia in the area, such as the Ogaden Force and the *Muaskar Ras Kamboni* (Ras Kamboni) Brigade in its war against *al-Shabaab*. We argue that the multimillion-dollar Lamu Port South Sudan Ethiopia Transport (LAPSSET) corridor, also known as the Lamu Corridor, has also brought a new dimension in the geo-strategic and geo-political strategic interdependence involving the countries in the region. More specifically, the leaders in the region driving the LAPSSET agenda are cognisant of the potential vulnerability of the project arising out of the terrorist activities of *al-Shabaab* among others, and as such, have to assess their strategic settings carefully in the prevailing strategic environment.[22]

Conclusion

This chapter has examined Kenya's foreign policy and foreign policy behaviour using realism as its theoretical point of departure. Kenya's unilateral (KDF) and multilateral (AMISOM) approach to diplomacy in Somalia has provided useful explanatory value in contextualising the relevance of realism in relation to the country's foreign policy and foreign policy behaviour. It is argued in the chapter, that irrespective of its multilateral approach to diplomacy through the AMISOM peacekeeping mission in Somalia, national interests understood in the context of realism underpin Kenya's strategic setting and foreign policy behaviour. Instability in Somalia and the *al-Shabaab* operations in the country, as well as in Kenya, explain the continued strategic interdependence involving a number of actors, including Kenya. The terrorist incursions by *al-Shabaab*, we have argued, rekindle the post-independence scenarios reminiscent of the *shifta* activities. This reinforces consistency in Kenya's foreign policy behaviour, driven by *realpolitik* national interests centred on the right to protect the country's sovereignty and territorial integrity.

In keeping with AU principles and ideals, Kenya commits to respect for sovereignty and territorial integrity of member states as articulated in the AU Constitutive Act. In addition, Kenya supports enhanced Pan-Africanism and regional integration through trade and multilateral engagements, towards regional peace and stability as part of her foreign policy endeavours. It is worth noting that the chapter's choice of realism as a framework of analysis does not negate the potential of liberal theoretical tenets in explaining Kenya's integration into AMISOM and the resultant multilateral approach to foreign policy, nor the social construction of the *al-Shabaab* as a threat to Kenya's national interests using the constructivist theoretical underpinnings. Such theories provide a basis for further theoretical and scholarly exploration and epistemological debate in explaining Kenya's foreign policy and foreign policy behaviour.

Notes

1 The objective of the Somali administrations was to unite all the areas in the Horn of Africa inhabited by Somali speaking peoples, namely Djibouti; Northern Frontier District (Kenya); Ogaden (Ethiopia); Italian Somaliland; and British Somaliland. This ideology-driven foreign policy objective was reinforced with a five-pointed flag depicting each of the regions.

2 The ICU was eventually defeated by the Ethiopian troops between 2005 and 2006.

3 Article 51 of the UN Charter provides, in part that: "Nothing in the present Charter shall impair the inherent right of individual or collective *self-defence* if an armed attack occurs against a Member of the United Nations" (our emphasis).

4 Al-Shabaab founded in Somalia in 2006 is also known variously as: Harakat al-Shabaab al-Mujahideen; Al-Shabaab Al-Islam; Al-Shabaab al-Islamiya; Al-Shabaab Al-Jihaad; Al-Shabaab; Ash-shabaab; Harakat Shabaab Al-Mujahidin; Harakat Shabaab al-Mujaahidin; Hizbul Shabaab; Hisb'ul Shabaab; HMS; Mujahideen Youth Movement; Mujahidin Al-Shabaab Movement; Mujaahiddin Youth Movement; Mujahidin Youth Movement; Shabaab; MYM; The Popular Resistance Movement in the Land of the Two Migrations; The Unity of Islamic Youth; The Youth; Young Mojahideen Movement; and Young Mujahideen Movement in Somalia, Youth Wing. For these details see, Parliament of Australia (n.d.). The movement pledged its allegiance to al-Qaeda.and the Islamic State of Iraq and al-Sham (ISIS).

5 See *Daily Nation* (2011).

6 On this issue see for example Pape (2003).

7 For details on this policy objective and other Al-Shabaab related issues, see, Australia, Parliament of Australia (n.d.). See also, Rudincova (2011).

8 *Uti possidetis juris*, in relation to Africa, is a principle which means the right of the newly independent sovereign states to retain their borders as acquired at the time of independence. The Organization of African Unity (OAU) adopted this principle during its Summit in 1964, Cairo, Egypt. This decision by the OAU prompted Somalia and Morocco to withdraw their membership from the organisation.

9 For more details on the epistemological contributions by Thucydides on realism, see also Connor (1984).

10 See African Union (March 2007). The Status of Mission Agreement (SOMA) between the Transitional Federal Government of the Somali Republic and the African Union Mission in Somalia (AMISOM), Chapter II, Article IV. African Union: Addis Ababa and African Union, Peace and Security Council (January 2007). Communique. Doc. PSC/PR/Comm (LXIX). African Union: Addis Ababa.

11 The Islamic Court Union (ICU) was destroyed by the Ethiopian National Defence Force (ENDF) in Somalia in 2006.

12 At the time of writing this chapter in November 2018, Kenya is still embroiled in military operations in Somalia, nearly a decade after its initial involvement in 2011.

13 Benin, Gabon, Ghana, Guinea, Malawi, Mali, Nigeria, Rwanda, Senegal, Swaziland, Tanzania, Tunisia and Zambia pledged support but failed to deploy their military contingents.

14 For details on the emerging role of the African Union and sub-regional organisation relation to African solutions to African problems, see for example Abatan & Spies (2016); Coleman (2011); and Dauda, Ahmad, & Keling (2018).
15 Article 240 of the Constitution establishes the Council which comprises of the President; the Deputy President; the Cabinet Secretary for Defence; the Cabinet Secretary for Foreign Affairs; the Cabinet Secretary for Internal Security; the Attorney-General; and the Chief of Kenya Defence Forces.
16 The study is not concerned with the other actors—Burundi, Djibouti, Ethiopia, EU, IGAD, Sierra Leone, Uganda and the UN—depicted in Figure 8.1. They are included in the figure mainly for purposes of illustration. For details on the meaning of strategy and strategic setting in relation to conflict, see for example Hart (1972); Schelling (1960); and Slaughter (2017).
17 For the meaning of just war theory, see Waltzer (2000).
18 For these debates see for example, Dinstein (2011) and Greig (1991).
19 For details on the meaning of "hot pursuit," see for example Poulantzas (2002).
20 For details on the statistical data used in this section see Kenya (2017a); Kenya, Kenya National Bureau of Statistics (2017b); and World Travel and Tourism Council (2017).
21 https://www.icj-cij.org/file/case-related/161/161-20170-22-JUD-01-00-EN.pdf. See also Kenya Law (2017)
22 It is estimated that the LAPSSET project will cost nearly $26 billion. These figures vary according to the sources used. For details on the LAPSSET Corridor project see for example Kasuku (2015) and Kenya, Lapsset Corridor Development Authority (2016).

References

Abatan, E. & Spies, Y. (2016). African Solution to African Problems? The AU, R2P and Coted'Ivoire. *South African Journal of International Affairs*, *23*(1): 21–38. doi:10.1080/10220461.2016.1153516.

Adar, G. (2007). Kenya's Foreign Policy and Foreign Policy-Making Process: An Analytical Context. In G. A. Korwa, G. Adar & P. J. Schraeder (eds.). *Globalization and Emerging Trends in African States Foreign Policy-Making Process: A Comparative Perspective of Eastern Africa*, Vol. 2. Lanham, MD: University Press of America.

Adar, K. G. (1994). *Kenyan Foreign Policy Behavior Towards Somalia, 1963–1983*. Lanham, MD: University Press of America.

Adar, K. G. (2011). Kenya's Foreign Policy and Geostrategic Interests: The Case of the Nile River Basin. In K. G. Adar & N. A. Check (eds.). *Cooperative Diplomacy, Regional Stability and National Interests: The Nile River and Riparian States*. Pretoria: Africa Institute of South Africa.

Adar, K. G. & Yoh, J. G. N. (eds.). (2006). *Somalia Peace Process: Challenges and Future Prospects for the Reconstruction and Restoration of Legitimacy*. Pretoria: Africa Institute of South Africa.

African Union. (March 2007). *The Status of Mission Agreement (SOMA) between the Transitional Federal Government of the Somali Republic and the African Union Mission in Somalia (AMISOM). Chapter II, Article IV*. Addis Ababa: African Union.

African Union, Peace and Security Council. (January 2007). *Communique*. Doc. PSC/PR/Comm (LXIX). Addis Ababa: African Union.

Ali, A. A. (n.d.). The Anatomy of al-Shabaab. TheAnatomyOfAlShabaab.pdf (Accessed 21 October 2018).

Anderson, D. M. & McNight, J. (2015). Kenya at War: Al-Shabaab and Its Enemies in Eastern Africa. *African Affairs*, *114*(454): 1–27. doi:10.1093/afraf/adu082.

Australia, Parliament of Australia. (n.d.). *Al-Shabaab, Unclassified*. https://www.aph.gov.au/~/media/wopapub/house/committee/pjcis/five_terrorist/sor/Al_Shabaab_pdf.ashx. Accessed 21 October 2018.

Botha, A. (2014). Political Socialization and Terrorist Radicalization among Individuals Who Joined al-Shabaab in Kenya. *Studies in Conflict & Terrorism*, *37*(11): 895–919. doi:10.1080/1057610X.2014.952511.

Cannon, B. J. & Pkalya, D. R. (2017). Why al-Shabaab Attacks Kenya: Questioning the Narrative Paradigm. *Terrorism and Political Violence*. doi:10.1080/09546553.2017.1290607.

Chaliand, G. & Blin, A. (2007). *The History of Terrorism: From Antiquity to al QAEDA*. Berkeley, CA: University of California Press.

Clinton, D. (1994). *Two Faces of National Interest*. Baton Rouge, LA: Louisiana State University.

Coleman, K. (2011). Innovation in African Solution to African Problems: The Evolving Practice of Regional Peacekeeping in Sub-Saharan Africa. *Journal of Modern African Studies*, *49*(4): 517–545. doi:10.1017/S0022278X11000462.

Connor, R. W. (1984). *Thucydides*. Princeton, NJ: Princeton University Press.

Crane, G. (1998). *Thucydides and the Ancient Simplicity: The Limits of Political Realism*. Berkeley, CA: University of California Press.

Daily Nation. (2011). UN Boss Lauds Kenya Sacrifice in Somalia. 08 December 2011. p. 1.

Dauda, M., Ahmad, M. Z. B. & Keling, M. F. (2018). Appraisal to African Solution to African Problems: An Empirical Analysis of African Union's Experience. *Asian Journal of Multidisciplinary Studies*, *6*(3): 60–69.

Dinstein, Y. (2011). *War, Aggression and Self-Determination*. Cambridge: Cambridge University Press.

Gayathri, A. (2012). AU Forces Capture Rebel Stronghold Kismayo. Says Kenya. *International Business Times*. 28 September. http://www.ibtimes.com/au-forces-capture-rebel-stronghold-kismayo-says-kenya-797219. Accessed 15 November 2018.

Greig, D. W. (1991). Self-Determination and the Security Council: What Does Article 51 Require? *The International and Comparative Law Quarterly*, *40*(2): 366–402.

Hart, L. B. H. (1972). *Strategy*. 2nd ed. New York: Praeger.

Kasuku, S. (2015). Lapsset Corridor Development Authority, Lapsset Presentation, Africa infrastructure and Power Forum, 15 October 2015, The Ritz Carlton Hotel, Beijing, China. www.energynet.co.uk/webfm_send/1005. Accessed 18 November 2018.

Kenya. (2010). *The Constitution of Kenya, 2010*. Nairobi: Government Printer.

Kenya, Lapsset Corridor Development Authority. (2016). *Brief on Lapsset Corridor Project*. Vision2030.go.ke/inc/uploads/2018/05/LAPSSET-Project-Report-July-2016.pdf.

Kenya, Ministry of Defence. (2017). *Defence White Paper*. Nairobi: Ministry of Defence.

Kenya. (2017a). *Sector Plan for Tourism, 2013–2017*. Nairobi: Government Pinter.

Kenya, Kenya National Bureau of Statistics. (2017b). *Kenya: Facts and Figures, 2018*. Nairobi: Kenya National Bureau of Statistics.

Kenya Law. (February 2017). *Court Declares It Has Jurisdiction over Somalia's Application against Kenya on Maritime Delimitation in the Indian Ocean and That It's Admissible*. KenyaLaw.org/kenyalawblog/court-declares-it-has-jurisdiction-over.somalias-application-against Kenya.pdf. Accessed 16 November 2018.

Kenya, Ministry of Defence. (2014). *Operation Linda Nchi: Kenya's Military Experience in Somalia*. Nairobi: Ministry of Defence.

Kenya, Ministry of Foreign Affairs and International Trade. (2014). *Kenya Foreign Policy*. Nairobi: Ministry of Foreign Affairs and International Trade. www.mfa.go.ke/wp-content/uploads/2016.09/Kenya-Foreign-Policy.pdf. Accessed 27 September 2018.

Kenya, National Assembly. (2011). *National Assembly Official Report, Wednesday, 7th December, 2011*. Nairobi: National Assembly

Makinda, S. M. (1983). From Quiet Diplomacy to Cold War Politics: Kenya's Foreign Policy. *Third World Quarterly*, *5*(2): 300–319. doi:10.1080/01436598308419697.

Mapendere, J. (2006). Track One and a Half Diplomacy and the Complementarity of Tracks. *Culture of Peace Online Journal*, *2*(1): 66–81.

Mburu, N. (2005). *Bandits on the Border: The Lost Frontier in the Search for Somali Unity*. Athens: The Red Sea Press.

Menkhaus, K. (2014). State Failure, State-Building, and Prospects for a "Functional Failed State" in Somalia. *The Annals of the American Academy of Political and Social Science*, *656*(1): 154–172. doi:10.1177%2F0002716214547002.

Meredith, M. (2011). *The State of Africa*. London: Simon & Schuster.

Morgenthau, H. J. (1948). *Politics Among Nations*. New York: Knopf.

Morgenthau, H. J. (1985). *Politics Among Nations*. 6th ed. New York: Knopf.

Mwagiru, M. (2000). The Elusive Quest: Conflict, Diplomacy, and Foreig Policy in Kenya. In P. G. Okoth & B. A. Ogot (eds.). *Conflict in the Contemporary Africa*. Nairobi: Jomo Kenyatta Foudation.

Mwanika, P. N. (2015). Kenya's Soft Power Dipomacy and Strategic Intervention in the Somali Conflict. *Occassional Paper No.1*. Africa Institute of South Africa.

O'Loughlin, J. (1989). World Power Competition and Local Conflicts in the Third World. In R. J. Johnson & P. J. Taylor (eds.). *A World in Crisis: Geographical Perspectives*. 2nd ed. Oxford: Basil Blackwell.

Organization of African Unity Secretariat. (1965). *Resolutions Adopted by the First Ordinary Session of the Assembly of Heads of State and Government Held in Cairo, UAR, From 17–21 July, 1964*. Addis Ababa: Organization of African Unity Secretariat.

Orwa, D. K. (1994). Continuity and Change: Kenya's Foreign Policy from Kenyatta to Moi. In W. O. Oyugi (ed.). *Politics and Administration in East Africa*. Nairobi: East African Educational Publishers.

Pape, R. A. (2003). The Strategic Logic of Suicide Terrorism. *American Political Science Review*, *97*(3): 343–361. doi:10.1017/S000305540300073X.

Philpott, D. & Powers, G. F. (eds.). (2010). *Strategies of Peace: Transforming Conflict in a Violent World*. Oxford: Oxford University Press.

Piazza, J. A. (2009). Is Islamist Terrorism More Dangerous? An Empirical Study of Group Ideology, Organization, and Goal Structure. *Terrorism and Political Violence*, *21*(1): 62–88. doi:10.1080/09546550802544698.

Poulantzas, N. M. (2002). *The Right of Hot Pursuit in International Law*. The Hague: Martinus Nijhoff Publications.

Robert, A. (2003). The Strategic Logic of Suicide Terrorism. *American Political Science Review*, *97*(3): 343–361. doi:10.1017/S000305540300073X.

Rudincova, K. (2011). Islamic Movements in Somalia: Global or Local Jihad? https://www.researchgate.net/publication/273806213_Islamic_Movements_in_Somalia_Global_or_Local_Jihad. Accessed 22 October 2018.

Schelling, T. (1960). *The Strategy of Conflict*. Cambridge: Harvard University Press.

Shaw, M. N. (1997). Peoples, Territorialism and Boundaries. *European Journal of International Law*, *3*: 478–507.

Slaughter, A. M. (2017). *The Chess-Board and the Web Strategies of Connection in a Networked World*. New Haven, CT: Yale University Press.

Tams, C. J. (2009). The Use of Force Against Terrorists. *European Journal of International Law*, *20*(2): 359–397. doi:10.1093/ejil/chp031.

The Military Balance. (2018). Chapter Nine: Sub-Saharan Africa. *The Military Balance, 118*(1): 429–498. doi:10.1080/04597222.2018.1416986.

United Nations Secretariat. (1948). *Charter of the United Nations and Statute of the International Court of Justice*. New York: United Nations Secretariat.

Waltzer, M. (2000). *Just and Unjust War: A Moral Argument with Historical Arguments*. New York: Basic Books.

World Travel and Tourism Council. (2017). *Travel and Tourism Economic Impact 2017: Kenya*. London: World Travel and Tourism Council.

Zartman, I. W. (1985). *Ripe for Resolution: Conflict & Intervention in Africa*. New York: Oxford University Press.

9 Addressing the conceptual void of African small state foreign policy in orthodox theory

A case study of Botswana's principled pragmatism

Kabelo M. Mahupela

Introduction

The ascendancy of small states and the manner in which they have come to matter in International Relations (IR) discourse has traditionally been diluted by the rationalist orthodoxies of the discipline (Lee & Smith, 2010: 1093). This has particularly been so for African small states. The paucity of literature on the subject is emblematic of the theoretical lacunae that persist in this respect. Neo-realist and neo-liberal scholarship is particularly culpable for marginalising the potential of small states, who after all, are capable of demonstrating political agency that affects their external environment. This, in part, is a consequence of the manner in which the field of IR treats Foreign Policy Analysis (FPA).[1] Unlike FPA, the dominant traditions of IR do not take into account the internal social processes that drive external state behaviour to produce in similarly positioned actors, quite different international outcomes. While FPA is viewed as a subfield of IR, it has, however, also been treated as separate from the field, leaving a gap between the two (Walker, 2011: 7). Houghton (2007) ventures to suggest that by drawing on social constructivism, FPA joins the mainstream to accommodate generally useful and fruitful explanations for IR of small state behaviour, including explanations on the domestic drivers of foreign policy (Houghton, 2007: 24). From this understanding, we posit that social constructivism is the most applicable avenue through which a meaningful foreign policy reading of small power agency can be realised.

Social constructivism is a theory of international relations that posits intersubjective relationships between structures and actors, in which states interact with each other and put across ideas, beliefs and assumptions that ultimately shape their identities and interests as perceived by actors in their external environment. The approach serves to analyse Botswana's foreign policy in its ability to oftentimes transcend its political and economic status as a small state. This is done by adopting what is here termed as "principled pragmatism", a descriptive appellation to describe the embodiment of Botswana's foreign policy since independence. "Principled pragmatism" is understood at two levels: how leadership

1) takes cognisance of its external environment to position itself with its preferences and interests, while 2) simultaneously expressing agency as driven by a set of principles that form the basis of the socio-cultural identity of the country as projected to the external world.

The principles driving foreign relations are primarily characterised by the promotion of democratic ideals. These include the respect for good governance, human rights and international law as a basis for achieving other principles such as equitable development and multilateral cooperation, as well as good neighbourliness and respect for sovereignty of nations.

This chapter draws on various examples that illustrate Botswana's use of principled pragmatism. This, in order to demonstrate how it is possible for small African states to leverage their identities with their foreign policies, giving them the ability to strike a chord with the international community to enable them to transcend their material status. In this regard, Botswana consistently defended liberal democratic ideals while -carefully projecting its position vis-à-vis its external environment. As such, this analysis arguably amounts to a constructivist reading of African small state foreign policy behaviour.

Constructivism: An appropriate theoretical framework

Social constructivism is presented here as the most apposite response to the shortcomings of rationalist theories in explaining foreign policy. It encapsulates the foundation upon which the analysis of small state agency, and indeed Botswana's foreign policy, can adequately be assessed.

Variations notwithstanding, constructivist scholarship tends to overlap on a number of core aspects. Constructivists first perceive of the world as being constituted by inter-subjective realities that expand the possibilities otherwise circumscribed by narrow rationalist interpretations of IR (Adler, 2002: 100). Second, constructivists are in concert about the distinction between brute facts (facts which constitute the material world) and social facts which are in existence as a result of human agreement. They believe that IR literature is mostly comprised of the latter (Adler, 2002: 100). Furthermore, constructivists promote the notion of agency and are in agreement that structure and agents are mutually constitutive and that one need not be privileged over the other (Houghton, 2007: 28).

Constructivists agree that the international arena is anarchic in nature; however, the contours of this environment need not lead to "self-help".[2] Wendt (1992) asserts that anarchy is what states make of it, and that instances of self-help are manifestations of "process", which in turn is a product of interactions and learning (1992: 394–395). The interaction process engenders perceptions of "self" and "others", leading states to interactively create expectations and understandings of each other's inter-subjectively defined interests as a result of the enactment of identities of states in the international arena. Structures are then formed from this conception of "interests" and "identities", and when these structures are relatively stable, they can be viewed as institutions that are governed by mutually agreed rules and norms (Wendt, 1992: 399, 404).[3]

In this regard, ideas and identities of elites can serve as drivers of foreign policy formulation. An elite's perception of its state's identity is then considered central to how it perceives of its state's interests, which in turn shapes behaviour against expected trends at the external level (Park, 2005: 231; Gvalia, Siroky, Lebanidze, & Isahvili, 2013: 106).[4]

Constructivism allows for an inclusive analysis since the social space for agency is an expansive one unrestricted by hierarchy and structure. In this respect, Botswana skilfully manipulated its situation vis-à-vis the apartheid state in its favour, which ultimately resulted in favourable outcomes. This approach also allows greater scope for the analysis of multilateralism within the context of conference diplomacy in that "what used to be typically offstage activity appears lately to be increasingly on-stage activities" (Jazbec, 2010: 71). Thorhallsson (2012: 152–158) and Jakobsen in Nasra (2011) have demonstrated how small states can use soft power[5] through conference diplomacy to influence the decision-making processes of powerful members of institutions, such as the United Nations Security Council and the European Union respectively.

Despite the Cold War, with its bloc politics and focus on strategic power relations, Botswana managed to transcend its unfavourable external and internal environments to secure its interests as defined by its socio-political identity. Botswana as a small state—with a small population and poor economy—faced existential and developmental challenges emanating from apartheid South Africa, its Western supporters and exploitative northern corporates. In navigating this terrain of blocs, alliances and disparate political groupings, Botswana was able to put forward a foreign policy based on pragmatism that ensured its survival. At the same time, it managed to simultaneously build up its credibility and credentials as a "shining example of liberal democracy" in the region and project these principles in its foreign policy approach (Tsie, 1996: 599). This reading of Botswana's foreign policy has not been adequately captured in IR literature.

Botswana's foreign policy and IR theory

The treatment of Botswana's foreign policy in literature

Literature on Botswana's foreign policy was dominated by neo-realist perceptions which posited Botswana as a "client", "captive" or "hostage" state to apartheid South Africa (Halpern, 1965; Dale, 1976: 69; Dale, 1987; Taylor, 1997: 77). Botswana suffered from internal and external vulnerabilities that threatened its survival, including a small population, low gross domestic product per capita, and merely a small mobile police force to defend the territory against external threats (Black, Mugyenyi, & Swatuk, 1988: 64–66). With the fall of apartheid South Africa, there was a great level of uncertainty about the implications for Botswana's external relations, with authors such as Claus and Weimer (1991) postulating on the role of Botswana in the changing landscape of Southern Africa. Their article is construed in a particularly neo-liberal temperament, conceiving of threats and opportunities that Botswana would need to grapple with if it was to participate in the reform and effective functioning of the then Southern African Development Coordination Conference (SADCC) (Claus & Weimer, 1991: 332).

Some of this older literature implicitly describes Botswana's foreign relations in constructivist terms. Henderson (1974), in seeking to assess foreign policy options for Gaborone, notes that Botswana, while cognisant of its vulnerabilities, manipulated its external environment in its favour and asserted its independence (1974: 49). Claus and Weimer also make reference to Botswana's exceptional negotiation skills in relation to transnational enterprises as well as the draconian apartheid government, which yielded outcomes that were favourable to its interests at the time (1991: 325). In more recent literature, Osei-Hwedie and Mokhawa (2014) analyse how the individual traits of the first four presidents of Botswana have shaped the foreign policies of these leaders.[6] Malila and Molebatsi (2014) also consider the role that Ian Khama's orientation has played in shaping what the authors refer to as an ethical foreign policy.

Botswana's foreign policy principles

In order to arrive at an analysis of Botswana's foreign policy orientation, a brief comment is necessary about its internal political and social milieu as forged by consecutive ruling elites throughout the country's history. In the eyes of the world, Botswana consistently positioned itself as a key success story as one of the oldest and most peaceful democracies on the continent. The orientation of the people of Botswana has consistently been in favour of liberal democratic ideals, from as early as the first general election that saw the Bechuanaland Democratic Party sweep aside socialist and Pan-African elements in a landslide victory (Parsons, 2008). Botswana's domestic landscape has generally been characterised by liberal democratic ideals, underpinned by multiparty contestation, the respect for civil liberties and human rights, the promotion of the rule of law, a largely independent press and a limitation of terms to presidential tenure (Sklar, 1989: 267). Botswana was an exemplary beacon of liberal democratic ideals at a time when the rest of the continent was plagued by one-party dictatorships, lifetime presidencies, suppression of political opponents and freedoms, a lack of accountability, transparency and the rule of law and personalisation of state political and economic capital (Nnoli, 1989: 266). The Batswana have continually accentuated their belief in the above democratic order. According to an Afrobarometer survey in 2016 (Afrobarometer, 2016), eight in ten Batswana claim to understand the term democracy; and two-thirds of the country prefer it to alternative forms of government, also rejecting non-democratic alternatives. The Batswana were also found to view democracy in its liberal and procedural conception, accentuating the elements outlined above (Lekalake, 2016: 2).

These principles filtered into the country's foreign policy objectives as noted by the Democratic Coalition Project (2002: 1):

> Botswana frequently has drawn on the prestige and capital it has acquired as a regional model of stability and democratic governance to exercise diplomatic

> leadership … [and has] used a range of policy tools to express its disapproval of violations of democratic governance.

It is here suggested that throughout its post-colonial history, Botswana's foreign policy has resolutely remained wedded to a number of principles. The principles of Botswana's foreign policy in this regard stem from a statement delivered by the first president, Seretse Khama, to the Botswana Democratic Party Congress on 28 March 1970 in Molepolole. The tenets include (1) the promotion of democratic ideals, the establishment of relations with democratic countries and peaceful resolution of conflicts; (2) unity and equitable development with as many countries as possible; (3) self-reliance and the reduction of external aid as well as the promotion of regional and bilateral cooperation; and (4) domestic territorial integrity, good neighbourliness and the promotion of sovereignty of nations (Legum, 1973: 179–181).

These principles have in subsequent administrations led by Masire, Mogae and Ian Khama formed the foundation of Botswana's internal social identity and helped project its foreign policy posture. As elucidated below, Seretse Khama (president from 1966–1980) pioneered the approach of pragmatism tempered with principle. He did this by positioning Botswana as a multiracial liberal democracy whose territorial security was threatened by tyrannical and immoral elements of white minority rule in the region. For his part, President Masire (1980–1998) followed the same foreign policy goals as his predecessor, accentuating the elements of Botswana's territorial security, economic development through international collaboration and continuing advancement of liberal democratic ideals. After the advent of South African democracy in 1994, Masire's foreign policy approach focused on the promotion and protection of human rights and the rule of law and good governance. He saw this preoccupation as necessary for the socio-economic well-being of the country and the overall stability of the Southern African region. Moreover, Masire's administration participated in a number of peacekeeping missions in Sierra Leone, Mozambique and Somalia as part of Botswana's overall orientation towards collective regional development, as a means of achieving the above principles (Osei-Hwedie & Mokhawa, 2014: 9–10).

Festus Mogae (president of Botswana from 1998–2008) followed a policy that was grounded in the pursuit of economic development and sought deeper regional integration through the Southern African Development Community (SADC) and the Southern African Customs Union (SACU). Mogae worked tirelessly to attract foreign investment and routinely sought to cultivate relationships through official visits and direct participation in international conferences. While Mogae traded on Botswana's image as a democratic showcase for emulation by others in the region, he remained preoccupied with the attainment of foreign economic goals amidst regional stability. To him, stability was more pressing than the public rebuke of tyrannical and illiberal elements. For example, Mogae acquiesced to SADC's collective position of silent diplomacy towards Zimbabwe (Democratic Coalition Project, 2002).

Ian Khama (president of Botswana 2008–2018) had a different orientation to his predecessors. As seen below, President Khama adopted an activist foreign policy predicated upon public rather than private diplomatic engagements. Ian Khama's government accentuated the promotion of liberal democratic ideals and placed less emphasis on the promotion of sovereignty. He was highly critical of counter-constitutional changes in elected governments, electoral irregularities, human rights abuses and reversals in the rule of law (Malila & Molebatsi, 2014: 12–15).

The appearance of this apparent variance within Botswana's long-established foreign policy record can be understood as "flexible and concrete actions by leaders who are pragmatic in responding to situations as they evolve" (Osei-Hwedie & Mokhawa, 2014: 6). In the main, however, it does not detract from the consistent thread of principles projected to the outside from the country's own internal social identity. Gaborone consistently positioned itself first and foremost as an advocate for liberal democratic ideals. Gaborone also followed a pragmatic approach underpinned by the identification of economic development needs, the strategic search for international cooperation partners and the respect for the sovereignty of nations. This is the context against which principled pragmatism operated.

Botswana's foreign policy: Principled pragmatism in practice

Posture towards white minority rule

Following independence from Britain in 1966, Botswana was a small, landlocked state surrounded by white minority rule.[7] It had a small population and vulnerable borders due to the lack of a professional armed force. The economy was heavily underdeveloped[8] and almost wholly reliant on South Africa for long term subsistence through the labour market, the South African Customs Union (SACU) for access to trade opportunities and a common monetary policy determined by Pretoria (Osei-Hwedie, 1998: 426; Black et al., 1988: 64–66). Notwithstanding these constraints, Gaborone carried out a pragmatically prudent, albeit principled foreign policy that incorporated defiance towards Pretoria, while still avoiding overtly provocative actions that would give South Africa and Rhodesia a pretext to respond coercively.[9] As Gvalia et al. (2013) hold, elite identities and ideas shape foreign policy perceptions. As such, it is necessary to analyse the founding president, Seretse Khama's views.

Khama had long been determined to wage a struggle against racial discrimination in the region. In 1948, he married Ruth Williams (a British Caucasian), occasioning remonstrations from the South African government, which had banned interracial marriages under its apartheid system.[10] This ultimately led to Khama's exile from Bechuanaland to Britain in the early 1950s (Henderson, 1990: 30). He garnered popular support amongst the British populace for what was seen as evidence of racism by the British government. Coupled with the refusal of the Bamangwato people, in defiance of the British colonial government to elect another chief, Khama and his wife eventually returned to Bechuanaland. Ultimately, he ascended to the centre of Bechuanaland politics, cementing his position in the 1965 elections

(Stevens, 1966: 15). The experience taught Khama that even in relations with more powerful counterparts, it was still possible to insist on one's principles and where necessary engage in dialogue to reach an acceptable end goal.

To Khama's administration, non-racialism was intrinsically linked to Botswana's internal social identity. At the same time, Khama remarked that his foreign policy would be directed by "reason and common sense" (Osei-Hwedie, 1998: 426). The independent Botswana sought to make its multiracial democratic identity attractive to the African continent, as well as to those elements that espoused similar values across the world (Henderson, 1990: 43). Botswana showed a level of defiance against its powerful neighbours in this regard. Thus, Gaborone resisted pressures to extend full diplomatic relations to Pretoria and Salisbury,[11] refused to accept official aid from apartheid South Africa and began pursuing its own monetary policy in the 1970s. Botswana denied diplomatic recognition to the homelands, thereby eschewing the legitimacy of the Bantustan system in which Pretoria created ethnic homelands as a way of showing that separate development could be achieved (Dale, 1976: 79).

Concurrently, Botswana also pursued a moderate policy towards South Africa, as seen in its decision to remain in the SACU and retain informal diplomatic backchannels for communication with Pretoria (Sekgoma, 1990). This prudence towards South Africa initially failed to inspire confidence from the more radical, anti-imperialist leaders on the continent who saw Botswana as a puppet of South Africa (Henderson, 1990: 43). This perception began to change as Khama drew on his long-standing friendship with President Kaunda of Zambia, who understood Gaborone's plight as the only black majority-led country that bordered Botswana. Zambia would serve as the interlocutor between Botswana and the rest of Africa, presenting Botswana as a country that favoured the end of white minority rule, but whose proximity to apartheid South Africa and settler-Rhodesia meant it had to be measured in its approach (Masire, 2006: 286–287). Botswana's search for allies on the continent led it to adopt a non-aligned stance in the Cold War, occasioning the establishment of ties with the Soviet Union and Yugoslavia in 1970. Having previously established relations with Japan and West Germany, this mitigated perceptions of radical socialism amongst South Africa and the Western world (Taylor, 1997: 77). In this respect, Botswana's internal social identity was becoming increasingly apparent.

Seretse Khama's government positioned itself as a leading member of the Frontline States (FLS). The FLS was a political alliance[12] based on the Lusaka Manifesto, which was the accepted strategy by the Organisation of African Unity (OAU) in 1969, on the process of liberating Southern Africa from white minority rule (Niemann, 1993: 29). Gaborone's geographic positioning was key to the activities of the FLS, but given its proximity to South Africa, Botswana could not allow the liberation war to be waged directly from its territory. However, Botswana did offer asylum to people that fled from tyrannical racist regimes through a revised refugee policy (Osei-Hwedie, 1998: 430). Gaborone facilitated meetings between the FLS and South Africa, at a time when hostilities did not favour direct diplomatic engagements between the parties (Masire, 2006: 275).

Khama played a pivotal role in uniting the FLS politically, by taking the lead in forming the SADCC and investing the majority of human resources for starting up the organisation. SADCC had the effect of advancing the economic development of the FLS by reducing dependency on South Africa (Masire, 2006: 277).

Botswana has been viewed by the international community as a leading example for the forging of multiracial societies and the promotion of liberal democratic ideals in the region. Dale (1976), for example, argues that Botswana was able to embolden its multicultural and non-racial identity to the world by harbouring schools such as Maru-a-Pula, which hosted local students, as well as black and white expatriates (Dale, 1976: 74–75). There had been a paucity of such symbiotic non-racialism in schools within the region following Botswana's independence. Vice-President Masire, in 1969, while addressing race relations in Francistown, made it clear that anti-racism was intimately linked to Botswana's principles and objectives that formed part of its internal social identity (Henderson, 1974: 39). The country also diplomatically profiled itself in multilateral settings such as at the OAU and at United Nations (UN) fora, to state its case on its geo-political vulnerabilities, while simultaneously demonstrating its commitment to the overall objective of national liberation and support for national liberation movements. Botswana, in projecting itself as a moderate but principled actor, straddled the sharp confrontational divide between South Africa as an internationally supported sub-regional hegemon, and itself, demonstrating that it had evolved its own diplomatic practice of predictable, principled pragmatism, one deeply embedded in its own internal social identity.

Botswana's conference diplomacy and negotiation skills

Botswana sought to make the most of multilateral conference settings by seeking to promote liberal democratic principles, while simultaneously looking to safeguard its survival through diplomacy and dialogue. Jazbec (2010), Jakobsen in Nasra (2011), and Thorhallsson (2012) demonstrate the role that multilateralism can play in the exercise of soft power, thereby providing small states with the opportunity to affect global agendas. In this respect, Botswana asserted itself in varying contexts against both the apartheid government and its Western allies, as well as radical and anti-imperialist forces. For example, in July 1970, Britain announced that its weapons manufacturers would consider doing business with South Africa. Seretse Khama prioritised this aspect at the Non-Aligned Movement (NAM) conference in Lusaka in September 1970 by publicly playing on the threat of entrenching white minority rule through a British and French arms race in Southern Africa (Tlou, Parsons, & Henderson, 1995: 291). Khama also prudently used the closed sessions of the conference to ease the tensions that had festered due to divergent views (Tlou et al., 1995: 292). He emerged from the conference as a leader who espoused reasonableness and this gave him support amongst liberals who opposed the apartheid regime and Western support for it (Henderson, 1990: 47).

Similarly, Botswana leveraged its growing prestige in the world in what Tsie (1996) refers to as a "shining example of liberal democracy", and appealed to the

UN Security Council to secure condemnation of violent reprisals emanating from Pretoria and Salisbury in the 1970s and 1980s. Botswana was able to secure a resolution in 1977 condemning Rhodesia for what the Security Council referred to as the actions of an "illegal racist regime" (UN Security Council, 1977). A similar resolution was adopted in June 1985 following a South African Defence Force attack on Gaborone seeking to destroy ANC strongholds (Dale, 1987: 83).

Botswana used its skilfully applied negotiating skills to manipulate its external environment to obtain favourable outcomes on the economic front as well. In the 1970s, South Africa had engaged in a policy of détente, seeking to obtain support from moderate African countries to divide the OAU in its opposition to Pretoria (Barber & Barratt, 1990). In this context, Botswana sought to tilt the terms of the SACU revenue-sharing formula in its favour. Botswana took the lead in the 1969 negotiations on behalf of the BLS states (Botswana, Lesotho and Swaziland). The delegation led by the then Minister of Finance, Quett Masire, was able to solicit the council of economic experts, who armed the Botswanan negotiators with relevant facts and arguments needed to obtain the outcomes sought (Masire, 2006: 257–258). This allowed Botswana to achieve an increase in the revenue formula, which compensated the BLS states for the negative effects of being in SACU, thereby reducing Gaborone's dependence on British aid (Landell-Mills, 1971: 76).

The above examples are illustrative of the positive image fostered by its ruling elite, emanating from Botswana's internal social identity. This was underpinned by a liberal democratic position on regional and global affairs fundamentally linked to its principles on the promotion of democratic ideals. This position is underscored by domestic considerations such as, *inter alia*, undisturbed elections, respect for civil liberties and human rights, the promotion of rule of law, and the chastisement of racialised societies and undemocratic bureaucratic machineries within the Southern African region. This disposition over a long period of time earned Botswana a high degree of political goodwill amongst its peers. Botswana has also been driven by its determination to be self-reliant and promote regional and bilateral cooperation. In this, Botswana has drawn upon its skilful diplomatic prowess to package its position in conference settings, appealing to a heterogeneity of audiences. To this end, its diplomats used measured and rational responses—as opposed to the rhetorical and emotive language adopted by some of its Pan-Africanist-African counterparts—as well as formal, business-like language, as opposed to indulging in symbolic sloganeering. This approach appealed to Africanist and Western liberal audiences alike, and simultaneously gave Gaborone a moderate appearance in its dealings with apartheid South Africa, setting the stage for a less hostile environment for negotiations.

Botswana and the norms and principles of SADC and the AU

Following the fall of apartheid in 1990, Botswana still enjoyed a large degree of international prestige. Gaborone saw itself playing an activist foreign policy role by ensuring that norms governing international regimes were respected and adhered to (Lekoa, 2017). In this regard, Gaborone's contributions towards conflict management organs and avenues of preventative diplomacy in both SADC and the OAU/African Union (AU) are well noted (Sekgoma, 1998: 483).

SADC norms and principles

The SADC Treaty provisions[13] have occasioned a bifurcation between those who privilege national sovereignty, regime solidarity, stability and anti-imperialism (as championed by South Africa and Zimbabwe) and those who underscore the value of liberal democratic ideals (such as Botswana and Zambia). SADC remains dominated by the former camp and this has contributed to the limited success of interventions with respect to crises of governance, democracy and the rule of law which manifest themselves within the region (The Nordic Africa Institute, 2018). Nevertheless, Botswana has managed to forge some alliances, for example with South Africa, in dealing with the Lesotho crisis of 1998 and with Zambia in condemning Mugabe's actions during the Zimbabwean electoral crisis of 2008.

AU norms and principles

As with SADC's political configuration, the Summit of the Heads of State and Government is the ultimate level of decision-making in the AU and has served as a bulwark against the operationalisation of the non-indifference principle.[14] Member state heads in this regard tend to shy away from decisions that could set precedents inimical to their own self-interests. Thus, for example, in 2016, against the backdrop of an evolving political and humanitarian crisis, the Summit of African leaders failed to dispatch an African Prevention and Protection Mission to Burundi as recommended by the Peace and Security Council of the AU (Dersso, 2016). Similarly, the AU took to a collective foreign policy approach which sought to delegitimise the International Criminal Court and called for a continent-wide withdrawal from the Rome Statute.

As with its participation in SADC, Gaborone imbued principles enshrined in the instruments of the AU as part of its identity. Botswana acceded to the Responsibility to Protect (R2P)[15] initiative under the UN, and co-hosted the fourth Annual Meeting of the Global Network for R2P Contact Points in June 2014 (Ntwaagae, 2015). Botswana also supported the AU's change in posture from non-interference to non-indifference under its Constitutive Act.[16] In the lead-up to the establishment of the AU, Botswana chaired the "International Panel of Eminent Personalities to Investigate the 1994 Genocide in Rwanda and Surrounding Events" (Kioko, 2003: 813).

While many of the obligations under international institutions necessarily involve deferring to supranational bodies for decisions that affect member state territories, it did not necessarily follow that Botswana was uncontestably in favour of surrendering its sovereignty to such bodies. This is especially the case with respect to African Institutions such as the AU and indeed SADC, where only four countries were classified by the Freedom House Survey in 2009 as being "free". This indicates stark contrasts in the socio-political orders of these states (Nathan,

2013: 881). Taking this context into account, the next section of this chapter turns to Botswana's post-1990 approach towards addressing various political crises that arose in Lesotho and Zimbabwe, as well as the AU and International Criminal Court (ICC) fallout over the prosecution of incumbent leaders indicted for gross human rights violations.

Lesotho's political crisis

With the fall of apartheid in South Africa, Botswana now had an ally—with a similar internal social identity—in a new liberal, democratic South Africa, which aligned with its principles of supporting democratic ideals in regional and global affairs.[17] Alongside the big powers of Southern Africa—Pretoria and Harare—Gaborone collaborated on the promotion of regional security, which was predicated on transparency, democracy and human rights (Khadiagala, 2001: 140). This context informed Botswana's foreign policy towards Lesotho in the 1990s.

In 1994, Botswana (under Masire), South Africa and Zimbabwe, as leading members of a "SADC troika", collaborated on addressing the problems that had started to plague Lesotho's political landscape. These problems included the army being at loggerheads with civilian administration, and the dissolution of the government by King Letsie III, culminating in nationwide protests and strikes (Selinyane, 2006: 68). In 1998, further pandemonium ensued, following electoral irregularities that led to a landslide victory for the Lesotho Congress for Democracy. In the wake of this chaos, junior army officers mutinied against senior officers, appointing a new commander. Under the auspices of SADC, Botswana (under Mogae) and South Africa carried out a joint military intervention to restore peaceful order to Lesotho.

Pretoria incurred criticism for using the intervention as a pretext to secure its interests in the Katse Dam, while Botswana was seen more as a peace keeping force, with its army entering the country flying a white flag (Neethling, 1999; Likoti, 2007: 256). In this regard, Botswana projected ideals commensurate with the promotion of liberal democratic principles.

The fallout with Zimbabwe

Botswana drew on its principles and long-standing credentials as an example of liberal democracy in the region, when Zimbabwe plummeted into crisis in 2008. Ian Khama stated that with regard to events in Zimbabwe, Botswana ascribed to the principles of good neighbourliness and the sovereignty of nations, as well as regional and global norms (Badza, 2009: 166). While Mogae's previous government had been critical of Mugabe's administration since 2002, it was cautious not to appear too antagonistic and sought to engage with Mugabe through exerting limited pressure in private, in what came to be known as "quiet diplomacy". Ian Khama departed from this approach and actively criticised the 2008 Zimbabwean elections, seen as irregular and unfair with a large degree of violence and intimidation against members and supporters of the opposition parties (Jonas, Mandiyanike, & Maundeni, 2013: 2). When the results were finally released after being withheld for an extended period of time, no party had acquired more than 50% of the vote, necessitating a run-off election (Nathan, 2012: 71). Ian Khama's government—along with Levy Mwanawasa's Zambian government—stood as lone voices in SADC, condemning Mugabe for seizing power through corrupt elections. Botswana announced that it would not recognise the government that Mugabe was on the point of forming, as the country had violated the principles of the AU, SADC and the UN. Ian Khama's government also recommended that Zimbabwe be barred from attending meetings at the SADC and AU levels (Badza, 2009, 166).

While the AU had failed to overtly condemn Mugabe's regime for its conduct, Botswana, like no other in the region, provided leadership in defending liberal democratic principles regarding individual freedoms and the holding of free elections—principles that were entrenched as part of its internal social identity. By doing so, it aligned itself with the concerns of similarly minded elites in Zambia, Kenya, Nigeria and Senegal, who all conveyed concerns about the legitimacy of Mugabe's government (Pambazuka News, 23 June 2008). Ultimately, a peace was brokered by South Africa, which saw Zimbabwe administered by a Government of National Unity (GNU), allowing for Morgan Tsvangirai to be sworn in as Prime Minister (Mmegi Online, 25 November 2008). While South Africa played a very important role in the formation of the GNU, Jonas et al. (2013) have credited Botswana's principled stand against the counter-democratic developments in Zimbabwe as having averted the prospect of civil war in the country, an event that would have had wide repercussions for the sub-continent and a wider world.

The AU and ICC crisis

Where multilateral fora have been at odds with Botswana's principled position on the promotion of liberal democratic ideals and the protection of human rights, Botswana has been willing to stand in opposition to collective decision-making processes. Under the stewardship of Ian Khama's administration, the country came to be at variance with the AU on the issue of the ICC. At times, this left the country in the political wilderness, trumpeting a principled stance that offended the collective voice of the institution.

Many African countries had initially been optimistic about the role the ICC could play in addressing the unchecked impunity associated with the large-scale carnage and human rights abuses historically visited upon the African populace, as endorsed by the AU's Peace and Security Council (Tladi, 2009: 59, Murithi, 2013: 2). These states, however, were disillusioned with the ICC when questions of its universal applicability began to arise. The Court, in the pursuit of its prosecution efforts, came to be accused of singling out the African continent. The accusation was odd in that African states themselves, on various occasions, had referred cases to the ICC. The recommendation from the Security Council on the issue of an arrest warrant for a sitting president, President Omar Hassan Al-Bashir of Sudan, for crimes against humanity, incensed African leaders. It led to a resolution that effectively shielded Al-Bashir from surrendering himself to the ICC (Sibalukhulu & Louw, 2010).

In projecting a dissenting view, Botswana stressed its commitment to the Rome Statute that had established the ICC. It further lamented that the AU was not acting in the interests of the Sudanese victims of conflict. In unequivocal terms, Botswana declared that it would arrest Al-Bashir. Later on, the declaration also covered Libya's Muammar Gaddafi (The Namibian, 8 July 2011). While South Africa remained silent on the issue, Malawi joined Botswana in taking a principled stance against Al-Bashir, leading to the 19th AU Summit being moved from Lilongwe to Addis Ababa in July 2012 (BBC News, 12 June 2012). Botswana also found allies in other AU states such as Niger, Gabon, Mali, Cote d'Ivoire, Ghana and Nigeria, who supported cooperation with the ICC, and like Botswana, considered the Court to have some relevance and value for international justice (Aggad & Apiko, 2016).[18] It is, however, also evident that Botswana did not always nor easily find allies amongst other African elites for the positions it took. It is therefore believed that its stance was detrimental to Botswana soliciting African endorsement for the positions of Secretary General of the Commonwealth in 2015 and Chairperson of the AU Commission in 2016 (Jimson, 2016; Keorapetse, 2016).

Domestic change and Botswana's international liberal credentials

While Botswana has enjoyed much international prestige for being a shining example of liberal democracy, increasingly there has been evidence of a growing trend of a non-accountable deep state at play within the country, especially under Ian Khama's administration.[19] Khama was criticised for fostering political intolerance and personalising state power (Botlhomilwe, Sebudubudu, & Maripe, 2011: 333), leading to the abuse of presidential edicts, the perpetration of state terrorism by security forces who carried out extrajudicial killings (Gwatiwa, 2011: 179–181) and the ill treatment of public sector employees who were paid low wages (CNN Online, 22 April 2011). This began to tarnish Botswana's image during Khama's administration.

Conclusion

Using constructivism, this chapter has sought to situate the analysis of Botswana's foreign policy record. This is because traditional IR theories with their objective, material emphasis have been inadequate to account for the foreign policies of small states and the potential for their subjective exercise of different levels of agency vis-à-vis their external environments. Constructivism, with its conception of a world constituted of inter-subjective realities, is a useful theory for foreign policy analysis. It aids in the understanding that aspects of ideology, identity and policy are conceptions constantly reinvented to overcome emerging threats and challenges by reading and taking advantage of developing opportunities over time.

Based on this theoretical framework, this chapter illustrates how depending on the ruling elite's perception of the circumstances of the day, each of the first four presidents accentuated different and various elements of the foreign policy principles originally articulated by the founding president, Seretse Khama. Predicated on Botswana's own enduring internal social identity as fostered by all four presidents, it is notable that foreign policy, despite variances, had a common approach: the promotion of democratic ideals as a necessary precondition for achieving any other objectives. A number of examples since independence illustrate how Botswana's foreign policy embedded in principled pragmatism, has had an enduring foreign policy posture.

What is articulated is a two-pronged approach to understanding Botswana's foreign policy direction as a small state in international relations.

First, there is the assessment of how Botswana's leadership took cognisance of its external environment to position itself in a manner that safeguarded its preferences and interests. Botswana pointedly read and understood its geo-political context during the apartheid era, cautious not to adopt a posture that would grant Pretoria or Salisbury the pretext to wage a military response. Botswana presented itself as a moderate, measured and rational voice in conference settings, which appealed to powerful liberal, potentially protective elements in the West. Further, it allowed for negotiations with Pretoria in an environment free of hostilities. In this regard, Botswana was able to safeguard its survival through how it positioned itself. This entailed the use of skilful diplomacy and committing itself to multilateral conference settings.

Second, in putting forward the notion of "principled pragmatism", Botswana's agency as projected to the external world was expressed in a set of principles derived from the socio-cultural identity of the country. Botswana in the main (notwithstanding instances during the Khama presidency, for instance), has managed to cultivate a liberal democratic ethos. This has been underpinned by regular, undisturbed electoral multiparty contestations, the respect for civil liberties, the practice of non-racialism, a respect for human rights and the promotion of the rule of law. These liberal democratic ideals were projected onto its foreign policy. Aware of its station as a small state during apartheid, Gaborone nevertheless exercised a level of defiance towards Pretoria and Salisbury, based on its disdain for racist, minority-led governments. Its central role in the FLS, which consolidated a concerted regional approach to opposing the apartheid-state, is well appreciated by Pan-Africanists. After the fall of apartheid, Botswana was prepared to stand in the wilderness and defend its principles. This, even where African counterparts chose to turn a blind eye towards violations of international law and the norms that govern their collective institutions.

Under changing conditions, the adherence to a principled stance is a key feature in the country's foreign policy posture. Botswana's intervention in Lesotho, the chastisement of Mugabe for bringing about the Zimbabwean electoral crisis of 2008 and its dissenting stance when the AU sought to sideline the ICC are all examples of this projected principled identity. Throughout its history, Botswana as a small African state succeeded in an international arena dominated by Western ideals because it visibly lived and espoused liberal democratic values. This was the antithesis of the general trend for many African states, which, to a large degree may explain why similarly situated small states on the continent have not boasted comparable levels of success.

While it is true that its long-standing image as a "shining example of liberal democracy" rewarded Botswana with positive political and economic outcomes, in recent times it has also led to a lack of solidarity with African counterparts and dented its image in Africa. This may explain the current approach adopted by the recently inaugurated president, Mokgweetsi Masisi, who has prudently sought to reposition Botswana's image amongst other African leaders as a bilateral and multilateral partner ("Masisi Quietly Resumes Silent Diplomacy", 2018). However, Masisi nevertheless reiterated his commitment to the promotion of human rights, democracy, good governance, the rule of law and the maintenance of international peace, in his inaugural address to parliament in 2018 (Masisi, 2018). Early indications suggest Masisi's foreign policy objectives, true to Botswana's steadfast tradition, will similarly ascribe to those of "principled pragmatism".

Notes

1 FPA is understood as the analysis of the political agency of states insofar as it is explained by the relationship between internal decision-making processes of actors and the external environment they face (Hudson, 2005: 2).
2 "Self-help" is understood as a situation that is brought about as a result of a central governing void that can guarantee collective security within the anarchic international system, promoting each state to provide for their own security (Waltz, 1988: 624).
3 Nathalie Tocci asserts foreign policies can be assessed to be driven by normative goals if they are motivated by, "democracy, human rights, the rule of law, international law and sustainable development" in contrast to strategic goals which entail, "protection of commercial interests, migration management or energy security" (Tocci, 2008: 6).
4 This is predicated upon two types of elite ideas: (1) state identity – the consolidation of the internal order preferred by an elite as the basis of the state's socio-cultural identity; and (2) the raison d'état or the purpose of the state—which drives the elite state to form alliances with countries that are constituted by similar socio-cultural dispositions (Gvalia et al., 2013: 108). The cumulative effect of these preferences will lead to an appraisal of the contours and perceptions of threats and opportunities persisting in an elite's external environment. Similarly, Ausra Park's individual-level approach to FPA requires the investigation of an elite's particular background, leading to an understanding of his beliefs, perceptions, motives and leadership style (Park, 2005: 233-234).
5 Joseph Nye (in Thorhallsson, 2012) defines soft power as those qualitative features of a country—such as diplomacy, reputation and culture—that grants the state with the ability to court other states into wanting what you want (Thorhallsson, 2012: 143; Chong, 2010: 3).
6 In this study, Osei-Hwedie and Mokhawa use descriptions to underscore the continuities and variance in approach of each president. This depicts Seretse Khama as a pragmatist who followed a realist external policy; Masire as a vector of reorientation that pursued an adaptive policy befitting of the changing post-apartheid environment; Mogae as the agent which sought the diversification of global development partners; and Ian Khama as the proponent of foreign policy activism in world affairs (Osei-Hwedie & Mokhawa, 2014: 8–14).

7 Botswana was surrounded by South Africa, Rhodesia and until the mid-1970s, minority white ruled Angola and Mozambique.
8 By 1970, the country's per capita income was USD 240 and government revenue and spending was USD 34 million (Maipose et al., 1997: 17).
9 Botswana did however experience reprisals from both South Africa and Rhodesia. There were numerous skirmishes on the border between the Botswana mobile police unit and Rhodesian forces in 1976 (Chipasula & Miti, 1989: 108; Dale, 1987: 85). The South African Defence Force also raided Gaborone in 1985 and 1986 looking for ANC strongholds (Dale, 1987: 78).
10 The marriage had also led to disdain from Bamangwato tribal elders in the Bechuanaland Protectorate as well.
11 Botswana did not wish to lend legitimacy to the racialist politics of South Africa and Rhodesia and the fact that they governed disenfranchised masses.
12 The FLS comprised of the core members of Botswana, Zambia, Tanzania, and later Angola and Mozambique.
13 The SADC Treaty establishing the regional economic community instructs that the conduct of member states must be commensurate with the values and norms of "sovereign equality … solidarity, peace and security… human rights, democracy, and the rule of law … equity, balance and mutual benefit … [and] peaceful settlement of disputes" (SADC, 1992: art 4).
14 Under the OAU, the inclination was to avoid engaging with activities that violated the domestic affairs of countries, through a principle of non-interference. Under the AU, the Heads of States and Governments are mandated under exigent circumstances to intervene in countries to ward off crimes against humanity, genocide and war crimes in what is known as this principle of non-indifference (Sharpe, 2017).
15 Botswana is a member of the Friends of R2P network. The R2P Initiative seeks to protect populations of the world from war crimes, genocide, ethnic cleansing and other crimes against humanity (Ntwaagae, 2015).
16 As early as 1975, Botswana had demonstrated its resolve to ensure that human rights issues are accorded the necessary attention when she—along with Mozambique, Tanzania and Zambia—boycotted a summit held in Kampala, remonstrating against Idi Amin's chairmanship of the OAU (Williams, 2007: 269).
17 In this regard, Mandela sought to reinvent Pretoria's image in the eyes of the world as an emerging liberal democracy whose foreign policy would be based on the promotion of human rights, democracy, respect for international law, peace and regional and international economic cooperation (Mandela, 1993).
18 For instance, Cote d'Ivoire handed Charles Ble Goude and Laurent Gbagbo to the ICC, while Niger surrendered war crimes accused Ahmad Al Faqi Al Mahdi to the court. Gabon also requested the ICC Prosecutor to open an investigation into international crimes committed in the country during the presidential elections of 2016 (Aggad & Apiko, 2016).
19 Botswana, since independence, is internationally seen as a liberal democracy where domestically, electoral democracy and the rule of law were firmly established. Botswana mounted a credible foreign policy advocating consensus politics and liberal principles to the world. A number of domestic events under the Mogae and Khama presidencies, however, attracted much criticism and dented Botswana's image. The resident expatriate academic, Kenneth Good, was by presidential fiat expelled from the country after being critical of government policy regarding the undemocratic nature of the country's automatic succession of the presidency. Survival International highlighted the displacement of a small minority population, the San people, from their land, in order to allow for formal and investment-bearing economic activity. Ian Khama was branded as a leader that personalised state power and governed by presidential edicts (Pegg, 2005: 829–830; Good, 2008: 4; Good, 2009: 320). Mogae was also seen to foster some level of political intolerance, as seen in the fact that he threatened to dissolve parliament

if his choice for vice president, Ian Khama, was not endorsed by parliamentarians as required by law. It is, however, noted by Botlhomilwe, Sebudubudu and Maripe (2011: 333) that political intolerance under Ian Khama reached extraordinary heights. Even more concerning was that under Ian Khama there were several reported incidents of state terrorism at the Directorate of Intelligence and Security Services (DISS), formed by the Khama presidency. In 2008 for example, following student demonstrations at the University of Botswana, DISS agents abducted the President of the Student Representative Council, issued death threats, and later abandoned him in the wilderness (Gwatiwa, 2011: 179–180). The DISS also engaged in overt extrajudicial killings and torture of various dissidents or criminal suspects, foregoing established procedures under the law. The most symbolic of these extrajudicial killings by the DISS was that of a suspect who was littered with armour-piercing bullets in full view of the public in 2009, after he was implicated in the robbery of a house belonging to a friend of the president (Gwatiwa, 2011: 181). Increasingly, it became evident that there was a growing trend of a non-accountable deep state at play within the country. Khama's government was also routinely criticised for its authoritarian treatment of public sector employees. Civil service remuneration had not increased for three years and relations reached a boiling point when in 2011, 90,000 workers downed tools and went on a strike that lasted longer than a month. The government subsequently refused the 16% salary increase that was sought and was criticised for occasioning a deadlock in subsequent negotiations (CNN Online, 22 April 2011).

References

Adler, E. (2002). Constructivism and International Relations. In W. Carlsnaes, T. Risse & B. Simmons (eds.). *Handbook of International Relations*. London: SAGE Publications Ltd.

Aggad, F. & Apiko, P. (2016). The International Criminal Court, Africa and the African Union: What way forward? Discussion Paper for the European Centre for Development Policy Management, No. 201. November 2016. Available from https://ecdpm.org/wp-content/uploads/DP201-ICC-Africa-AU-Apiko-Aggad-November-2016.pdf (Accessed 15 May 2019).

Badza, S. (2009). Zimbabwe's 2008 Harmonized Elections: Regional and International Reactions. In E. Masunungure (ed.). *Defying the Winds of Change. Zimbabwe's 2008 Elections*. Harare: Weaver Press.

Barber, J. & Barratt, J. (1990). *South Africa's Foreign Policy: The Search for Status and Security 1945–1988*. Cambridge: Cambridge University Press.

BBC News. (2012). Ethiopia to Host Africa Union Summit After Omar al-Bashir Malawi Row. *BBC News Online*. 12 June 2012. Available from http://www.bbc.co.uk/news/worldafrica-18407396 (Accessed 14 July 2018).

Black, D., Mugyenyi, J. & Swatuk, L. (1988). *Foreign Policy in Small States: Botswana, Lesotho, Swaziland and Southern Africa*. Halifax, NS: Centre for Foreign Policy Studies, Dalhousie University.

Botlhomilwe, M., Sebudubudu, D. & Maripe, B. (2011). Limited Freedom and Intolerance in Botswana. *Journal of Contemporary African Studies*, *29*(3): 331–348. doi:10.1080/02589001.2011.581501.

Chipasula, J. & Miti, K. (1989). *Botswana in Southern Africa: What Lies Ahead*. Delhi: Ajanta Publications.

Chong, A. (2010). Small State Soft Power Strategies: Virtual Enlargement in the Cases of the Vatican City State and Singapore. *Cambridge Review of International Affairs*, *23*(3): 383–405. doi:10.1080/09557571.2010.484048.

Claus, O. & Weimer, B. (1991). Changing Southern Africa: What Role for Botswana *Africa Spectrum*, *26*(3): 315–334.

CNN. (2011). 90,000 Botswana Government Workers on Strike. *CNN Online*. 22 April 2011. Available from http://edition.cnn.com/2011/WORLD/africa/04/21/botswana.civil.servant.strike/index.html (Accessed 26 January 2018).

Dale, R. (1976). President Sir Seretse Khama, Botswana's Foreign Policy and the Southern African Subordinate State System. *Plural Societies*, *7*(1): 69–87.

Dale, R. (1987). Not Always so Placid a Place: Botswana Under Attack. *African Affairs*, *86*(342): 73–91.

Democracy Coalition Project. (2002). *Defending Democracy: A Global Survey of Foreign Policy Trends 1992–2002*. Democracy Coalition Project: University of California.

Dersso, S. (2016). To Intervene or Not to Intervene? An Inside View of the AU's Decision-Making on Article 4(h) and Burundi. *Occasional Paper for the World Peace Foundation*. Available from https://sites.tufts.edu/wpf/files/2017/05/AU-Decision-Making-on-Burundi_Dersso.pdf (Accessed 15 May 2019).

Good, K. (2008). *Diamond, Dispossession and Democracy in Botswana*. Johannesburg: Jacana Media.

Good, K. (2009). Briefing the Presidency of General Ian Khama: The Militarization of the Botswana "Miracle". *African Affairs*, *109*(435): 315–324. doi:io.io93/afraf/adpO86.

Gvalia, G., Siroky, D., Lebanidze, B. & Isahvili, Z. (2013). Thinking Outside the Bloc: Explaining the Foreign Policy of Small States. *Security Studies*, *22*(1): 98–131. doi:10.1080/09636412.2013.757463.

Gwatiwa, T. (2011). Intelligence Operations as Terrorism: Emerging State Terrorism in Botswana. *Journal of African Studies and Development*, *3*(9): 167–186. doi:10.5897/JASD.

Halpern, J. (1965). *South Africa's Hostages*. Harmondsworth: Penguin.

Henderson, W. (1974). Independent Botswana: A Reappraisal of Foreign Policy Options. *African Affairs*, *73*(290): 37–49.

Henderson, W. (1990). Seretse Khama: A Personal Appreciation. *African Affairs*, *89*(354): 27–56. doi:10.2307/1161426.

Houghton, D. (2007). Reinvigorating the Study of Foreign Policy Decision Making: Towards a Constructivist Approach. *Foreign Policy Analysis*, *3*: 24–45.

Hudson, V. (2005). Foreign Policy Analysis: Actor-Specific Theory and the Ground of International Relations. *Foreign Policy Analysis*, *1*: 1–30.

Jazbec, M. (2010). Small States and Diplomacy: An Indispensible though Much Diversified Relation. *Administrative Culture*, *11*(1): 66–83.

Jimson, K. (2016). Are we a Nation of Failures? *Botswana Guardian Online*. 26 July 2016. Available from http://www.botswanaguardian.co.bw/news/item/2074-are-we-a-nation-of-failures.html (Accessed 20 July 2018).

Jonas, O., Mandiyanike, D. & Maundeni, Z. (2013). Botswana and Pivotal Deterrence in the Zimbabwe 2008 Political Crisis. *The Open Political Science Journal*, *6*: 1–9.

Keorapetse, D. (2016). Khama's Foreign Policy is Flawed. *Mmegi Online*. 4 March 2016. Available from http://www.mmegi.bw/index.php?aid=58292&dir=2016/march/04 (Accessed 15 July 2018).

Khadiagala, G. (2001). Foreign Policy Decision Making in Southern Africa's Fading Frontline. In G. Khadiagala & T. Lyons (eds.). *African Foreign Policies: Power and Process*. London: Lynne Rienner Publishers.

Kioko, B. (2003). The Right of Intervention Under the African Union's Constitutive Act: From Non-Interference to Non-Intervention. *International Review of the Red Cross*, *85*(852): 807–826.

Landell-Mills, P. (1971). The 1969 Southern African Customs Union Agreement. *Journal of Modern African Studies*, *9*(2): 263–281. doi:10.1017/S0022278X00024939.

Lee, D. & Smith, N. (2010) Small State Discourses in the International Political Economy. *Third World Quarterly*, *31*(7): 1091–1105. doi:10.1080/01436597.2010.518750.

Legum, C. (1973). The Problems of the Land-Locked Countries of Southern Africa in the Confrontation Between Independent Africa and South Africa, Rhodesia and Portugal. In Z. Cervenka (ed.). *Land-locked Countries of Africa*. Uppsala: The Scandinavian Institute of African Studies.

Lekalake, R. (2016). Botswana's Democratic Consolidation: What Will It Take? *Afrobarometer Policy Paper No. 30*, January 2016. Available from http://afrobarometer.org/sites/default/files/publications/Policy%20papers/ab_r6_policypaperno30_democracy_in_botswana.pdf (Accessed 17 November 2018).

Lekoa, L. (2017). Botswana's Foreign Policy is Predicated on Multilateralism (part 2). *Botswana Guardian Online*. 15 December 2017. Available from http://www.botswanaguardian.co.bw/news/item/3116-botswana-s-foreign-policy-is-predicated-on-multilateralism-part2.html (Accessed 19 November 2018).

Likoti, J. (2007). The 1998 Military Intervention in Lesotho: SADC Peace Mission or Resource War? *International Peace Keeping*, *14*(2): 251–263. doi:10.1080/13533310601150875.

Maipose, G., Somolekae, G. & Johnston, T. (1997). Effective Aid Management: The Case of Botswana. In J. Carlsson, G. Somolekae & N. van de Walle (eds.). *Foreign Aid in Africa: Learning from Country Experiences*. Motala: Motala Grafiska.

Malila, I. S. & Molebatsi, R. M. (2014). Botswana's Experimentation with "Ethical Foreign Policy". *Southern African Peace and Security Studies*, *3*(1): 5–25.

Mandela, N. (1993). South Africa's Future Foreign Policy. *Foreign Affairs*, *72*(5): 86–97. doi:10.2307/20045816.

Masire, Q. (2006). *Very Brave or Very Foolish: Memoirs of an African Democrat*. Gaborone: Macmillan Botswana.

Masisi, M. (2018). *Inauguration Address by Mokgweetsi Masisi, the Fifth President of Botswana*. 1 April 2018. National Assembly of Botswana. Available from https://www.mmegi.bw/index.php?aid=75087&dir=2018/april/01 (Accessed 9 January 2020).

Mmegi. (2008). "Homeboy" Khama Ventures Out. *Mmegi Online*. 25 November 2008. Available from http://www.mmegi.bw/index.php?sid=1&aid=6&dir=2008/November/Tuesday25 (Accessed 20 October 2013).

Murithi, T. (2013). The African Union and the International Criminal Court: An Embattled Relationship. Institute for Justice and Reconciliation, 8. Available from https://www.africaportal.org/publications/the-african-union-and-the-international-criminal-court-an-embattled-relationship.

Nasra, S. (2011). Governance in EU Foreign Policy: Exploring Small State Influence. *Journal of European Public Policy*, *18*(2): 164–180. doi:10.1080/13501763.2011.544490.

Nathan, L. (2012). *Community of Insecurity: SADC's Struggle for Peace and Security in Southern Africa*. Burlington: Ashgate.

Nathan, L. (2013). The Disbanding of the SADC Tribunal: A Cautionary Tale. *Human Rigths Quarterly*, *35*(4): 870–892. doi:10.1353/hrq.2013.0059.

Neethling, T. (1999). Military Intervention in Lesotho: Perspective on Operation Boleas and Beyond. *The Online Journal of Peace and Conflict Resolution*, *2*(2). Available from http://www.operationspaix.net/DATA/DOCUMENT/6107~v~Military_Intervention_in_Lesotho__Perspectives_on_Operation_Boleas_and_Beyond.pdf (Accessed 8 October 2013).

Niemann, M. (1993). Diamonds Are a State's Best Friend: Botswana's Foreign Policy in Southern Africa. *Africa Today*, *40*(1): 27–47.

Nnoli, O. (1989). Democracy in Botswana: A Pan-African Perspective. In J. Holm & P. Molutsi (eds.). *Democracy in Botswana: The Proceedings of a Symposium Held in Gaborone*. Gaborone: MacMillan Botswana.

Nordic Africa Institute. (2018). Peace and Security Challenges in Southern Africa Governance: Deficits and Lacklustre Regional Conflict Management. *Policy Note No. 4, 2018*. Available from https://reliefweb.int/sites/reliefweb.int/files/resources/FULLTEXT01.pdf (Accessed 13 May 2019).

Ntwaagae, C. (2015). Informal Interactive Dialogue on the Responsibility of States to Protect their Populations by Preventing Genocide, War Crimes, Ethnic Cleansing, and Crimes against Humanity. *Statement by the Ambassador and Permanent Representative to the United Nations, to the UN General Assembly, New York*. 8 September 2015. Available from http://www.responsibilitytoprotect.org/botswana-2.pdf (Accessed 20 November 2018).

Osei-Hwedie, B. (1998). The Role of Botswana in the liberation of Southern Africa since 1966. In W. Edge & M. Lekorwe (eds.). *Botswana: Politics and Society*. Pretoria: J.L. van Schaik Publishers.

Osei-Hwedie, B. & Mokhawa, G. (2014). Continuity and Change: The Influence of the Presidents on Botswana's Foreign Policy. *Afro Asian Journal of Social Sciences*, *5*(1).

Pambazuka News. (2008). Zimbabwe: Memo to African Leaders. 23 June 2008. Available from http://www.pambazuka.org/en/category/racism/48972 (Accessed 8 December 2013).

Park, A. (2005). Starting from Scratch: The Role of Leadership in the Foreign Policymaking of the Baltic States, 1991–1999. *East European Quarterly*, *XXXIX*(2): 229–270. doi:10.1017/S1049096505210430.

Parsons, N. (2008). Seretse Khama: 1921–80. University of Botswana History Department website. Available from http://www.thuto.org/ubh/bw/skhama.htm (Accessed 17 November 2018).

Pegg, S. (2005). Presidential Succession and Academic Freedom: Botswana Deports Leading Political Scientist. *Political Science and Politics*, *38*(4): 829–831. doi:10.1017/S1049096505210430.

Sekgoma, G. (1998). New Dimensions in Botswana's Foreign Policy. In W. Edge & M. Lekorwe (eds.). *Botswana: Politics and Society*. Pretoria: J.L. van Schaik.

Sekgoma, G. (1990). A Note on Botswana's Foreign Policy and Ideological Stance. *Transafrican Journal of History*, *19*: 152–164.

Selinyane, N. (2006). Lost Between Stability and Democracy: South Africa and Lesotho's Constitutional Crises of the 1990s. In R. Southall (ed.). *South Africa's Role in Conflict Resolution and Peacemaking in Africa*. Cape Town: Human Sciences Research Council Press.

Sharpe, M. (2017). From Non-Interference to Non-Indifference: The African Union and the Responsibility to Protect. *Report Prepared for the International Refugees Rights Initiative*. September 2017. Available from https://reliefweb.int/sites/reliefweb.int/files/resources/AU%20R2P%20-%20final.pdf (Accessed 15 May 2019).

Sibalukhulu, N. & Louw, A. (2010). The AU and the ICC Still Not the Best of Friends. *Institute for Security Studies*. Available from http://www.issafrica.org/iss-today/the-au-and-the-icc-still-not-the-best-of-friends (Accessed 5 April 2012) doi:10.1177/0047117819842294.

Sklar, R. (1989). On Democracy and Development in Botswana. In J. Holm & P. Molutsi (eds.). *Democracy in Botswana: The Proceedings of a Symposium Held in Gaborone*. Gaborone: MacMillan Botswana.

Stevens, R. (1966). The New Republic of Botswana. *Africa Report*. October 1966. Available from http://www.aaionline.org/wp-content/uploads/2017/02/Botswana-1.pdf (Accessed 16 September 2018).

Sunday Standard. (2018). Masisi Quietly Resumes Silent Diplomacy. *Sunday Standard Online*. 15 April 2018. Available from http://www.sundaystandard.info/masisi-quietly-resumes-silent-diplomacy (Accessed 15 July 2018).

Taylor, I. (1997). The Captive States of Southern Africa and China: The PRC and Botswana, Lesotho and Swaziland. *Journal of Commonwealth and Comparative Politics*, *35*(2): 75–95. doi:10.1080/14662049708447746.

The Namibian. (2011). Botswana Supports ICC Warrant for Gaddafi. *The Namibian Online*, July 8 2011. Available from http://www.namibian.com.na/indexx.php?archive_id=82287&page_type=archive_story_detail&page=1604 (Accessed 10 October 2013).

Thorhallsson, B. (2012). Small States in the UN security Council: Means of Influence? *The Hague Journal of Diplomacy*, *7*: 135–160. doi:10.1163/187119112X628454.

Tladi, D. (2009). The African Union and The International Criminal Court: The Battle of the Soul of International Law. *South African Year Book of International Law*, *34*: 57–69.

Tlou, T., Parsons, N. & Henderson, W. (1995). *Seretse Khama: 1921–80*. Johannesburg: MacMillan.

Tocci, N. (2008). *Who Is a Normative Foreign Policy Actor? The European Union and Its Global Partners*. Brussels: Centre for European Policy Studies.

Treaty of the Southern African Development Community. (1992). Available from http://www.sadc.int/files/9113/5292/9434/SADC_Treaty.pdf (Accessed 10 April, 2019).

Tsie, B. (1996). The Political Context of Botswana's Development Performance. *Journal of Southern African Studies*, *22*(4): 519–616. doi:10.1080/03057079608708514.

United Nations Security Council. (1977). *Resolution 406: Botswana-Southern Rhodesia*. Available from http://unscr.com/en/resolutions/doc/406 (Accessed 15 November 2013).

Walker, S. (2011). Foreign Policy Analysis and Behavioural International Relations. In S. Walker, A. Malici & M. Schafer (eds.). *Rethinking Foreign Policy Analysis: States, Leaders, and the Microfoundations of Behavioural International Relations*. New York: Routledge.

Waltz, K. (1988). The Origins of War in Neorealist Theory. *The Journal of Interdisciplinary History*, *18*(4): 615–628. doi:10.2307/204817.

Wendt, A. (1992). Anarchy Is What States Make of it: The Social Construction of Power Politics. *International Organisation*, *46*(2): 391–425.

Williams, P. (2007). From Non-Intervention to Non-Indifference: The Origins and Development of The African Union's Security Culture. *African Affairs*, *106*(423): 253–279. doi:10.1093/afraf/adm001.

10 Tunisia's foreign policy towards France before and after an undemanding "revolution"

A theoretical explanation of the An-Nahdha-led interim governments' soft policy

Ahmed Ali Salem

Introduction

Tunisia is considered to have staged a revolution that brought a democratically elected government to power which fundamentally changed the domestic order of things. However, there was no major reordering of its external relations. This is most obvious in the relationship with France, the former colonial power which still holds a preeminent position, as Tunisia continues to depend on France by way of economic ties of tourism, investment and aid. Tunisia's foreign policy underwent no radical restructuring with France, which remained as influential as before. Using the prism of foreign policy, this raises questions about the nature of change in Tunisia.

France was taken aback by the uprisings in Tunisia and other Arab Spring countries in late 2010 and early 2011. Well after the uprisings began, the French government maintained its support for long-ruling dictators in the region, including Tunisia's Zine El Abidine Ben Ali, who had served the interests of the West in general and France in particular. After he fled Tunisia on 14 January 2011, there followed a provisional government led by his long-standing prime minister Mohamed al-Ghannouchi. This government was short-lived and replaced on 27 February by another provisional government led by Caid Essebsi, a former minister prior to Ben Ali's rise to power. This government was also replaced by three other provisional governments until Essebsi was elected as a president by the end of the transitional period in December 2014.

During the transitional period, Tunisia experienced free and fair elections for the first time since independence in 1956 when voting for a National Constituent Assembly (NCA) in October 2011. The turnout of over 49% meant that more Tunisians than ever had participated in the elections. The outcome was one where the Islamist party, *An-Nahdha* (Renaissance), came first, with 35% of the popular vote, winning 89 seats in the NCA. The Congress for the Republic came second, with 8.2% of the popular vote (29 seats), followed by the Democratic Forum for Labour and Liberties, with 6.6% of the popular vote (20 seats), then the Progressive Democratic Party, with 3.7% of the popular vote (16 seats). After long negotiations, a coalition government was formed; an An-Nahdha leader, Hamadi Jebali, chaired the cabinet and the leaders of the second- and fourth-winning parties were elected as president of the republic and speaker of the NCA respectively (Aghrout, 2011). In March 2013, the same coalition formed a new interim government, led by Ali Larayedh—another An-Nahdha leader.

Under the An-Nahdha-led interim governments, Tunisia's foreign relations with France cooled at times, but the country's strategic foreign policy outlook continued to accommodate France's preeminence in Tunisia's affairs throughout this immediate post-uprising period. The An-Nahdha-led interim governments had in no way been challenging of France and its privileged position of influence in Tunisia. As a matter of fact, even though the new governments were made up of parties repressed under the French-supported Ben Ali regime, their position towards France hardly differed from that of the old regime or the two interim governments before the 2011 elections (Lesch, 2014).

Instead of drawing attention to France's erstwhile support for Ben Ali, in order to extract leverage from France to materially support democratisation under the new dispensation, the An-Nahdha-led interim governments adopted a foreign policy of sweet-talking and cosying up to the French government. They pursued business-as-usual, aiming basically to convince France of the economic and security benefits of supporting Tunisia. They made no hard demands, such as compensating the Tunisians for France's enduring support of the deposed dictator and his brutal policies up until his last day in office. Ironically, while the An-Nahdha-led interim governments' policies towards France softened, the gap between what France announced and what its actual policies on democratisation in Tunisia amounted to, widened.

This soft policy towards France is not puzzling for some political theorists. For example, structuralists who locate the source of state preferences in the international political or economic system would not be surprised by this policy. For them, Tunisia's uprising did not change the structures of international systems, and so no foreign policy change could be expected. However, structuralist theorists do not contribute, or even aspire to contribute, to foreign policy theorising. The theorists who aspire to contribute to foreign policy theorising, and must be puzzled by this soft policy towards France, are those who locate the source of state preferences inside the state. They normally expect post-revolution governments to make radical changes in foreign policies. For example, democratic-peace theorists attribute the improved relations between the West and the East European states that underwent democratic revolutions in the late 1980s partly to those revolutions (Russett, 1993). Post-revolutionary Iran also experienced a radical shift in foreign policy, especially towards the states perceived as adamant supporters of its deposed dictator (Terhalle, 2015). Egypt under Nasser in the 1950s and 1960s was another example of a revisionist state in regional and world politics. Its foreign policy turned against its former coloniser, the United Kingdom, and its Western allies. Thus, it not only refused to join the US-engineered Baghdad Pact Organisation in 1955 but also concluded an arms deal with the Soviet-controlled Czechoslovakia in the same year. Moreover, Egypt advocated a progressive view of Pan-Arab nationalism that inspired Arab masses but was perceived as threatening by Arab monarchies (Salem, 2008).

Tunisia is obviously an anomaly. This chapter proves that the An-Nahdha-led interim governments did not challenge French policies towards Tunisia and in the region more generally for more than two years, apart from the French intervention in Mali. The foreign policies of those governments were hardly revolutionary, especially towards France. In this chapter, I offer a blended realist-constructivist explanation of the continuity in foreign relations with France by governments brought to power by a national uprising against a repressive regime that France (and the West) had uncritically supported for many years. An-Nahdha's soft policy towards France, I argue, was partly a result of the ideology and social nature of its leadership and the need for compromise in domestic politics. My contention is that neoclassical realism and non-structural constructivism can together provide an explanation of this anomaly. To apply this hybrid approach to An-Nahdha's soft policy towards France, An-Nahdha's ideology, leadership and domestic political calculations will be taken into consideration.

The chapter is structured in two main parts. The first empirical part discusses the particulars of Tunisia's relations with France under the post-uprising, An-Nahdha-led interim governments between 2011 and 2014, which show no radical change. The analysis highlights Tunisia's agency (or lack thereof) vis-a-vis the governments of two French presidents: Sarkozy and Hollande. The second theoretical part attempts to solve this puzzle by dismissing structuralist explanations, building a realist-constructivist approach and applying it to Tunisia's case. The chapter, however, begins with a brief history of Tunisia's relations with France before the uprising.

Tunisia's foreign policy towards France before the uprising

Since France occupied Tunisia in 1881, the two countries never considered their relations "foreign" in the strict sense of the term. Tunisia's formal independence in 1956 only opened a new chapter in this special relationship. The French colonial administration not only established "a fairly large number of settlers", but also paved the way for the emergence of a Tunisian national movement that was heavily influenced by the French model of state (Ayubi, 1995: 199–120). A familiarity with French culture and an advocacy of the French modernist character were foundations of that movement (Powel, 2009). Its leader, Habib Bourguiba, who later became Tunisia's first president, believed in a strong cordial relation with France (Murphy, 2014: 235–236) and was so cooperative with the French authorities that he accepted the autonomous status that France offered Tunisia in 1954 and imposed it against the wishes of many Tunisians and at the risk of a civil war (Micaud, 1968). Despite clashes over the last French military base in Tunisia and a territorial dispute in occupied Algeria in 1961, Bourguiba maintained a close relationship with France, especially in the field of education, to "save Tunisia from the winds of the Orient", as he once said. Admiring the secular culture of France's Third Republic, he also adopted extremist measures against public religious symbols and behaviours. This was criticised by the later Islamist movement that gave birth to the An-Nahdha Party (Burgat, 1998).

The winds of the Orient did not only refer to Islamic ideals but also to the then rising ideologies of Pan-Arab and Pan-African nationalisms. Bourguiba strongly upheld Tunisia's sovereignty and warm relations with the West against Nasser's, and later Qaddafi's unionist and anti-Western versions of these ideologies (Deeb, 1989). He opposed their anti-Israel rhetoric and aspirations to dominate the Pan-Arab and Pan-African institutions (Salem, 2007), and preferred to join the French-friendly Brazzaville Group over the anti-French Casablanca Group before the creation of the Organisation of African Unity (Zartman, 1987). Despite improved security relations with the United States, Bourguiba sought France's support against Libya in the 1980s. This brought them both to the brink of rupture (Balta, 1986: 243) and rivalled Algeria and Morocco for privileged relations with their former common metropole (Balta, 1986: 15)—Tunisia's first arms supplier and major commercial partner throughout the Cold War (Balta, 1986: 26).

Local, regional and global events contributed to opening another chapter in Tunisia's relations with France in the late 1980s and early 1990s. Senile Bourguiba was bloodlessly ousted in 1987 by his prime minister and former interior minister, Zine El Abidine Ben Ali; the Cold War came to an end; and the Maghreb states gave up their malicious strategy of allying against each other, initially to build an (ineffective) Arab Maghreb Union in 1989, then to focus on their individual crises such as Algeria's military coup and the embargo on Libya in 1992. In this environment, Ben Ali was relieved of any serious external threat and turned against the internal threats to his rule, mainly the new popular forces that could rise to power democratically. The 1989 elections, though not fully free or fair, only confirmed his suspicions, so he retreated to dictatorial rule and mass violations of human rights in the name of fighting extremism and terrorism.

In response, and surprisingly to idealists, France, the European Union and the United States did not defend their democratic and liberal ideals; rather, they succumbed to Ben Ali's claims and supported his rule to varying degrees, especially after the terrorist attacks on the United States in 2001. Addressing the Western audience, Ben Ali always stressed not only Tunisia's indisputable economic success but also its stability in an unstable region and "willingness to cooperate in the war on terrorism" (Wood, 2002: 108). In his visit to France in October 1997, for example, Ben Ali responded to the hostile campaign of the French press and international and French human rights groups, claiming that there were no political detainees in Tunisia. In turn, President Chirac congratulated him for "the exemplary success of Tunisia's experience over the past ten years" (Wood, 2002: 100–101). In short, Ben Ali drew on Western fears of "Islamist terrorism" to build partnerships around a securitised agenda that boosted his regime. Meanwhile, France's economic assistance to Tunisia was "the highest to any country in terms of contribution per capita", and remained Tunisia's first trade, investment, and loan partner (Murphy, 2014: 240–241).

Post-uprising cooperation with Ben Ali's main international ally, 2011–2014

When France realised the initial success of Tunisia's uprising after Ben Ali fled, French officials pledged support of Tunisia's democratisation. Not necessarily signifying any true shift in French foreign policy, it was an attempt to cope with the new status quo, to continue to further long-standing French interests in Tunisia, and also to minimise perceived security threats such as illegal immigration and Islamism in all its forms.

Despite claims to support democratisation in Tunisia, deeds did not follow words because French presidents and governments feared that democratisation might in fact give birth to a hostile regime in what was, after all, a neighbouring country. During Tunisia's transitional period between 2011 and 2014, French presidents and their governments did not support the outcome of the 2011 elections, and Tunisia's relations towards France cooled due to France's increasingly uncooperative policies towards Tunisia during this phase of democratic transition. Nevertheless, the An-Nahdha-led interim governments continued to cooperate with France on several issues, such as fighting what France considered terrorist threats. Even though France claimed to be committed to a democratised Tunisia, the French government nevertheless viewed An-Nahdha as suspect and a potential security threat.

First An-Nahdha-led government and President Sarkozy

The results of the 2011 election alarmed some, both internally and abroad. President Sarkozy, for example, said that France should closely follow the conditions of freedoms and human rights in Tunisia after An-Nahdha won. French foreign minister Juppé confirmed this implicit warning, saying that "there are red lines that must not be crossed; those of human rights, democratic alternation and gender equality". He denounced claims of contradictions between Islam and democracy and in a phone call with An-Nahdha's leader, Al-Ghanouchi, expressed his personal trust in Ennahda and the democratic transition in Tunisia. The French warning was read as French economic support to Tunisia being made conditional on respecting those "red lines" (Tunisia Live, 2011a).

For months after the election, no Western official visited Tunisia. It was only in January 2012 that France's Prime Minister Juppé became the first Western official after the elections to visit Tunisia (Tunisia Live, 2011b). While promising to boost French aid and to fully support the democratic transition, he again emphasised the need to respect freedom and women's rights (Tunisia: French back new leaders, 2012: 51), indicating that aid was conditional on this. Tunisia's government not only failed to condemn this clear meddling in its domestic affairs, but also expressed its willingness to serve France's Arab policy by hosting a meeting of the French-proposed "Friends-of-Syria Group" in February 2012 (Tunisia Live, 2012c).

The positive attitude of the Tunisian government towards France was at odds with the sentiments of many Tunisians towards France. For example, many

Tunisians were inflamed by a French book accusing French businesses, politicians and diplomats of complicity with the Ben Ali regime (Tunisia Live, 2012b). Also, a group of Tunisians gathered in front of the French embassy in Tunis to protest against the ban of the *niqab* (or full-face veil) in France and to defend a Moroccan-French national arrested for sporting a *niqab* in public and refusing to remove it (Tunisia Live, 2012a). Tunisia's Independence Day, 20 March, was another occasion for Tunisians to express a desire to end the psychological, cultural and economic dependence on France, as many of them publicly debated how they should describe the French presence of the past in their country: whether it amounted to occupation, colonialism or protectionism. For some, the history learnt in schools, language policies and lifestyle, all coloured by France, needed to change (Tunisia Live, 2012d).

First An-Nahdha-led government and President Hollande

The election of François Hollande to the French presidency was received by the Tunisian government with relief. Facing financial difficulties and having yet to see any of the billions pledged by the Group of 8 (G8) at its summit at Deauville, France, in May 2011 (Alderman, 2011), Tunisia expected President Hollande to fulfil his promise of a partial write off of its debt or a suspension of interest payments—a promise he had made in Tunis a year earlier after the uprising. Tunisians were encouraged by a statement of Hollande's special envoy in Tunis after he became president, in which he stressed France's "wishes to encourage a new start of the French-Tunisian relations", and readiness to contribute to the economic development process in Tunisia and participate in large-scale projects in underprivileged regions (Tunis Afrique Presse, 2012a). However, when Germany wrote off Tunisia's debt to Berlin, French diplomats in a change of mind undertook to persuade the Tunisian government unsuccessfully that wiping off debt was not at all a good idea and ultimately to the detriment of Tunisia since "it would propel Tunisia immediately into the ranks of customer nations of the Club de Paris and that would mean far higher interest rates on capital markets" ("Paris & Berlin in clash on debt", 2012). Although this French position was a sign of the new president's turnaround and reluctance to fulfil his promise, the Tunisian government did not react publicly, and continued to exert efforts to improve and placate relations with France. This was done by appointing a new ambassador to Paris, someone who held dual Tunisian and French citizenship and was well known in Franco-Tunisian business circles ("Left-wing businessman named envoy …", 2012).

By June 2012, Tunisia's prime minister, Hamadi Jebali, wished to take his government's concerns on the general relationship with France to Paris. His visit was postponed on several occasions by the French government and was made possible only after the prime minister himself reportedly requested an invitation from France's General Confederation of Small and Medium Companies (PME) and the French Employers Federation. As such, the visit took place without an invitation from the French Republic. Presented with a fait accompli and anxious to avoid a diplomatic snub, the French foreign ministry quickly set up a meeting between Tunisia's prime minister and his French counterpart ("Bosses prod Ayrault …", Paris, 2012). In a conference on Tunisia's economy, Jebali asserted that Tunisia possessed all assets to succeed and its partnership with France was a win-win partnership (Tunis Afrique Presse, 2012b). Tunisia's diplomatic effort at this time was aimed at boosting economic cooperation with France, because according to Jebali, his government counted on partners to help "overcome the hardship" (Tunis Afrique Presse, 2012c). This diplomatic effort continued with rapid progress, with Tunisia's caretaker President Moncef Marzouki visiting Paris the following month. However, like his prime minister, he was not successful on the critical issue of Tunisia's debts (Tunis Afrique Presse, 2012d). France refused to write off Tunisia's debt and only undertook to "identify the appropriate mechanisms to convert it into development projects" (Tunis Afrique Presse, 2012e).

With increasing French anxieties about Tunisia-related security threats, the Tunisian government turned more defensive. It had to address rising worries about Western nationals and diplomats in Tunisia after the attacks on the United States Embassy and the American School in Tunis in September 2012 in response to a crudely produced US-made anti-Islam film. Thus, the Tunisian foreign minister met Western ambassadors, voicing his government's regret and strong condemnation of the attacks (Tunis Afrique Presse, 2012f). French concerns of Tunisians being involved in plans of terrorist attacks in France grew after the discovery of a terrorist cell with ties to elements in Tunisia (Magharebia, 2012).

The bilateral relationship was put under more strain with the French military intervention in Mali in early 2013, something which the Tunisian government opposed publicly. With many Tunisians demonstrating against the French intervention, the government was under popular pressure to take this position. To address Tunisia's displeasure with the French measures in Mali, a French minister visited Tunisia and met its prime minister, asserting that the situation in Mali should worry Tunisia and all neighbouring countries (Tunis Afrique Presse, 2013a). However, in a rare moment of openly challenging France and displaying a strong sign of Tunisia's agency, its foreign minister, Rafik Abdessalem, chose to disagree and expressed his government's opposition to all non-African military operations in Mali (Reguly, 2013: A3). Unlike Algeria, Tunisia refused to open its airspace to French forces intervening in Mali (Brahem, 2013: 22). The French reaction was immediate and sharp: The French interior minister announced that cooperation with Tunisia on the economy and tourism industry was only possible where there was respect for democratic principles (Interior minister sees France as "trailblazer" in Mali, 2013).

This implied once more that French assistance was conditional, not only on Tunisia's democratisation and record on human rights but also in its agreeing to France's security policy in the region and toeing the line in fighting against what France considered terrorism in Africa.

The assassination of a leading opposition politician, Chokri Belaid, on 6 February 2013, gave France a new opportunity to meddle in Tunisia's internal affairs. The French president not only condemned this murder but also expressed concerns over "the mounting political violence in Tunisia" (Tunisia protests after assassination of opposition politician Chokri Belaid, 2013). Moreover, his interior minister, Manuel Valls, accused the Tunisian government of Islamic fascism (Radio France Internationale, 2013). Protesting against this interference, crowds burned the French flag in Tunisian streets, shouting "Get out!" (Murphy, 2014: 254–255). However, Tunisia's caretaker president, Moncef Marzouki, who was visiting France at that time, did not respond publicly and cut his visit short ("French foreign minister …", 2013). The Tunisian government's passive stance was also evident in the way it glossed over France's open siding against the Tunisia's ruling coalition. For example, France hosted Nessma TV which came out strongly against An-Nahdha (Nessma TV to broadcast in France, 2013). French interference was criticised by Tunisian journalists who lamented that French officials "openly disregarded the people's choices by offering opposition figures logistical support and preferential treatment" (Brahem, 2013: 22).

Despite the tensions, the Tunisian government continued to request French support. For example, the speaker of the National Constituent Assembly (NCA), when visiting Paris, stressed that Tunisia needed further support from France on the rescheduling of its debt and the bilateral achievement of a new balance in economic bilateral relations (Tunis Afrique Presse, 2013b). President Hollande's answer the next day was that France wanted first to see Tunisia finish off the transition process by adopting a constitution that suited the Tunisian people's revolution (Tunis Afrique Presse, 2013c).

Second An-Nahdha-led government and President Hollande

Partly in response to the repercussions of the assassination of Chokri Belaid, Tunisia's ruling coalition formed the second An-Nahdha-led interim government in March 2013 with a new prime minister, Ali Larayedh, and a new foreign minister, Othman Jerandi. After meeting the new prime minister, the French ambassador claimed that France supported the Tunisians in their democratic transition without any interference in their domestic affairs (Tunis Afrique Presse, 2013d). Nevertheless, the French government did not miss any opportunity to involve itself in Tunisia's internal affairs.[1] For example, a French minister at a meeting with Tunisia's prime minister again hinted that a conditionality regime was at play by emphasising "the drafting of the constitution and next elections as well as the priorities of the new cabinet" (Tunis Afrique Presse, 2013e).

President Hollande's long-awaited, repeatedly postponed visit to Tunisia to improve Franco-Tunisian relations happened on 4 July 2013. The first by a French president since the toppling of Ben Ali (Tunis Afrique Presse, 2013i), the visit held promise for Tunisian officials. In a build-up to the visit, Tunisia's Forum for Investment preceded it, attended by nearly a hundred heads of French enterprises enthusiastic about economic cooperation (Tunis Afrique Presse, 2013j). At the forum, the speaker of the NCA demanded deeds, not words, to strengthen the cooperation and partnership ties between France and Tunisia (Tunis Afrique Presse, 2013k).

Hollande's visit occurred a day after the military coup that ousted the first democratically elected president in Egypt. This dramatic end of Egypt's democratisation process gave French politicians an excellent opportunity to maintain their policy of verbal support for Tunisia's democratisation. Contrasting Tunisia's democratic progress with the military takeover in Egypt, Hollande called the latter a failed democracy. In a news conference, he addressed Tunisians and said "there is an obligation for you to succeed, because you are an example. You give many people in the Arab world hope" (Bouazza, 2013: A07). This direct appeal to Tunisians, however, amounted to a calculated, indirect snub to the Tunisian government.

In fact, Hollande's visit gave considerable prominence to the Tunisian opposition, more than to the Tunisian government. While the French president held just one set of talks with Prime Minister Larayedh, he went on to receive the main opposition leaders at a meeting held at the French embassy. No representative of An-Nahdha was invited to the latter (Power Brokers, 2013). Moreover, after meeting Laarayedh, Hollande again emphasised how Tunisia needed to finish off with the constitutional drafting process and organise free elections. Instead of criticising France's overt demands made on Tunisia's domestic affairs, the prime minister confirmed the government's readiness to conclude the present stage of the process by starting a debate on the constitution, setting up a body of electoral law and organising free elections (Tunis Afrique Presse, 2013k). In what appeared to be an apologetic and defensive stance, the prime minister went on to praise the French role in supporting Tunisia, acknowledging the existence of difficulties and lapses along the path (Magharebia, 2013).

Aware of popular criticisms of French interference in Tunisia's domestic affairs and unwillingness to accept its Islamist party as a legitimate democratic player, Hollande claimed that France cared greatly about Tunisia's transition process without interference, but also without indifference (Tunis Afrique Presse, 2013l). Addressing the NCA, he acknowledged that Islam and democracy are compatible, and that his visit testified to the will to rebuild Franco-Tunisian relations (Tunis Afrique Presse, 2013m). Hollande summarised the goals of his trip: backing up Tunisia's democratic transition and reaffirming friendship to all Tunisian people, clearly hinting to the opposition (Tunis Afrique Presse, 2013n). To achieve these goals France had to honour its old pledges of economic support. Thus, Hollande and the ministers and businesspeople who accompanied him signed a string of cooperation agreements (Tunis Afrique Presse, 2013o). Nevertheless, on the key issue of debt, he declared France's willingness to convert only a part of the Tunisian debt into investment projects (Tunis Afrique Presse, 2013p).

Despite the objective grounds for unhappiness regarding France's political and economic actions regarding Tunisia—something expressed by popular opinion though not overtly by the Tunisian government—the only seemingly real stumbling block to France Tunisia relations became the issue of Mali. For Tunisia, unable to confront France directly, this became an indirect way of upholding the principle of state sovereignty, thereby sending a message regarding Tunisia's wish to be recognised for now having a more independent foreign policy towards France. Hollande, in turn, was keen to explain to a sceptical Tunisian audience why France had intervened in Mali and wanted to develop cooperation with the Tunisian government in the fields of intelligence, training and equipment, to fight terrorism in the Maghreb, West Africa and Sahel regions (Tunis Afrique Presse, 2013q).

A subsequent event helped the French to obtain a more cooperative stance from Tunisia. Ironically, the French goal was achieved shortly after Hollande's visit, when, on 25 July, a second Tunisian opposition leader, Mohamed Brahmi, was assassinated, and clashes between terrorists and the Tunisian army increased in mountainous terrain in summer 2013 ("Tunisia declares Ansar al-Sharia ...", 2013). After an incident in which eight Tunisian soldiers were killed, Prime Minister Larayedh assured the French foreign minister that his government was open to "all constructive initiatives" to fight terrorism (Tunis Afrique Presse, 2013r).

Unlike the French stance, however, President Marzouki considered fighting terrorism a challenge which needed both countries to address its socio-economic causes, not only its outcomes. Thus, after meeting the French president in Paris, he announced that Tunisia relied on France's friendship to collectively fight against not only terrorism, but also its root causes, stressing the duty to find "good answers to true problems like ignorance, poverty, misery and cultural alienation" (Tunis Afrique Presse, 2013s). Tunisia's diplomatic attempt to use a broader understanding of terrorism to obtain French economic aid did not succeed. Hollande preferred to ignore the root causes for terrorism and only offered to help Tunisia with expertise and the equipment needed to combat terrorism (Tunis Afrique Presse, 2013t).

At that time, the French government was taking advantage of the Tunisian government's weak hand in the aftermath of the assassination of Mohamed Brahmi, which resulted in a political crisis that the Tunisian government could not survive. While some opposition deputies boycotted the NCA, which was thus suspended (Tunisia basks in praise over its new constitution, 2014), the Tunisian government began a national dialogue with the opposition, promising to resign once the new constitution was drafted and approved. An agreement was reached on 14 December 2013 to form a new interim government, the fifth since Ben Ali fled the country. This agreement paved the way for adopting a new constitution consensually on 26 January 2014 (France: Egypt should look to Tunisia's example, 2014).

While France waited for the outcomes of the national dialogue (Tunis Afrique Presse, 2013a), it added to the crisis, demonstrating again its meddling in Tunisia's internal affairs. For example, amid political wrangling between Tunisia's various parties, Hollande praised the boycott of the NCA by opposition parties as a strong message that the new constitution should be drafted in a consensual spirit (Tunis Afrique Presse, 2014). After the constitution was adopted consensually, Hollande addressed a ceremony in Tunis, calling the new constitution a proof that Tunisia was "on the right road to conclude this difficult transition".

A realist-constructivist explanation of the puzzle

The anomaly of a post-revolution government cozying up to the main ally of the previous oppressive regime in the face of public opposition needs an explanation that can contribute to foreign policy theorising. I argue that a realist-constructivist approach that combines classical realism's emphasis on power struggle and constructivism's emphasis on actor's ideology is better suited than structuralist theories to offer such explanation. While structuralists offer explanations of this anomaly, they stop short of contributing to foreign policy theorising.

Economic structuralists, such as dependency theorists, would attribute this policy to Tunisia's heavy economic dependence on France.[2] Indeed, on the eve of the uprising, Tunisia was relying on foreign, especially French aid, to cover its serious trade deficits (Lesch, 2014: 76). According to the French Ministry of Foreign Affairs, between 2006 and 2010, France allocated 950 million Euro in foreign assistance, including loans and grants, to Tunisia (Tunisia Live, 2011a). France was also Tunisia's greatest tourist market with an annual average of 1.4 million French tourists visiting Tunisia ("France Hopes to Lift 'Very Soon' Its Travel Restrictions to Nation", 2011). In addition, France was Tunisia's largest investor, with 1,250 French enterprises constituting the core of the country's economy. These enterprises covered practically all economic sectors, ranging from the textile and apparel industry to automobiles, microelectronics, aeronautics and services. According to official figures, French investments in Tunisia amounted to 140 billion Euro in 2009, making France Tunisia's main economic partner.[3] Dependency theory, however, is hardly convertible into state policy. In Latin America, where this theory emerged, International Relations scholars mixed it with Morgenthauian assumptions about the state, the statesman and the national interest to create a foundation for suppositions about foreign policy and peripheral state dependence (Tickner, 2008: 739–740).

Political structuralists such as Waltz, within neo-realism, also present theories of international politics that neither imply nor require a theory of foreign policy. His balance of power theory "cannot answer questions about matters at a different level of generality", and must therefore not be criticised for not explaining particular policies of states (Waltz, 1979: 72).

> A theory of international politics … can tell us what international conditions national policies have to cope with. To think that a theory of international politics can in itself say how the coping is likely to be done is the opposite of the reductionist error.
>
> (ibid.: 121)

Like Waltz' theory, Alexander Wendt's social constructivist theory is systemic in the sense of making the international system both the dependent and independent variable, and is therefore not about explaining state interests, preferences or identities. Wendt is not interested in foreign policy; rather, his interest is in international politics only (Wendt, 1999: 11) His version of constructivism treats the state as "an actor which cannot be reduced to its parts" (Smith, 2001: 50), thus offering little scope for foreign policy analysis. Accordingly, a state's interests and preferences are formed by interacting with other states, not through debates between domestic actors or as a result of domestic political process.

[Wendt's] actors are not the officials who make decisions, or the interest groups or companies, or political parties or military juntas. Rather, the actors are the states-as-persons, and there is no need to look into the black box of the foreign policy process. It is in this sense that foreign policy is what states make it (ibid.).

Contrary to structural constructivists and similar to most foreign policy analysts, non-structural constructivists employ the assumption that actors make their worlds emphasise foreign policy as a realm of choice where "actors interpret, decide, pronounce, and implement" (ibid.: 38). Non-structural constructivists define policies as declarations of an agent's intentions linked to its interests, and thus pave the way to offer a theory of agency and make a vital contribution to a theory of foreign policy.[4] This theory stresses that actors such as foreign policy decision-makers, and structures such as states and the international political and economic systems, are mutually constituted, as actors are not mere agents of structures. While structures constrain and enable actors, actors constitute structures through norms, rules and cultures (Hopf, 1998: 172–173).

Thus, non-structural constructivists move beyond the decades-old split of the two fields of international politics and foreign policy analysis, which laid the foundation of the distinction between foreign policymakers as agents on the one hand and the structure of the international system on the other (Kubalkova, 2001b: 15–19).

A constructivist strand that opened room for foreign policy analysis is the one founded by Nick Onuf and carried on by the Miami IR Group. Like foreign policy analysts, this group focuses exactly on the linkage between social structures and calculating agents, and "looks at the interface between institutions, agents and rules, with the aim of showing how these led to the foreign policy choices made by the collective agents known as states".

Onuf defines a rule as "a statement that tells people what we should do", and argues that actors follow rules because they live in a world that is socially constructed by these rules, but actors also interpret rules and make choices over whether to follow particular rules (Smith, 2001: 51–53). Nevertheless, this group focuses exclusively on agent preferences driven externally through international institutions and rules and ignores agent preferences driven internally.

A neoclassical realist analysis of foreign policy can fill in this gap because it considers domestic politics as an important factor in foreign policy analysis.[5] It is based on the conception of foreign policies as responses of leaders to international events and actions of other states shaped by expectations regarding the domestic political support or opposition that a policy is expected to produce. In other words, political leaders view foreign policy as both a potential threat to, as well as an opportunity to strengthen their domestic political position (Huth, 1996: 185–186), and must therefore take domestic political institutions and rules seriously.

This approach builds on Putnam's conception of international politics as a two-level game of bargaining between and within states (Putnam, 1993), and thus theorise foreign policy as partly shaped by the domestic political concerns of leaders. It also rests on Morgenthau's proposition that contingent contexts are an important element in foreign policy analysis (Salem, 2012). Morgenthau's assumption of rationality in foreign policy decision-making (Kubalkova, 2001b: 26), however, often overshadows his emphasis on the political and cultural context within which foreign policy is formulated. For example, Kowert criticises rationalists for their inability to contribute to a theory of preferences or foreign policy because they exclude national interest formation from their research agendas (Kowert, 2001: 281). Finnemore also takes issue with two assumptions shared by rationalist theorists of international politics: first, the preferences of states and other actors are unproblematic, as actors are claimed to "know what they want and that those wants are readily discernable to researchers", and second, those preferences can be simply deducted from objective conditions and material characteristics of a state (Finnemore, 1996: 7–8). Morgenthau's assumption of rationality does not lead necessarily to these faults. He distinguishes between "good, that is rational, foreign policy and foreign policy as it actually is", that is foreign policies that follow such irrational elements as emotion, personality, prejudice, and subjective preference. This distinction is aimed at highlighting the contingency of a rational foreign policy that "ought to be rational in view of its own moral and practical purposes" (Morgenthau, 1960: 5–9). Thus, two types of foreign policy analysis can be discerned: a normative analysis of how decision-makers ought to act, and an explanatory analysis that takes into consideration the ideational elements which furnish the ultimate goals of a particular foreign policy and the practical constraints that shape it.[6] As Keohane correctly puts it, Morgenthau never declared ideals as unimportant in determining state goals; he only claimed that foreign policymakers can ignore ideals because power is a necessary means and therefore the immediate aim (Keohane, 1984: 121).

Theory application to the Tunisian case

To apply this realist-constructivist approach to An-Nahdha's soft policy towards France, An-Nahdha's ideology and domestic political calculations must be taken into consideration. Its ideology represents a hybrid of reformism and pragmatism. Indeed, An-Nahdha has never been a revolutionary party, at least in terms of methods if not also goals. Although its leader, Rashid al-Ghannouchi, claims that his revolutionary thinking is documented in a set of unpublished papers, he admits that his "radical" positions were not always welcomed by the party's institutions and leaders, who before the uprising, used to blame him for deviating from its official policy of leaving a margin for reconciliation with the Ben Ali regime (Jebnoun, 2014: 15–16).

Reformism and pragmatism were evident in An-Nahdha's compromising and tolerant approach towards other parties with different ideologies before and after the uprising. For example, in June 2003, while still exiled in France, representatives of An-Nahdha and three Tunisian secularist parties negotiated and signed The Call from Tunis, which endorsed four principles of a post-Ben Ali government, namely sovereignty of the people as the sole source of legitimacy; full equality of women and men; guaranteed liberty of beliefs to all; and political neutralisation of places of worship. This commitment was reiterated in later documents and declarations of the opposition parties, including the 18 October Coalition for Rights and Freedoms in Tunisia (Stepan, 2012: 96–97), and reached a peak unfamiliar to an Islamist party in An-Nahdha's 2016 Congress when its leader, al-Ghannouchi, told the crowd, "we must keep religion far from political struggles" (Filali-Ansary, 2016: 99). Accordingly, An-Nahdha would split into two separate bodies: a political and electoral formation and a religious, social and cultural movement.

An-Nahdha was no less pragmatic in practice during the transitional period. It joined all opposition parties and civil society organisations in forming a commission, that according to a democratisation scholar, was "one of the most effective consensus-building bodies in the history of "crafted" democratic transitions" (Stepan, 2012: 96–97). An-Nahdha's behaviour in power was unrestrained by any policy programme or revolutionary declaration, responding to grass roots demands in general and external relations in particular. Neither was it committed to a thought-out and agreed-upon vision on how to reorganise economic and social life. Thus, following its reformism, An-Nahdha adopted no policy of exclusion, retaliation or revenge normal in post-revolution regimes. To the contrary, it permitted the parties associated with the old regime to revive and organise. Ironically, and to the disappointment of revolutionaries, this policy of inclusion eventually enabled elements of the old regime to form the *Nidaa Tounes* (Tunisia's Call) Party and return to power after winning the parliamentary and presidential elections in 2014 (Jebnoun, 2014: 26).

Consistent with this reformism and pragmatism in domestic politics, the foreign policy of An-Nahdha's governments was unsurprisingly compromising, including towards Western states and France in particular. This lenient policy is also rooted in the hardships that An-Nahdha's leaders and cadres had to face, following Ben Ali's systematic oppression in the early 1990s. According to al-Ghannouchi, many of them took refuge in Western states, hence their gratitude to them after the uprising. As pragmatists, An-Nahdha leaders disregarded their treatment in those states first as a security concern, then as a humanitarian case. Although they expressed a keen interest in building good relations with their host governments as exiled representatives of a political party, those governments refused to recognise them as such and began to deal with An-Nahdha as a political body only after the uprising (ibid.: 30–32). Hence its leadership's immeasurable indebtedness to the revolution.

An-Nahdha's electoral victory and empowerment in 2011 was a path to recognition not only by Western governments but also of Tunisia's state bureaucracy, which had considered the party as backward and inferior. An-Nahdha's leaders calculated that this recognition could only be maintained if it remained in power, and to achieve this goal, they were willing to make compromises with secular forces. The experience of life under dictatorship, imprisonment and exile convinced the party's leaders that sharing power might be their only way to survive and "close off the dire possibility of renewed persecution" (Netterstrøm, 2015: 121). Thus, An-Nahdha's soft policy towards France was partly a result of compromises in domestic politics to accommodate the expectations of the secularist elite. Compared to the Muslim Brotherhood in Egypt, An-Nahdha's leaders were keener not to antagonise the secular forces, both in the opposition and the ruling coalition (Murphy, 2014: 251). Its coalition partner, caretaker president Moncef Marzouki, for example, had close links in France where he was exiled and was "most closely associated with the liberal democratic trend informed by his roots in human rights activism" (Miller & Martini, 2012: 61).

Indeed, relations with France was not the only foreign policy issue on which An-Nahdha compromised with its coalition partners. Other instances include relations with Algeria, Syria, Palestine and the Arab Gulf monarchies. For example, against An-Nahdha's Islamist ideological commitment, its interim governments collaborated with Algeria's military junta that led the 1992 coup and cancelled the elections that Islamists won overwhelmingly. These governments were also committed to a political rather than a military solution in Syria, although An-Nahda's ideals would arguably dictate an endorsement of jihad there (ibid.: 252–253).

Undermining human agency, structuralists argue that Tunisia had to act pragmatically in foreign relations because of "the constraints imposed by resource scarcity and location in a problematic neighbourhood" (ibid.: 257). They, however, conflate foreign policy analysis and prescription. Like empowered Islamists and other ideologues elsewhere, An-Nahdha's leadership could have opted for another foreign policy orientation, irrespective of any consequences, and the realist-constructivist approach proposed in this chapter demonstrates that its pragmatism was a foreign policy choice, not a necessity.

Conclusion

After the Tunisian uprising, the Islamist An-Nahdha party came first in the election of the NCA in October 2011 and led the winning coalition and its interim government. Despite its revolutionary credentials, this government sought French support and challenged no French foreign policy. The French government, however, did not welcome this government in practice, and Franco-Tunisian relations therefore cooled. President Sarkozy warned against violations of freedoms and human rights in Tunisia, making the French economic support to Tunisia conditional on respecting these "red lines". A change in the French leadership—Hollande's victory in the presidential elections of 2012—made only a little difference in this regard. Challenged by mounting financial difficulties and having yet to see the billions pledged in the Group of 8 summit in 2011, the Tunisian government expected Hollande to fulfill the promise he made a year earlier, that is, a partial write-off of Tunisia's debt, or at least a suspension of interest payments. But Hollande refused to fulfill this promise. Despite all efforts of the Tunisian government to mend relations with France, Franco-Tunisian relations moved from cool to tense with increasing French anxiety about alleged Tunisia-related security threats. Still, these relations suffered more with Tunisia's opposition of the French military intervention in Mali in 2013.

A new An-Nahdha-led interim government was formed but barely improved relations with France, which continued its mainly verbal support for Tunisia's democratisation while meddling with its domestic affairs. During a long-awaited, repeatedly postponed visit to Tunisia, Hollande announced France's readiness to convert only a part of Tunisia's debt into investment projects. With a serious political crisis evolving after the assassination of two opposition leaders, the Tunisian government had a weak hand and was taken advantage of by France. Thus, Hollande encouraged the opposition parties to boycott the NCA, which added to the economic crisis. In short, despite French good talk of supporting democratisation in Tunisia, French aid was limited and conditional. No matter how noble the French conditions were, the message was clear: Tunisians must fulfill French expectations if they wished to maintain French aid, thus only confirming their suspicions of "Western hypocrisy" respecting the results of free and fair elections in democratising nations. The Tunisian government, however, never criticised this implicit message openly. The experience of An-Nahdha in power demonstrated its willingness to compromise on most issues with France, its reluctance to take a firm stand or make strong demands on France, and a preference to yield rather than to fight.

The foreign policies towards France under the An-Nahdha-led interim governments were too soft and lenient. In this chapter, I applied a blended approach combining neoclassical realism and non-structural constructivism to explain this soft policy. Better suited than structuralist theories to explain *and* theorise foreign policy, this hybrid approach applies classical realism's emphasis on power struggle and constructivism's emphasis on actor's ideology. Accordingly, this soft policy is partly attributed to An-Nahdha's unrevolutionary and persistently reformist and pragmatist ideology that was evident in its positions both before and after the uprising. On the other hand, An-Nahdha's leaders perceived their political, and perhaps physical survival, as conditional on compromising with secularist parties and Francophile politicians of the opposition, on domestic and foreign policies, including policies towards France.

Notwithstanding its causes, this soft policy sheds doubt on the nature of change in Tunisia after the uprising. Though clearly a revolutionary moment, the uprising did not develop into a full revolution and stopped short of making radical changes in Tunisia's foreign policy. This is also true regarding Tunisia's foreign policy towards African states and the African Union. As Murphy puts it succinctly, "Revolutionary Tunisia's foreign policy has been anything but revolutionary" (ibid.: 255). Tunisia obviously missed the opportunity of its revolutionary momentum to reestablish relations with France (and the West) on a more balanced, let alone equal basis.

Notes

1 This official French position towards Tunisia and other Arab Spring countries was criticized by a delegate of the French Senate Foreign Affairs commission that met Tunisian politicians, including the new prime minister. See: Tunis Afrique Presse (2013f, g).

2 For a discussion of the premises and expectations of the dependency theory within the broader context of Latin American theorising on international relations, see: Tickner (2008).

3 Many French enterprises in Tunisia enjoyed close links to Ben Ali and his family. For instance, 49% of the telecommunications operator Orange Tunisie belonged to the former French state monopolist France Telecom. The other 51% belonged to Investec, the investment company owned by Marwan Mabrouk, Ben Ali's son-in-law, who was accused of corruption. In other words, France was a major economic partner of Tunisia's corrupt regime. See: Godoy (2011).

4 Kowert (2001, p. 281). For a different view of constructivism as merely a way of studying social relations and a system of concepts and propositions that offers no theory of international relations or foreign policy, see: Kubalkova (2001a, p. 71)

5 For rich discussions and assessments of combining or even synthesizing classical realism and constructivism, see: Barkin (2004, 2010); Salem (2008).

6 Thus, Dougherty and Pfaltzgraff's criticism of realism as failing "to provide an adequate explanation as to why political leaders sometimes do not adhere to realist tenets in foreign policy" is simply misplaced. Dougherty & Pfaltzgraff (1996, p. 92).

References

Aghrout, A. (2011). The National Constituent Assembly election in Tunisia. *Electoral Studies*, *34*(2014): 294–299.

Alderman, L. (2011). G-8 pledges to aid stability in Egypt and Tunisia. *The International Herald Tribune*, 28 May 2011.

Ayubi, N. N. (1995). *Over-stating the Arab State*. London: I.B. Tauris.

Balta, P. (1986). French policy in North Africa. *Middle East Journal*, *40*(2): 238–251. Retrieved from http://www.jstor.org/stable/4327308.

Barkin, J. S. (2004). The forum: Bridging the gap: Toward a realist-constructivist dialogue. *International Studies Review*, *6*: 337–352.

Barkin, J. S. (2010). *Realist Constructivism: Rethinking International Relations Theory*. Cambridge, UK: Cambridge University Press, 154–173.

Bosses prod Ayrault to receive Jebali; Prime minister's residence, Paris. (2012). *Maghreb Confidential*, 28 June 2012.

Bouazza, B. B. (2013). France calls Tunisia's transition an example for Arab world. *The Washington Post*, 5 July 2013.

Brahem, S. (2013). Comment: France must let Tunisia go: Independence was won in 1956, yet French politicians and media still meddle in our affairs. *The Guardian (London)* – Final Edition, 18 February 2013.

Burgat, F. (1988). *L'Islamisme au Maghreb: La Voix du Sud* (Paris: Editions Karthaka), translated into Arabic by Lauren Zakary in 1992. Chicago: Third World Publishing House.

Deeb, M. J. (1989). Inter-maghribi relations since 1969: A study of the modalities of unions and mergers. *Middle East Journal*, *43*(1). doi:10.1017/S0022278X00054252.

Dougherty, J. & Pfaltzgraff, R. (1996). *Contending Theories of International Relations: A Comprehensive Survey*. New York: Longman.

Filali-Ansary, A. (2016). Tunisia: Ennahda's new course. *Journal of Democracy*, *27*(4): 99–109.

Finnemore, M. (1996). *National Interests in International Society*. Ithaca, NY: Cornell University Press.

France: Egypt should look to Tunisia's example. (2014). *The New Zealand Herald*, 18 January 2014.

France hopes to lift "very soon" its travel restrictions to nation. (2011). *Tunisia Online (Tunis)*, 12 February 2011.

French foreign minister hopes Tunisians to "get grip on themselves". (2013). *BBC Monitoring Europe – Political*, 8 February 2013.

Godoy, J. (2011). France Plays Suspicious Role in Countries in Crisis, *Inter Press Service* (Johannesburg), 27 January.

Hopf, T. (1998). The promise of constructivism in International Relations theory. *International Security*, *23*(1): 171–200.

Huth, P. (1996). *Standing Your Ground: Territorial Disputes and International Conflict*. Ann Arbor: The University of Michigan Press.

Interior minister sees France as "trailblazer" in Mali. (2013). *BBC Monitoring Europe – Political*, 12 February 2013.

Jebnoun, N. (2014). Tunisia at the crossroads: An interview with Sheikh Rachid al-Ghannouchi. *ACMCU Occasional Papers*, April 2014, 15–16.

Keohane, R. (1984). *After Hegemony: Cooperation and Discord in the World Political Economy*. Princeton, NJ: Princeton University Press.

Kowert, P. (2001). Toward a constructivist theory of foreign policy. In V. Kubalkova (ed.), *Foreign Policy in a Constructed World*. London: M.E. Sharpe.

Kubalkova, V. (2001a). A Constructivist Primer. In V. Kubalkova (ed.), *Foreign Policy in a Constructed World*. London: M.E. Sharpe.

Kubalkova, V. (2001b). Foreign policy, international politics, and constructivism. In V. Kubalkova (ed.), *Foreign Policy in a Constructed World*. London: M.E. Sharpe.

Left-wing businessman named envoy; Tunisian embassy, Paris. (2012). *Maghreb Confidential*, 7 June 2012.

Lesch, A. M. (2014). Troubled political transitions: Tunisia, Egypt and Libya. *Middle East Policy*, *21*(1): 62–74. doi:10.1111/mepo.12057.

Magharebia (Washington DC). (2012). Tunisia Combats radical speech. *Africa News*, 6 November 2012.

Magharebia (Washington DC). (2013). Hollande backs democratic Tunisia. *Africa News*, 8 July 2013.

Micaud, C. A. (1968). Tunisia's foreign policy: Independence and development. *Africa Today*, *15*(6). African Non-Alignment and Foreign Policies (Dec.1968–Jan. 1969): 12–15

Miller, L. E., Martini, J., Larrabee, F. S., Rabasa, A., Pezard, S., Taylor, J. E. & Mengistu, T. (2012). *Democratization in the Arab World: Prospects and Lessons from Around the Globe*. Rand Corporation. Retrieved from https://www.rand.org/content/dam/rand/pubs/monographs/2012/RAND_MG1192.pdf (Accessed 9 January 2020)

Morgenthau, H. J. (1960). *Politics Among Nations: The Struggle for Power and Peace*. 3rd ed. New York: Alfred Knopf.

Murphy, E. C. (2014). The foreign policy of Tunisia. In R. Hinnebusch and A. Ehteshami (eds.), *The Foreign Policies of Middle East States*. Boulder, CO: Lynne Rienner.

Nessma TV to broadcast in France. (2013). *Maghreb Confidential*, 28 February 2013.

Netterstrøm, K. L. (2015). After the Arab Spring: The Islamists' compromise in Tunisia. *Journal of Democracy*, *26*(4): 110–124.

Paris & Berlin in clash on debt. (2012). *Maghreb Confidential*, 24 May 2012.

Powel, B. T. (2009). A clash of norms: Normative power and EU democracy promotion in Tunisia. *Democratization*, *16*(1): 193–214. doi:10.1080/13510340802575924.

Power Brokers. (2013). A lost occasion for Hollande. *Maghreb Confidential*, 4 July 2013.

Putnam, R. (1993). Diplomacy and domestic politics: The logic of two-level games. In P. Evans et al. (eds.), *Double-Edged Diplomacy: International Bargaining and Domestic Politics*. Berkley: University of California Press, *42*(3): 427–460.

Radio France Internationale. (2013). Hollande visits Tunisia Amid Turmoil in Egypt. *Africa News*, 4 July 2013.

Reguly, E. (2013). Tunisia takes measures to prevent spillover from conflict in Mali. *The Globe and Mail* (Canada), 18 January 2013.

Russett, B. (1993). *Grasping the Democratic Peace: Principles for a Post-Cold War World*. Princeton, NJ: Princeton University Press.

Salem, A. A. (2007). Inter-Arab conflictual interactions. In A. Y. Ahmed and A. A. Salem (eds.), *The League of Arab States in Sixty Years*. Cairo: Institute of Arab Research and Studies. [in Arabic].

Salem, A. A. (2008). *International Relations Theories and Organizations: Realism, Constructivism and Collective Security in the League of Arab States*. Saarbruecken, Germany: Verlag Dr. Muller.

Salem, A. A. (2012). *What Is Constructivist About Realism? Constructivist Critiquing of the Realist Paradigm. in International Relations*. Saarbruecken, Germany: LAP Lambert Academic Publishing.

Smith, S. (2001). Foreign policy is what states make of it: Social construction and International Relations theory. In V. Kubalkova (ed.), *Foreign Policy in a Constructed World*. London: M.E. Sharp.

Stepan, A. (2012). Tunisia's transition and the twin tolerations. *Journal of Democracy*, *23*(2): 96–97.

Terhalle, M. (2015). International relations theory and the moderation of revolutionary states. *International Politics*, *52*(5): 589–593. doi:10.1057/ip.2015.22.

Tickner, A. B. (2008). Latin American IR and the primacy of lo práctico. *International Studies Review*, *10*(4): 739–740.

Tunis Afrique Presse. (2012a). "Paris wishes new start for French-Tunisian relations", says special envoy of French President. *Africa News*, 22 May 2012.

Tunis Afrique Presse. (2012b). "Tunisia does have all assets of success", says Premier Jebali. *Africa News*, 28 June 2012.

Tunis Afrique Presse. (2012c). PM – " stakes in Tunisia have nothing to do with religion and doctrine". *Africa News*, 28 June 2012.

Tunis Afrique Presse. (2012d). Tunisia, France willing to turn Tunisian debt into development projects. *Africa News*, 18 July 2012.

Tunis Afrique Presse. (2012e). Maghreb summit, BCT governor and Marzouki's visit to France, focus of Adnan Mansar's press conference. *Africa News*, 23 July 2012.

Tunis Afrique Presse. (2012f). Foreign minister meets with ambassadors of U.S., France, Germany, Great Britain and EU. *Africa News*, 17 September 2012.

Tunis Afrique Presse. (2013a). François Hollande visits nation "when agendas of Presidents Hollande and Marzouki Coincide" - French minister. *Africa News*, 15 January 2013.

Tunis Afrique Presse. (2013b). Tunisia needs more support from France (ben Jaafer). *Africa News*, 5 March 2013.

Tunis Afrique Presse. (2013c). Ben Jaafar meets with François Hollande. *Africa News*, 6 March 2013.

Tunis Afrique Presse. (2013d). François Gouyette – France will not interfere in Tunisia's domestic affairs. *Africa News*, 26 March 2013.
Tunis Afrique Presse. (2013e). PM confers with French Minister in charge of development. *Africa News*, 29 March 2013.
Tunis Afrique Presse. (2013f). 'France needs to rethink co-operation with Tunisia, Libya and Egypt' —Jean Glavany. *Africa News*, 23 April 2013.
Tunis Afrique Presse. (2013g). Peace and stability in Southern Mediterranean depend on guarantee of peace and stability in Tunisia (French Senate). *Africa News*, 6 May 2013.
Tunis Afrique Presse. (2013h). Hollande expected in Tunisia on July. *Africa News*, 7 May 2013.
Tunis Afrique Presse. (2013i). "We are the first partner of Tunisia" – Laurent Fabius. *Africa News*, 14 May 2013.
Tunis Afrique Presse. (2013j). France should Remain Tunisia's 1st economic partner (Rhone-Alpes Region President). *Africa News*, 15 June 2013.
Tunis Afrique Presse. (2013k). "I came to Tunisia bearer of positive messages from France to friendly country" – Laurent Fabius. *Africa News*, 14 May 2013.
Tunis Afrique Presse. (2013l). France Remains fully committed to the Tunisian people – François Hollande. *Africa News*, 5 July 2013.
Tunis Afrique Presse. (2013m). France is following up transition process without interference. *Africa News*, 5 July 2013.
Tunis Afrique Presse. (2013n). France willing to work with all Tunisian people's representatives. *Africa News*, 5 July 2013.
Tunis Afrique Presse. (2013o). Hollande – France ready to convert part of national debt into investment projects. *Africa News*, 5 July 2013.
Tunis Afrique Presse. (2013p). Hollande visits Tunis Town Hall. *Africa News*, 5 July 2013.
Tunis Afrique Presse. (2013q). France is following up transition process without interference. *Africa News*, 5 July 2013.
Tunis Afrique Presse. (2013r). Building-up new partnerships between France and Tunisia for joint development – Francois Hollande. *Africa News*, 6 July 2013.
Tunis Afrique Presse. (2013s). Larayedh/Fabius phone talk. *Africa News*, 31 July 2013.
Tunis Afrique Presse. (2013t). France's confidence in Tunisia destination unaltered – Hollande. *Africa News*, 6 November 2013.
Tunis Afrique Presse. (2013u). Marzouki in Paris – Tunisia will establish a democratic and non-corrupt state in answer to terrorism. *Africa News*, 6 November 2013.
Tunis Afrique Presse. (2013). France calls for quick resumption of national dialogue in Tunisia - Quai d'Orsay. *Africa News*, 6 December 2013.
Tunis Afrique Presse. (2014). "Tunisia embodies hope in Arab world" – Hollande. *Africa News*, 7 February 2014.
Tunisia basks in praise over its new constitution. (2014). *The New Zealand Herald*, 8 February 2014.
Tunisia declares Ansar al-Sharia a terrorist group. *BBC News*, 27 August 2013. Retrieved from https://www.bbc.com/news/world-africa-23853241.
Tunisia: French back new leaders. (2012). *The Advertiser* (*Australia*), 7 January 2012.
Tunisia Live. (2011a). France shifts positions, Ennahda copes – Tunisian foreign affairs. *Africa News*, 13 November 2011.
Tunisia Live. (2011b). French Foreign minister to visit nation in January. *Africa News*, 28 December 2011.
Tunisia Live. (2012a). Salafists protest in front of French embassy in Tunis. *Africa News*, 20 January 2012.

Tunisia Live. (2012b). New book accuses French journalists of complicity with former president Ben Ali. *Africa News*, 24 January 2012.

Tunisia Live. (2012c). Nation will host first meeting of international Pro-Syria organization. *Africa News*, 13 February 2012.

Tunisia Live. (2012d). This independence day, locals must end dependence on France. *Africa News*, 20 March 2012.

Tunisia protests after assassination of opposition politician Chokri Belaid. (2013). *The Times*, 6 February 2013.

Waltz, K. (1979). *Theory of International Politics*. New York: Random House.

Wendt, A. (1999). *Social Theory of International Politics*. New York: Cambridge University Press.

Wood, P. C. (2002). French foreign policy and Tunisia: Do human rights matter? *Middle East Policy*, *IX*(2): 92–110.

Zartman, I. W. (1987). Foreign relations of North Africa. *The Annals of the American Academy of Political and Social Science*, *489*(1). doi:10.1177%2F0002716287489001002.

11 Straddling between convergence and divergence

A constructivist's view of Malawi's foreign policy in post-independence Africa

Eugenio Njoloma

Introduction

Mainstream approaches to international relations such as neo-liberalism and neo-realism privilege structure over agency in a state's foreign policy choices. Yet their interpretation of state relations as driven by an inherent desire for material power overlooks the significance of social interactions among individuals and states in explaining state behaviour. Constructivism offers a critical perspective that ideas and beliefs are key in informing and shaping the behaviour of actors on the world stage (Steans et al., 2010). The ideas and beliefs include "mental constructs held by individuals, sets of distinctive beliefs, principles and attitudes that provide broad orientations for behaviour and policy" (Tannenwald, 2005: 15). Constructivism is agency-oriented, and fundamentally holds that people act towards objects, including other actors, based on the meanings that the objects have for them (Wendt, 2010). Accordingly, the billiard ball imagery of international relations offered by traditional approaches loses significance for its lack of capacity to reveal the thoughts, ideas and beliefs of the actors (Houghton, 2017). In other words, it obscures the fact that "decision-makers act in accordance with their perception of reality, not in response to reality itself" (Adogamhe, 2003: 82).

Social interaction among states and individuals in international relations is important in explaining foreign policy in a (Southern) African context. Since the 1955 Bandung Conference, Third World states have come together on common issues to exercise agency. The consequence of this has been to develop both the agency and profile of states in the South. According to Grovogui (2003: 31), these states congregate on issues of identity, autonomy and will to choose by "conventionalising systems of ideas … or languages, and of politics that emerged from the collective ethos and style of anticolonialism". It was within this spirit in mind that the emergence of the Organisation of African Unity (OAU) in 1963 provided African leaders with a critical platform upon which collective responses to various issues of common concern could be advanced (Wright, 1999). According to Finnemore (1996), such solidarity constitutes a critical element in a constructivist take, where the norms of behaviour advocated for in the international system by international organisations influence to shape state identities, interests and foreign policy behaviour. Despite this general assumption, the African continent, however, offers evidence for inconsistency in individual states demonstrating consistent solidarity. Malawi, in adhering to collective norms and principles advanced by African regional organisation, is a case in point. Since attaining independence from British rule in 1964 and in the face of the forces of colonialism, apartheid and neo-imperialism, the state has pursued a varied foreign policy path characterised by both convergence and divergence from developing norms around African unity. This, amidst concerns on how best to evolve common understandings for the advancement of socio-economic development, in response to the challenges generated by the forces above.

Malawi demonstrated agency in its commitment to regional integration with its participation in the Southern African Development Coordination Conference (SADCC)—later the Southern African Development Community (SADC)—and expressions of regional inter-state solidarity. This was seen, when for more than two decades after 1997, in concert with other SADC members, it supported the actions of President Robert Mugabe's regime despite international criticism. Yet, while agreeing with the general principles of the OAU, later the African Union (AU), Malawi, nevertheless, could also choose to ignore regional prescriptions. Significantly, Malawi opposed the collective call for sanctioning apartheid South Africa. Instead, the country chose to enter into diplomatic and economic relations with the pariah state. Similarly, when the AU condemned the International Criminal Court (ICC), Malawi was supportive of the Court and its indictments of African leaders.

Mainstream approaches favour the centrality of structure in determining state foreign policy behaviour; a structural explanation would have Malawi subordinate its foreign policy to the sources of structural power: the donor community and international (regional) organisations. This obscures an explanation for the foreign policy dichotomy expressed by a small state such as Malawi. Neo-realism puts emphasis on a foreign policy informed by the national interest of material resources and incentives given by an international power structure. Neo-liberalism instead values the power of international cooperation in informing a state's foreign policy choices (Dunne, 2008). On the other hand, constructivist analysis explains Malawi's agency without recourse to what Barry Hindes (1989: 1–3) terms a "portfolio" of interests independent of social context. Social political actors formulate their peculiar interests when they define their own situations. This is underscored by Foote's (1951: 15) proposition that "a human being, as a participant in the ongoing social process in which he necessarily finds himself, defines a problematic situation as calling for the performance of a particular act, with more or less anticipated consummations and consequences".

Ordinarily, structuralist approaches would assume that a small state such as Malawi consistently aligns its foreign policy choices with the common practices found at a multilateral level. Neo-liberalism, for example, sees the benefits of multilateralism for small states in the way it helps them to define norms; create, monitor, and enforce rules; settle disputes; allocate resources and act as a platform for the exchange of views and decision-making (Karns & Mingst, 2004). Although Malawi seems to live up to the characteristics of a small state preoccupied in optimising its national interest using multilateral membership, at the same time, it does show agency in that it chooses to both accept and defy the prescriptive behaviour suggested by the African organisations to which it belongs. The foreign policy behaviour of convergence or divergence from multilateral norms is arguably effectively shaped by a socio-cultural context defined by interpersonal and cultural relationships among Malawian and African leaders.

While constructivist explanations of state behaviour disregard the role of culture, Uemura (2015) sees the significance of culture in explaining identity formation. As argued by Gray (1999), the relevance of culture in a state's foreign policy behaviour is embedded in the way interactions among individuals and groups exhibit distinct behaviour patterns and meanings across cultural boundaries. This can be suitably understood by what Jack Snyder (1977) conceptualised as strategic culture, which entails the socialisation of individuals into a distinctive mode of strategic thinking. The socialisation process results in a set of general beliefs, attitudes and behavioural patterns (Snyder, 1977). Strategic culture is given meaning by various attributes such as geography, history and narratives of the actors involved (Howlett, 2006). Accordingly, Johnson (2006: 5) defines strategic culture as "shared beliefs, assumptions, and modes of behaviour, derived from common experiences and accepted narratives (both oral and written), which shape collective identity and relationships to other groups, and which determine appropriate ends and means for achieving security objectives". The prevalence of cultural relations among Malawian and (Southern) African leaders is seen here as key in attaching meaning to Malawi's international relations.

Work on Malawi's foreign policy decision-making, by Sagawa (2011), Patel and Hajat (2007), and Kaunda (2002) point to the dominance of Malawi's political leadership as a single agent in shaping the country's foreign policy choices. Lantis (2006) acknowledges the role of political leadership. He explains that leaders are seen as having a momentous responsibility in defining and ensuring the different scope and direction countries face in confronting new challenges. As Gaddis (1992: 55) contends, leaders are "by nature conscious entities capable of reacting to, and often modifying, the variables and conditions they encounter. They can at times see the future taking shape; they can devise, within limits, measures to hasten, retard, or even reverse trends". This exposition of foreign policy analysis focused on the personality attributes of leaders and often accompanies descriptions of leaders who wield significant authority and personal control over government machinery (Hermann, 1976). This is true and has been the norm throughout the five regimes Malawi has had since independence, including those of Kamuzu Banda (1964–1994), Bakili Muluzi (1994–2004), Bingu wa Mutharika (2004–2012), Joyce Banda (2012–2014) and Arthur Peter Mutharika (2014 to the present). As such, Malawian leaders have all retained the prerogative to choose their (presidential) staff and set in place norms and rules that determine the organisational culture of a presidency. All this has considerable bearing on Malawi's foreign policy path.

Feldman (1990: 17) observes that (foreign policy) staff increase the leader's "available attention, knowledge and expertise" and extend the leader's capabilities.

The social context of the entire decision-making process is the basis for constructivism's description of inter-subjectivity. This includes the ideas shared among people and/or states (Hurd, 2008) and the institutionalised ideas expressed as practices and identities. Accordingly, Legro (2005: 6) holds that "ideas are not so much mental as symbolic and organisational; they are embedded not only in human brains but also in the 'collective memories', government procedures, educational systems, and the rhetoric of statecraft". It is therefore possible to suggest that constructivism borders largely on the interaction between or among individuals, thus implying that the ideas under reference may not necessarily be those of an individual or that of a single state. This, therefore, suggests that Malawian leaders consolidate their thoughts and actions in concert with those around them.

In defiance of African unity?

Malawi's singular and idiosyncratic foreign policy stems from the early post-independence period when Malawi took issue with the OAU's stance on decolonisation. As Omari and Macaringue (2007) contend, the failure of a negotiated transition to independence in the Portuguese colonies of Mozambique and Angola, the existence of settler colonialism in Southern Rhodesia (Zimbabwe), and the institutionalisation of racism as apartheid in South Africa, brought about the armed struggles for the independence of these territories.

Like many African leaders, President Hastings Banda was supportive of the OAU's call for the complete liberation of all those countries still under the colonial yoke. This was evident when he openly declared that:

> the independence of Malawi would be meaningless as long as there is an inch of African soil under colonialism and imperialism. I share the views already expressed in this conference and elsewhere that all independent African states and all African leaders must do everything possible in their power to help those [southern African] countries which are still under the colonial yoke.
>
> (Banda in Patel & Hajat, 2007: 384)

However, President Banda became disinclined to the idea of Malawi becoming one of the frontline states in the region's liberation warfare, leaving only Botswana, Tanzania and Zambia eventually to lead what was to become the Frontline States (FLS) movement in the 1970s. The change of foreign policy stance did not necessarily emanate from his personal preferences. It largely came about from him privileging domestic priorities. According to Short (1974), these priorities had to do with Malawi's socio-economic development plans, including the enhancement of agricultural production, diversification of manufacturing and industrial processing, and measures set in place to eliminate ignorance, disease and poverty.

One way of harnessing resources to support these socio-economic development plans was by choosing to consolidate diplomatic and all other relations with South Africa's apartheid regime (McMaster, 1974). President Banda openly declared his preferences to "alliances with the devil" (Malawi Government, 1966: 411). As such, his government was the first of all black independent states to formalise diplomatic relations with apartheid South Africa (Ihonvbere, 2003), a move that contravened the OAU's concerted norm for African unity against apartheid. For President Banda, isolating South Africa was "dishonest and devoid of integrity", perhaps because many African leaders surreptitiously engaged in economic dealings with the apartheid regime (McMaster, 1974: 99). It thus became apparent that President Banda's main concern with regard to relations with apartheid South Africa centred on the positive socio-economic outcomes diplomatic relations could offer. This became apparent when he argued that "sending a mission, goodwill, trade ... to South Africa [did] not mean [Malawi agreed] with apartheid" (Malawi Government, 1967: 362). Therefore, by proposing that "economic unviability and political instability" (Malawi Government, 1967: 362) constituted the central concerns the continent had to address, Banda was able to isolate his beliefs from those collectively held by the majority of African leaders who regarded colonialism, neo-imperialism and apartheid as main impediments to the continent's socio-economic and political progress.

President Hastings Banda's agency in leading Malawi to a foreign policy position out of kilter with the regional and continental consensus was, in the main, underlined by a three-pronged foreign policy approach. This included 1) "non-interference in the affairs of other countries", 2) an assessment of individual situations based on their merits rather than being held by pre-existing alignments of countries and 3) a willingness to accept the aid of "any country prepared to help Malawi" (Patel & Hajat, 2007: 385). This foreign policy stance in several ways proved beneficial to Malawi's socio-economic development aspirations. South Africa provided financial assistance to assist in major projects, including the relocation of Malawi's capital from Zomba to Lilongwe and the construction of a railway line connecting Malawi with Mozambique's port of Nacala, something which eased transport costs and opened up the landlocked Malawi to international markets (Ihonvbere, 2003). Moreover, both South Africa and minority-ruled Southern Rhodesia (Zimbabwe) were prepared to host thousands of Malawian migrant workers in their economically vibrant agricultural and mining sectors (McMaster, 1974).

Following Zimbabwe's independence in 1980 and with the concomitant emergence of the Southern African Development Coordination Conference (SADCC), Malawi contemplated a switch to have its foreign policy converge with that of the region. According to Gwaradzimba (1993), membership of SADCC was intended to facilitate the realignment of economic relations among and between members, and change the pattern of asymmetrical economic relations with South Africa. President Banda demonstrated agency by embracing the ideals of SADCC as a means to diversify economic relations and moderate Malawi's heavy reliance on the South African economy. Moreover, the newly formed grouping prioritised transport links, including railway lines, which President Banda believed would serve to unlock Malawi further to international markets through seaports in Mozambique and Tanzania (Kadyampakeni, 1985). For the first time, therefore, President Hastings Banda was able to re-identify with fellow leaders of the majority ruled states only because of the broader prospects of socio-economic development that SADCC promised to offer. Nonetheless, membership of SADCC with its aim of economic de-linkage from apartheid South Africa that accompanied the official political and diplomatic isolation of the regime did not prevent Malawi from continuing to maintain diplomatic ties with South Africa. President Banda's agency in this regard prevailed as most member states both surreptitiously and openly still showed varying degrees of dependence or economic engagement with South Africa (Kadyampakeni, 1985; Gwaradzimba, 1993). Moreover, SADCC's focus on economic development was initially rhetorical and considered more of a platform upon which to counter South Africa's regional destabilisation scheme, as evidenced by Tanzania's President Julius Nyerere's pronouncement that:

> The basic reason for SADCC's strength is the political commitment that underlines its existence. For SADCC was created by the Frontline States out of their own felt need; although now it has a somewhat wider membership, the Frontline States still provide its core, are still the guardians of its objectives, and are still its main energies.
>
> (Nyerere in Gwaradzimba, 1993: 52)

Banda's recalcitrant stance is to be viewed through the lens of pragmatism, necessitated by the country's own relative socio-economic weakness and peripheral status on the continent. Malawi's foreign policy under President Hastings Banda was "more attuned to low-politics than to political-military geopolitics", one where political leaders sought to satisfy domestic imperatives rather than to build concern for the people of other states or amity with them (du Plessis, 2006: 132).

A similarly singular foreign policy position by Malawi manifested itself in 2012 during President Joyce Banda's short tenure of office. Her government defied the spirit of African unity in the wake of the ICC's demand for the arrest of Sudan's President Omar al-Bashir. Malawi's departure from the common African cause did not only antagonise a July 2009 declaration by the AU, which encouraged member states to boycott the ICC's demands for "the arrest and surrender of African indicted personalities" (Reuters, 2009). Importantly, it demonstrated considerable agency by Malawian leaders in their ability to isolate the country's foreign policy choices from those advanced collectively at the continental level. Malawian leaders demonstrated this agency by objecting to President al-Bashir's attendance of an AU summit planned to take place in Malawi's capital, Lilongwe, in July 2012. The decision was an intersubjective one, taken by the entire cabinet and supported by members of the political opposition. While acknowledging Malawi's obligations to the AU, the Malawian leaders realised that accommodating the Sudanese leader on Malawian soil would not only contravene the country's obligation to the Rome Statutes, but would importantly also jeopardise its relations with Western donor countries (The Guardian, 2012). Malawi's position contradicted that assumed by the majority of African states, which regards the

ICC's indictment of perpetrators of war crimes and crimes against humanity as machinations of the West (Bako, 2012).

With the AU apparently unwilling to accede to Malawi's position, in solidarity with the Sudanese leader, the summit shifted to Addis Ababa. The AU's high regard for harmonised state behaviour became apparent when it indicated to Malawi that its leaders did not have any "right to dictate who could attend the summit" (The Guardian, 2012). This lends credence to the proposition that foreign policy choices of the AU's member states are often constrained by the multilateral setting. However, the agency of Malawian leaders, it is argued, was underpinned by Resolution 911 of the AU which provides liberty to member states to balance their interests in terms of obligations to the AU and their national interests (Nyasa Times, 2012). In the knowledge of its rights as a member, Malawian leaders chose to override the majority AU view. Following the economic decline that followed President Bingu wa Mutharika's poor political and economic policies between 2009 and 2012, domestic socio-economic concerns became paramount. Malawian leaders feared that appearing to support the impunity of the perpetrators of human rights abuses by conceding to the AU's demands could possibly prevent the flow of financial assistance from Western donors and impede Malawi's socio-economic recovery. This agency on the part of Malawi was emphasised by President Joyce Banda in her argument opposing the AU's demands:

> In the interest of Malawi and Malawians … I respect that decision [moving the summit to Addis Ababa]. I respect Sudanese President Omar al-Bashir as head of state of Sudan, but … my main agenda right now is economic recovery. How did the AU support us and who supported us [when the former President Bingu wa Mutharika hosted President al-Bashir the previous year]? And who lost? We lost in the end.
>
> (Capital News, 2012)

> Malawi is already going through unprecedented economic problems and it would not be prudent enough to take a risk by allowing one person to come and attend the summit against much resistance from our cooperating partners and donors … It is about the nation; … It is not Malawi hosting the summit but rather it is a question of African Heads of State meeting in Malawi. But at the end of the day, Malawi will have to seriously take into consideration the economic repercussions of hosting President al-Bashir in Malawi.
>
> (Nyasa Times, 2012)

The agency shown by Malawian leaders on the issue happened when they were addressing some of the socio-economic failures left by Bingu wa Mutharika's administration. The near immediate resumption of financial support by the International Monetary Fund (IMF) and Western donor countries, as well as the need for the country to resume having a (relatively) uninterrupted power and electricity supply, were key elements of this. Malawi's foreign policy position indicated adopting pragmatism over the ritual of keeping up formal inter-African governmental relations, that in the short-term threatened the country's financial and economic welfare.

Embracing African unity

Unlike under the Hastings Banda and Joyce Banda presidencies, Malawi's foreign policy choices have generally reflected the spirit of collectivism advanced by the AU. Under Presidents Bakili Muluzi, Bingu wa Mutharika and Peter Mutharika, the Malawian leadership showed considerable zeal for African unity. The changing foreign policy context in the period from 1989 to 1994 coincided with some important events at both the regional and domestic level in Malawi. For one, there was the political change towards democracy in South Africa; this effectively removed the basis upon which President Hastings Banda had obtained financial support (Ihonvebere, 2003). At this time, President Banda's health had also significantly deteriorated and his regime under challenge spelt the re-introduction of a multiparty democracy in 1993.

This political change reshaped Malawi's foreign policy path. In particular, the country's new President, Bakili Muluzi, in his resolve to shed Malawi's image of "pariah statehood" inherited from the country's go-it-alone foreign policy towards apartheid South Africa, demonstrated agency by trying to build good neighbourly relations. Early in his presidency, he embarked on a series of goodwill missions to several southern African states. In trying to overcome Malawi's previously tattered image on the continent, Muluzi sought to assure Africa of the country's commitment to regional cooperation and integration. In the five years of his presidency, his visits to Mozambique, South Africa, Tanzania, Zambia and Zimbabwe were reciprocated by visits from regional leaders Joaquim Chissano, Benjamin Mkapa, Frederick Chiluba and Robert Mugabe. Close friendships with a number of African leaders, particularly Benjamin Mkapa, Frederick Chiluba and Joaquim Chissano, resulted from these engagements. As Heimann (2012: 30) contends, friendship possesses considerable impact on the foreign policymaking process, because leaders "may know each other well, and share a common worldview and common values. They may support each other regularly in international fora, and enjoy an intense, varied, and close bilateral relationship". Indeed, the presence of Presidents Robert Mugabe, Frederick Chiluba, Pierre Buyoya (Burundi), King Mswati III (Swaziland) and Joaquim Chissano at President Muluzi's wedding in 1999 gave credence to the power of the friendship factor. Arguably, foreign policy in the context of Bakili Muluzi's presidency was one characterised by a significant affinity towards the region, given further meaning by the strong bonds of friendship that prevailed between him and a number of other (Southern) African leaders. Against the background of family ties and a wider socio-cultural context, this personal friendship factor can be said to have influenced Malawi's favourable foreign policy stance towards the admonished regime of President Robert Mugabe during the long-standing Zimbabwe crisis.

The personal friendship between President Bingu wa Mutharika and Robert Mugabe formed the basis upon which Malawi's solidarity with Zimbabwe came to be measured. A few months after assuming office in May 2004, President Bingu wa Mutharika openly "assured [President Mugabe] and the people of Zimbabwe that Malawi will stand by [Zimbabwe] and will provide its support in all international and regional issues" (Malawi Government, 2004). President Mutharika's friendship with President Mugabe manifested itself through reciprocated visits—an extraordinary fifteen visits took place between 2006 and 2010 (Masina, 2006). Wa Mutharika publicly defended his decision to name a road in Malawi after the Zimbabwean leader even though this proved unpopular and was mainly opposed by many of Malawi's civil rights groups and the Western community. President wa Mutharika argued:

> Who else, and I repeat, who else is more eligible to have this honour of this highway than Comrade Robert Mugabe? There [are] many streets in Malawi named after colonialists perhaps for killing more blacks… Here we are, we have a hero, an African hero, and someone in his proper sense of mind, born here in Malawi, will come and say "no it is not right and proper to honour Robert Mugabe". Are you serious? If we cannot honour Robert Mugabe and other true sons of Africa, who can we honour? Europeans we don't know? When are we going to end colonial domination?
>
> (Mutharika in Masina, 2006)

Moreover, the aspect of the prevalence of mixed marriages between the peoples of Malawi and Zimbabwe reflects the socio-cultural context that informed Malawi's solidarity with Zimbabwe. President Bingu wa Mutharika himself had married a Zimbabwean woman, Ethel Zvauya. As a consequence he maintained some property (Bineth Trust) and held financial shares with one of the leading commercial banks in Zimbabwe. In turn, it is widely believed that President Mugabe's father was an immigrant from Malawi. These cases reveal the prevalence of intermarriage arrangements between the peoples of Malawi and Zimbabwe, which mainly resulted from patterns of economic migration and settlement in Zimbabwe (Mashiri, 2002). The unofficial but common identification of a specific population of Zimbabweans seen as being of Malawian origin (Mabeza, 2017) reinforces the depth of socio-cultural relations between the peoples of the two countries. The existence of mixed marriages can be argued to have significantly increased the probability of social cohesion (Smits, 2010), which can be seen to be an intervening factor in helping to shape Malawi's foreign policy choices on the issue of Zimbabwe.

The apparent indifference with which the Bingu wa Mutharika administration treated the Zimbabwe issue at a time when thousands of Malawians came to be displaced following the land reform programme started in the late 1990s seemingly did not disturb the continuing amity between the two leaders. Significantly, not only did this speak to the depth of socio-cultural integration of Malawians in Zimbabwe society, but also to Malawian fears of the economic fallout from Zimbabwe deciding on a mass repatriation of large numbers of Malawians. These fears were expressed by a former Cabinet Minister, Patricia Kaliati:

> should Malawi interfere with internal matters of Zimbabwe? If some countries have problems with Zimbabwe, that should not concern Malawi. Zimbabwe

> has been a friend of Malawi for a long time and it is playing host to over five million Malawians. If we quarrel with Mugabe, where will these Malawians go? Will some of these Western countries host them? Malawi is a sovereign state fully entitled to choose its friends freely.
>
> (Kaliati in Masina, 2006)

With the exception of President Muluzi who, in 2001, as chairperson at one SADC summit said that the negative effects of the Zimbabwe crisis would affect the entire region (Berries, 2002), Malawian leaders have, in the main, demonstrated significant reluctance to admonish the Mugabe regime over the ongoing crisis in Zimbabwe. Malawi's approach to Zimbabwe can be said to have subsisted within a multilateral context defined by SADC's quest for regional solidarity. This reflected a particular strategic culture in the leaders' considerable resolve to disregard external (Western) influence on (Southern) African issues. This became apparent when Malawi's former Foreign Minister, Lilian Patel, dismissed Western pressure on SADC to act against President Robert Mugabe by arguing that "SADC would not go along with (the) evil machinations of some Western powers using the neo-colonialist press locally and internationally" [to criticise President Mugabe]. "SADC would remain on Zimbabwe's side because blood is thicker than water" (Patel in Sachikonye, 2005: 573).

Perhaps because of the amity between Presidents Bingu wa Mutharika and Robert Mugabe, the British government attempted to persuade the Malawian leader to directly confront President Mugabe regarding the controversial land reform programme and human rights abuses. However, President Bingu wa Mutharika disregarded this attempt and emphasised the centrality of African unity within SADC's multilateral context by holding that:

> The British government has always wanted me to speak out against Robert Mugabe, but I have always kept quiet, because during one SADC summit, we agreed that we should speak with one voice through SADC and not just individually. And for your own information, you should know that SADC is a highly disciplined entity …We [Malawi] shall always speak through SADC and not on our own.
>
> (Malawi ruler blasts Britain …, 2009)

Malawi's position resulted from the country's professed commitment to regional integration, which it considers vital for socio-economic development. As former Foreign Affairs Minister Davis Katsonga argued:

> Malawi's participation in SADC affairs has a huge potential to assist in fulfilling the mission and objective [of the country]. This is because SADC has developed a very comprehensive regional integration agenda which Malawi has already benefitted from…. There is high potential for additional development opportunities in the medium to long term.
>
> (Malawi Government, 2006)

Malawian leaders had thus, at this time, following the difficult years of pariah statehood under President Hastings Banda, come to see SADC (and in all probability the AU) as an important vehicle for re-establishing Malawi's regional credibility. Importantly, SADC also came to be regarded as a crucial platform on which Malawi's socio-economic development aspirations could be promoted. Malawi's regard for the convergence of its foreign policy interests with other (Southern) African states is also explained by the social unity among its leaders, expressed in them cooperating against (Western) external influence. Ani (2015) sees this within a context where there are growing misgivings about external interventions in Africa, as well as the dominant belief and activism among African thinkers and politicians that only African oriented solutions can secure lasting solutions to Africa's challenges.

Conclusion

This chapter has shown that, since independence, Malawi's foreign policy choices had as their premise the country's quest for socio-economic development.

On the one hand, Malawian leaders have consistently professed their entrenched desire for the country's socio-economic stability. Limited financial and economic resources at Malawi's disposal have driven the country into seeking external assistance. This encompassed a diplomacy aimed at mobilising aid from bilateral partners both from within and outside the continent. This long-standing approach eventually found its way into the country's official foreign policy document (Malawi Government, 2010). On the other hand, Malawi has also used the multilateral platform offered by Africa's regional organisations to advance its foreign policy aspirations. Against the background of a socio-cultural mesh of trans-border relations, Malawian leaders have been able to use personal friendship elements with other (Southern) African leaders to obtain favourable foreign policy outcomes.

However, the attainment of a critical domestic socio-economic imperative has not been straightforward. At times, it has meant having to maintain a bifurcated foreign policy approach. This has seen the country converge towards and diverge away from the social political prescriptiveness suggested by Africa's multilateral context. Malawi's at times errant foreign policy behaviour therefore defies conventional wisdom which suggests small states such as Malawi stand only to benefit from and therefore need to consistently pursue their interests within a multilateral context (Graham, 2017).

Malawi's foreign policy behaviour exposes inconsistencies in the formal principles that guide inter-state relations on the continent and the Pan-African wish for collective foreign policy. The principles include ones to do with non-interference by any member state in the internal affairs of another, the respect for borders inherited at independence and sovereign equality and interdependence among member states (SADC, 2015; AU, 2000). Given these principles, it is structurally difficult for any regional body to push or pull an apparently deviant member towards a collective path of foreign policy. Socio-cultural factors, however, can play a persuasive part. Malawi's long-term foreign policy behaviour presents a theoretical challenge to neo-liberal institutionalist literature (Stein, 2008), which has the behaviour of small states in international relations shaped by structural and material factors skirting the issue of the socio-cultural layer, where intersubjective understandings make a difference to small state behaviour in the Global South. Interpersonal and cultural relationships among Malawian and African leaders have, as indicated, significantly informed Malawi's foreign policy choices and help explain the dichotomy of Malawi's foreign policy on the continent. Constructivism and a focus on the centrality of social interactions among individuals and states in explaining state behaviour enhances our understanding of ambiguous, in this case, bifurcated foreign policy behaviour departing from expected norms.

References

Adogamhe, P. (2003). African Foreign Policy: Integrating Political Economy and Decision-making Perspectives. In J. A. B. Wagner (ed.). *The Foreign Policies of the Global South: Rethinking Conceptual Frameworks*. Boulder, CO: Lynne-Rienner.

African Union. (2000). *Constitutive Act of the African Union*. Addis Ababa: African Union.

Ani, N. C. (2015). African Solutions to African Problems: Assessing the African Union's Application of Endogenous Conflict Resolution Approaches. A PhD Thesis submitted at the University of Kwa-Zulu Natal, Pietermaritzburg, South Africa. https://www.academia.edu/31240137/African_Solutions_to_African_Problems_Assessing_the_African_Unions_Application_of_Endogenous_Conflict_Resolution_Approaches, Accessed on 02 October 2019.

Bako, J. P. (2012). Towards Justice for Grave Human Rights Violations: The African Union vis-à-visthe International Criminal Court. https://ssrn.com/abstract=2808378. doi:10.2139/ssrn.2808378. Accessed on 24 July 2018.

Berries, C. P. (2002). The Zimbabwe Crisis and SADC: How to Deal with a Deviant Member State? In D. Hansohm, C. P. Berries, W. Breytenbach, T. Hartzenberg, W. Maier & P. Meyns (eds.). *Monitoring Regional Integration in Southern Africa Yearbook* (Vol. 2). Windhoek: Gamsberg Macmillan.

Capital News. (2012). Malawi Economy More Important than Bashir. *Capital News*. https://www.capitalfm.co.ke/news/2012/06/malawi-economy-more-important-than-bashir/. Accessed on 15 July 2018.

Dunne, T. (2008). Liberalism. In J. Baylis, S. Smith & P. Owens (eds.). *Globalization of World Politics* (4th ed.). New York: Oxford University Press.

Feldman, M. S. (1990). Organization Theory and the Study of the Presidency. *Paper Presented at the Institute for Public Policy Studies*, University of Pittsburgh.

Finnemore, M. (1996). *National Interests in International Society*. Ithaca/London: Cornell University Press.

Foote, N. (1951). Identification as the Basis for Theory of Motivation. *American Sociological Review*, *16*: 14–21.

Gaddis, J. L. (1992). International Relations Theory and the End of the Cold War. *International Security*, *17*(3): 5–58.

Graham, S. (2017). Drivers of the Foreign Policies of Southern African Small States. *Politikon*, *44*(1): 133–155. doi:10.1080/02589346.2017.1279802.

Gray, C. S. (1999). Strategic Culture as Context: The First Generation of Theory Strikes Back. *Review of International Studies*, *25*: 49–69.

Grovogui, S. N. (2003). Postcoloniality in Global South Foreign Policy: A Perspective. In J. A. Braveboy-Wagner (ed.). *The Foreign Policies of the Global South*: *Rethinking Conceptual Frameworks*. Boulder, CO: Lynne Rienner.

Gwaradzimba, F. (1993). SADCC and the Future of Southern African Regionalism. *African Studies Association*, *21*(1/2): 51–59.

Heimann, G. (2012). Can States be Friends? The Relevance of Friendship to International Relations. http://www.ipedr.com/vol48/007-CHHSS2012-A00023.pdf. doi:10.7763/IPEDR.2012.V48. 7.

Hermann, M. G. (1976). When Leader Personality Will Affect Foreign Policy: Some Propositions. In J. Rosenau (ed.). *In Search of Global Patterns*. New York: Free Press.

Hindes, B. (1989). *Political Choice and Social Structure*. Aldershot: Edward Elgar.

Houghton, D. (2017). Constructivist Analyses of Foreign Policy. *Oxford Research Encyclopedia of Politics*. http://politics.oxfordre.com/view/10.1093/acrefore/9780190228637.001.0001/acrefore-9780190228637-e-400. Accessed on 22 August 2018. doi:10.1093/acrefore/9780190228637.013.400.

Howlett, D. (2006). The Future of Strategic Culture. *Defense Threat Reduction Agency*. Contract No. DTRA01-03-D-0017. https://fas.org/irp/agency/dod/dtra/stratcult-future.pdf. Accessed on 15 May 2018.

Hurd, I. (2008). Constructivism. In C. Reus-Smit & D. Snidal (eds.). *The Oxford Handbook of International Relations*. New York: Oxford University Press.

Ihonvbere, J. O. (2003). Background: From Independence to a One-Man Dictatorship. In J. O. Ihonvbere & J. M. Mbaku (eds.). *Political Liberalization and Democratization in Africa: Lessons from Country Experiences*. London: Praeger.

Johnson, J. L. (2006). *Strategic Culture: Refining the Theoretical Construct*. SAIC. https://fas.org/irp/agency/dod/dtra/strat-culture.pdf. Accessed on 15 May 2018.

Kadyampakeni, J. G. (1985). Banda, Balanced Development and Disengagement. *Africa Insight*, *15*(2): 89–98.

Karns, M. P. & Mingst, K. A. (2004). *International Organizations*. Boulder, CO: Lynne Rienner.

Kaunda, M. (2002). Continuity and Change in Malawi's Foreign Policy-making. In K. Adar & R. Ajulu (eds.). *Globalisation and Emerging Trends in African States' Foreign Policy-making Process: A Comparative perspective of Southern Africa*. Aldershot: Ashgate.

Lantis, J. S. (2006). *Strategic Culture: From Clausewitz to Constructivism*. SAIC. https://fas.org/irp/agency/dod/dtra/stratcult-claus.pdf. Accessed on 10 April 2018.

Legro, J. (2005). *Rethinking the World: Great Power Strategies and International Order*. Ithaca, NY: Cornell University Press

Mabeza, C. M. (2017) *Water and Soil in Holy Matrimony? A Smallholder Farmers' Innovative Agricultural Practices for Adapting to Climate in Rural Zimbabwe*. Bamenda: Langaa RPCIG.

Malawi Government. (1966). *Malawi Hansard*, 18 January. Zomba: Malawi National Assembly.

Malawi Government. (1967). *Malawi Hansard*, 29 March. Zomba: Malawi National Assembly.

Malawi Government. (2004). Speech by His Excellency the President of the Republic of Malawi Dr. Bingu wa Mutharika at a State Banquet Hosted by President Robert

Mugabe, Harare, Zimbabwe. http//www.malawi.go.mw/presidential.../state%20 Banquent%20in%20ZIMBABWE.pdf. Accessed on 14 August 2009.

Malawi Government. (2006). *Talking Points for Honourable Davies Katsonga, M.P., Minister of Foreign Affairs and Chairperson of the SADC National Committee during the SADC National Committee Meeting*. Lilongwe: Ministry of Foreign Affairs Conference Room.

Malawi Government. (2010). *The Foreign Policy of the Government of Malawi*. http://www.foreignaffairs.gov.mw/phocadownload/publications/Foreign%20 Policy%20of%20the%20Republic%20of%20Malawi.pdf. Accessed on 24 July 2018.

Malawi Ruler Blasts Britain on Mugabe. (2009). *The Zimbabwean*, 12 February. https ://www.thezimbabwean.co/2009/02/malawi-ruler-blasts-britain-on-mugabe/. Accessed on 15 March 2010.

Mashiri, M. (2002). *The Language of ethnic contempt: Malawian Zimbabwean-Shona Rivalry*, Department of African Languages and Literature, Harere: University of Zimbabwe.

Masina, L. (2006). African Hero Honoured. *New Africa*, June. http://www.africasia.com/ newafrican/recent.php?back_month=58. Accessed on 23 April 2009.

McMaster, C. (1974). *Malawi Foreign Policy and Development*. London: Julian Friedmann Publishers Ltd.

Nyasa Times. (2012). Bashir not Welcome to Malawi President Banda. *Nyasa Times*. https://www.nyasatimes.com/bashir-not-welcome-to-malawi-president-banda/. Accessed on 25 July 2018.

Omari, A. H. & Macaringue, P. (2007). Southern African Security in Historical Perspective. In G. Cawthra, A. du Pisani & A. Omari (eds.). *Security and Democracy in Southern Africa*. Johannesburg: Wits University Press.

Patel, N. & Hajat, R. (2007). Foreign Policy. In N. Patel & L. Svasand (eds.). *Government and Politics in Malawi*. Zomba: Kachere Series.

Reuters. (2009). AU Will Not Cooperate with ICC on Bashir: Draft. https://www.reuters. com/article/ozatp-sudan-darfur-au-idAFJOE5610FV20090702. Accessed on 20 July 2018.

Sachikonye, L. M. (2005). South Africa's Quiet Diplomacy: The Case of Zimbabwe. In J. Daniel, J. Lutchman & R. Southall (eds.). *State of the Nation: South Africa 2004–2005*. Cape Town: HSRC Press.

Sagawa, M. D. (2011). Power Politics or Personality? Re-Visiting Malawi's Foreign Policy Conception and Strategy under Kamuzu Banda, 1964–1994. *Forum for Development Studies*, *38*(2): 131–156.

Short, P. (1974). *Banda*. London: Routledge and Kegan Paul.

Smits, J. (2010). Ethnic Intermarriage and Social Cohesion. What Can We Learn from Yugoslavia? *Social Indicators Research*, *96*(3): 417–432. doi:10.1007/ s11205-009-9485-y.

Snyder, J. (1977). *The Soviet Strategic Culture: Implications for Nuclear Options*, R-2154-AF. Santa Monica, CA: Rand Corporation. https://www.rand.org/content/dam/ rand/pubs/reports/2005/R2154.pdf. Accessed on 15 May 2018.

Southern African Development Community. (2015). *Consolidated Text of the Treaty of the Southern African Development Community*. Gaborone: SADC.

Steans, J., Pettiford, L., Diez, T. & El-Anis, I. (2010). *An Introduction to International Relations Theory: Perspectives and Theme* (3rd ed.). London: Pearson.

Stein, A. (2008). Neoliberal Institutionalism. In C. Reus-Smit & D. Snidal (eds.). *The Oxford Handbook of International Relations*. Oxford University Press. http://www

.oxfordhandbooks.com/view/10.1093/oxfordhb/9780199219322.001.0001/oxfordhb-9780199219322-e-11. Accessed on 29 October 2018. doi:10.1093/oxfordhb/9780199219322.003.0011.

Tannenwald, N. (2005). Ideas and Explanation: Advancing the Theoretical Agenda. *Journal of Cold War Studies*, *7*(2): 13–42. doi:10.1162/1520397053630619.

The Guardian. (2012). African Union Pulls Summit from Malawi in Row Over Sudan's President. https://www.theguardian.com/world/2012/jun/08/african-union-malawi-summit-sudan. Accessed on 20 July 2018.

Uemura, T. (2015). Understanding Chinese Foreign Relations: A Cultural Constructivist Approach. *International Studies Perspective*, *16*(3): 345–365.

Wendt, A. (2010). Anarchy Is what States Make of it: The Social Construction of Power Politics. In H. R. Nau (ed.). *International Relations in Perspective*. Washington, DC: CQ Press.

Wright, S. (1999). The Changing Context of African Foreign Policies. In S. Wright (ed.). *African Foreign Policies*. Boulder, CO: Westview Press.

12 Strategies of a small state between realism and liberalism

Sixty years of Guinea's diplomacy and foreign policy (1958–2018)

Issaka K. Souaré

Introduction

When in 1958, French president General de Gaulle put to a referendum his new French constitution providing for France's then "African colonies" to remain with France in a sort of commonwealth, Guinea was the only "territory" that voted "no" on 28 September, and so becoming a sovereign state on 2nd October 1958. Relations with the former colonial power thus started on a rocky basis, to the point that France nearly opposed Guinea's membership application to the United Nations a month later. This, together with the Cold War politics and the strong Pan-African penchant of Guinea's first president, Ahmed Sékou Touré, strongly influenced the country's diplomacy and foreign relations until Touré's passing in 1984. After this, and setting aside a two-year military transition (2008–2010), two further political regimes have ruled Guinea, those of Lansana Conté (1984–2008) and of Alpha Condé (2010–2020). Each of the three regimes had its own political and historical context, and this has had a bearing on its changing foreign policy orientations.

In retrospect, one can argue that Guinea's foreign policy under Touré mainly followed a realist script, particularly the concept of alliance building for balance of power and the notion of national interest. The two subsequent regimes after Touré's passing departed from the strong doctrinal/ideological justifications of foreign policy and embraced forms of liberalism aligned more with economic than with political thought.

This chapter looks at the changing and constant aspects of foreign policy orientations of the Guinean state and its three political dispensations. An initial realist postulate on the national interest and alliance building in the country's foreign policy is followed by considerations of a mix of realist and liberal positioning under three different administrations. A country may be endowed with great resources, but still be considered poor if there is no effective transformation of these resources into actual wealth. Guinea is such a country. It is thus a small and "poor" country. However, the three successive leaders of the country used various ways to deploy policy agency in order to compensate for this; albeit the First and Third Republics were more successful in this regard than the second one. In the case of the First Republic, which had more constraints than the other two, it resorted to the practice of alliance building. It entered pacts with the Eastern bloc while dealing with the West, to the point at times of confusing some observers who did not know where to place the country. This confirms the positions of small state theorists who argue that it is not necessarily a country's smallness that matters, but the strategies it adopts to interact with the outside world.

Realism, liberalism and small states: Theoretical underpinnings of Guinea's foreign policies

Realist postulates in Guinea's foreign policy

Through his seminal book, *Politics among Nations*, Morgenthau (1948) defines realism as a school that believes in the world as the result of forces inherent in human nature. This being essentially a world of opposing interests and of conflicts amongst those living in it, moral principles can never be fully realised, but must at best be approximated through the constantly short-term balancing of interests and eternally precarious settlement of conflicts. There is a clear centrality of power in realist thought. However, the concept of balance of power and alliance building allows the appropriate juggling of power by state actors of the international system. This is true for both where you have a "simple balance" in a bipolar world and "complex balance" in a multipolar system (Nicholson, 1998: 93). Bulls (1977: 97) refers to the US-USSR rivalry during the Cold War as an illustration of the first scenario. He calls to mind mid-18th century Europe to illustrate a complex balance of power, when France and Austria were joined by England, Russia and Prussia as big powers. The multipolar system that we have been living in since the beginning of the new millennium with the rise of China and other powers is another illustration of this scenario.

Dunne and Schmidt (2001) recognise the same advantages in a balance of power in the mitigation of the negative effects of the uncertainties created by the security dilemma, itself induced by the phenomenon of "self-help" coined by Waltz in his *Theory of International Politics* (1979). In the realists' "anarchical society", they add, "alliances will be formed that seek to check and balance the power against threatening states". In this regard, "a fortuitous balance will be established through the interactions of states in the same way that an equilibrium is established between firms and consumers in a free economic market—according to classical liberal economic theory" (Donne & Scmith, 2001: 153).

Indeed, alliance formation is an inevitable consequence of interaction among sovereign political units driven by the motivation of either dominating or balancing the power. For Mearsheimer (2001), weaker states generally forge alliances to balance power and protect themselves against the dominating tendency of a strong (hegemon) or a group of strong states. Stronger ones, on the other hand, often form alliances to increase their share of world power and dominate it, sometimes in a zero-sum game. Walt (1985: 5–6) elaborates on these two scenarios and the positioning of various states vis-à-vis alliance building through two hypotheses. He terms the two hypotheses as "balancing" and "bandwagoning". He explains the first hypothesis by the proposition that "states will join alliances in order to avoid domination by stronger powers [...] to protect themselves from states or coalitions whose superior resources could pose a threat".

Bandwagoning behaviour occurs when states tend to ally *with* rather than against the dominant side. The underlining logic behind this hypothesis is that

> the more powerful you are and the more clearly this is demonstrated, the more likely others are to ally with you. By contrast, a decline in relative position will lead one's allies to opt for neutrality at best or to defect to the other side at worst.
>
> (ibid: 7–8)

In the final analysis, in Walt's view "states facing an external threat overwhelmingly prefer to balance against the threat rather than bandwagon with it". To him, this situation can primarily be explained by the fact that "an alignment that preserves most of a state's freedom of action [which is joining with weaker or equal partners] is preferable to accepting subordination under a potential hegemon" (Walt, 1985: 16).

This debate is very apt in describing the situation of most African countries during the Cold War. In this bipolar world, most African countries joined either the camp between the Washington-led Western capitalist alliance or the Moscow-led Soviet Communist bloc and from this emerged a third alliance called the "Non-Aligned Movement" (NAM).

A liberal ethos in Guinea's foreign policy

Liberalism is a school that believes that a rational and moral political order derived from universally valid abstract principles can be achieved. It assumes the eternal goodness and infinite malleability of human nature and blames the failure of the social order to measure up to these standards on a lack of knowledge and understanding. It trusts in education, reform and the sporadic use of force to remedy these effects. As such, the liberal view about diplomacy is that it is an integral part of the process seeking to bring about harmony and cooperation among members of the international society.

Doyle and Recchia (2011: 1434) argue that liberalism is generally associated with an essential principle, the importance of the freedom of the individual. "This is a belief in the importance of moral freedom, of the right to be treated and a duty to treat others as ethical subjects and not as objects or means only". Talking about diplomacy and foreign policy, they highlight the insistence of liberal thought on the state of being "subject to neither the external authority of other states nor the internal authority of special prerogatives held, for example, by monarchs or military bureaucracies over foreign policy" (Doyle & Recchia, 2011: 1434). According to Jonsson and Hall (2005: 17), liberals tend to progress from methodological individualism and conceptualise International Relations (IR) as the sum total of state or actor behaviour, which is thought to be shaped by state-society relations. According to this view, diplomacy "takes place within a context of international rules, institutions, and practices, which affect the incentives of the actors".

A neo-liberal reformulation of these tenets is offered by Marovcsik (1997). To him, liberal IR theory contends that "state-society relations … have a fundamental impact on state behaviour in world politics". Societal ideas, interests and institutions influence state behaviour by shaping state preferences, that is, the fundamental social purposes underlying the strategic calculations of governments. He identifies three main strands of liberalism: ideational, commercial and republican. As we will see later, the Guinean foreign policy in the Second and Third republics aspired more to this thinking, particularly as regards to the economic aspects of foreign policy.

The advent of the third wave of democratisation in most African countries from the early 1990s made many of them, willingly or unwillingly, follow at least some tenets of this liberal view. With the rise of civil society organisations and international advocacy groups, more and more states, even hypocritically, try to align their foreign policy engagements with liberal principles. This is also true even for big powers that try to follow what can be termed as "principled opportunism", but hiding behind liberal ideals to advance "Machiavellian" policies.

What is the impact of Guinea's "small state" status on its foreign policy orientations?

Scholars talking about big powers have always been conscious about categorising states as "small" and "big". The formal development of a body of literature about "small states" in IR theory is however relatively recent and there is now increasing literature on "small states studies". Nevertheless, one big challenge in this sub-field is the definitional dilemma, as the criteria for qualifying a state "small" are not consensual. For example, Keohane (1969) defines small states based on their political capabilities. To him, small states are those that are "system ineffectual", meaning that they are unable to influence the international system. Vital (1967) has the same view about a state's capabilities, seen in terms of its economic endowment and demographic and military resources. Rothstein (1968), however, prefers to defer to the states themselves: do they perceive themselves as weak within the international system and require the security of outside help? Then they are small. Do they think and try to act otherwise, regardless of their size and other resources? Then they should be viewed as such.

What matters for us is the impact of such status on a country's foreign policy actions. Vital (1967) basically argues that small states do not have agency in this regard. For him, the choice of strategy is not a mere decision made within the small state, but more like a consequence of its location and role in the international arena: countries located within the sphere of interest of great states prefer to follow a passive or defensive policy, because whatever opportunity they may have to manoeuvre is narrower. The predominant choice of a small state, in Vital's view, is the strategy of forming alliances (multilateral) or choosing a protector (bilateral).

In a recent article on the small island state of Iceland, Thorhallsson (2018) reformulates this in what he calls "shelter theory", based on three forms of protection: political, economic and societal. Applying this to his case study, he looks at the long-standing relationship that Iceland enjoyed with the US until the latter closed its military base there in 2006, and in 2008 refused to provide Iceland with assistance following its economic collapse. Thorhallsson (2018) then shows how Iceland has since made new security and defence arrangements with its neighbouring states, applied for membership of the European Union and became the first European country to conclude a free-trade agreement with China. Its president has also pressed for closer political and economic ties with Russia. In the African context, the defence agreements signed between France and a number of African countries since the 1960s (e.g. Côte d'Ivoire, Gabon, Djibouti, Senegal) and more recently (e.g. Mali and Niger) are similar to Iceland in the search for protection. The pacts with France have allowed for the establishment of military bases, purportedly to protect these countries in case of need.

It goes without saying that such protection comes at a price. Vital (1967: 79) rightly argues that "where the quest for protection and insurance is successful, a price must normally be paid in terms of sacrifice of autonomy in the control of national resources and loss of freedom of political manoeuvre and choice". In the same vein, but focusing on the African and Asian states, Wong (2018: 31) notes that "the small powers are forced to engage in a structurally dependent relationship with the great powers by engaging in unfair and exploitative trade relations".

But do such relationships take away from expressions of real agency by small states? If this is so, why should some small states with similar characteristics and challenges then play a more active role than others in both regional and international politics? Compare a more passive Kuwait to a hyperactive Qatar; a more assertive Rwanda to the big, very rich and militarily more able Angola; a very dynamic Morocco neighbouring a less dynamic yet richer neighbour in Algeria ... in fact, the same country may be more active at one period of its history than at another. This appears to give credence to the critical view recently expressed by Long (2017: 146–147) through what he calls an "asymmetrical relationship". In Long's view, the analysis of small states should move away "from the poorly specified category of smallness to instead prioritise the dynamics of the relationships in which these states are engaged [...] What matters is not 'size', however defined, but the relationships between states". He rightly calls for a shift of "focus from the power that states possess to the power that they exercise" and to acknowledge that "relationship may be overwhelmingly asymmetrical in military terms, but less so economically, diplomatically, or institutionally".

With its estimated 12 million people in 2018 (and far fewer during the First and Second Republics), a land mass of 258,852 square km and its small economic resources, it is evident that Guinea in relative terms belongs to the league of small states. But how has the country acted on its agency?

Guinea's realist foreign policy in action under the First Republic (1958–1984)

The First Republic was born out of the referendum vote organised by the colonial power France in 1958. It should be recalled that a new devolution act was adopted in France under the name of *Loi cadre* (sponsored by Gaston Deferre, then minister of overseas territories) in June 1956. This act offered a level of autonomy to French colonies in Africa, Asia and the Caribbean. In May 1958, General de Gaulle returned to power in France with the objective of embarking on profound political and institutional changes in France. De Gaulle's constitutional reform bill ushered in the constitution for the Fifth French Republic. For the French colonies, the new constitution proposed a form of association within a "French Community" à la commonwealth. The African territories were to become autonomous republics with the theoretical opportunity for (some of) them to form a confederation, though still under the aegis of the French state.

Touré tried to negotiate the draft constitution to provide for the right to independence, which General de Gaulle rejected. He likened it to secession and rupture with France and its community. Because of this, Touré and his président-directeur général (PDG) campaigned for a "no" in the referendum and Guinea voted overwhelmingly (95%) against the proposed constitution. This paved the way for the country's independence on 2nd October, thereby becoming the first sovereign country amongst the French colonies in Africa (Kaba, 1990: 147–79; Devey, 1997: 135–37).

France strove to punish its "audacious former colony" so as not to encourage others to follow suit. It severed relations with it by repatriating all its technical personnel, taking away all archives and even removing some material installations. Most importantly, it sought to diplomatically isolate the newly independent state and came close to opposing Guinea's membership application to the United Nations, although it eventually abstained from voting (Lewin, 2009). As Muehlenbeck (2008: 72) recalls, "upon leaving, the French vindictively launched a 'scorched-earth' policy to punish Guinea for having left the French Empire". He adds: "Departing colonial officials stripped their offices of all administrative records, as well as anything else potentially useful to the Guineans, including telephones and telephone wires, typewriters, maps, and medical supplies". Formal diplomatic relations were established between the two countries in January 1959, but they were severed in 1969 with the recall of their respective ambassadors. It was only in 1975 that the two countries established normal diplomatic relations.

This was the context in which the first Guinean post-independence regime had to forge a new set of foreign relations. It coincided with the Cold War and East-West rivalries. But this context contributed to a deteriorating economy and the attempt by the state to politically control domestic economic and political life, resulting in nationalisation, the establishment of a one-party state, strong security systems and a suppression of dissent. As most dissidents sought refuge in neighbouring countries, particularly Senegal and Côte d'Ivoire, relations with these neighbouring states were often rocky until the passing of Touré. The latter frequently accused the leaders of the two countries of colluding with France and Guinean dissidents for subversive activities aimed at overthrowing his regime (Keita, 2002).

Strongly nationalistic and Pan-Africanist, Touré appears to have been forced into the arms of the Communist bloc, while he continued courting the western countries as a true realist who only follows his national interest in his alliance-makings. It is against the background of this dialectic that the non-alignment position of the country's foreign policy under Touré's regime should be read. Terming it as "positive neutralism", Touré himself theorised this in the following terms:

> we state vigorously that we shall never accept subjugation to any bloc, or any nation, while reaffirming our determination to play our part, in all circumstances, in the action conducted by the peoples of the world for democratic freedom, social progress and international security [...] Positive neutralism is the choice of states which are resolved to respect the personality of their peoples and to safeguard their originality in assuring and conducting their evolution, while letting them benefit from the technical, scientific and cultural contributions of other peoples, in order to permit the rapid evolution and constant improvement of their living conditions.
>
> (Touré, 1979: 592–93)

This also shows agency on the part of a small state which is aware of its weaknesses but striving to overcome them. It was a balancing act, often tilting towards the Soviet bloc, but not always and not necessarily because they were communist, but because they happened to stand for the same principles on a number of issues, such as anti-colonialism and the fight against apartheid. Yet he continued courting the Western bloc, because he realised they could also offer him as much development assistance as the Socialist bloc—or even more in some cases. This was realism at the core—no permanent enemy or friend, everything hovering around national interest. Thus, during the Kennedy presidency in the United States, and thanks to the latter's use of personal diplomacy with the Guinean leader, the relationship between Conakry and Washington became very warm, to the point that Touré became slightly pro-Western (Muehlenbeck, 2008: 82).[1]

The position of non-alignment in Guinea's foreign policy was mostly expressed in the country's dynamism in promoting South-South and Afro-Asian cooperation, particularly through the NAM. This movement espoused a position of neutrality vis-à-vis the two dominant blocs, but it was a bloc in its own right advocating for the sovereignty and independence of states of the South to choose their own path to development and an expanding nuclear free zone. Although hard at times to preserve in the face of pressure from the two camps, members of the NAM insisted on entertaining good relations with members of both alliances in their foreign relations.

Beyond this, one of the country's foreign policy goals was to contribute to the liberation of other African territories under colonial domination or minority domination and segregation, particularly in Lusophone and Southern Africa. Very active in the National Liberation Committee of the OAU, the country hosted many dignitaries of these movements, including Amilcar Cabral, who led the liberation struggle in Guinea-Bissau. Cabral was eventually assassinated in Conakry in January 1973. These personages also included Govan Mbeki and Miriam Makeba from South Africa. Kozo Zoumanigui, who served as Guinea's foreign minister for several years in the 1990s, argues that 1% of the country's national budget was earmarked for liberation movements until 1991 (Zoumanigui, 2013: 18–19).

Inconsistent liberalism in Guinea's foreign policy since 1984

There were two subsequent political regimes of the Second and Third Republics that ruled Guinea after the passing of Sékou Touré in 1984. The two are discussed together because the differences between them are far fewer than what unites them in comparison to the previous regime whose ideological leanings were very different.

The Second Republic was characterised by three main factors. The first is that it was a military regime that came to power through a putsch staged on 4 April 1984. General Lansana Conté led the coup-makers and became the head of state. Dominated by military officers, the regime "civilianised" itself in preparation for multiparty elections in December 1993. It nevertheless continued to be viewed by many as a military regime led by a (former) army general.

The second characteristic—compared to the Touré regime—is a lack of ideological grounding, since military officers constituted the bulk of the leadership of the regime. Another element was that those who supported this regime were those who had been at loggerheads with the preceding regime. In foreign policy terms, France and the neighbouring states who had experienced difficult relations with the Touré regime were both approached by, and welcomed, the new military regime in the spirit of "one's enemy's enemy is one's friend".

The first actions of this regime consisted of going against almost everything the previous one stood for. This posturing was considered important in order to clearly show their difference and distance from the previous regime. Foreign policy was one of the most prominent fields to show up this "paradigm shift".

First, the regime broke ranks with some of Guinea's long-standing bilateral partners under the old regime who numbered several in the Eastern bloc, in order to look westwards. From the nationalistic state-controlled and socialist-oriented economy, liberal principles in terms of market-driven economy were now espoused. As many countries in the NAM remained considerate of the defunct regime, the new leadership also disengaged from these alliances.

A brief contextualisation of the coming of the Third Republic under the leadership of Alpha Condé can further explain changes in agency. The regime came to power in December 2010, having won the second round of a very competitive presidential election and following a transitional period that had begun in December 2008 (Souaré, 2009). The marked difference between this regime and that of Conté is that it was a civilian-elected regime from the start. With this and the international outlook of its president, it has managed to reassert Guinea's presence on the regional and continental scene to a degree not reached by the Second Republic, but nevertheless short of what was achieved by the First Republic.

The Third Republic is closer to its immediate predecessor in terms of the ideological framing of its foreign policy actions, which are also couched in liberal terms. The democratic credentials of the country have certainly increased with the introduction of a multiparty system in 1992. In writing on Guinea's foreign policy under the Second Republic, Cissé (2012: 23) observes that this regime coincided with a new world order characterised by a unipolar system, marked by American supremacy and an expanding liberal capitalist economy. Guinean foreign policy reflected this new order. "It is pragmatic and less charged ideologically compared to the past [regime]" (Cissé, 2012: 24).

Indeed, the leadership of the Second Republic came up with the term "economic diplomacy" to describe their foreign policy orientation, away from what they considered as the ideologically and politically-led state-centred development policies of the previous regime. The Third Republic has continued with the same concept. Ordinarily, this would mean an emphasis on promoting citizens' economic interests in other countries, such as assisting business people and entrepreneurs or state companies to obtain good markets and contracts abroad. In the Guinean context, as in that of many other African countries, however, foreign policy has become largely driven by the search for aid. This overshadows any other non-economic concerns of foreign policy and happens against the background of no meaningful home-grown economic prosperity (Akokpari, 2001: 45–46).

Promotion of regional integration in Africa

The issues of regional integration can be explained, at least in part, by theories of regime formation. It should be admitted that there is a lack of consensus on the conceptual definitions of international regimes, mainly because most authors mean different things when they use the concept of "international regime" (Strange, 1983; Gilpin, 2001: 342–43). In any case, what really matters for the purpose of this chapter is why states form and/or join regional and international organisations in what is essentially a foreign policy decision.

Theories about regional integration

Virtually every theoretical school in IR attempts to describe some or other aspect of international institutions (Hasenclever, Mayer, & Rittberger, 2000). Some of this is of importance in looking at Guinea's foreign policy orientation regarding international and regional organisations.

Both realism and liberalism depart from the same premise—that international institutions are an important feature of the contemporary international system. They also agree that states are rational actors when committing themselves to creating international institutions to facilitate cooperation. Differences, however, emerge in their explanation of why states commit themselves to creating institutions. Realists contend that the anarchical nature of the international system encourages states to commit themselves to institution building only if their relative gains—vis-à-vis other states in the proposed institution—are assured (Martin & Simmons, 1998). From this, one could also argue that a realist would view regional integration processes, as with Mearsheimer (2001), as a form of alliance building for balance of power purposes.

To the liberal-institutionalists, however, states commit themselves to creating international institutions out of their realisation that these mechanisms could help them to overcome problems of collective action, high transaction costs and information deficits. They see their benefit in terms of absolute gains; that is what they expect to gain from their adherence to the institution proposed and not how they will be better off compared to others, as realists maintain states do. As a result of this, liberal-institutionalists argue, the main concern of states in this process is whether they will get the best deal possible (Keohane, 1984).

Regional integration in Guinea's foreign policy

Looking at regional integration processes in Africa and how Guinea has engaged with them in its foreign policy, one could argue that all three republics view them through a liberal-institutionalist lens in the African context. In addition to this, however, it is not far-fetched to assume that the Touré regime viewed regional organisations, particularly the continental ones, as alliances for achieving a balance of power on the international stage. The Condé regime sometimes toes this line, thereby uniting with the First Republic in emphasising that "Africa must speak with one voice". I have considered above, albeit briefly, the country's participation and role in the NAM. Let us now consider its role in the creation and functioning of the OAU/AU and ECOWAS (Economic Community of West African States) in the light of these theories about regime formation.

The establishment of the OAU, 1963

It would appear that the first leaders of independent Guinea had a natural disposition for regional if not continental integration. This is because the first constitution of the country, adopted a month after independence, included a clause that provided for the possibility of Guinea ceding a part or the whole of its sovereignty in favour of a greater African entity. Subsequent constitutions in 1982, 1992 and 2010 have carried forward the same spirit in various forms. The last two constitutions stipulate in their preamble, the country's "attachment to the cause of African unity, sub-regional and continental integration" (Guinea's Constitution of 2010: 3).

Guinea's first attempt at regional integration was its joining hands with Nkrumah's Ghana to form the Ghana-Guinea Union in February 1959. This became the Ghana-Guinea-Mali Union when the latter country, under Modibo Keita, joined the confederation in April 1961. This union did not last long, like many similar ones in Africa and around the world, as it collapsed in 1962. It nevertheless contributed to the efforts for the creation of a similar entity at the continental level, which would become the OAU.

Guinea's foreign policy orientations made sure that it played a pivotal role in these processes. Thus, in addition to the advocacy for the formation of the OAU and contribution to this, Conakry also ensured that the first substantive Secretary General of the organisation hailed from Guinea, in the person of Telli Diallo, who served two terms from 1964 to 1972. Diallo had been Guinea's first permanent representative to the UN (United Nations) in New York. A brilliant lawyer by training, and armed with the New York experience, Diallo was indeed the ideal candidate to interpret these principles of Guinean foreign policy at the helm of the first continental organisation in Africa.

Guinea's involvement in continental matters did see a decline during the Second Republic, which accounts for the country's absence in the major debates on the continent in the 1990s and particularly at the turn of the century. These included, for example, the entire debates about the New Partnership for Africa's Development (NEPAD) and the transformation of the OAU into the AU. It took the advent of the Third Republic for the country to become aware of a level of "come-back" on the continental and international diplomatic scenes. This was marked particularly with the election of President Condé as the chair of the AU during the year 2017.

Partly because of his poor health, Lansana Conté had been absent from AU summits for several years. With the advent of Condé, he rarely missed one. Also, during his chairmanship of the AU in 2017, he advocated for the idea of "continental champions", designating individual leaders to champion specific thematic areas, such as energy (himself), youth, infrastructure, etc. He also insisted on Africa "speaking with one voice" on global matters, particularly in support of African candidates for top jobs at international organisations. One can question the weight of Guinea's singular role in processes to have African candidates winning international positions such as the Directorship General of the World Health Organisation in 2017 and Secretary General of the International Organisation of the Francophone in 2018. This is because the countries of origin of the contenders played a bigger role in campaigning than what the Guinean leader might have done as chair of the AU.

It is worth mentioning though, how the Guinean leader, in a relentless effort, campaigned to ensure that Guinea hosted the headquarters of the newly formed African Minerals Development Centre (AMDC). Created in 2013, AMDC is the AU's specialised institution tasked with implementing the Africa Mining Vision (AMV), developed in 2009 for "a transparent, equitable and optimal exploitation of mineral resources to underpin broad-based sustainable growth and socio-economic development" by 2050. Guinea won this in a fierce competition with Zambia at the 31st Summit of the Heads of States and Governments of the AU held in Mauritania in June/July 2018. Significantly, this was the first time the country hosted such a continental body. Albeit unsuccessfully, it did bid for two AU Commissioners in 2017 and 2018. Moreover, its membership and presidency of the AU Peace and Security Council at the height of the Central African crisis of 2015 brought its continental diplomacy new prominence.

But while there was a relative absence of a forceful Guinean diplomacy at the continental level after the First Republic, the situation differed at the West African level. This is perhaps because the immediate neighbourhood and some of the issues at stake directly affected Guinea's own security.

The formation of ECOWAS, 1975

The treaty establishing ECOWAS was signed on 28 May 1975 in the then Nigerian capital Lagos. Its establishment was the culmination of a series of high-level meetings initiated in 1972 by two young military leaders, namely Yakubu Gowan of Nigeria and Gnassingbé Eyadéma of Togo. Nevertheless, Guinea's Sékou Touré, who was consulted very early on, "gave the initiative his unqualified support" according to Adebayo Adedeji, who led the joint Nigerian-Togolese ministerial delegation that toured the region to sell the idea of these two leaders (Adedeji, 2004: 30).

Indeed, when the organisation was finally launched in May 1975, Guinea was at the forefront of its founding members. The Second Republic, under Lansana Conté, continued with the same involvement. A turn of events saw Guinean foreign policy under Conté come to play an even bigger role in the functioning of ECOWAS than that of his predecessor. This is because it coincided with the transformational challenge of the engulfment of the region in armed conflicts, particularly in Guinea's immediate neighbourhood in Liberia (1989–1996; 1999–2003), Sierra Leone (1991–2002), Guinea-Bissau (1998–99) and Côte d'Ivoire (2002–2007). These challenges forced a shift in the focus of the regional organisation, through a revision in 1991 of the founding Treaty of ECOWAS. This reform incorporated issues of conflict prevention, resolution and peacekeeping at a more prominent level.[2] This was followed immediately by the establishment of the ECOWAS Peace Monitoring and Ceasefire Group (ECOMOG), which intervened in these countries (Adebajo, 2002; Souaré, 2006).

The same practice has continued under the Third Republic. The country has consequently remained at the frontline of almost all the peacekeeping troops deployed by ECOWAS, including Mali recently, both as part of the African-Led International Support Mission for Mali (AFISMA), co-deployed by the AU and ECOWAS from January to June 2013, and the UN Multidimensional Integrated Stabilization Mission in Mali (MINUSMA) that replaced the latter from July 2013.

The main reference for the resolution of the serious political crisis in Bissau was the Conakry Agreement signed by the Bissau-Guinean actors in October 2016. The role played by Alpha Condé in the epilogue of the Gambian crisis in January 2017 is a further successful illustration of the country's regional diplomatic pushes. Moreover, two executive secretaries of ECOWAS have hailed from Guinea: Edouard Benjamin (1993–1997) and Lansana Kouyaté (1997–2002).

Conclusion

This chapter looked at Guinea's foreign policy orientations and practices under three successive political regimes. One common thread across all three successive regimes in Guinea is their consistent involvement in regional integration processes in Africa. The differences are found in their degree of emphasis on one level or the other of this cooperation. The First Republic was an all-embracing one, playing an active role in both regional and continental integration processes and not shying away from diving into the hot waters of international politics beyond Africa. The Second Republic limited itself to the regional sphere, for the obvious considerations concerning its nature as a military regime, but also the limited continental and international ambitions of its top leadership. The current and third regime tries to emulate the first one, but tends to look more at the continental level, and in some respects, global affairs, without the charisma or the doctrinal foundations of the First Republic.

As a small state, the country tried to complement its relative weakness by entering into alliances. The dynamism of the agency underpinning this depended on the nature of each regime. While the First Republic managed to sail on the East-West rivalry to eat at both tables, it suffered because of its authoritarian politics at home. The Second Republic threw itself into the arms of the West and adopted uncontrolled liberal economic policies. While this appeared attractive at the beginning, the absence of a strong economic base at home hit the country hard. The military nature of the regime also reduced its legitimacy in the eyes of other nations. The Third Republic has benefitted from its civilian nature and the fact that the president is the first democratically elected leader in the country. After several years in opposition and travelling between various countries, President Condé developed a wide personal network of contacts that he appears to have been using to build more bilateral alliances, with some mixed results in terms of concrete economic dividends.

Notes

1 Touré eventually died in a Cleveland (Ohio) clinic in March 1984.

2 It should be acknowledged that peace and security concerns had never been absent in the calculus of West African leaders, even before 1990. The extent of peace and security concerns, however, expanded greatly after 1990 (see Souaré, 2007).

References

Adebajo, A. (2002). *Building Peace in West Africa: Liberia, Sierra Leone and Guinea-Bissau*. Boulder, CO/London: Lynne Rienner.

Adedeji, A. (2004). ECOWAS: A Retrospective Journey. In A. Adebajo & I. Rachid (eds.). *West Africa's Security Challenges: Building Peace in a Troubled Region*. Boulder, CO London: Lienne Rienner, 22–50.

Apokpari, J. K. (2001). Post-Cold War International Relations and Foreign Policies in Africa: New Issues and New Challenges. *African Journal of International Affairs*, *4*(1–2): 34–55. doi:10.4314/ajia.v4i1-2.458.18.

Bull, H. (1977). *The Anarchical Society: A Study of Order in World Politics* (2nd ed.) with a new foreword by Stanley Hoffmann. London: Macmillan Press.

Cissé, M. L. (2012). *La Politique extérieure de la Guinée. Les fondements*. Paris: Editions Publibook.

Devey, M. (1997). *La Guinée*. Paris: Karthala.

Doyle, M. & Recchia, S. (2011). Liberalism in International Relations. In B. Badie, D. B. Schlosser & L. Morlino (eds.). *International Encyclopaedia of Political Science*. Los Angeles, CA: Sage, 1434–1438.

Dunne, T. & Schmidt, B. C. (2001). Realism. In J. Baylis & S. Smith (eds.). *The Globalization of World Politics: An Introduction to International Relations*. Oxford/New York: Oxford University Press, 141–161.

Gilpin, R. (2001). *Global Political Economy: Understanding the International Economic Order*. Princeton, NJ/Oxford: Princeton University Press.

Guinea's Constitution of 2010. (2010). https://www.constituteproject.org/constitution/Guinea_2010.pdf?lang=en.

Hasenclever, A., Mayer, P. & Rittberger, V. (2000). Integrating Theories of International Regimes. *Review of International Studies*, *26*(1): 3–33.

Jönsson, C. & Hall, M. (2005). *Essence of Diplomacy*. London: Palgrave McMillan.

Kaba, L. (1990). *Le "non" de la Guinée à De Gaulle*. Paris: Editions Chaka.

Keita, S. K. (2002). *Des complots contre la Guinée de Sékou Touré (1958–1984)*. Conakry: Les Classiques Guinéens.

Keohane, R. O. (1969). Lilliputians' Dilemmas: Small States in International Politics. *International Organization*, *23*(2): 291–310.

Keohane, R. O. (1984). *After Hegemony: Cooperation and Discord in the World Political Economy*. Princeton, NJ: Princeton University Press.

Lewin, A. (2009). *Ahmed Sékou Touré (1922–1984): Président de la Guinée*, Tome 3 (1958–1960). Paris: l'Harmattan.

Long, T. (2017). It's Not the Size, It's the Relationship: From "Small States" to Asymmetry. *International Politics*, *54*(2): 144–160. doi:10.1057/s41311 0170028x.

Martin, L. L. & Simmons, B. A. (1998). Theories of Empirical Studies and International Institutions. *International Organization*, *52*(4): 729–758. doi:10.1162/002081898550734.

Mearsheimer, J. J. (2001). *The Tragedy of Great Power Politics*. New York: W.W. Norton & Company.

Moravcsik, A. (1997). Taking Preferences Seriously: A Liberal Theory of International Politics. *International Organization*, *51*(4): 513–553.

Morgenthau, H. J. (1948). *Politics Among Nations: The Struggle for Power and Peace*. New York: Knopf.

Muehlenbeck, P. E. (2008). Kennedy and Touré: A Success in Personal Diplomacy. *Diplomacy & Statecraft*, *19*(1): 69–95. doi:10.1080/09592290801913734.

Nicholson, M. (1998). *International Relations: A Concise Introduction*. London: McMillan Press.

Rothstein, R. 1968. *Alliances and Small Powers*. New York: Columbia University Press.

Souaré, I. K. (2006). *Civil Wars and Coups d'Etat in West Africa: An Attempt to Understand the Roots and Prescribe Possible Solutions*. Lanham, MD: University Press of America.

Souaré, I. K. (2007). Regional Integration in Africa: The Case of ECOWAS. In B. Moyo (ed.). *Africa in Global Power Play: Debates, Challenges and Potential Reforms*. London: Adonis & Abbey, 215–230.

Souaré, I. K. (2009). Explaining the December 2008 Military Coup d'État in Guinea. *Conflict Trends*, *1*: 26–33.

Strange, S. (1983). Cave! Hic Dragones: A Critique of Regime Analysis. In S. D. Krasner (ed.). *International Regimes*. Ithaca, NY: Cornell University Press, 337–354.

Thorhallsson, B. (2018). A Small State in World Politics: Iceland's Search for Shelter. *Icelandic Review of Politics and Administration*, *14*(1): 61–82. doi:10.13177/irpa.a.2018.14.1.3.

Touré, A. S. (1979). *Africa on the Move*. London: Panaf Books.

Vital, D. (1967). *The Inequality of States: A Study of the Small Power in International Relations*. Oxford: Oxford University Press.

Walt, S. M. (1985). Alliance Formation and the Balance of World Power. *International Security*, *9*(4): 3–43.
Waltz, K. (1979). *Theory of International Politics*. Reading, MA: Addison-Wesley.
Wong, P. N. (2018). *Destined Statecraft: Eurasian Small Power Politics and Strategic Cultures in Geopolitical Shifts*. Singapore: Springer Nature.
Zoumanigui, K. (2013). *La politique étrangère de la République de Guinée de 1958 à nos jours*. Conakry: Editions Verdure.

13 Rethinking SADC

A mixed actor approach to collective policymaking on external relations[1]

Cecilia Lwiindi Nedziwe

Introduction

There is a growing scholarship that has dismissed a depiction of the African continent as lacking in agency in International Relations (Bischoff, Aning & Acharya, 2016; Chipaike & Bischoff, 2018; Chipaike & Knowledge, 2018). An examination of African agency in two selected states, Angola and Ghana, has Chipaike and Bischoff note that "Africa is a heterogeneous space with different states and non-state actors". With reference to the participation of non-state actors, they point out the differences in the existing capacities driving (foreign policy) agency in the above two, more or less democratic African states. Studies reflecting African agency in policymaking usually focus on the elite, their institutions, or on local and external factors shaping collective foreign policy on external relations (Adibe, 2001; Iyob, 2001; Khadiagala & Lyons, 2001). In addressing security, a bulk of these studies reveal policymaking as state-centred (Khadiagala, 2012; Bischoff, 2014; Van Nieuwkerk, 2014). Compelling as these studies may be, there is a need to deepen the analysis about Africa's agency. It is an agency that is to be seen as dynamic and one that goes beyond the traditional linearity inherent in the study of international relations (IR); one that talks to composite or collective agency where both state and non-state actors play their respective parts in crafting external relations. A collective policy on regional security are the norms towards member states as put together by states and/or non-state actors that cover various issue areas, including gender. The notion of security here transcends conventional state-military conceptualisation to encompass the broader non-military security dimension in areas of food security, HIV/AIDS, gender and climate change. In Southern Africa, policymaking on regional security concerns is more complex or intertwined than normally presented.

The evolution of the Southern African Development Community's (SADC) security architecture is not only limited to inter-state policies/interactions as portrayed in mainstream analyses. SADC's history of policymaking towards achieving liberation and end minority rule can be traced to the mixed actor interactions involving state and non-state actors of the mid-1970s, to formal rules-based processes beginning in the 1980s and consolidated from the 1990s onwards.

Acharya (2013: 466) has pointed out that norms have "multiple sources and contexts". The OAU's liberatory ideals as they diffused into Southern Africa's collective policy were raised in the informal talks of the Mulungushi club of the early 1970s and carried forward by Africa's two prominent heads of state, Zambia's Kenneth Kaunda and Tanzania's Julius Nyerere (ISS, 1999; Vale & Matlosa, 1995: 53; CCR, 2013: 36; Bischoff, 2014: 61). Over time, the two leaders were joined by Botswana's Sir Seretse Khama to establish the informal interstate grouping of the Frontline States (FLS) (Bischoff, 2014: 61). Countries such as Angola and Mozambique became members in the late 1970s after attaining independence. Bischoff (2014: 61) notes that "the FLS was driven by the good relationship among its founding leaders ... in opposition to an apartheid South Africa". Here the coming together of Heads of State that sought to bring to an end minority rule across Southern Africa, and South Africa's apartheid system, signifies African agency.

Importantly, both state and non-state actors formulated the policies emerging from the interactions of the FLS to achieve regional security. It points to an important, composite form of African agency in the international relations of the time. Historically in inter-governmental deliberations, anti-colonisation sentiments were not only championed formally and informally, but also saw the inclusion of policymaking representatives of non-state national liberation struggle movements (ISS, 1999). The coming together of state and non-state actors point to their ability to work together to address regional security issues.

Khadiagala and Lyons (2001: 3) have pointed out that foreign policymaking is a prerogative of the state elite that has reinforced the dominance of presidents and prime ministers. While this observation may not altogether be dismissed, processes and interactions from the colonial to the post-colonial era also do reveal *a mixed actor approach* involving state and non-state representatives seeking to address regional security issues. For example, South Africa's two main national liberation movements, the African National Congress (ANC) and the Pan-Africanist Congress (PAC), participated in the OAU's policymaking spaces at a continental level to push for the end of the racist policy and rule of apartheid South Africa. Indicative also is the example where a non-state actor representative such as South Africa's Nelson Mandela used his first international trip after his release from prison in February 1990 to address the OAU. According to Maloka, Mandela used this inter-governmental policymaking arena to request, through the OAU's ad hoc committee and through the Secretary-General of the OAU, financial assistance to re-vamp the ANC's legal structures (2017: 292). This then is to add to Chipaike and Bischoff's point (2018) that African agency strengthens when state and non-state actors combine on (democratic) foreign policy positions. In our case, African agency is enhanced where non-state actors and an Intergovernmental Organisation (IGO) combine to make policy which the IGO implements in the conduct of its external relations with member states.

The interface of state and non-state regionalism within inter-governmental policymaking to formulate or diffuse norms in Southern Africa is traceable to the era of decolonisation (Khadiagala, 2012). Given the significance of decolonising the region against a background of wider continental norms, building alliances between non-state actors and governments became an important strategy to end colonialism and push for the development of the newly independent but weak states.

A *mixed actor approach* to policymaking involving non-state actors is evident in some academic discourses. Maloka (2017: 300) notes the participation of South Africa's business sector played a role in the development of the New Partnership for Africa's Development (NEPAD) policy—the Millennium Africa Recovery Plan (MAP) —as well as in pushing for its integration into the OAU/AU policy framework. These included the NEPAD Business Group, South Africa's parastatals and financial institutions such as Eskom, the Development Bank of Southern Africa (DBSA), Transnet, the Industrial Development Cooperation (IDC) and Telkom. At the initiative of South Africa, there was the establishment of a private sector-led African Renaissance Fund put in place to push for continental infrastructural development (Maloka, 2017: 300). At the same time, in inter-governmental policymaking spaces, exclusive non-state practices persist. For instance, while private business actors were invited to participate in the development of the NEPAD policy document, civil society actors noted their exclusion, labelling the process as elite-driven. The neo-liberal linear market approach adopted by most of Africa's regional and sub-regional bodies in their policy documents have tended to prioritise private business. Yet, a closer examination points to *mixed actor* processes of IGOs and multiple non-state actors in addressing both economic and non-economic security issues.

There exists a strong link between policies initiated at a national level and those evolving at a continental level. For example, the NEPAD policy of 2001 was crafted outside OAU processes by South Africa's Thabo Mbeki's presidency, in consultation with countries such as Nigeria and Algeria. The NEPAD then found its way into the echelon structures of the AU (Maloka, 2017: 296–297). The diffusion of norms emerging from localised contexts into regional or global policy frameworks point to Africa's agency in its international relations (Bischoff, Aning & Acharya, 2016). The integration of the NEPAD policy met with resistance and was viewed with great suspicion by other African member state countries, however. Maloka noted:

> the unveiling of the MAP by Mbeki was viewed with suspicion by some actors, with a rumour circulating that some member states were creating a parallel continental body. The fear was allayed, partially when the plan was adopted as a programme of the OAU. The integration of NEPAD into the AU was … a painful and divisive process due to competing interpretations.
>
> (Maloka, 2017: 297)

Article 22 of the Constitutive Act of the African Union points to the importance of collaborative efforts between civil society and governments in the AU's processes, and those to do with democratisation efforts. Representatives from civil society organisations with a gender bias have been invited to participate in policy formulation as it relates to gender. For instance, the AU recognised Southern African-based NGO, Gender Links, for championing women's rights at the continental level within and outside its structures. In 2011, another Southern African NGO, Ditshwanelo, participated as an expert resource in the establishment of the African Commission on Human and People's Rights (ACHPR), the working group on Indigenous Populations, and the working group of Experts on Economic, Social and Cultural Rights. The involvement of non-state actors within inter-governmental policymaking points to their ability to work with the state in a variety of fields and issue areas, all to address Africa's security issues. While challenges remain, the interface of state and non-state regionalism and its outcome—a collective policy—is illustrative of proven African agency in addressing collective insecurities.

This chapter intends to contribute to the academic discourse advancing the notion of African agency in international relations; one between state and non-state actors that is effective as it is composite (Bischoff, Aning & Acharya, 2016; Chipaike & Bischoff, 2018; Chipaike & Knowledge, 2018). What is explored is how the SADC's policymaking attempts have evolved from the colonial, to the post-colonial era, and how continental liberatory ideals help signify a collective policy which finds expression in the external relations of the SADC, not least within its own region. What is argued is that the SADC is an inter-governmental body with a collective policy on external relations whose policymaking processes regarding wider notions of security, notably on gender, have involved a mixed actor approach.

SADC's history of policymaking: Policymaking under the FLS to the SADCC

Agency within the Southern African context can be traced to the informal interactions and norms of the FLS of 1975, and those of its successor, the Southern African Development Coordination Conference (SADCC) of 1980. Within this context, having a collective policy constituted an important mechanism to struggle against minority rule, to strengthen national liberation movements, as well as to address the challenges that confronted newly independent weak states. The FLS' collective policy on external relations was shaped by the continental ideals of Pan-Africanism as propagated by the African Union's (AU) forerunner organisation—the Organisation for African Unity (OAU)—of 1963, to decolonise the continent. According to Khadiagala (2012: 33), "decolonisation regionalism" played a profound role in pushing for the liberation of African countries from colonial and minority regimes. The liberatory norms advanced by the OAU spread across the African continent, influencing the emergence of inter-governmental bodies such as the FLS. The military insecurities presented by apartheid South Africa, further shaped the FLS's policymaking approaches and its evolving security architecture.

The remnants of the colonial legacy, as well as the brutality of South Africa's apartheid regime, drove the idea to establish the FLS. FLS policymaking reflects *a mixed actor* approach. It involved representatives of Southern Africa's national liberation movements and those of newly independent governments. The leaders of the national liberation movements followed invitations to participate at the summits and other high-level meetings of the FLS and in the development of its policies on regional security (ISS, 1999; CCR, 2013). The role of Robert Mugabe as head of the national liberation movement—the Zimbabwe African National Union (ZANU) —in the development of the FLS military security wing, and the Inter-State Defense and Security Committee (ISDSC), formed in 1976. As a non-state representative, Mugabe chaired the ISDSC meetings (CCR, 2013: 36). Non-state actors not only contributed to the development of a collective policy on military-security matters, but they also presided over these inter-governmental structures. The emerging ISDSC's policies on external relations to address the then regional military insecurities was made possible from combined forces of state and non-state actors.[2]

With the incorporation of countries such as Malawi, Lesotho and Swaziland, and following Zimbabwe's independence in 1980, the FLS evolved from politically-oriented cooperation to economic coordination under a newly established Southern African Development Coordination Conference (SADCC). Khadiagala (2012: 33) notes that "the FLS began with a political dimension and consequently combined with the economic aspects as a response to the multiple insecurities presented by the apartheid system". The loosely organised SADCC's economic objective was driven by the desire of newly independent weak states to industrialise through an elaborate sectoral coordination programme (Amin, Mandaza & Chitala, 1987). Khadiagala (2012: 25) further notes, "Through the sector-led coordination approach to integration, SADCC was an attempt to transcend the post-colonial approaches to regionalism by emphasising trade and market integration". Unlike the mainstream linear progression to integration from economic to political cooperation, policymaking from the FLS to emerging rules-based processes of the SADCC began with the political objectives and gradually added economic elements.

Yet, while earlier policymaking of the FLS was inclusive of non-state actors, it was not so with the SADCC. According to Khadiagala (2012: 25), the SADCC "adopted ... state-centric and highly individualised regionalism, owing to the circumstances surrounding Southern Africa's decolonisation processes". Khadiagala and Lyons (2001: 2) note, "For a majority of weak African states, regions are sources of authoritative foreign policies, places where power is displayed and exerted". However, civil society actors have played important roles in various fields and issue areas, working together with African states in policymaking, and in reinforcing African agency at various levels. Scholars highlighted the surrounding hostile environment from apartheid South Africa and narrow nationalism as having significantly shaped the SADCC's policymaking strategies (Van Nieuwkerk, 2014; Bischoff, 2014). Mandaza (1987: 214) points out that SADCC's state-centric orientation was inevitable: "It is a natural and legitimate desire of any young state to strengthen itself. The SADCC states' wishes [were] to promote a regional industrial strategy, however, narrow nationalism present[ed] ... a problem". Yet, strong nationalistic tendencies prevailed over a more inclusive approach to policymaking. Due to the narrow developmental focus, Mandaza points out that the "SADCC... remain[ed] quite divorced from the very masses that could provide the political basis and framework for economic disengagement from South Africa" (1987: 218). However, African agency can be strengthened by combining forces of state and non-state actors in the formulation and implementation of policies.

Scholars have noted the constraints to policymaking that newly independent states faced in consolidating power, in building regional organisation, reducing dependence on apartheid and in addressing social-economic demands (Adedeji, 1996; Chitala, 1987). The coming into existence of the SADCC was met with counter-resistance from South Africa's apartheid government. As part of its destabilisation strategies to contain the threats from across the region, the then South African government established a counter organisation to the SADCC—the Constellation of Southern African States (CONSAS) —in the early 1980s. The SADCC member states perceived CONSAS as a body established to advance the interests of apartheid South Africa and rejected it (Chitala, 1987). In turn, South Africa waged a destabilisation war across Southern Africa that resulted in the loss of about one million lives and at a cost of an estimated $60 billion in damages in the 1980s alone (Adedeji, 1996: 9). The South African government further implemented coercive measures to destabilise the SADCC's industrialisation programme by engaging and trading with its individual member states (Chitala, 1987: 31). With little to no international donor support for industrialisation, the SADCC achieved very little in terms of its economic agenda (Bischoff, 2014: 61).

The regional military insecurities presented by South Africa limited the SADCC's effective implementation of its industrialisation programme. Instead, the opposition to apartheid, including its counter-responses and actions, formed significant aspects of the SADCC's policy (Khadiagala, 2012: 33; CCR, 2013: 36; Bischoff, 2014: 61). For example, the security wing of the FLS, the ISDSC, was retained as the SADCC's military structure. Further, despite the elaborate sectoral programme to industrialise and develop the various economies of the newly independent states, the SADCC's policy implementation attempts faced limitations in that they relied heavily on donor funding (Amin, Mandaza & Chitala, 1987). For example, while the SADCC's industrialisation policy addressed coordination in a number of sectors, in practice, regionalisation only increased in the transport sector, an area that was also of interest to the West and their extractive agenda (Chitala, 1987). Africa's limitation to addressing wider socio-economic security concerns is embedded in its prolonged history of over reliance on donor funding. If African agency is to be reinforced, more attempts are to be channelled toward self-sustaining funding projects, as well as those drawn from solidarity groups and individuals.

In the immediate post-independence period, narrow nationalism shaped much of the SADCC policymaking approaches. Given the gendered nature of immediate post-independence African states, there is equally no mention of women's participation in the FLS policymaking summits. Notably, the SADCC's sectoral coordination economic strategy excluded individual women and women groups from participation in inter-governmental processes. Attempts by women groups to push for the establishment of a regional gender desk as a framework for addressing gendered insecurities within a regional framework under the SADCC came to nothing and could only be realised under the new policies of SADCC's successor organisation, the SADC (Roadmap to Equality Report, 2009). Yet, as shown below, the participation of women in composite forms of policymaking has proven effective in strengthening forms of African agency in addressing gendered insecurities across the region. Here, I seek to show African agency through policymaking as not only limited to state interactions, but also as involving a *mixed actor approach* of state and non-state actors.

SADC's policymaking and power relations

After the end of apartheid in 1994, South Africa joined the SADCC's successor, the SADC, formed in 1992. This new development also entailed the SADC redefining its policies and role to correspond with a post-apartheid world. The end of the apartheid era also marked the end of minority governments across Southern Africa. The coming on board of South Africa, previously the region's giant enemy, was not without challenges. Adedeji (1996: 9) highlights that the damage caused by South Africa's apartheid regime during the war of destabilisation remained fresh in the minds of Southern African leaders. He notes that levels of distrust, even toward South Africa's new black majority government headed by Nelson Mandela, were high (Adedeji, 1996: 9). This distrust manifested itself in various forms, and brought to the fore the significant role of strong personalities in shaping what was to be adopted as collective SADC policy to address regional security.

South Africa's push to re-conceptualise SADC's notion of security in line with a neo-liberal paradigm resulted in serious differences between two strong heads of state: Zimbabwe's Robert Mugabe and South Africa's Nelson Mandela (CCR, 2013: 36). Mugabe held a reactionary position, pushing for a narrow and patriarchal kind of security with a view that the ISDSC is maintained as a separate military security wing with its own summit, while Mandela pushed for a broader notion of peace that included a non-military security dimension. The latter approach pushed for the ISDSC security organ to be integrated into the new SADC policy framework and report to the summit of heads of state (CCR, 2013: 36). Mandela's South Africa was perceived as a "norm entrepreneur" and its external policy anchored on pushing a liberal-human rights agenda in Southern Africa and the Great Lakes region (Louw-Vaudran, 2016: 1–4). The tension between a state militaristic-centred approach to security and one centred on social welfare continued with emphasis being put on one or the other policy instrument. Given these tensions, it took close to five years to put in place the SADC's new security policy framework. For example, while the decision to establish the SADC Organ on Politics, Defense, and Security (OPDSC) happened in 1996, it only came into force in 2001.

In line with a neo-liberal focus, South Africa played a leading role in pushing for the inclusion of new security issues, and the broadening of the notion of security beyond a military-centred definition. South Africa, for example, pushed for the establishment of the OPDSC, which was to replace the ISDSC at an extraordinary summit in Botswana on June 28, 1996. According to Khadiagala (2001: 141), the OPDSC was to function as the security arm of SADC, concerned with regional security, political cooperation such as democracy and human rights, conflict prevention and resolution, peacekeeping and collective security and defence. Under the auspices of the OPDSC, South Africa and Botswana conducted a poorly organised military mission to a politically embattled Lesotho in 1998 until 1999 that exposed the SADC's failure to institutionalise the very policies it had developed.

Not only were collective SADC policies towards the region at the level of the OPDSC not effected as planned, the SADC's security architecture was highly personalised by the domination of Mugabe and his country's Ministry of Foreign Affairs. For instance, Mugabe rammed through and rationalised SADC's intervention in the Democratic Republic of Congo (DRC) in August 1998. In this, Angola's and Zimbabwe's involvement in the DRC were largely perceived as driven by far narrower national and personalised interests. Mugabe, argues Khadiagala, used the "SADC Organ as a unilateral instrument for his own aggressive foreign policy" (2001: 145). Between 1975 and the 1990s, Zimbabwe also played a key military role in securing the Limpopo corridor linking South Africa, Swaziland, DRC, Zambia and Zimbabwe to Maputo in Mozambique (Khadiagala, 2012: 25–38; Mbuende, 2012: 39–60). Narrow personal interests preoccupied most newly independent states, driven by its elite leadership point to what has become the legacy of national liberation struggle in addressing regional insecurities across Southern Africa.

The SADC's collective policies on regional security expanded over time to include the Mutual Defence Pact of 2003, the Strategic Indicative Plan for the Organ (SIPO) of 2004, and its revised version of 2012. The OPDSC as outlined in the SIPO highlights an expanded regional policy in the political, defence, public security sector and state security spheres (Revised edition SIPO, 2010). The security threats addressed within the SIPO policy framework included human trafficking, organised crime, illegal migration, maritime piracy, economic threats, foreign interference, HIV/AIDS and the smuggling of goods. Further, within the evolved SIPO of 2012, regional security focus areas include "providing and ensuring services in law enforcement, public safety, corrections/prisons, immigration, parks and wildlife, customs and refugees" (Revised edition SIPO, 2010). The SIPO document equally accommodates for non-state participation within SADC's broader policymaking framework in order to ensure their contribution to community building, and to addressing issues around security and governance (CCR, 2013: 37). Importantly, the SIPO further calls for collaboration with non-state actors in areas of research, public debates, seminars, as well as in conflict prevention, management and resolution (Revised edition SIPO, 2010).

This emergent regionalism recognises mixed approaches that includes the participation of non-state actors within the SADC's inter-governmental structures to promote greater security and development. Equally, the SADC Treaty of 1992 made progress to acknowledge and recognise the role of non-state actors in collective region building. The SADC's policy approaches to region-building have in this way differed from those of the Southern African Customs Union (SACU) and Common Market for Eastern and Southern Africa (COMESA), due to the different contexts in which the latter organisations emerged. SACU and COMESA have evolved as economic regional bodies, while the SADC began as a politically oriented, inter-governmental organisation, which, only over time, came to include economic and social functions. Since the 1990s, African agency reflects in the growing recognition of non-state actors as key partners in inter-governmental policy documents, as well as in state and non-state combined policymaking efforts to address regional security.

SADC's policies and non-state actors

Overall, the context of democratisation and liberalisation, and the shift from the SADCC to the SADC, opened up space for the recognition of non-state actors in policymaking. The Windhoek Treaty of 1992, establishing the SADC, redefined previously non-legal forms of cooperation within the SADCC into a legally-binding regional policy framework (SADC Treaty, 1992). Unlike the SADCC's highly exclusive state-centric and personalised approaches, the SADC Treaty attached importance to non-state actors in addressing regional security. Paragraph 23 of the Treaty provides that:

> SADC shall seek to involve fully the peoples of the region and non-governmental organisations in the process of regional integration … SADC shall cooperate with and support the initiatives of the peoples of the region and non-governmental organisations, contributing to the objectives of this Treaty in the areas of cooperation in order to foster closer relations among communities, associations and the peoples of the region.
>
> (SADC Treaty, 1992)

Providing an inside perspective, the SADC's former Executive Secretary, Kaire Mbuende (2012: 56), notes that:

> There [was] a recognition that the legitimacy of regional integration depends on support from the peoples of the region. Regional integration by its very nature encroaches on the space of ordinary citizens in different ways and must therefore be acceptable to the citizens of member states … the peoples of the region can make a significant contribution to the formulation of policies based on their experiences from their various walks of life. It is against this background that provisions were made for the participation of non-state actors in community-building.

Mbuende (2012: 56) has further pointed out that non-state actors possess expertise and knowledge in the various issue areas of the SADC's programme of action including in the field of gender. While SADC constitutes an inter-governmental body dominated by member states, it is important to highlight that its policymaking on external relations has also involved non-state actors involved in a variety of issue areas and fields. The recognition and increasing involvement of non-state actors in SADC's inter-governmental policymaking to address regional security points to growing African agency in (regional)(international) relations. It debunks narratives that suggest this body as a mere instrument of an exclusive club of heads of state.

The SADC Treaty of 1992 was amended further in 2001. It restructured the SADC according to a new institutional framework and governing structure. This included the Summit, the supreme policymaking institute led by Heads of State and Government, a Council of Ministers that oversees functioning of the SADC, a Standing Committee of Officials as technical advisory committee of the Council of Ministers and the Executive Secretariat that provides secretariat services (Amended SADC Treaty, 2001). While the SADC Treaty recognises a broad spectrum of non-state actors to community building, its 2003 blueprint—the Regional Indicative Strategic Development Plan (RISDP)—tends to prioritise private business as key to regional growth. Yet in practice, SADC reveals a *mixed actor* approach involving multiple private business and civil society actors in pushing for regional development in both economic and non-economic issue areas.

SADC's collective mixed actor approach on gender security

In the immediate post-independence phase, the majority of newly formed African governments reinforced gendered politics, leaving women behind in the new governance structure. The male-dominated leaders tended to be hostile towards women (Mama, 2001). As a result of the gendered nature that characterised the early post-independence period, women from Southern Africa suspended their political activism temporarily within their local communities. Instead, they turned to the global women's structuring and restructuring spaces, where they participated in norm development at the United Nations (UN) (Van der Westhuizen, 2005: 10; Lowe-Morna, 2004; Marchand & Runyan, 2011; Marchand, 1996).

In contrast to post-independence gendered structures of exclusion and marginalisation, the SADC from the 1990s onwards adopted inclusive measures to policymaking. First, an eminent group of commissioners was put in place in the early 1990s to review the situation of women across Southern Africa. Second, a task force was created in the post-1995 Beijing International Women's Conference to draft a Regional Plan of Action to begin to address gender security. Finally, a first meeting of the SADC Ministers Responsible for Women and Gender Affairs was held in 1997 (Roadmap to Equality Report, 2009: 34). The SADC's evolving norms point to inter-connections to changing global policies on gender. The latter norms have been infused into regional and local policy on gender, thereby working around an evolving norm cycle from local-global-regional-local levels. The norm cycle on gender further points to the interlinkages of gendered insecurities to SADC's expanding policy architecture.

The changing character and move to recognise non-state actors in community-building, as encapsulated in SADC's 1992 Windhoek Treaty, further opened up space for gender and women-focused civil society groupings to begin to participate within its inter-state policy frameworks in order to address gendered insecurities (SADC Treaty, 1992). In contrast to the 1980s, this marked a real shift when, following Zimbabwe's independence, inward nationalistic tendencies predominated and regional women's organisations' efforts to push for a regional gender desk at the level of SADCC—the predecessor to the SADC—could simply go unnoticed. After 1992, however, there was the increasing mobilisation and participation of women and gender-focused civil society groups in global and regional policymaking arenas.

With the presence of a democratic South Africa and general shift towards political pluralism in the region, a remembrance of previous non-state participation by national liberation movements in regional determinations amidst a new, expanding culture of democratisation opened up the political space for further non-state participation. This enabled organised civil society working on gender to begin to work with states of the region to formulate policies that addressed gender security. From this time onwards, state and non-state actors in mutual consultation formulated a number of key SADC policies on gender.

All this pointed to the newly proven abilities and prominence of organised gender groups. It also signified their newfound agency both in regional and global international relations.

SADC's key policies on gender

The increasing interface between state and non-state actors pursuing gender security within the SADC's policy structures can be summed up in a three-phase process between the 1990s to 2015. This process culminated in the development of SADC's three key policies addressing gender security.[3]

The first policymaking phase resulted in the first regional policy on gender, the 1997 SADC Declaration on Gender and Development. This collective policy of 1997 sought to contribute to improved security through fostering closer regional cooperation and action among state and non-state actors in achieving gender equality (SADC Declaration on Gender, 1997). Through this collective gender policy, the SADC in its external relations with member states committed to establishing regional advisory structures with governments and Non-Governmental Organisations (NGOs) to monitor gender-related concerns across the region, as well as to establish a Gender Unit within its Secretariat (SADC Declaration on Gender, 1997). In 1998, an Addendum was crafted to address violence against women and children, and this formed a key feature of the 1997 Declaration (SADC Addendum, 1998). Particularly, Article 26 of the Addendum pointed to the critical need of urgently putting in place a legally binding SADC gender instrument on "Preventing Violence Against Women and Children" (SADC Addendum, 1998).

The second phase can be traced from 2003, when gender and women-focused civil society groupings were invited to the Botswana-based SADC Secretariat to participate in the review process of the 1997 Declaration and its 1998 Addendum.

The coming together of civil society actors and regional governments led to the development and adoption of the SADC's first legally binding gender policy, the SADC Protocol on Gender and Development of 2008 (Roadmap to Equality Report, 2009: 12–13). The 2008 Gender Protocol sought to integrate gender in all SADC's region-building structures, actions and policies (SADC Protocol on Gender, 2008). The 2008 Gender Protocol provided for steps to increase gender security through the empowerment of women, the elimination of all forms of discrimination in order to achieve gender equality, and to diffuse its content into legislation, programmes and projects, particularly at the national level (SADC Protocol on Gender, 2008).

The evolving SADC policies on gender point to their link to global, regional and local policies. SADC's 2008 Gender Protocol was further aligned to the United Nations (UN) Convention on the Elimination of All Forms of Discrimination against Women (CEDAW) of 1979, and the Millennium Development Goals (MDGs) of 2000, including its targets and timeframes up to 2015. As the expiration date of the MDGs approached in 2015, and in what would constitute the third phase, regional gender and women-focused civil society groups began to push for a review of the 2008 SADC Protocol on Gender and Development to be in line with the changing global, continental and regional norms (SADC Gender Protocol Barometer, 2016: 14).

SADC's Post-2015 Protocol on Gender and Development was a successor to the 2008 policy discussed above. The Post-2015 gender policy was shaped by global and continental norms such as the 2015–2030 United Nations Sustainable Development Goals (SDGs), the Beijing Plus 20 of 2015, the African Union's Agenda 2063, as well as by the SADC's twenty-seven protocols (SADC Protocol Barometer, 2016: 14). The evolving regional gender policy in Southern Africa reveal their strong link to global, regional and sub-regional norms. As noted by Acharya, norms have "multiple sources and contexts" (2013: 466). The Post-2015 policy embraced the values and language of the SDGs with the motif "Leaving No One Behind". This includes the inclusion of often neglected issues and/or communities, such as men in the conversations on women and gender issues, and those advanced by the transnational queer movement on lesbian, gay, bisexual, transgender and intersex (LGBTI) rights.[4] The actions of gender and women-focused civil society groups who work closely with the SADC Secretariat and states at multiple levels to produce policies to push for their diffusion at a regional and at local levels, point to non-state agency in addressing gendered insecurities in the intra-national, international and transnational relations of the sub-region.

The opening up of democratic spaces characterised by growing non-state actor participation in politics has been perceived as a security threat by some SADC member-states. Owing to the thesis of declining state capacity, and in turn, the promotion of non-state actors in governance and democratic issues, the 1990s were characterised by the channelling of resources by donors directly to NGOs. NGO activities were in turn perceived as donor-funded, thereby regarded as a national security threat by some SADC member states such as

Zimbabwe, Zambia, Botswana and Swaziland (CCR, 2013: 17). Mbuende (2012: 56) relates that:

> There has been apprehension among SADC governments about foreign-funded NGOs in a number of countries. NGOs are seen either as pursuing a foreign agenda or as opposition in disguise. One of the liveliest debates that I witnessed at SADC summits was when the Secretariat tabled a report on SADC cooperation with NGOs. Most of the heads of state who participated in the meeting expressed apprehension about the role of NGOs.

According to Landsberg (2012: 12), the SADC to some degree practices its own exclusive forms of region-building in that it mostly interacts with its preferred non-state actors in line with its own interests that nonetheless overlook or neutralise others. For example, while NGOs running shelter programmes in Botswana have received financial support from the government, those with a human rights focus have faced challenges accessing such funding. Further, the human rights case between *Mike Campbell (Pvt) Ltd and Others v the Republic of Zimbabwe* over the seizure of land as part of Zimbabwe's land reform programme without compensation brought to light the manner in which non-state actors are neutralised when they challenge state interests. Despite the fact that the SADC Tribunal in 2012 ruled in favour of the individual applicant (Campbell), the Zimbabwean government disregarded this ruling (Ndlovu, 2011). Article 16 of the SADC Treaty provides for the constitution of the SADC Tribunal to ensure the adherence to, and proper interpretation of, SADC's legal instruments (SADC, 1992). Yet, the 2012 ruling that reflects the scaling up of human rights protection did not receive any support. Member states, including a democratic South Africa and SADC as a whole, buckled to a rearguard action fought by the Zimbabwean Mugabe-led state. As a result, the SADC's Summit decision simply suspended the Tribunal (former President Jacob Zuma's government decision to support this action was subsequently overruled by South Africa's Constitutional Court in 2018).

Notwithstanding such an anomaly, the impressive growth of regional policies by SADC in Southern Africa points to a softening of the region's gendered structures. While the implementation of policies on gender in the SADC's external relations with member states has been key in promoting gender security, having some African governments positively respond has been lamentably slow. While there exists an active network of non-state actors interfacing with regional governments, there is, overall, however, still a lack of clarity "on the modalities for civil society participation in SADC's activities" (CCR, 2013: 16). While the SADC recognises non-state actors as vital partners in community building, there is also a persisting degree of marginalisation of non-state actors in its policymaking spaces. Since 2016, nationalistic tendencies in terms of state to non-state relations within the SADC's policymaking structures began to re-surface. The fall back into narrow nationalism points to retrogressive changes: to roll back non-state participation within SADC's policymaking structures developed since the 1990s, rooted in a collective agenda, particularly in the area of gender (SADC Gender Protocol Barometer, 2017: 335). If left unchecked, these tendencies potentially spell greater insecurity across Southern Africa and curtail the organisation of SADC in its external relations role on seeing to the implementation of regional policy by member states.

Seemingly in an effort to neutralise "these developments" to mean parochial nationalistic ones, counter-measures were devised. A process towards re-engagement with civil society by the SADC Secretariat was commissioned in 2016 (SADC Gender Protocol Barometer, 2017: 335). The re-engagement process seeks to consult widely with various stakeholders within, and outside, Southern Africa in order to develop a legal framework agreement to guide non-state participation within the SADC's policy structures (SADC Gender Protocol Barometer, 2017: 335). The need for clear modalities for non-state participation within inter-governmental structures is stressed in civil society research reports and academic discourse. The legal framework formulated is necessary and, as it relates to strengthening non-state relations between the SADC Secretariat and member states, is a potential game-changer. Mbuende (2012: 57) notes:

> There is no doubt that various non-state actors can add value to the process of regional integration in Southern Africa. It is important to underscore the differential roles of NGOs and governments. NGOs cannot substitute for governments even in areas where government institutions are weak. The challenge is to work towards strengthening such institutions. There are functions that can be carried out effectively by civil society, while others remain the preserve of the state. What is of cardinal importance, however, is to design appropriate mechanisms to institutionalise the involvement of non-state actors in the process of regional integration. Thus far, this involvement has been sporadic and unpredictable.

While SADC policy frameworks accommodate non-state engagement within its broader region-building agenda, in reality, African agency can only be strengthened within regional spaces if there are institutionalised or set-down modalities for non-state-state interactions (CCR, 2013: 16).

Concluding reflections

SADC's collective policy and external relations with its members reflects a *mixed actor approach* involving the region's state and non-state actors. Unlike conventional analyses, SADC's policymaking has not merely been state-driven, but has involved state and non-state actors in tandem developing collective policy to address issues of regional security. What are commonly described as elitist state-centred practices, these only partially uncover the actual dynamics and complexities of African agency in the international relations of the region. The role played by non-state actors toward Southern Africa's liberation instinctively made them natural partners in developmental issues, as well as in pushing for even greater regional security. The collective policy structure such as the ISDSC Committee that addressed military-security under the FLS was a product of a mixed actor approach to policymaking involving state and non-state actors. SADC's 1992 Treaty revealed important aspects of inclusion and the recognition of non-state actors in community building and to addressing regional security. Challenges, however, remain in theory and practice. Generally, IR analyses overlook African dynamic agency and mixed actor approaches to policymaking, and to the impressive increasing interface of state and non-state regionalism, leading to a collective policy on external relations. In the context of the SADC region, growing African agency is highly notable in non-military security areas such as gender and HIV/AIDS.

The norms with a gender and women-focus emerging at a regional level of analysis have been aligned to those at a global and continental level. For example, the 2008 SADC Protocol on Gender and Development, and its revised version, the Post-2015 Gender Protocol, was aligned to the MDGs, and subsequently, to the evolved SDGs. The expanding collective policy emerging from state and non-state interactions within inter-governmental policy spaces addressing Southern Africa's regional security point to the existence of Africa's agency in international relations. Non-state regional bodies at a SADC level have also played key policymaking roles within global spaces, pointing to Africa's agency in global international relations.

While accounts on the SADC's evolution as a body to remind and prompt member states into implementing policies taken at a regional level reveals a growing state-non-state regionalism and a sense of regionness, it is also true to say that states' relations to non-state actors have been erratic at times. While some scholars have argued that the exclusive narrow nationalism exhibited by SADC member states have been shaped by surrounding insecurities, these tendencies have at the same time accounted for SADC's detachment from the very people whose standard of life it seeks or claims to improve. Attempts to exclude non-state actors from participating in inter-governmental affairs instead point to some of the shortcomings to African agency. Nationalistic proclivities characterised by exclusive approaches toward civil society actors, including those with a gender and women focus, reveal a potential rollback of gains achieved since the 1990s. At the same time, a spirit of persistence and resistance is visible from the responsive efforts championed by SADC's Secretariat and civil society groups. Improving non-state-state relations is vital in ensuring more effective African agency in the external relations of African IGO such as the SADC. While far from perfect, the ways in which a mixed actor approach has unfolded within the Southern African context holds important lessons for invigorating policymaking structures at the level of the AU on human (including women's) security matters. In terms of demonstrating a developing state-non-state actors' collaboration point, what has happened at the SADC level carries model character for the type of African agency that aims at more inclusive, participatory policymaking at the AU and in other African sub-regions.

Notes

1 This chapter draws on debates and discussions advanced in my PhD thesis titled: Regional thickening as game-changing: Examining transnational activities of gender and women-focused civil society actors for region-building in Southern Africa (2018).
2 The Nigerian government, as an associate member of the FLS, was also invited to sit and participate in the FLS informal meetings (ISS, 1999). Policymaking spaces, as such, are more inclusive of norms and actors beyond the state-centric confines of a region.
3 At a regional level, other norms on gender have included the SADC Gender Policy, the SADC Regional Indicative Strategic Development Plan (RISDP), as well as the RISDP's Women Empowerment Programme.
4 In the SADC region, however, while countries such as South Africa, the DRC and Mozambique have decriminalised homosexuality, there remain differences across the region in terms of sexual orientation. For example, in countries such as Zambia, Malawi, Madagascar and Zimbabwe, LGBTIs are not tolerated.

References

Acharya, A. (2013). The R2P and norm diffusion: Towards a framework of norm circulation. *Global Responsibility to Protect*, *5*(4): 466–479. doi:10.1163/1875984X-00504006.

Adedeji, A. (ed.). (1996). *South Africa in Africa: Within or Apart?* London: Zed Books.

Adibe, C. A. (2001). Foreign policy decisionmaking in Anglophone West Africa. In G. M. Khadiagala & T. Lyons (eds.). *African Foreign Policies: Power and Process*. Boulder: Lynne Rienner.

Amin, S., Chitala, D. & Mandaza, I. (eds.). (1987). *SADCC: Prospects for Disengagement and Development in Southern Africa*. Tokyo: United Nations University Press.

Bischoff, P. H. (2014). How much its own and to what end? SADC and the culture of security and regional organisation in Southern Africa. In S. Aris & W. Wenger (eds.). *Regional Organisations and Security Conceptions and Practices*. New York: Routledge.

Bischoff, P. H., Aning, K. & Acharya, A. (2016). *Africa in Global International Relations: Emerging Approaches to Theory and Practice*. London/New York: Routledge.

CCR. (2013). Governance and security challenges in post-apartheid Southern Africa. *Policy Seminar Report*. Cape Town, South Africa. September 2013.

Chipaike, R. & Bischoff, P. H. (2018). A challenge to conventional wisdom: Locating agency in Angola and Ghana's economic engagements with China. *Journal of Asian and African Studies*, *53*(7). doi:10.1177%2F0021909618763922.

Chipaike, R. & Knowledge, M. H. (2018). The question of African agency in international relations. *Cogent Social Sciences*, *4*(1): 1–16.

Chitala, D. (1987). The political economy of SADCC and imperialism's response. In S. Amin, D. Chitala & I. Mandaza (eds.). *SADCC: Prospects for Disengagement and Development in Southern Africa*. London: ZED/UNU Press.

Convention on the Elimination of all Forms of Discrimination against Women (CEDAW). (1979). http://www.un.or/womenwatch/daw/cedaw (Accessed 10 March 2016).

Ditshwanelo – The Botswana Centre for Human Rights. http://www.ditshwanelo.org.bw (Accessed 18 November 2017).

ISS. (1999). The Legacy of the Front-Line States. Institute for Security Studies Monograph. *Building Security in Southern Africa*, *43*. www.iss.co.za/pubs/monographs/no43/Thelegacy.htmlweb (Accessed 21 March 2019).

Iyob, R. (2001). The foreign policy of the Horn: The clash between the old and new. In G. M. Khadiagala & T. Lyons (eds.). *African Foreign Policies: Power and Process*. Boulder: Lynne Rienner.

Khadiagala, G. M. (2001). Foreign policy decisionmaking in Southern Africa's fading Frontiers. In G. M. Khadiagala & T. Lyons (eds.). *African Foreign Policies: Power and Process*. Boulder: Lynne Rienner.

Khadiagala, G. M. (2012). The SADCC and its approaches to African regionalism. In C. Saunders, G. A. Dzinesa & D. Nagar (eds.). *Region-Building in Southern Africa: Progress, Problems and Prospects*. London: Zed Books.

Khadiagala, G. M. & Lyons, T. 2001. Foreign policy making in Africa: An introduction. In G. M. Khadiagala & T. Lyons (eds.). *African Foreign Policies: Power and Process*. Boulder, CO: Lynne Rienner.

Landsberg, C. (2012). The Southern African Development Community's decision-making architecture. In C. Saunders, G. A. Dzinesa & D. Nagar (eds.). *Region-Building in Southern Africa: Progress, Problems and Prospects*. London: Zed Books.

Louw-Vaudran, L. (2016). Is South Africa a norm entrepreneur in Africa? *Institute for Security Studies Policy Brief*, 94. https://issafrica.s3.amazonaws.com/site/uploads/policybrief94.pdf (Accessed 23 October 2018).

Lowe Morna, C. (2004). *Gender in Southern African Politics: Ringing up the Changes*. Johannesburg: DS Print Media.

Lowe Morna, C., Makamure, L. & Glenwright, D. (2009). *Roadmap to Equality: Lessons Learned in the Campaign for a SADC Protocol on Gender and Development Report*. Southern African Gender Protocol Alliance.

Maloka, E. (2017). South Africa and the African Union. In A. Adebajo & K. Virk (eds.). *Foreign Policy in Post-Apartheid South Africa: Security, Diplomacy and Trade*. London/New York: I.B. Tauris.

Mama, A. (2001). Challenging subjects: Gender and power in African contexts. *African Sociological Review*, *5*(2): 63–73.

Mandaza, I. (1987). Perspectives on economic cooperation and autonomous development in Southern Africa. In A. Amin, D. Chitala & I. Mandaza (eds.). *SADCC: Prospects for Disengagement and Development in Southern Africa*. London: Zed Books.

Marchand, M. H. (1996). Reconceptualising "gender and development" in an era of globalisation. *Journal of International Studies*, *25*(3): 577–603. doi:10.1093/acrefore/9780190846626.013.4.

Marchand, M. H. & Runyan, A. S. (2011). *Gender and Global Restructuring: Sightings, Sites and Resistances* (2nd ed.). London/New York: Routledge.

Mbuende, K. M. (2012). The SADC: Between cooperation and development – an insider perspective. In C. Saunders, G. A. Dzinesa & D. Nagar (eds.). *Region-Building in Southern Africa: Progress, Problems and Prospects*. London: Zed Books.

Mike Campbell (Pvt) Ltd. and Others v. Republic of Zimbabwe. (2008). http://www.saflii.org/sa/cases/SADCT/2008/2.pdf (Accessed 30 April 2019).

Ndlovu, P. N. (2011). *Campbell v Republic of Zimbabwe*: A moment of truth for the SADC Tribunal. *SADC Law Journal*, *78*(1): 63–79. https://www.kas.de/c/document_library/get_file?uuid=23dd33c8-5d5a-cc64-b2b9-dbd58449ca67&groupId=252038 (Accessed 11 March 2019).

SADC. (1992). Windhoek Treaty. http://www.sadc.int/about-sadc/overview/history-and-treaty (Accessed 12 March 2018).

SADC. (1997). Declaration on Gender and Development. http://www.sadc.int/documents/publications/show/Declaration_on_Gender_Devlopment_1997.pdf (Accessed 10 December 2018).

SADC. (1998). Addendum on Gender. https://www.justice.gov.za/docs/other-docs/1998_SADC%20DeclarationAddendum.pdf (Accessed 11 July 2019).

SADC. (2001). Treaty of the Southern African Development Community – as Amended. *Gaborone*. http://www.sadc.int>files>Agreement_Amending_the_Treaty-2001.pdf (Accessed 10 December 2018).

SADC. (2008). Protocol on Gender and Development. https://www.genderlinks.org.za/page/sadc-protocol-policy (Accessed 10 December 2018).

SADC. (2010). Strategic Indicative Plan for the Organ on Politics, Defence and Security Cooperation (Revised Edition). https://www.sadc.int/files/6313/6880/3040/03514_SADC_SIPO_English.pdf (Accessed 11 July 2019).

SADC. (2012). Regional Indicative Strategic Development Plan (RISDP). http://sadc.int/about-sadc/overview/strategic-pl/regional-indicative-strategic-development-plan (Accessed 10 December 2018).

SADC. (2016). *SADC Gender Protocol 2016 Barometer*. Johannesburg: Gender Links.

SADC. (2017). *SADC Gender Protocol 2017 Barometer*. Johannesburg: Gender Links.

Vale, P. & Matlosa, K. (1995). Beyond the nation-state: Rebuilding Southern Africa from below. *Harvard International Review*, *17*(4): 1–7.

Van der Westhuizen, C. (2005). Beijing+10, the AU Women's protocol and beyond. In C. Van der Westhuizen (ed.). *Gender Instruments in Africa: Critical Perspectives, Future Strategies*. Midrand: Institute for Global Dialogue.

Van Nieuwkerk, A. (2014). The strategic culture of foreign and security policymaking: Examining the Southern African development community. *African Security*, *7*(1): 49–69.

14 Ghana

Identity formation and the foreign and defence policies of a small state

Kwesi Aning and Kwaku Danso

Introduction

Ghana's formal entry into the international system came in 1957, following its transition as a British colony of the Gold Coast into a sovereign entity. In a sense, the sovereign state established following the rejection of colonial rule presupposed the emergence of a new political space for autonomous action. While this was true in principle, Ghana's independence did not necessarily come with the freedom of manoeuvrability to pursue such policies as its citizens had reason to believe and expect; even if they sought to do so within the parameters of the "sovereignty regime" (Clapham, 1996; Jackson, 1991). As a small post-colonial state, Ghana emerged on the margins of the international system with severe constraints that circumscribed the decision-making options opened to it. Notable among them were the country's diminutive size and population, its agrarian economic base and technological backwardness, its strategic insignificance and path dependency, and consequently, its lack of requisite power resources to assure effective national defence (Boafo-Arthur, 1999; Clapham, 1996; Thompson, 1969).[1] These constraints, however, impelled Ghanaian governments to experiment with a variety of defence and foreign policy measures designed to assure security, while transforming the post-colonial state's marginal and inconsequential image into one of a viable actor in regional and global politics.

Under President Kwame Nkrumah, Ghana's founding leader, the country had visions of itself as a continental leader and sought to modernise its armed forces in order to demonstrate power abroad through peacekeeping and support to like-minded radical Pan-African states and groups. It was therefore no coincidence that the first decades of independence saw Ghana become an active participant in the affairs of the international system. Nkrumah was an avid supporter of multilateral diplomacy and a co-founder of the Organisation of African Unity (OAU), the antecedent of the African Union (AU). Believing and proclaiming that his country had security interests in common with states and colonies on the continent, Nkrumah projected Ghana as the "vanguard force" in the process of African decolonisation (Nkrumah, 1973: 163). To an extent, his anti-colonial politics and the narrative of Pan-Africanism seemed to provide Ghana with the legitimacy it needed to mobilise anti-colonial nationalists and anti-apartheid activists in Africa (Ahlman, 2011) and to influence events and processes across the continent and further afield. Nkrumah's vision in terms of the leadership role he wanted Ghana to play in African affairs and the strategy for achieving that objective was well articulated and clearly laid out. This continental leader image proved ephemeral, however. Following the departure of Nkrumah in 1966, the country was compelled to reassess its bloc leadership aspirations as economic debility forced a retreat from the external scene, resulting in a general erosion of the country's initial pre-eminence in the African regional system. Ghana's waned influence created a role identity crisis as the conception of the nation's role, or what it represented in international affairs, became indistinct.

While abandoning the offensive aspects of his policy, Nkrumah's successors have tended to favour multilateral approaches in their external relations. This has, in turn, resulted in a foreign-defence policy interface that presents Ghana's defence policy as an extension of its foreign policy. Moreover, Ghanaian elites have been unanimous in their commitment to Ghana's participation in international peacekeeping, perceiving it as a role type germane to the nation's interest, including its interest in constructing and projecting a favourable image. In fact, peacekeeping has been Ghana's most visible diplomatic-military engagement since independence in 1957 and the most active role type enacted by the country on the international scene. Peacekeeping is seen by Ghanaian elites as a role congruent with universal norms, institutions and mechanisms, and hence, a responsibility that might enhance its self-placement in the external world. Not only, therefore, has peacekeeping participation had special appeal for policymakers, but Ghana has always agreed to contribute troops for peace operations irrespective of their political hue. In spite of the centrality of peacekeeping to the country's foreign and defence policies, the idea of *Ghana as a peacekeeper* (and not merely as a troop contributor) has yet to be established. Saying Ghana is a peacekeeper does not currently project for the country the kind of identity its orientation as a liberation supporter, a Pan-Africanist or an anti-imperialist/anti-colonialist mobiliser, for example, once bestowed on the state. What explains this state of affairs?

We argue that the post-Nkrumah regimes have not fully thought out a peacekeeper role that will tie Ghana's security interests to regional stability, and thereby, open up and legitimise new military and diplomatic responsibilities in the context of peace and security promotion in (West) Africa and further afield. As a result, Ghana's peacekeeping involvement has been confined mainly to the supply of troops, denying it the potential of playing a greater role as a mediator or a civilian protector, for example, that is based on a broader approach to peace.

Drawing on national role conceptions as advanced by K.J. Holsti (1970), this chapter examines the interplay between Ghana's foreign and defence polities in relation to the country's search for external identity. Following this introduction, the chapter proceeds with an explanation of the ideational basis of Ghana's foreign and defence policy orientations, drawing on insights from national role conceptions. This is followed by an analysis of Ghana's foreign and defence policies. The chapter then examines the interplay between the foreign and defence policies of Ghana with a focus on the country's participation in international peacekeeping. Finally, the chapter reflects on the idea of Ghana as a peacekeeper through a broader approach to peace, enabling Ghana to enact greater roles that elevate its external self-placement and provides it with a stable and more valued sense of international identity, while strengthening African agency in the maintenance of international peace and security.

National role conceptions as ideational bedrock of foreign and defence policies

That policy elites perceive value in the participation of their states in the affairs of the international system seems incontrovertible. An immediate question prompted by this claim is: What roles do policymakers expect their states to play in the international system or subordinate regional systems? This suggests the further question: What ideational precepts inform the roles held or enacted by policy-makers? One of the approaches in International Relations that reflect most systematically on these questions is national role conceptions as developed by Holsti (1970). The notion of national role conceptions has its roots in role theory, which, in turn, derives from a range of theoretical perspectives common in sociology and social psychology (Mead, 1934; Parsons, 1951). Role theory explains how the behaviours and attitudes of individuals are framed by expectations held by the individuals themselves and society. Among other assumptions, the theory rests on the claim that individuals or actors define for themselves and others specific roles that are based on social learning; and that these individuals form expectations regarding the roles that they and others will enact (Merton, 1957; Pfeffer & Salancik, 1975).

Role theory, when applied as an analytical framework in International Relations, assumes that states "behave consistent with specific roles with which they identify" (Chafetz, Abramson & Grillot, 1996: 732). A role can be understood as self-assigned behavioural and attitudinal categories that are consistent with a status and the expectations of the environment in which they manifest (Holsti, 1970; Walker, 1987). Like individuals, these categories "provide states with a stable sense of identity", guiding their actions through the complex terrain of international politics (Chafetz et al., 1996: 733). State identity being "one kind of identity that refers to the image of individuality and distinctiveness held and projected by the state within particular international contexts.... [It] connotes a conception of what the country is and what it represents" (Ashizawa, 2008).

In terms of its constituent elements, a role represents a synthesised triad of ideas, blending together an actor's own subjective understandings or perceptions of what its behaviour should be, its role conceptions, society's demands, role expectations, and the contextual environment in which the role is enacted and its context (Aras & Gorener, 2010; Chafetz et al., 1996). The most coherent application of role theory to the study of foreign policy (and defence policy) can be seen in Holsti's (1970) work on the roles that states play in international affairs, which he explores within the framework of national role conceptions. Holsti (1970: 247) defines national role conceptions to include:

> the policymakers' own definitions of the general kinds of decisions, commitments, rules and actions suitable to their state, and of the functions, if any, their state should perform on a continuing basis in the international system or in subordinate regional systems. It is their "image" of the appropriate orientations or functions of their state toward, or in, the external environment.

Thus, national role conceptions represent the general perceptions of the policy elites regarding their nation's position or identity in the international system, and what role they should play in its affairs (Holsti, 1970; Wish, 1980). They serve as the ideational or intellectual determinants that condition specific diplomatic-military policies and actions. At the same time, they reflect the nation's identity within the society of states, specifying its long-term functions. Nkrumah had no doubts regarding the vanguard role he wanted Ghana to play in African international relations. His vision of African unity rooted in the ideal of Pan-Africanism served as the basis for constructing African solidarity in response to the continent's marginalised and dependent position in the political economy of global capitalism. Liberation, freedom and unity, which were central to his external policy, are virtuous categories, which, since they are difficult to oppose without appearing immoral or misguided, were leveraged by Ghana in the process of continental mobilisation and the construction of a common African diplomacy. In turn, this projected for Ghana the image of a Pan-Africanist liberator, turning Accra into an "extra-metropolitan centre" for "African anti-colonial nationalists and anti-apartheid activists during the so-called first wave of Africa's decolonisation" (Ahlman, 2011: 23).

Ghana's foreign and defence policies

The international system in which states interact is an inherently unequal environment characterised by differential levels of participation among actors. Ideationally constructed under the intellectual hegemony of political realism, the system is thought to provide the context for state interactions, with security represented as a derivative of power. This implies a positive relationship between power and security (and ultimately survival). In other words, power-possessing and knowledge-producing states have political clout, greater security and better chances of survival. They dominate the global order and affect the system in much the same way as they are affected by it. This representation, by extension, renders power-deficient and knowledge-consuming states weak, subordinate and peripheral, implying greater risk to their independence, security and survival. The essence of Nkrumah's foreign and defence policies was to transform the weak and subordinate image of Ghana and, indeed, the other states on the continent, through the complete decolonisation and unification of African states, guided by the idea of Pan-Africanism. The pursuit of these goals, in turn, bestowed on Ghana a number of closely linked identities such as continental bloc leader, liberation supporter and Pan-Africanist. Ghana had a fully developed national role in international affairs that derived from Nkrumah's understanding of his country's position in the international system, a clear vision of what he wanted Ghana and Africa to become, and a systematic mobilising strategy for achieving his vision that was closely linked to narratives of decolonisation and Pan-Africanism.

Foreign and defence policies under Nkrumah

As noted above, Ghana emerged on the international scene as a small, subordinate state with limited power resources, political clout and influence. Certainly, upon independence Ghana's economy and institutions were in relatively good shape, compared to other African states. According to Thompson (1969), Ghana, in 1957, supplied over 30% of the global cocoa demand while it featured as the fifth biggest exporter of gold. With over half a billion dollars in foreign reserves—more than India had at the time—Ghana's economy was in a relatively good position. When placed on a global scale, however, Ghana fell within the category of weak states that occupied the bottom rung of global power, importance and prestige (Clapham, 1996). In Nkrumah's view, Ghana's marginal position in the world meant that it could not assure its security or develop according to its own needs, nor could it further its interests apart from the rest of Africa (Mbalia, 2011; Nkrumah, 1957; Nkrumah, 1973). He recognised that under prevailing circumstances, "Ghana could never hope to defend herself against determined attack by a major power" (Ghana National Defence Policy Ministry of Defence, 2012: 8). In spite of this, Nkrumah still sought to use Ghana's independence to re-establish Africa's position in the world. Ghana's independence, therefore, was to serve as a "Vanguard force to offer what assistance we can to those now engaged in the battles that we ourselves have fought and won. Our task is not done and our safety is not assured until the last vestiges of colonialism have been swept from Africa" (Nkrumah, 1973: 163).[2]

This commitment was made against the backdrop of two major international processes that combined to exert great influence on the general orientations of Nkrumah's foreign policy. The first related to the Cold War confrontations between the East and the West for dominance in international affairs, while the second concerned the process of decolonisation (Boafo-Arthur, 1999). The fact that Nkrumah could leverage on the goal of continental decolonisation and unity within the constraints of Cold War politics is a key factor that allowed Ghana to develop and have a recognised, high profile national role. By virtue of Ghana's birthright as the first sovereign actor south of the Sahara, Nkrumah felt the need to lead the process of liberation of Africa from colonial domination in ways that would eventually culminate in the economic and political unification of the African continent. On the eve of independence, therefore, Nkrumah tied the independence of Ghana to the broader aspirations of African liberation and continental unity when he declared that "the independence of Ghana is meaningless unless it is linked up with the total liberation of the African continent". For Nkrumah, the fact that the post-colonial state could not assure its own survival meant it was "a political experiment that had already failed" (Moss, 1970: iii) and had to be reconstructed (Nkrumah, 1963). Nkrumah did this in dramatic ways by building the largest army in West Africa prior to his overthrow in 1966. This he thought was necessary for the liberation of the continent and the subsequent establishment of a union government.

In the view of Nkrumah, the best alternative to the balkanised states created by colonial action in Africa was to be found in a continental union government which could obviously only happen after the total decolonisation of the African continent (Nkrumah, 1963). While the process of liberation in some instances required resorting to arms which Nkrumah was committed to provide, the limits on his own power impelled him to concurrently seek ideational or non-material power resources in some moral or value constructs. As he observed, "Force alone is no longer a decisive factor in world affairs" (Nkrumah, as cited in Thompson, 1969: xi). As noted above, Nkrumah's pursuit of Pan-Africanism and the corresponding narratives of decolonisation enabled him to transform Ghana into a Pan-Africanist mobiliser (Ahlman, 2011). However, the anti-colonial and Pan-Africanist politics that underpinned the role of the mobiliser meant that Ghanaian external policy was perceived as subversive for some, and liberationist for others on the continent, making it stand out for Britain, France, USSR and the US.

Nkrumah and Pan-Africanism

Pan-Africanism is an intellectual perspective that envisions the liberation of peoples of African descent from foreign domination and the eventual unification of the African continent into a single sovereign entity. The ideal of Pan-Africanism was, therefore, intimately connected with the idea of the unity of Africa. African states had emerged with arbitrary frontiers that hardly corresponded to "pre-colonial social or geographical identities" (Clapham, 1996: 4). Nkrumah drew a link between the problems associated with domestic integration and consolidation on the continent with the "artificial" nature of the African state, and advanced the idea of continental unity as the only solution to the survival of African states and their societies (Nkrumah, 1963). As such, the idea of continental unity became a central element of his foreign and defence policies, under the broader umbrella of Pan-Africanism.

The pursuit of Nkrumah's unification projects, while receiving support from some of the African states, faced opposition from others, and eventually divided the continent into three main blocs. The OAU, which was established in 1963 to organise Africa's international relations while reflecting a modicum of compromise between the diverging blocs, could not provide the foundation for the construction of a continental union. As such, the objective was pursued through a form of Pan-Africanist mobilisation strategy that involved the hosting of conferences, propaganda and the forging of personal alliances with heads of state such as Sekou Toure of Guinea and Patrice Lumumba of the Congo (Rooney, 1988; Thompson, 1969; Moss, 1970). Within the framework of Pan-Africanist mobilisation, Nkrumah was accused of using subversive measures such as support for opposition leaders from the neighbouring countries of Togo and La Côte d'Ivoire (Aluko, 1975; Austin, 1963). Moreover, he sought to equip the

Ghana Armed Forces (GAF) with offensive and defensive capabilities that would position the forces to defend the country, but also conduct operations elsewhere on the African continent (Addae, 2005).

Nkrumah and non-alignment

The second ideational signpost that guided the foreign policy pursued under the Nkrumah administration was the principle of non-alignment, which required independent judgement and complete freedom from the policy dictations of the Cold War protagonists. According to Holsti (1970: 233), a state that classifies itself as non-aligned would typically exhibit diplomatic behaviours and attitudes that include "anti-colonial predispositions and policies, unwillingness to enter into bloc-sponsored military alliances, receipt of foreign aid from a variety of sources, [and] prohibition against maintenance of other countries' forces on the state's territory". These elements made non-alignment particularly attractive to Nkrumah not only because they helped to assert a modicum of freedom of action, but they also enabled him to play one of the superpower rivals against the other while augmenting his diplomatic stature (Clapham, 1996). Within the abrasive context of Cold War politics, Nkrumah's non-aligned credentials enabled him to mediate in international conflicts both on the African continent and beyond. On the crisis in the Middle East, for example, he consistently emphasised the need for Israel to remain "within the limits laid down by the United Nations" (Nkrumah, as quoted in Thompson, 1969: 286).

Nkrumah's capacity to pursue genuine non-alignment was, however, curtailed by economic exigencies (Thompson, 1969, Aning, 2018). In particular, his adoption of socialist political and economic models and his establishment of closer ties with the Soviet Union, especially from 1961, meant that Ghana became "less and less objectively non-aligned, even if it remained subjectively committed to the policy" (Thompson, 1969: 280). Aluko (1975) attributes Nkrumah's drift to the East partly to the triumph of the left-wing faction within the ruling Convention People's Party (CPP) and Ghana's differences with the West on the Congo crisis.

This notwithstanding, Nkrumah's policies positioned Ghana as the most influential state in sub-Saharan Africa, playing prominent roles in continental affairs (Chazan, 1984). Desirous of seeing Ghana take the identity of the defender or protector of the black race, Nkrumah proceeded to assume the mantle of leadership in African international relations in ways that went well out of proportion to its economic base (Boafo-Arthur, 1999; Thompson, 1969). By 1966, when Nkrumah exited the scene, the economy was on the verge of collapse. Nonetheless, his conceptions of the role Ghana ought to play in the international system continues to influence the approaches adopted by his successors, including their commitment to the AU and its institutions. However, the harmony of security and economic interests that Nkrumah identified between Ghana and the rest of the African continent, the importance of multilateralism and the clarity with which these were articulated remains exceptional to his administration.

The centrality of multilateralism in Ghana's foreign policy can be traced to the immediate post-independence administration of the CPP led by Dr Nkrumah. For him, the constraints imposed on Ghana as a post-colonial state possessing no significant power meant that the country could not wholly assure its own security (Ministry of Defence, 2012) . To that end, Nkrumah started an aggressive programme of training, education and international exchanges for his security forces (Clune, 2014). At the same time, he thought a measure of power and influence could be obtained by joining and sharing in the working of international organisations. It is, therefore, not a coincidence that Ghana joined the United Nations (UN) on 8 March 1957, a day after attaining independence. Nkrumah's influence on Ghana's foreign policy remains unrivalled by any of his successors, if for no other reason than that he established the intellectual signpost that continues to guide successive Ghanaian regimes in their external relations since he was ousted in 1966. What is clearly lacking is a broad conception and approach to the promotion of peace in the sub-region and further afield that is based on a well-articulated policy of what roles Ghana should play in stabilising the rather troubled region of Africa.

Defence policy in the immediate post-independence era

Upon independence, Nkrumah quickly modernised and expanded the military, and established an air force and a navy to complement the army to reflect Ghana's new status as a sovereign state. The Ghanaian leader sought to build the best equipped and most efficient armed forces on the continent (Baynham, 1988). In keeping with his Pan-Africanist agenda, including his objective to help transform the remaining colonies in Africa into sovereign entities, Nkrumah sought to equip the GAF with both defensive and offensive capabilities that would enable them to provide effective national defence, while conducting operations elsewhere on the African continent (Addae, 2005; Thompson, 1969). To this end, Nkrumah sought extensive International Military Education and Training (IMET) support from Canada, US and the UK (Clune, 2014). This enabled him to use the GAF in external operations. The use of the GAF under the Nkrumah administration is best exemplified by the deployment of Ghanaian forces to the United Nations Operation in the Congo (ONUC) during the Congo crisis, which erupted following the country's attainment of independence (Aning, 2018). Although Nkrumah sought to aid the colonised states to independence, the officer corps of his armed forces were totally European. This obvious paradox became even more embarrassing when Ghana intervened in the Congo, compelling Nkrumah to Africanise the leadership of the armed forces. The presence of Ghanaian officer corps projected the image of an African authority, capacity and competence.

According to Addae (2005: 125), Nkrumah also sought to equip the GAF with offensive capabilities that included "torpedo and missile firing equipment", while orders for offensive aircrafts were placed. It is significant to note that Nkrumah's policy to develop offensive capabilities has since remained the exception to the rule. Undoubtedly, all his successors have had in common a tendency to favour "purely defensive" and collaborative security policy orientations in their international relations. With very few exceptions, the post-Nkrumah administrations have emphasised the policy of good neighbourliness as a strategy to obviate the need for engaging the armed forces in inter-state conflicts. The policy of good neighbourliness remains a core feature of the 2012 security policy. Also, the participation in international peacekeeping represents a major element in the current defence policy (Aning, 2000).

Foreign and defence policies after Nkrumah

In its relations with the outside world, Ghana has traditionally operated without a codified foreign policy. Since 1992, following the restoration of constitutional rule, the fundamental principles guiding the country's relations have derived from the 1992 Constitution of Ghana. Article 40 of the Constitution provides that the government of Ghana in its conducts and determinations with "other nations" shall (Constitution of Ghana, 1993: Art. 40):

1. promote and protect the interests of Ghana;
2. seek the establishment of a just and equitable international economic and social order;
3. promote respect for international law, treaty obligations and the settlement of international disputes by peaceful means; and
4. adhere to the principles enshrined in, or as the case may be, the aims and ideals of the Charter of the United Nations; the Charter of the Organisation of African Unity [the African Union]; the Commonwealth; the Treaty of the Economic Community of West African States; and any other international organisation of which Ghana is a member.

Although the constitution makes reference to other "nations" as the referent in Ghana's interaction with its external environment, it would be misleading as point four above clearly shows, to conclude that it downplays the role played by non-state actors and intergovernmental organisations (IGOs) such as the UN, the AU and the Economic Community of West African States (ECOWAS) on the world stage. Indeed, a consistent theme linking Ghana's external policies since independence has been the commitment on the part of successive administrations to engage with multilateral organisations and broader institutions of global governance as a strategy for achieving national and collective interests, particularly in the area of security. However, no distinct national role and corresponding image has been distilled from these proclamations. While the country's involvement in international peacekeeping has remained consistent, the identity of Ghana as a peacekeeper, and not merely a troop contributing country, has not been established.

Ghana's foreign policy in the post-Nkrumah era (1966–2019) has been marked by a general erosion of the country's initial pre-eminence in regional affairs (Chazan, 1984) as economic debility continues to force elite retreat from the external political environment. Following his removal from office in 1966, the view was widely held that Nkrumah's extensive involvement in African and global affairs had undermined the Ghanaian economy (Aluko, 1975). As such, the priority accorded to political goals in the first decade of independence gave way to the search for economic support as an approach to domestic transformation (Boafo-Arthur, 1999; Aning & Lartey, 2009). The growing salience of economic foreign policy in Ghana is clearly in evidence when one considers the emphasis placed on "economic diplomacy" by President Nana Addo Dankwa Akufo-Addo of the New Patriotic Party (NPP) since he assumed office on 7 January 2017.

The foreign policy of the party, as stated in Chapter 15 of its 2016 Manifesto, has as its main objective the use of foreign policy resources as "the principal agents of Ghana's socioeconomic resurgence" (Manifesto of New Patriotic Party, 2016: Chap. 15). As such, the establishment of new markets and the broadening of existing markets have been central elements of the NPP's foreign policy. A related priority can be found in the government's "Ghana Beyond Aid" agenda, which seeks to reduce the country's dependence on economic charity and handouts originating from outside, by prudently managing the country's resources. The feasibility of this project remains unclear, however, given that the Ghanaian economy has yet to undergo a major transformation.

On the whole, in spite of occasional deviations, Ghana's diplomatic engagements have been marked by recurring relationships centred on multilateral diplomacy, particularly since the adoption of the fourth republican constitution in 1992 and the subsequent transition from military to democratic rule (Aning & Lartey, 2009). The emphasis on multilateral diplomacy as the preferred instrument for policy implementation appears to be guided by the logic that effective diplomatic engagements will serve defence policy goals by fostering greater understanding and cooperation with Ghana's contiguous neighbours and other states in the international system. By working through bilateral or multilateral institutional channels, Ghana can obviate or minimise the likelihood of conflict and associated costs, as well as the corresponding burden on the armed forces. A dominant policy stance which reflects this tendency is the good neighbourliness policy which seeks to sustain peaceful and cordial relations with Ghana's West African neighbours including Togo, Burkina Faso, La Côte d'Ivoire and Nigeria.

Although the domestic transformation goal has come to occupy the centre stage of external policy, the Ghanaian elite recognise that economic diplomacy and development is possible only in an atmosphere of peace and security. This has become particularly important in the context of the changing nature of conflict and the threat to security following the demise of the Cold War. In keeping with its obligations under Article 40 of the Constitution, the two leading political parties in Ghana, the National Democratic Congress (NDC) and New Patriotic Party (NPP), have supported joint international and regional efforts at ensuring peace and security on the African continent, mainly through the deployment of Ghanaian troops to AU and UN-mandated peacekeeping missions on the continent and elsewhere. Peacekeeping participation has remained a core element of the foreign and defence policies of successive regimes since Nkrumah (Aning & Aubyn, 2013). Arguably, the most critical peacekeeping duty undertaken by the GAF since the Congo crisis happened when former President Jerry John Rawlings of Ghana, serving as the Chairman of the Authority of ECOWAS Heads of State and Government, deployed Ghanaian troops to the ECOWAS Cease-fire Monitoring Group (ECOMOG) established to restore stability to Liberia in the early 1990s. Ghana has also mediated conflicts involving West African states such as Liberia and La Côte d'Ivoire.

West Africa's interconnected and changing conflicts, structurally embedded in regional security complexes, destabilise the entire region, generating adverse implications for states and societies. The majority of these conflicts generally occur within states, with high proclivity to spill over into neighbouring states. The spillover potential of conflicts and the threat they pose mean that Ghana participates in peacekeeping operations to, among other objectives, mitigate the spread of conflicts and "prevent them from jeopardising its security" (Aning & Aubyn, 2013: 274). In addition to its commitment to contribute to the maintenance of international peace and security, peacekeeping is seen as an instrument for enhancing Ghana's image and prestige in the wider world, while helping to assure its security. Other motivations for Ghana's peacekeeping participation include the financial and technical incentives secured through the compensation packages and the training or professional support received mainly from the UN. However, a systematic policy linking regional instability to specific peacekeeping role types that legitimise greater diplomatic and military support have yet to be framed.

Indeed, until 2012, Ghana did not have a codification of her defence policy, implying that defence policy articulation and implementation was for the most part marked by adhocracy. Moreover, beyond the broad assertion that the defence police are "firmly grounded in our foreign policy" (Ministry of Defence, 2012: 5), it is difficult to understand the operational relationship between the Ministry of Foreign Affairs (MFA) and the Ministry of Defence (MOD). The 2012 defence policy, which derives its legitimacy from Article 84 of the 1992 Constitution of Ghana, outlines the tasks and objectives of national defence and the guidelines for the management of the GAF to achieve effectiveness and efficiency at all performance levels of the armed forces. The policy provides the framework for the protection of strategic national resources; the protection of the rights, safety and security of Ghanaians; and fulfilment of Ghana's commitments towards the UN, AU and ECOWAS, among others. These priorities and others are subsumed in Ghana's national security, which is defined as "the aggregate of the security interest of all individuals, communities, ethnic groups and political parties that exist in Ghana" (Ministry of Defence, 2012: 9).

The strategies by which Ghana seeks to further its interests depend on the nature of the threat to its security that needs to be addressed, and whether it relates to the individual, state or international level. Although Ghana does not appear to face an imminent threat from an external aggressor, the country faces multiple sources of security threats in its external environment that include the many unresolved conflicts in Ghana's neighbouring states, terrorism and religious fanaticism, illicit arms trafficking, environmental stresses and strains and human trafficking. Given the generally cordial relations between Ghana and its neighbours, and given the fact that Ghana has not experienced any major attacks from maritime sources, there appears to be no major attempt at establishing a powerful navy. Ghana's new status as an oil exporting country—which the current defence policy rightly acknowledges—suggests the need for greater attention to the sea. While the policy recognises the porous nature of Ghana's borders as a source of threat, it is virtually silent on the issue of cross-boundary ethnic groups that straddle Ghana and its contiguous states, particularly to the east. The long-standing and growing demand by a segment of the Ewe ethnic group in the Volta Region of Ghana to secede and either join their kinsmen in the Republic of Togo or establish an independent state poses a potential major challenge to the territorial integrity of Ghana, particularly given that Togo has a long-standing bilateral defence pact with France (Austin, 1963).

The interplay between Ghana's foreign and defence policies

Ghana's preference for defensive security and the commitment to multilateral diplomacy as the underpinning of external relations have combined to evolve a foreign policy-defence policy interface that projects Ghana's defence policy as an extension of its foreign policy. Consistent with this policy arrangement, the role played by the GAF has largely been one of supporting the implementation of foreign policy initiatives. This has been portrayed most visibly by Ghana's contribution to the maintenance of global and regional peace and security through the deployment of its military forces to international peacekeeping missions mandated by the UN, AU or ECOWAS (Aning & Aubyn, 2013).

Ghana's participation in international peacekeeping lies at the interface between the country's foreign policy and defence policy, which, while the nation is at peace, seems to represent the best alignment of the diplomatic-military resources to its interests abroad. In the absence of a comprehensive national security framework that conceptualises and bridges the two policy strands, the point of intersection has remained indistinct.

As a developing country lacking preponderant power resources and facing no eminent military threats, Ghana however falls within the categories of states for whom foreign policy objectives take precedence over defence objectives. Although the 1992 Constitution from which Ghana's foreign policy and defence policy derive their source does not make this explicitly clear, there are phrases in the 2012 national defence policy that indicate that the country's defence policy derives from its foreign policy. Aside from the claim that the defence policy is firmly grounded in Ghana's foreign policy, the defence policy also stresses the importance of multilateral cooperation in addressing contemporary security challenges through close collaboration with the UN, AU and ECOWAS. The policy, in various sections, reaffirms Ghana's continuous support to regional and global peacekeeping efforts.

Ghana as a peacekeeper

Undoubtedly, Ghana's peacekeeping initiatives have been accompanied by the offering of other forms of political support, particularly to the ECOWAS and the

AU Peace and Security Council (PSC). These have mostly involved the mediation and negotiation of conflict, hosting refugees from warring states in Africa, the provision of personnel towards the deployment of the African Standby Force (ASF) (through the ECOWAS Standby Force (ESF)), regular financial contribution to the AU Peace Fund and the mounting of a consistent campaign for the reform of the UN Security Council in keeping with the provisions of the Ezulwini Consensus (African Union, 2005). Such activities have, however, remained isolated and uncoordinated in the absence of a coherent national role conception. While Ghana's participation in international peacekeeping remains the country's most visible military-diplomatic engagement, its linkages to the above activities have been indistinct. In the absence of any likelihood of external aggression against Ghana, peacekeeping is likely to remain the single most important and visible initiative around which its foreign and defence policies converge. This, in turn, suggests that Ghana will remain a principal troop contributing country to ECOWAS, AU and UN-mandated peace operations in the foreseeable future.

Despite its centrality to Ghana's foreign-defence policy mix, peacekeeping has yet to be developed into a national role conception articulated as the synthesised or abstracted ideational base grounding specific peacekeeping enactments. In other words, the idea of *Ghana as a peacekeeper* has yet to crystallise into a national role conception, understood as the policymakers' perception of the general and long-term role their nation should play in the affairs of the international system (Holsti, 1970).

Ghana's current role as a peacekeeper simply does not live up to its past role as a Pan-Africanist leader willing to oppose the big powers. Thus, saying that Ghana is a peacekeeper does not project for the country the kind of image or identity its orientation as a liberation supporter, a Pan-Africanist or an anti-imperialist/anti-colonialist mobiliser, for example, once bestowed on the state.

Moreover, given the ongoing prioritisation of domestic transformation goals, Ghanaian elites appear unclear in their minds as to which specific national role conceptions they should identify with and what further roles Ghana's diplomatic and military conduct can fulfil in international affairs. As Ghana's traditional decoloniser and non-aligned identities become anachronistic, and as its image of continental unifier proves difficult to sustain, peacekeeping has come to occupy the centre stage of Ghana's international diplomatic and military enactments. This suggests the potential for a new and positive international identity of a peacekeeper.

But transforming Ghana's identity from a troop contributor to a peacekeeper requires the elevation of Ghanaian peacekeeping role from a functional imperative to a cognitive orientation that provides the intellectual context for shaping elite perceptions and policies around conflict, peace and security on a general basis. This can only happen when peacekeeping is connected with the idea that effective national security can best be achieved in a safe and secured neighbourhood. This will, in turn, require a broader notion of peace conceived in terms of the absence of threats to regional stability, at least from a national perspective. Conceiving peace as the absence of threat to regional stability will correspondingly widen its approach to making and keeping peace. Thus, a peacekeeper idea can tie Ghana's security interests in common with other states in (West) Africa, opening up and legitimising new military and diplomatic responsibilities that may for example include the roles of a mediator and a civilian protector. Not only is a peacekeeper international identity or role consistent with the broader interests of the international community or universal norms, institutions and mechanisms, it will also enable the pursuit of defence and foreign policy goals that further the interests of Ghana, while addressing the gap in Ghana's current international role.

Conclusion

The external posturing of Ghanaian governments since independence has been guided by the national role conceptions adopted in the first decade following independence. These have typically included Pan-Africanism, positive neutrality and non-alignment, good neighbourliness, and economic diplomacy (Chazan, 1984). Certainly, Ghana's security and broader international relations have been far from static. Over the years, specific decisions and actions taken by policymakers in a variety of domestic and global contexts have differed from regime to regime. Moreover, particular administrations have experimented with multiple and sometimes contrasting policy choices in response to changing currents internal or external to the Ghanaian state. However, the variations in official stance have taken place alongside fundamental elements of continuity, resulting in recurring trends. On the whole, Ghanaian elites have tended to favour multilateral approaches to national security and defence, resulting in a foreign-defence policy interface that projects Ghana's defence policy as an extension of its foreign policy. The interplay between Ghana's foreign and defence policies is depicted most visibly by the country's peacekeeping participation, through which Ghana helps to maintain international peace and security while furthering its own interests. Despite its centrality to Ghana's diplomatic-military enactment, peacekeeping has yet to evolve into a national role conception.

Unlike Nkrumah's national role conception, which was firmly grounded in the vision of African unity that was itself rooted in the ideal of Pan-Africanism—bestowing on Ghana the identity of continental unifier and anti-colonialist mobiliser—there has been a deficit of national role identity following his departure. While Nkrumah's successors have tended to prioritise issues around domestic transformation at the expense of external participation, they have been consistent in their support to international peacekeeping. Nonetheless, the idea of Ghana as a peacekeeper has not been established. Ghana can evolve an identity of a peacekeeper and not merely a troop contributor, when the peacekeeper idea effectively ties Ghana's security interests in common with other states in (West) Africa, thereby opening up and legitimising new military and diplomatic commitments that may include the roles of a mediator and a civilian protector. This will come about when peacekeeping is conceived, articulated and enacted as a synthesised ideational base grounding specific decisions and actions around conflict, peace and security; in effect, transforming Ghana from a peacekeeping troop contributor to a peacekeeper.

Notes

1 Certainly, the Ghanaian economy and institutions, upon independence, were relatively well-formed when compared to those of other African states (Hutchful, 2006; Thompson, 1969). At the global level, however, Ghana ranked as a small and weak state.
2 Nkrumah (1973, p. 163).

References

Acland, A. & Tuzo, H. (1983). The relationship between foreign and defence policy. *The RUSI Journal, 128*(2): 3–6. doi:10.1080/03071848308523518.

Addae, S. (2005). *A Short History of Ghana Armed Forces*. Accra: Ministry of Defence of Ghana Armed Forces.

African Union. (2005). *The Common African Position on the Proposed Reform of The United Nations: "The Ezulwini Consensus"*. Addis Ababa. https://www.un.org/en/africa/osaa/pdf/au/cap_screform_2005.pdf. Accessed 14 January 2020.

Ahlman, J. (2011). Road to Ghana: Nkrumah, Southern Africa and the eclipse of a decolonizing Africa. *Kronos, 37*(1): 23–40.

Aluko, O. (1975). After Nkrumah: Continuity and change in Ghana's foreign policy. *A Journal of Opinion, 5*(1): 55–62. doi:10.1017/S1548450500000111.

Aning, K. (2000). Ghana election 2000—Implications and significance for the future. *Africa Security Review, 10*(2). doi:10.1080/10246029.2001.9627934.

Aning, K. (2018). The impact of security force assistance: The curious case of Ghana. *Text of Paper to Be Delivered at a Conference on Security Force Assistance in Fragile States*, Oslo, Norway, 5–7 December, 2018.

Aning, K. & Aubyn, F. (2013). Ghana. In B. Alex & P. Williams. (eds.). *Providing Peacekeepers: The Politic, Challenges and Future of United Nations Peacekeeping Contributions*. Oxford: Oxford University Press, 269–290.

Aning, K. & Lartey, E. (2009). Presidential transitions in Ghana's politics: Lessons from the 2008 elections. *African Renaissance, 6*(1): 7–12.

Aras, B. & Gorener, A. (2010) National role conceptions and foreign policy orientation: The ideational bases of the Justice and Development Party's foreign policy activism in the Middle East. *Journal of Balkan and Near Eastern Studies, 12*(1): 73–92. doi:10.1080/19448950903507453.

Ashizawa, K. (2008). When identity matters: State identity, regional institution-building, and Japanese foreign policy. *International Studies Review, 10*(3): 571–598. doi:10.1111/j.1468-2486.2008.00805.x.

Austin, D. (1963). The uncertain frontier: Ghana-Togo. *The Journal of Modern African Studies, 1*(2): 139–145. doi:10.1017/S0022278X00001026.

Baynham, S. (1988). *The Military Politics in Nkrumah's Ghana*. Boulder, CO: Westview Press.

Boafo-Arthur, K. (1999). Ghana's politics of international economic relations under the PNDC, 1982–1992. *African Study Monographs, 20*(2): 73–98.

Chafetz, G., Abramson, H. & Grillot, S. (1996). Role theory and foreign policy: Belarussian and Ukrainian compliance with the nuclear nonproliferation regime. *Political Psychology, 17*(4), 727–757. doi:10.2307/3792136.

Chazan, N. (1984). Ghana. In T. Shaw & O. Aluko (eds.). *The Political Economy of African Foreign Policy: Comparative Analysis*. London: Gower, 94–121.

Clapham, C. (1996). *Africa and the International System: The Politics of State Survival*. Cambridge: Cambridge University Press.

Clune, J. V. (2014). *The Abongo Abroad: Military Internationalism, Travel, Training, and Peace in Ghana and the United States, 1960–1992*. PhD Dissertation University of Kansas.

Ghana. (1993). *Constitution of the Republic of Ghana.* 7 January 1993. http://www.refworld.org/docid/3ae6b5850.html. Accessed 17 November 2018.

Holsti, K. J. (1970). National role conceptions in the study of foreign policy. *International Studies Quarterly*, *14*(3): 233–309. doi:10.2307/3013584.

Hutchful, E. (2006). Ghana. In W. Omitoogun & E. Hutchfu (eds.). *Budgeting for the Military Sector in Africa: The Processes and Mechanisms of Control*. Oxford: Oxford University Press, 72–97.

Jackson, R. (1991). *Quasi-States: Sovereignty, International Relations and the Third World*. Cambridge: Cambridge University Press.

Mbalia, D. (2011). *Kwame Nkrumah, Contributions to African Revolution*. Bedford: Panaf.

Mead, G. (1934). *Mind, Self, and Society*. Chicago, IL: University of Chicago Press.

Merton, R. (1957). *Social Theory and Social Structure*. New York: Free Press.

Ministry of Defence. (2012). *Promulgation Instructions: Ghana National Defence Policy*. Unpublished document.

Moss, R. (1970). *To Move a Continent: Kwame Nkrumah's Role in African Affairs 1957–1966*. Dissertation Presented for the Degree of Master of Arts to the Australian National University.

New Patriotic Party. (2016). *2016 Manifesto of New Patriotic Party*. http://www.codeoghana.org/assets/downloadables/npp_2016_manifesto.compressed.pdf. Accessed 10 June 2018.

Nkrumah, K. (1957). *Ghana: The Autobiography of Kwame Nkrumah*. Edinburgh: Thomas Nelson and Sons.

Nkrumah, K. (1963). *Africa Must Unite*. London: Heinemann.

Nkrumah, K. (1973). *The Autobiography of Kwame Nkrumah*. London: Panaf.

Parsons, T. (1951). *The Social System*. Abingdon: Routledge and Keagan Paul Ltd.

Pfeffer, J. & Salancik, G. R. (1975). Determinants of supervisory behavior: A role set analysis. *Human Relations*, *28*: 139–153.

Rooney, D. (1988). *Kwame Nkrumah: The Political Kingdom in the Third World*. London: I.B. Taurus.

Thompson, S. (1969). *Ghana's Foreign Policy 1957–1966: Diplomacy, Ideology and the New State*. Princeton, NJ: Princeton University Press.

Walker, S. G. (1987). *Role Theory and Foreign Policy Analysis*. Durham, NC: Duke University Press.

Wish, N. (1980). Foreign policy makers and their national role conceptions. *International Studies Quarterly*, *24*(4): 532–554. doi:10.2307/2600291.

15 Conclusion

Paul-Henri Bischoff

After the end of the Cold War in 1990, expansive liberalisation changed conditions and structures across the world and engendered greater state and non-state agency. The consequences of these global developments saw an increase in wealth for many, but also a rise in relative poverty and inequality for many others; in short, it accelerated uneven development. These shifts challenged the post-1945 hierarchy of states, institutional politics and global governance. In the twenty-first century, Asia became Africa's biggest source of trade when the locus of growth, production and accelerated development in the world began to tilt towards the Asia-Pacific region. The diversification and intensification of relations with China and a host of other new actors in a changing world order calls for the study of a differentiated African response, new African initiative in world politics and the greater studied exercise of African foreign policy choices.

For the African continent, a globalist, neo-liberal political and economic opening in the world after 1990 promoted a plurality of actors—domestic, regional and global. Greater plurality prompted a greater African response. At the turn of the century, African states, regional institutions and non-state actors increasingly began to face off on international, multilateral and global initiatives. On the continent, the increased exposure expanded the foreign policy choices of states and Inter-Governmental Organisations (IGOs). Similarly, non-state actors became part of expansive transnational relations (as well as intraregional and non-state-IGO-state relations). As such, the latter began to engage in their own, external relations. To obtain an overall understanding of a myriad of foreign policy or external dispositions, there is a need for a holistic, organic or "cultural" understanding of the regional and the domestic. The study of reactions and initiatives towards external forces is to identify the signifiers that trigger types of actions or dispositions and define actorness.

A pluralising region in Southern Africa, for instance, means exposure to global and regional norms that invigorates non-state agency. This finds its own resonance in the collective policymaking and the intra-regional external relations of regional organisation. One regional signifier for the present is the regionalism of liberation of the recent past, which admitted national liberation movements as non-state actors. This has come to inform the present actorness of SADC. With erstwhile national liberation movements/non-state actors now constituted as governing parties, some civil society actors, Cecilia Nedziwe shows (see Chapter 13), have stood to benefit. SADC's recognition of non-state actors in community building has opened up *a mixed actor space* for gender and women-focused civil society groupings as participants in the inter-state policy frameworks of the organisation. The result, a collectively arrived at policy implemented in SADC's "external relations" with member states, enhances regional (gender) security in society.

African foreign policymaking increasingly has to do with capacitating agency. While lacking an expansive and intensive tradition of legitimated state control, African states traditionally relied on the international recognition sovereignty afforded them. Outside recognition to strengthen the government's hand on a domestic front has been key to the political survival of a regime. In an environment of multiplying actors, including those by the market, however, encourages choices beyond mere political survival. The exposure to the world market has also spelt more differentiated and uneven development within and between African states. More than ever, the descriptions of country-specific contexts that take into account individual political, cultural, historical and circumstantial factors on engagements with the world are signifiers for foreign policy explanations marking differences in dispositions. The study of African specificities provides new insights and expands on a globally informed, more diverse study of foreign policy. By way of illustration, scholars look at the prevalence of the long-standing dialectics of tension and conflict in Africa between the project of nation-state making and the counterclaims of ethno-nationalism (Malaquias, 2013: 14).

Signifiers to explain agency in this volume fall under the groupings of culture, identity and ideology; leadership, roles and strategy; social factors and the social nature of African organisation, and collective foreign policy actorness.

Culture and identity as foreign policy drivers

International Relations (IR) literature has traditionally glossed over the importance of identity, culture and ethnic division as sources of foreign policy. Instead, much of IR theory proposes states motivated by a desire to protect themselves from external threats or increase material prosperity at home. Yet, many states and the ethnic and regional groups of which they are constituted are greatly concerned with the vitality of their cultures and the ways in which foreign policy strengthens or weakens these cultures and the identities to which they are attached (Shulman, 1998: 111). "Culture, not the number of actors and their relative capabilities, determines who counts as an actor and how those actors define and pursue their interests" (Lebow, 2008: 442). As such, an actor-centred study of foreign policy is well positioned to distance itself from the hegemonic structures of political and economic structuralism and normative assumptions of rational actor model explanation.[1] Mike Mavura in his contribution suggests African ways of being allows us to think of new ontologies and epistemologies around the "cultural turn", the role and value assigned to culture in foreign policy.

Culture as a domestic source of foreign policy has Mike Mavura (see Chapter 7) talk to the use of the spirit world embedded in local culture as a driver of foreign policy: "the spiritual, metaphysical and symbolic force of totemic and clan names in relation to Robert Mugabe offer an alternative analytic window to understand some of the seemingly 'illogical' or 'ill-informed' Foreign Policy choices that Zimbabwe made". What is highlighted are deep cultural and social identity factors to explain the vagaries of foreign policy conduct that do not "live up to" rational actors' assumptions. This serves to expose a deeper state by looking at the depth of ideology and culture as a constituent part of the underbelly of foreign policy.

Culturally grounded conceptual tools build alternative understandings of foreign policy. The proposition made is that culturally grounded foreign policy analysis falls outside the hegemonic norms established by mainstream foreign policy analysis. Individuals involved in making foreign policy are not necessarily rational subjects reacting to objective factors as understood by mainstream theory. Instead, it may be that the individual decision-makers' experiences in everyday life governed by the logic of ancestral and spiritual intercession can be a guide. Mavura refers to this as "the cultural turn framework in foreign policy study".

A strategic culture approach to Ethiopia's foreign policy towards Israel and Middle Eastern Arab countries has historical, cultural, and strategic and *real-politik* foreign policy determinants speak to each other. Makonnen Tesfaye (see Chapter 5) takes a broad definition of the concept and argues that strategic culture variables such as history, geography, culture, identity, ideology and religion combine with domestic politics and institutions and material factors such as preponderant military power, technology, demography or economic resources to shape national security decisions and strategic behaviour. All this has to be balanced against preponderant environmental influences to explain the art and logic of conducting foreign relations.

A complementary approach to conventional explanations, a strategic culture approach provides for an overarching understanding of Ethiopia's decisions and strategic behaviour towards Israel and the Middle Eastern Arab countries. The aim is to provide a holistic understanding of Ethiopia's foreign policy. Tesfaye finds only in those periods when domestic pressures challenge the regime's security is Ethiopia closely aligned with a pro-Israeli foreign policy. Conversely, when the state domestically feels relatively secure, it is able to conduct cordial relations with neighbouring Arab and Muslim states. Ethiopia's strategic culture, combined with prevalent geo-political considerations and the material resources forced at its disposal to promote its national interest, provides a consistent and overarching understanding of Ethiopia's complex foreign policy towards Israel and Middle Eastern Arab countries.

Ideology, leadership, identity, roles and strategy

Ideology, leadership and strategy are domestic indicators of either weak or strong foreign policy choices. Post-revolutionary Tunisia, under the ostensibly revolutionary rule of the An-Nadha party, chose not to make any radical foreign policy changes. Even though, in the aftermath of the revolution, ordinary Tunisians expressed a desire to end the psychological, cultural and economic dependence on France, the revolutionary government took an apologetic and defensive stance towards France.

An-Nahdha's soft policy towards France expresses an ideology that represents a hybrid of both reformism and pragmatism that is not the hallmark of a revolutionary party. Ahmed Salem (see Chapter 10) applies a realist-constructivist approach to interpret Tunisia's foreign policy choice. He takes issue with structuralists who argue Tunisia had to act pragmatically in foreign relations because of resource constraints and geo-economic factors. In looking at rationality and power as sources of explanation, he finds that foreign policies do contain irrational elements influenced by emotion, personality, prejudice and subjective preference. Where foreign policymakers seemingly do ignore ideals because objective power considerations are seemingly an automatic given, Salem contests the view that conflates foreign policy analysis with foreign policy prescription. Like empowered Islamists and ideologues elsewhere, An-Nahdha's leadership, irrespective of any consequences, could realistically have opted for quite another foreign policy orientation. The realist-constructivist approach proposed by Salem demonstrates that pragmatism signifies following a distinct foreign policy choice not given by any objective necessity.

The use of ideology in foreign policy which initially promoted state-led development, as opposed to market-led development and its reversal, is the subject of Issaka Souaré's disposition on Guinea (see Chapter 12). He argues that the foreign policy under President Sekou Touré followed a mainly realist script with a reliance on alliance building, to achieve balances of power best seen to promote the national interest of strengthening state-led development. The two subsequent regimes departed from the strong doctrinal and ideological justifications of foreign policy. Both abandoned notions of state-led development and strategic alliance building. Instead, they embraced forms of liberalism aligned with market-friendly economic, not overt political thought. Thus, the leaderships of both the Second and Third Republics emphasised the role of "economic diplomacy" in describing their foreign policy orientation. However, without much success in attracting private investment and achieving economic expansion, the principal purpose of economic diplomacy has simply translated into a nominal role played by Guinea's current foreign policy: the search for foreign aid assistance.

Nigeria has been unequivocal of its desire and resolve—constitutionally enshrined—to provide a leadership role in West Africa and on the African continent, Olumuyiwa Amao holds (see Chapter 6). Neither a structural realist analysis of Nigeria's foreign policy and intervention behaviour in Africa, seeking power and relative gains within the West African sub-region or on the African continent, nor a constructivist analysis that points to cross-national solidarity, shared aspirations or expressions of collective identity, can explain Nigeria's foreign policy and intervention behaviour in Africa. What is key is the highly personalised foreign policymaking process, somewhat modified by whether a leader heads a military or civilian government, that best accounts for the vagaries in foreign policy. While an interventionist approach suited the often imperial and idiosyncratic dispositions of decidedly unrestrained military presidential leaders, dwindling economic resources over the last twenty-five years have significantly constrained the state's capacity to deliver on its self-imposed subregional policing role in conflicts.

Under military rule, we observe how unidirectional and autocratic Nigeria's foreign policy and intervention behaviour was. While Nigeria's regime and military, socio-economic and political resources serve as backdrop to projecting foreign policy influence—even under democratic dispensations with the competing demands on a leader—the characteristics of individual leadership consistently remains a key driver. This brings to the fore a plain agency perspective to signify a state's foreign policy behaviour.

Changing leadership, the lack of ideology and a change in domestic institutions are foreign policy drivers for Mzukisi Qobo's writing on South Africa under President Jacob Zuma (see Chapter 4). It is a government characterised by unprincipled pragmatism, occasioned by an anti-colonial rhetoric accompanied by domestic governance failure. A foreign policy stance that cloaks personal and particularistic interests as the country's own national interest privatises foreign policy and dispels or undermines any defined set of ideas on principled foreign policy conduct. The consequences have been considerable—a loss in the moral and political authority of South Africa as an erstwhile global actor and aspirant middle power under the presidencies of Mandela and Mbeki. Unless arrested under the current presidency of Cyril Ramaphosa, the liabilities inherited from the Zuma period has the country face further loss in projecting an independent foreign policy or aspirant middle-power status. Instead, there is the prospect that South Africa incrementally becomes subject to the design of authoritarian big powers in their quest for regional and international prominence.

For Kwesi Aning and Kwaku Danso, a national role conception represents the general idea of self that policy elites hold about the identity of a country (see Chapter 14). Diplomatic-military policies derive from this sense of self, and condition with what relevance you are able to choose to position yourself. Despite or because of being small, with an agrarian base, dependent on external support and without being of strategic importance, successive Ghanaian governments experimented with a variety of defence and foreign policy measures designed to assure security, while attempting to transform the post-colonial state's marginal and inconsequential image into that of a recognisably viable actor in regional and global politics. Here President Kwame Nkrumah's avid support for multilateral diplomacy and regional organisation carried over into successive administrations. The national policy elite found that Ghana serving in the role of an international peacekeeper was foundational to determining the national interest. This went hand in hand with constructing and projecting a favourable image outside. However, the quest remains largely elusive. Only a broader, deeper conceptual and strategic approach to global peace could elevate Ghana, give it more of an international identity and add to African agency on promoting international peace and security.

African foreign policy issues prompted by the transnational invites responses that are predictably mixed and complex. Korwa Adar and Mercy Kathambi Kaburu point to the strategic-military response by Kenya in confronting a transnational threat to its stability (see Chapter 8). While Kenya positively embraced the renewal of Pan-African institutions and opened up to liberal forms of integration, it held to a military-led response towards Somalia. Such a response bases itself on a realist reading of an old security threat—dating back to confronting the transnational marauders or *shiftas* in the 1960s–1970s—presently dressed up in the post-modern, post 9/11 narrative of *al-Shabaab*'s dreams for a regional Islamic Emirate of Somalia. Although the short-term objective of Kenya's military involvement in Somalia had to do with the perception of needing to protect its territory and citizens from threats posed by *al Shabaab*, the emerging interest in oil exploration along the Kenya-Somalia coastal region is an economic consideration coming into play and quite another of Kenya's long-term strategic objectives.

Social factors and foreign policy: The social nature of African organisation

Social inter-governmental, trans-governmental and transnational interaction is important in the validation of common norms. The social factor allows actors to attach meaning to inter-state relations and helps channels their foreign policy behaviour. Eugenio Njoloma shows that since independence, Malawi has pursued a foreign policy path characterised by both convergence and divergence from the concerted norm for African unity, signified by the concern for a collective, multilateral approach (see Chapter 11). Convergence implies socially and normatively identifying with fellow African states on matters of common concern, while divergence individually defies collective social expectations of common and predetermined outcomes of state behaviour. The promotion of convergence has been ideological as it has been political: to achieve Pan-African unity and inter-nationalist solidarity norms as well as the benefits derived from regional integration and regionally sourced aid. Errant foreign policy behaviour, however, defies the general assumption that small (African) states only pursue their interests for anticipated benefits from within a multilateral context (Graham, 2017). In explaining deviations from the norm, indicators include specific domestic-socio-economic factors to do with stabilising the economy, social bonds given by personal, kinship and marital ties between presidents and their families or, identifying the otherwise untrodden path, in order to diversify sources of foreign aid.

The social type of foreign relations practised relates to a material world. The mutual material weakness of African states is enabling of African cooperation and allows African diplomacy to seek consensus and employ mediation in foreign policy. There is the long-standing propensity to converge in multilateral bodies and adopt collective foreign policy positions (Zartmann, 1973: 377–387). Global hierarchies of power encroach on the continent and fuel an ongoing collective sense of relative economic deprivation. National liberation movements now in power are reminders of past common struggles against colonialism, oppression and exclusion. Their presence and a common past facilitates finding collective policy responses.

A material and normative basis for the promotion of social inter-state cohesion at a regional society level has its own foreign policy consequences. Whereas mainstream foreign policy description puts the exercise of power and influence at the centre of analysis, material attributes are not necessarily the basis for describing African diplomacy. Norms of mutual respect and reciprocity and a similar ideology help mobilise and resist outside pressures (Mahmud, 2013: 138; 143).

Collective foreign policy actorness

Driving collective African foreign policymaking has been the revival of a sense of (Pan-) African agency. During the 1990s, a politically and strategically absent International Community (IC) saw Nigeria lead the ECOMOG interventions in Sierra Leone and Liberia. This helped (re-)kindle African agency. The emergence of South Africa as an aspirant emerging middle power, albeit of a different type with asymmetrical capacities from the traditional middle-power within a Western-led international order (Jordaan, 2003), added to Africa's presence and new sense of sovereignty in the world. South African President Thabo Mbeki's "African Renaissance" led Africa to show strategic initiative in and around the UN's Millennium Development Goals (MDPS), the constitution of the African Union (AU), in part an African response to neo-liberalism and globalisation and African participation of meetings at the G7 (G8) in the early 2000s.

Agency is explicit political action relayed through both rhetoric and action. Tsepho Gwatiwa shows how the African Union as a new foreign policy actor in its own right demonstrates agency (see Chapter 3). Yet, this agency and associated actorness takes place in a context where individual states such as Libya or Zimbabwe can make use of Pan-Africanism as a lever to simply promoting personal leadership and influence. As an ideology, Pan-Africanism needs rethinking on how to become more inclusive and participative beyond a state-centric context. Importantly, political support by the two biggest African powers for the AU's norm entrepreneurship is found wanting. Importantly, enduring political support by the two biggest African powers for the AU's norm entrepreneurship is lacking. Arguably, it would be easier for a charismatic leader of one or the other of the two "pivotal powers"—Nigeria or South Africa—to be an agentic pivot. Given the specific cultural and political context, it would, however, equally be possible for a smaller state to be the custodian of African agency on matters to do with international politics and security.

The AU is responsible for negotiating and implementing agreements on global issues such as international trade, international law, international security and other important crosscutting issues such as migration, humanitarian aid and protection of vulnerable groups. However, precepts and codes in these areas originate from abroad. Key strategic African powers such as South Africa and Nigeria, though initially important, have not consistently provided transformative leadership and practical support for autonomous regional organisation and political plurality. It is a challenge for the AU to reconcile African preferences and interests from fifty-four member states so that these are relevant for African constituents. In addition, while member states support the African Union in its promotion of standardising norms on integration, governance and democracy, for reasons of self-interest they have also undermined the AU as an independent, socialising foreign policy actor (Landsberg, 2018: 50). As such, needful to protect its agency, the AU exists in essentially defensive mode.

Conclusion

Aware of Africa's exposure and its effects, individual and collective African foreign policy positioning in a complex and dynamically changing world needs its own, full description.

Contributors in this volume all engage in assessing domestic explanations for plotting differing African responses to the international. In terms of the use of theory, this proceeds in a rather eclectic manner. With exceptions, contributors eschew political and economic structuralism as explanatory frameworks. With the emphasis on agency, constructivism and Foreign Policy Analysis (FPA) serve as the principal constructs to explain African foreign policy agency. In addition, the use of mid-level theory helps in terms of African specificities to characterise the domestic and its importance for explaining the international. Where culture is emphasised, the plea is for new ontology, new paradigms and epistemologies.

This is an opportune moment to signify African foreign policy: how foreign policy on the African continent in an emerging post-Western—say inter-polar or multiplex world deserves ongoing study and how this may inform the study of foreign policy in general. This kind of intellectual endeavour opens up "a pluralistic space for theoretical intervention" (Dunn & Shaw, 2013: 5) to question, abrogate or generate middle-range theory or new paradigms at a global level.

South Africa making foreign policy in response to changing configurations in the world serves as an example of the parameters of this research:

> South Africa's more independent, cosmopolitan, bridge-building posture under Mandela—through which it accrued considerable soft power—has increasingly given way to a flip-flopping between liberationist and liberal democratic values and soft balancing against the OECD world. Whether this move has resulted in *unequivocal* African followership as a form of soft power that is distinct from the soft power contemplated in Western media discourses remains uncertain.
>
> (van der Westhuizen, 2016: 465)

Correspondingly, Lopez-Lucia, looking at Nigeria and Brazil as similarly placed regional powers holds material factors are not to be discounted, but—

> ideational and material factors are intertwined and made meaningful through representations, which for writers such as Kevin Dunn are "concerned with how names, meaning, and characteristics are attached to the world around us" These representations influence regional powers' policies towards the region but always in interaction with policy dilemmas arising in an ever-changing context which can trigger creative and adaptive practices by the actors. Foreign policy decision-makers in the foreign policy machineries of regional

> powers are thus "situated agents" who draw on, and sometimes adapt, foreign policy traditions in response to dilemmas.
>
> (Lopez-Lucia, 2015: 349; 351)

The focus on optimising agency, given the constraints imposed by structure, is about a systematic rediscovery of the possibilities given by the descriptions and meanings of African actorness.

We suggest two avenues of study. The one eclectically draws from an existing IR toolbox to fill accounts of foreign policy with African content. To reflect African reality, this may mean, as done in this book, to mix approaches—realist with liberal, realist with constructivist, strategic with cultural. The aim is to show how African state and collective foreign policy actors, preferably assisted by civil society in a democratic dispensation, ought to better their position in the world. The study of foreign policy that works within the purview of Westphalian state-centredness largely takes this route in this volume.

The other is to centre analysis of agency on African ontology informed by a collectively oppressive, culturally similar but also specific past. The latter puts the structurally inherited, real and existing human condition of Africans on the continent and its living African voice at the centre of a normative account. This has state and non-state actors respond accordingly to the human subject in international relations. Cecilia Nedziiwe and Tshepo Gwatiwa hint at this.

With an IR shaped by Western and US concerns, an interpretive approach can help explain how, beyond the West, even if only at a local, regional level, small states, for instance, draw up their own foreign policy accounts. As Neufeld (1993: 43; 44; 47; 58) has put it, for "interpretive theorists, the object of study of social science must include the interpretations and definitions of the human subjects whose interaction makes up the social world". "[They] conceive of the 'web of meaning' … as being comprised of 'intersubjective meanings' which are the product of the collective self-interpretations and self-definitions of human communities … that takes place in relation to a concrete historical context (material and social)". Intersubjective meanings open the prospect for change and emancipation from existing structures themselves seen as "the product of an on-going process of self-definition and self-reflection".

Part of negotiating a self-tailored African position in the world is under the condition of *interpolarity* (Grevi, 2009),[2] where state-actors from the South are unwilling to enter into any serious conflict with the West over core principles regarding the present world order. Instead, the agency of the global South consists of obtaining a greater say in pre-existing institutions of global governance. Another is the condition of *multiplexity*, where in a world of multiple modernities—the West constitutes one of several modernities—African actors have a choice of actors and scenarios as never before in a greatly differentiated, competitively composite world order where there are new risks and opportunities for managing international stability (Acharya, 2017).

Whatever the condition subscribed to, African foreign policy derives greater choices. African foreign policy needs, consistently and in a rounded way, to be able to foreground a recommitment to international institutions, the provision of international public goods, more inclusive global problem solving and the insistence on the legitimacy of multilateral diplomacy. Together with the credibility and moral standing that comes from practising greater democracy, respecting human dignity and freedom, and inclusive citizen participation at home, this is to help place a new and more diverse set of non-Western actors at the centre of power. Together with greater regional organisation, this opens up new avenues for the foreign relations of African states and African continental or regional organisations.

The argument here is that an interpretivist analysis as a guide to action under conditions of multiplexity or interpolarity opens up the continental and international political policy space. As opportunities for African diplomacy increase, so does the need for studying African foreign policy.[3] While after the economic crisis of 2008, a pluralising international system, now in flux, did not create scope for major acts of agency in the hope of substantial gains and a more equal, redistributive international order, the period has shown it did not preclude that absolute gains for weak or emergent states were possible (Andreasson, 2013: 25). These evolving world scenarios, however, present ongoing opportunity for the study of African foreign policy and its signifiers.

Notes

1 Here synergies exist between constructivist take and Foreign Policy Analysis (FPA).

2 "The description of a multipolar system captures many dimensions of the emerging international environment. However, emphasis on the relative power of competing actors offers only a partial insight into this new environment. Deepening interdependence is the second basic trend shaping the international system, and provides the new context of power relations. Economic growth, energy security and environmental sustainability are the three interconnected issues at the core of complex interdependence. All major powers are exposed to the unprecedented conjunction of the economic, energy and environmental crises and none of them can successfully confront these challenges on its own" Grevi (2009).

3 Norm promoting agents situated within various social, political, bureaucratic, intellectual, security and business contexts at various levels of organised society and that of the 'peri-state', the state itself, the formal and informal region, as well as the international, promote a diversity of foreign policy initiatives and responses.

References

Acharya, A. (2017). After liberal hegemony: The advent of a multiplex world order. *Ethics & International Affairs*, *31*(3): 271–285.

Andreasson, S. (2013). Elusive agency: Africa's persistently peripheral role in international relations. *Mimeo*: 1–25. http://works.bepress.com/stefan_andreasson/16. Accessed 23 June 2019.

Dunn, K. C. & Shaw, T. M. (eds.). (2013). *Africa's Challenge to IR Theory*. Basingstoke: Palgrave.

Graham, S. (2017). Drivers of the foreign policies of Southern African small states. *Politikon*, *44*(1): 133–155. doi:10.1080/02589346.2017.1279802.

Grevi, G. (2009). The interpolar world: A new scenario (Occasional Paper, European Union of Security Studies, 2009). https://www.iss.europa.eu/sites/default/files/EUISSFiles/op79.pdf. Accessed 5 June 2019.

Jordaan, E. (2003). The concept of a middle power in international relations: Distinguishing between emerging and traditional middle powers. *Politikon*, *30*(2): 167–169.

Landsberg, C. (2018). The troubled socialising agent: Democratic governance and the African Union's quest to become and independent foreign policy actor. In J. Warner & T. Shaw (eds.). *African Foreign Policies in International Institutions*. London: Macmillan, 49–62.

Lebow, R. N. (2008). *A Cultural Theory of International Relations*. Cambridge: Cambridge University Press.

Lopez-Lucia, E. (2015). Regional powers and regional security governance: An interpretive perspective on the policies of Nigeria and Brazil. *International Relations*, *29*(3): 348–362.

Mahmud, S. (2013). Controlling African states' behavior. In K. C. Dunn & T. M. Shaw (eds.). *Africa's Challenge to International Relations Theory*. Basingstoke: Palgrave, 129–145.

Malaquias, A. (2013). Reformulating IR theory: African insights and challenges. In K. C. Dunn & T. M. Shaw (eds.). *Africa's Challenge to International Relations Theory*. Basingstoke: Palgrave, 11–28.

Neufeld, M. (1993). Interpretation and the "science" of international relations. *Review of International Studies*, *19*(1): 39–61.

Shulman, S. (1998). National integration and foreign policy in multiethnic states. *Nationalism and Ethnic Politics*, *4*(4): 110–132.

van der Westhuizen, J. (2016). South Africa's soft power conundrum: How to win friends and influence people in Africa. *Journal of Political Power*, *9*(3): 449–465.

Zartmann, W. (1973). Africa as a subordinate state system in international relations. In R. Falk & S. Ilendlovitz (eds.). *Regional Politics and World Order*. San Francisco: Freeman, 387–397.

Index

For Product Safety Concerns and Information please contact our EU representative GPSR@taylorandfrancis.com
Taylor & Francis Verlag GmbH, Kaufingerstraße 24, 80331 München, Germany

www.ingramcontent.com/pod-product-compliance
Ingram Content Group UK Ltd.
Pitfield, Milton Keynes, MK11 3LW, UK
UKHW020014200926
475702UK00014B/1874
9781032400266